Financial Market Complexity

# Financial Market Complexity

**NEIL F. JOHNSON, PAUL JEFFERIES**

*Clarendon Laboratory*
*University of Oxford*

**PAK MING HUI**

*Department of Physics*
*The Chinese University of Hong Kong*

OXFORD

UNIVERSITY PRESS

# OXFORD

UNIVERSITY PRESS

Great Clarendon Street, Oxford OX2 6DP

Oxford University Press is a department of the University of Oxford.
It furthers the University's objective of excellence in research, scholarship,
and education by publishing worldwide in

Oxford  New York

Auckland  Bangkok  Buenos Aires  Cape Town  Chennai
Dar es Salaam  Delhi  Hong Kong  Istanbul  Karachi  Kolkata
Kuala Lumpur  Madrid  Melbourne  Mexico City  Mumbai  Nairobi
São Paulo  Shanghai  Taipei  Tokyo  Toronto

Oxford is a registered trade mark of Oxford University Press
in the UK and in certain other countries

Published in the United States
by Oxford University Press Inc., New York

A catalogue record for this title is available from the British Library

Library of Congress Cataloging in Publication Data

Johnson, Neil F., 1961–
Financial market complexity / Neil F. Johnson, Paul Jefferies and Pak Ming Hui.
Includes index.
1. Finance–Statistical methods.   2. Finance–Mathematical models.
3. Statistical physics.   I. Jefferies, Paul.   II. Hui, Pak Ming.   III. Title.

HG176.5.J64 2003        332.5'01'519–dc21        2002044694

ISBN 0 19 852665 2

10 9 8 7 6 5 4 3 2 1

Typeset by Newgen Imaging Systems (P) Ltd., Chennai, India
Printed in Great Britain
on acid-free paper by
Biddles Ltd., Guildford & King's Lynn.

# Preface

Theory is of value in empirical science only to the extent to which it connects fruitfully with the empirical world.

(Herbert Blumer (1954) 'What is wrong with social theory?',
*American Sociological Review* **19**, 3)

This is a book about financial markets . . . written by physicists. It is not surprising to find books on quantitative finance written by economists, mathematicians, and even computer scientists—but physicists? There is a simple reason, or rather a simple 'complex' reason. Financial markets are complicated, dynamical systems which are continually generating high-frequency data series. This data records the aggregate action of the market's many participants, each of whom is trying to win in this vast global 'game'. In fact it can be argued that financial markets provide the most well-documented, and longest running, record of a large-scale 'complex system'. In short, financial markets constitute a real-world complex system which is continually evolving, which has significant practical importance, and which produces an enormous amount of data—and that's the appeal.

It has been said that being a successful investor is like being a successful burglar. Most burglars know how to get into a building, and what to take, but only the successful ones know how, and most importantly *when*, to get out. 'Time' is therefore crucial in financial markets. Since our goal is to understand *real-world* markets as opposed to idealized ones, time also takes centre-stage in this book. Time relates to dynamics, and it is this evolving complex-system dynamics which underpins our scientific interest in financial markets.

Most, if not all, standard finance textbooks make some kind of apparently innocuous assumptions about market dynamics. For example, they assume that the markets are in some kind of steady-state or represent a stationary process, and that there are no implicit temporal correlations—or at best, that these correlations are of a specific type. As we show in the present book, these assumptions can give misleading answers to practical problems such as minimizing financial risk, coping with extreme events such as crashes or drawdowns, and pricing derivatives in non-ideal markets. Having said this, standard finance theory usually works. But it is the 'usually' that we are interested in—or rather the 'unusually'. We focus on how and why real financial markets deviate from the standard finance theory paradigm of random-walk behaviour, and the consequences of such deviation. In particular, we will be interested in the tails of the distribution of price returns, and in the dynamics induced by crowd-like behaviour in markets. The consequences for managing risk will also feature quite prominently. In short, the following questions provide the focus of this book: *How* do financial markets behave? *Why* do financial markets behave in the way that they do? *What* can we do to minimize risk, given this behaviour?

The relationship between science, and in particular physics, and finance is still in the courtship phase—hence the (not so) occasional squabbles. Despite the immaturity of this so-called Econophysics field, there are many people interested in knowing more about it, including practitioners and students. A common request is 'Where can we learn about these Econophysics ideas, and how to implement them?' The latter part of this request, concerning implementation, motivated us to prepare this book. In particular, we felt that there was a need to produce a textbook which takes a relatively small number of topics—the essential ones in our opinion—and treats them as thoroughly as possible. We have tried to make the book as pedagogical as we could, so that readers would feel comfortable about trying out some of the ideas for themselves in a real financial setting. The net effect is, we believe, a reasonably cohesive story yet clearly one which is still in the process of evolving. This story-so-far unfolds as follows. After discussing the background to the concept of complexity and the structure of financial markets in Chapter 1, Chapter 2 examines the assumptions upon which standard finance theory is built. Reality sets in with Chapter 3, where we analyse data from two seemingly different markets and uncover certain universal features which cannot be explained within standard finance theory. Chapters 4 and 5 mark a significant departure from the philosophy of standard finance theory, being concerned with exploring microscopic models of markets which are faithful to real market microstructure yet which also reproduce the real-world statistical features discussed in Chapter 3. Chapter 6 moves to the practical problem of how to quantify and hedge risk in real-world markets. Chapter 7 discusses deterministic descriptions of market dynamics, incorporating the topics of chaos and the all-important phenomena of market crashes. We both hope and believe that these chapters combine to provide a unified framework for developing future research in this interdisciplinary field. At the same time, the chapters themselves were constructed to be fairly stand-alone for the benefit of the practitioner who may only be interested, say, in implementing a derivative scheme which goes beyond Black–Scholes theory (Chapter 6).

This endeavour to produce a pedagogical book which introduces essential topics at the frontiers of finance, yet provides sufficient detail such that the reader can implement the ideas presented, is a zero-sum game in terms of space. Hence our textbook provides neither a review of the whole Econophysics literature, nor does it cover all the standard formalism and references expected of a classical finance textbook. We believe this is acceptable for the following reasons. Regarding Econophysics, the website *www.unifr.ch/econophysics* provides a daily record of the rapidly expanding body of research. In terms of classical finance theory, there are plenty of comprehensive textbooks already available. Many of these are, we feel, somewhat removed from the real goings-on in a market, whereas we wanted to refer to the 'experimental system' as much as possible. Hence we see the present book as complementary to these standard finance texts, rather than incorporating or replacing them. In terms of the technical skill required to read the book, we have aimed it at graduate students or final year undergraduates, and practitioners with a working knowledge of calculus and probability. For this reason, we believe that the book can be followed as part of a course or for private study by students, academics, and practitioners alike. In order to encourage further discussion of the ideas and models presented, we have set up a book website at *www.occf.ox.ac.uk/books/fmc*.

We are very grateful to Michael Hart, David Lamper, Larry K. F. Yip, and Chen Xu for their contributions in terms of ideas and material. We would also like to thank Sam Howison, Jeff Dewynne, Damien Challet, Andre Stern, Steve Mobbs, Vladimir Montealegre, Jose Pablo Mesa, Bing Hong Wang, and DaFang Zheng for many discussions which have helped us understand the complexities of the financial world. Together with workers in the Econophysics community at large, their comments have taught us how even the most realistic sounding theories are sometimes not that realistic, and that one always needs to be pushing further. Finally, we are extremely grateful to our families and friends, and the editors at Oxford University Press, for their faith and patience.

April 2003                                                                N. F. J., P. J., and P. M. H.
Oxford

# Contents

# 1. Financial markets as complex systems

## 1.1 Real problems in finance

Suppose we have an interest in a dot-com company *risk-e.com* that has been around on the stock market for a few years. The 'we' could be private investors who hardly ever buy stocks, online traders who trade several times a day for a living, pension-fund managers looking to the longer term, finance officers in a multinational company looking to speculate with some extra funds, or traders in a commercial bank looking to either balance portfolio risk for customers or carry out proprietary trading. We all have different time horizons in mind, different capital, different ease of access to the market, different levels of transaction costs, different minimum execution times, and different perceptions and definitions of potential risk. But we all have one thing in common: *we certainly do not want to lose any money.* After all, if we expected to lose money in the market then we should either put our cash in a bank account, or stick it under the bed. Suppose *risk-e.com* had its Initial Public Offering (IPO) in January 1996, hence there is some limited history available of past performance. The history of the stock price to date is shown in Fig. 1.1.

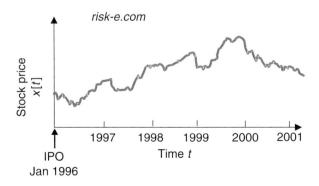

**Fig. 1.1**   Past price series for the dot-com company *risk-e.com*.

We may not just be looking to buy stock in the hope that the price will go up, although it would be nice if it did of course. We might also be wanting to assess future risk, hedge risk, or compare performance to that of other supposedly similar companies. While we could, and should, check out the company's earnings and growth reports, we also know that this information is limited. And anyway, according to standard finance theory, since this information is essentially public, surely it will already have been incorporated into the current price? While pondering the situation and staring at the price chart, we can not help but noticing the roller coaster ride that the stock seems to have had since the IPO. Questions start popping into our heads:

Does any of that roller coaster ride in the stock price $x[t]$ actually tell us anything? If so, what? Should we buy (i.e. go long) the stock? Or sell it (i.e. go short)? Maybe we want to use this stock to hedge our risk in other dot-com companies, or in other technology sectors, or in another market. What should we then do to minimize our risk? What do we each mean by 'risk'—risk of what exactly? Is there any predictability in the stock's behaviour? How, and to what extent, would such predictability manifest itself on the hourly, daily, or monthly scale? Is the roller coaster ride driven by crowd behaviour? Can we infer what the crowd is thinking? If so, might we then be able to forecast the future based not on the past price series, but on what we believe the crowd will do?

These are a sampling of the types of practical questions that anyone interested in the markets faces regularly, from large investment institutions through to the private investor. These questions are however not the types of questions that are easily answered, or even easy to address, within standard finance theory. Why? Embedded in each of these questions is the issue of *time*, and timing of decisions or actions. Hence, in order to really address these questions, we will need to understand something about the time evolution of the particular asset's price, and probably also the market in general. But, surely it is impossible to say exactly what will happen to a given asset or market in the future? Yes, of course—but even a limited quantitative description might be useful, assuming that we understand what these limitations are. The big problem is that it is very difficult to make even reasonably accurate statements about the future time evolution of such a system, because that time evolution is generally so complicated. In fact, it would be hard to find anyone who disagreed with the statement that a financial market is indeed a 'complex' system. This underlies why standard theory falls short: it has nothing to do with the ability of finance theorists, but instead has to do with the fact that nobody yet knows how to describe mathematically the time evolution of such complex systems in a general yet useful way. And herein lie the academic and practical motivations for this book: across a broad range of disciplines, researchers are now realizing that some of the hardest problems that they each face have key common elements. These elements are the key elements of what is now being called a 'complex' system. So in order to understand the claim that a financial market is also such a complex system, we will spend a few moments looking at what these key ingredients are.

## 1.2    Complex systems and complexity

When we say 'financial markets are complex systems', we mean more than just 'complicated systems'. Making a pizza or fixing a bike puncture are both 'complicated', but neither is 'complex'. However, put these tasks together, and let the next step in one task depend on the present state of the other, and you start to incorporate at least a glimmer of complexity. Although there is no universally accepted definition of 'complexity' or 'complex system', most people would agree that any candidate complex system should have most or all of the following ingredients:

1. *Feedback*. The nature of the feedback can change with time—for example, becoming positive one moment and negative the next—and may also change in magnitude and importance. It may operate at the macroscopic or microscopic level, or both. The presence of feedback implies that on some level, buried in the details of the dynamics, the system is 'remembering' its past and responding to it, albeit in a highly non-trivial way.
2. *Non-stationarity*. We cannot assume that the dynamical or statistical properties observed in the system's past, will remain unchanged in the system's future.[1]
3. *Many interacting agents*. The system contains many components or participants, known as 'agents', which interact in possibly time-dependent ways. Their individual behaviour will respond to the feedback of information, which is possibly limited, from the system as a whole and/or from other agents. Since these agents may effectively be competing to win, it is unlikely that there is any such thing as a 'typical' agent.
4. *Adaptation*. An agent can adapt its behaviour in the hope of improving its performance.
5. *Evolution*. The entire multi-agent population evolves, driven by an ecology of agents who interact and adapt under the influence of feedback. The system typically remains far from equilibrium and hence can exhibit 'extreme behaviour'.[2]

---

[1] In financial calculations, for example, historic volatility levels obtained from past price series may be poor estimates of future volatility. In a complex system, statistical niceties such as stationarity cannot be taken for granted. As suggested by the disclaimer in financial advertisements, past performance provides no guarantee as to future success.

[2] The financial example of such extreme behaviour, is a market crash. See Chapters 3–5 and 7.

6. *Single realization*. The system under study is a single realization, implying that standard techniques whereby averages over time are equated to averages over ensembles, may not work.

7. *Open system*. The system is coupled to the environment, hence it is hard to distinguish between exogenous (i.e. outside) and endogenous (i.e. internal, self-generated) effects.

Most, if not all, these criteria are applicable to a financial market, implying that a financial market can be thought of as a complex system. The market price series provide a record of the system's global dynamics, while the market's participants (traders) represent the agents. Given the above criteria, it is often said that such complex systems are *more than the sum of their parts*. In other words, just as we say 'two's company, but three's a crowd' to denote how a collection of $N$ people changes its character and behaviour as $N$ increases from 2 to 3 or more, so a complex system exhibits so-called emergent properties which could not be easily predicted based on the behaviour of the individual constituent parts. A crowd of people is a good example of an emergent property. Certainly there are many, often tragic, examples in history of the power of a crowd. In fact, the connection to financial markets is quite direct, since it is often claimed that crowd behaviour causes crashes. This topic will be discussed in more detail in Chapters 4, 5, and 7. For now, having dealt with the idea of complexity, we spend the rest of this chapter reviewing the nuts and bolts of a financial market (e.g. see Pilbeam (1998) for an indepth account).

## 1.3    Financial market overview

### 1.3.1    The role of financial centres

Financial centres are places where the demand for financial services, both within the domestic and international communities, is met. Examples of financial centres worldwide include London, New York, and Tokyo. Financial centres increasingly find themselves competing in a global marketplace both to retain their domestic market and to win international business. Governments seek to promote their financial centres, not only because of the influx of substantial amounts of foreign capital but also because they provide employment for vast numbers of people. Effective financial centres can also help the economy by channelling capital into investments with high returns. In general, the most important role of a financial centre is to transfer funds or goods from agents with a surplus to agents with a deficit, in the most efficient way possible. In order for such transfer to be efficient, the financial centre must offer a diverse range of products and services to meet the diverse range of borrowers' and investors' needs. Among the services most in demand are: primary and secondary markets in bonds and equities, foreign exchange, risk management, derivative products, domestic and international bank lending.

### 1.3.2    Types of financial market

A distinction is made between primary and secondary markets: a primary market deals in issues of new assets whereas in a secondary market, existing assets are traded. In a primary market, the issuer of the asset benefits directly from the capital raised by its sale. In a secondary market, the issuer does not receive any proceeds from the resale of the asset. The secondary market is nonetheless important to the original issuer. The price of the issuer's asset in the secondary market reflects how willing financial agents are to buy the asset and hence how much capital could be raised by the original issuer through a further new sale on the primary market. A secondary market also provides what is known as liquidity. Liquidity is essentially the freedom to transact assets. Without a liquid secondary market, investors would not be willing to pay as much for new assets on the primary market since they know it would be difficult to sell the assets again. Vital to the provision of liquidity in the secondary market is the presence of so-called 'market-makers'. A market-maker will quote buy and sell prices for assets and be willing to accept large trades in either direction in response to market supply and demand. Consequently, it is usually easy for a buyer or seller of the asset to find a counter-party for the trade, thus allowing high 'volumes' of transactions and increased liquidity. We will henceforth only consider secondary financial markets, since their dynamics are a direct result of these interactions between buyers and sellers. Not only is there competition between buyers of the asset, but also between sellers. The nature of this two-sided competition will be of great importance in casting the financial market into the form of a general complex system. We henceforth refer to secondary financial markets simply as 'financial markets'.

Secondary markets can have diverse forms in terms of both their macroscopic character and microscopic structure. In 'screen-based markets', trading takes place electronically through an (possibly geographically dispersed) IT infrastructure. In a 'call market', orders are batched together at infrequent intervals (just once a day in some markets) and a market price is decided by an auction process, either oral or written. In a 'continuous market', prices are quoted continuously by market-makers throughout the trading day. Some markets have a mixture of systems.

### 1.3.3    Financial assets

A financial asset is simply a legal claim to a future cash flow. Financial assets are interchangeably referred to as financial securities, financial instruments, financial products, or financial claims. The issuer of the financial asset undertakes a legal agreement to make cash payments to the holder (interchangeably referred to also as the investor) of the asset in the future. Financial assets, and hence the financial markets that trade them, are named according to the details of the contract for future cash flow. Broadly speaking, financial assets can be classified according to the following criteria.

**1.3.3.1   Debt, equity, and foreign exchange.**   With debt claims, the holder has two pre-determined sources of future cash flow. At the 'maturity time' of the contract, the issuer must deliver back the original value of the claim. Also, at regular fixed times until maturity, the issuer must pay the holder interest on the loan—this interest may be fixed or variable. Typically, holding a debt claim will be lower risk than holding an equity claim since the debt claim will usually be secured against the assets of the issuer. For this reason, debt instruments are often referred to as 'fixed-income' since the future cash flow is more assured than for equity instruments. Examples of debt instruments are: government bonds or bills, corporate bonds, mortgages, and bank loans. Debt instruments with less than one year maturity are known as 'bills' and are traded on 'money markets', whereas debt instruments with more than a year's maturity are known as 'bonds' and are traded on 'capital markets'. Cash and foreign exchange can be viewed as debt instruments issued by the central bank of the country in question. For this reason, they are viewed as the simplest and most secure financial assets available, since repayment is (almost always!) definite and the interest rate is fixed at zero.

With equity claims, the holder also has two sources of future cash flow, but neither is guaranteed in terms of the actual amount. First, the holder has the right to a regular dividend payment, which is paid once the holders of all the issuer's debt claims have been paid. Second, the holder has the right to a portion of the value of the issuing institution should it be sold or placed in liquidation. Of course, the holder of an equity claim has no guarantee that there will be *any* future cash flow. Equity claims are thus more risky instruments than debt claims since the future cash flow will depend on the issuing institution's financial success. By far, the most prevalent form of equity instruments is ordinary company shares (common stock).

**1.3.3.2   Time of settlement.**   If the details of the financial asset contract stipulate that settlement should be made at the time the contract is agreed between the two parties, then the asset is a 'cash (or spot) asset' and as such is traded on a 'cash (or spot) market'. If however the contract is settled at some time in the future from the time it was agreed, the asset is known as a 'forward contract' or 'future contract'. Forward and future contracts can be made on a wide range of financial asset types such as foreign exchange, stock, bonds, and even indices (i.e. assets whose value depends on the collective value of a basket of other assets). A forward contract is usually an agreement forged between two distinct parties, hence the contracts cannot easily be sold on to a third party. This is in contrast to futures contracts that are usually for set contract sizes, based on set delivery dates and sold by a 'futures exchange'. Futures contracts can be sold from party to party and do not usually end in the delivery of the 'underlying asset' (i.e. the currency, stock, or bond). They are used by investors more for speculation and risk management than for future delivery of the underlying asset. Because the delivery of an underlying asset is secondary to a futures contract, it is classed as a 'derivative instrument' since its value is derived from an underlying asset.

**1.3.3.3 Obligation to exchange.** For some financial assets, the contract has an associated obligation to deliver another product immediately, or at some time in the future. For example, a bond contract has associated with it the obligation for the issuer to pay to the holder the original bond value at maturity, plus interest at regular intervals. For a currency forward, there is the obligation that the issuer must deliver the holder a quantity of currency at a given future time. However, some financial assets simply give the holder the *right*, but not the *obligation*, to exchange one product for another at a certain time. An example of this financial asset type is the 'option'. The holder of an option contract has the right but not the obligation to buy the 'underlying asset' for a given price (the strike price). As such, an option contract is a derivative instrument just as for the future contract described above.

### 1.3.4 Financial market agents

The participants who are active in any given financial market, can be loosely split into those whose job it is to provide the service and those who seek to use the service. The main providers of the service will be the brokers, market-makers, and regulators. The main users of the service form a wide group and may include: individuals, invest-ment and commercial banks, investment companies, insurance and pension funds, businesses, local and central governments, and international institutions such as the World Bank.

**1.3.4.1 Market service providers.** 'Brokers' act as the legal agents of investors, and as such can be more closely regulated than the investors themselves. A broker is the intermediary between the investor and the financial assets. The brokers not only offer a service for the buying and selling of financial assets, but may also offer relevant market news, research reports, and custody of the asset. Brokers make their money by charging a commission for their services. 'Market-makers' act as dealers for particular financial assets. Market-makers will offer a 'bid price' at which they are prepared to buy the financial asset from the investors (or other market-makers) and an 'ask price' at which they are prepared to sell the financial asset. The difference between the ask and bid price is known as the 'spread' and represents the profit margin of the market-maker. The market-maker's job is to aid in the efficient running of the market by offering competitive prices for the financial asset, and also to act as a source of liquidity. 'Market regulators' aim to guarantee the legality and correct execution of all market interactions. Further to this role, regulators may try and ensure a degree of stability in the market. For example, if the movement in a particular financial asset (or the market as a whole) exceeds certain bounds, the regulator may seek to intervene and halt trading in that asset (or the whole market) in the hope that subsequent trading will be calmer.

**1.3.4.2   Market service users.**   Although market users are diverse in size, time horizon, and objective, they can usefully be divided into three main groups depending on their motivations and preferences for return on their investment versus risk. The three main groups are:

1. *Speculators*. These are market agents who are aiming for return on their financial investment above all else. Speculators will have a view of the future evolution in price of a financial asset and will consequently buy the asset if they decide it is undervalued with respect to their beliefs, and sell the asset if they decide it is overvalued.
2. *Hedgers*. These are market agents who choose to participate in the market in order to reduce the risk of their uncertain portfolio value. These agents are consequently not as concerned with absolute return as the speculators, but instead choose to buy or sell financial assets whose movement in price they believe will dampen out the movement in value of their existing portfolio.
3. *Arbitrageurs*. These are market agents who are concerned not only with attaining a high return from their investments, but also doing so with minimal (or zero) risk. Arbitrage has a specific meaning within the context of finance: it is the process of exploiting mis-pricing of financial assets in order to gain riskless profit. Suppose an asset has price $X_A$ on market A but price $X_B < X_A$ on market B—the arbitrageur would, at the same point in time, buy the asset on market B and sell it on market A. The arbitrageur thus makes $X_A - X_B$ profit without risk. The very presence of arbitrageurs implies that the opportunities for arbitrage are scarce, since the action of buying on market B forces the price $X_B$ upwards whereas selling on market A forces the price $X_A$ downwards until $X_A = X_B$. This is known as the principle of no arbitrage.[3]

---

[3]   O'Hara, M. (1995) *Market Microstructure Theory*, Blackwell Publishers.

### 1.3.5 The price of an asset

One of the most important roles of a financial market is to supply, on a continuous basis, a price for a financial asset at which both buyers and sellers are willing to trade. Classically the 'value' of a financial asset is the current value of the total expected future cash flow from that asset. This is the 'rational expectations' price of the asset and there are many models in the economics and finance literature for calculating this price (e.g. see Campbell *et al*. 1997). However, it is an obvious fact that the price of every financial asset moves on a day to day, hour to hour, and often second to second basis and that usually there is very little relation between the mean price of the asset and the 'rational expectations' price. The question therefore arises as to what determines the price of a financial asset in practice.

**1.3.5.1 Role of the market-maker.** We have already discussed the important role of the market-maker in the process of setting a price level for financial assets at which buyers and sellers are willing to trade. The market-makers supply a willing counterparty for each trade, at a price set by themselves. In the simplest scenario, a market-maker, by contrast to the other market participants, will have no interest in generating a financial return from holding a position in the financial asset and then raising its price. Ideally, the market-maker's manipulation of the price should be solely for the purposes of matching the supply of assets from willing sellers, with the demand for assets from willing buyers. In this way, market-makers can maximize the number of assets traded (i.e. the volume) hence generating market liquidity, and at the same time maximizing their own profit. (Recall that market-makers set a spread between bid and ask prices which generates revenue for them from each traded asset). It is a fairly undisputed fact[4] that *on average*, the market-maker will raise the asset price in the presence of an excess of buyers, and will lower the asset price in the presence of an excess of sellers. This follows from the assumption that fewer agents will be willing to buy the asset if the ask price is raised, though more agents will be willing to sell it if the bid price is raised as well. Although this assumption is not necessarily always true, it serves as a good approximation. Hence, we have the scenario wherein the demand for assets largely determines the traded price through the action of the market-maker. In order to pursue our goal of understanding what determines the price level of financial assets in the market, we must therefore answer the question: 'what determines the demand for assets?'

**1.3.5.2 Demand for assets.** We will refer to the number of financial assets sought minus the number offered, as the 'excess demand' for the asset. The excess demand,

---

[4] Chordia, T., Roll, R., and Subrahmanyam, A. (2001) *J. Fin. Econ.* **56**, 501. See also Lillo, F., Farmer, J. D., and Mantegna, R. N. (2003) *Nature* **421**, 129; Plerou, V., Gopikrishnan, P., and Stanley, H. E. (2003) *Nature* **421**, 130.

by construction, will be a very complex function of the investors' beliefs about the asset: in particular, its expected future price levels and its expected future earnings. These two issues are the principal factors that will be in investors' minds when they decide to place an order with their broker to buy or sell the asset. How important each of these issues is to an investor, and how his/her individual perception of these issues arises, will in turn be a function of very many possible parameters. For example, while one investor may view a news bulletin about the performance of company $X$ as a deciding influence on the future price movement of company $X$'s assets, another investor may see this news as neutral or may even believe it will have the opposite effect. Consequently, any realistic model of the excess demand for a financial asset, and hence a model for the asset price itself, must capture these possible behavioural issues in a very general way.

### 1.3.6    Orders and market clearing

Financial market investors who wish to buy or sell assets, do so by contacting their broker who acts as their legal agent in the market. However, there are different types of request an investor can make of his/her broker. Broadly speaking, investors can place an order with their broker to execute a trade irrespective of the price at which the trade is made, or they can place an order which is dependent on the traded price which can be achieved. We refer to the first (unconditional) type of order as a 'market order' and the second (conditional) type as a 'limit order'. The existence of these different types of order arises from the fact that investors cannot immediately execute their desired trade at the current price they observe. It will physically take a certain amount of time for the broker to be contacted and for the trade to be secured. Within this time interval, which is small nowadays but still non-zero, the price may well move away from the value the investor saw at the time the order was placed. In addition, the price observed by the investor at the time of placing the order may not be an accurate representation of the current asset price. The reasons why this might be so are many. For example, the price observed by the investor may be delayed by the data provider, be an average over the last few traded prices, be an average over the bid and ask prices or simply be incorrectly recorded. These factors contribute to create the situation whereby an investor may not have accurate knowledge of the traded price. However, there is a third and more fundamental reason why the actual traded price can be different from the asset price observed at the time of the order. This is due to the mechanism by which the price is set in the market. When the order is placed by the broker, it enters the market-maker's 'order book'. The market-maker must then update his/her calculation of the excess demand in the market, by adding up all the buy orders in the order book and subtracting all the sell orders. Due to the revised calculation of the excess demand, the market-maker may then consequently wish to move the price of the asset. All this will be done *prior* to the execution of the orders. *The temporal ordering of this entire process is central to the task of constructing a useful model of the complex system represented by the financial market.* We reiterate this temporal ordering in the schematic representation shown in Fig. 1.2.

**1.3.6.1   Market impact.** The mechanism of the market-maker moving the asset price in response to the excess demand *prior* to executing the orders, leads to a very important feature of the complex system representing the financial market: this feature is termed 'market impact'. Broadly speaking, market impact is the adverse affect of an order on its own traded price. To recap, the market-maker moves the price up in the presence of a positive excess demand, and down in the presence of a negative excess demand. Let us imagine a scenario where the order $a_i$ placed by one investor $i$ is statistically independent from the order $a_j$ placed by another agent $j \neq i$. The act of agent $i$ placing an order to buy assets ($a_i > 0$) will, when we average over all the possible orders from agents $j \neq i$, increase the excess demand $D = \sum_k a_k$. The opposite is also true, that is, agent $i$ placing an order to sell assets ($a_i < 0$) will on average lower the excess demand. The consequence of this is that an order to buy assets will on average raise the price at which they can be bought, and an order to sell assets will on average lower the price at which they can be sold. This is the market impact effect.

**1.3.6.2   Clearing the market.** We have discussed the fact that orders can be placed by an investor in two distinct ways, either as 'market orders' or 'limit orders'. Whether the order is a market or limit order determines how it is treated by the market-maker and hence how the order itself affects the market. A general framework for the way orders are placed with the market-maker is as follows. An order $a_i$ (whether it be a market or limit order) represents the willingness of an investor $i$ to either buy ($a_i > 0$) or sell ($a_i < 0$) a quantity $|a_i|$ of financial assets. In general, we can say[5] that the order at time $t$, which is $a_i[t]$, is a function of the price at which the order will be executed, which is $x[t+1]$. Hence, the general order $a_i[t, x[t+1]]$ can now be defined mathematically in terms of the preferences of the investor. For example, a simple market order that says 'transact at any traded price' has the form $a_i[t, x[t+1]] = a_i[t]$, and a simple limit order that says 'transact only if the traded price is equal to or greater than value $y_i$' has the form $a_i[t, x[t+1]] = a_i[t]H[x[t+1] - y_i]$, where $H[x]$ is the Heaviside function.[6] In most circumstances, the market is dominated by market orders together

---

[5] Units of time are arbitrary here, and reflect the discrete nature of the process of placing an order and having it executed, as demonstrated schematically in Fig. 1.2.    [6] $H[x] = 1, 0$ for $x \geq 0, x < 0$, respectively.

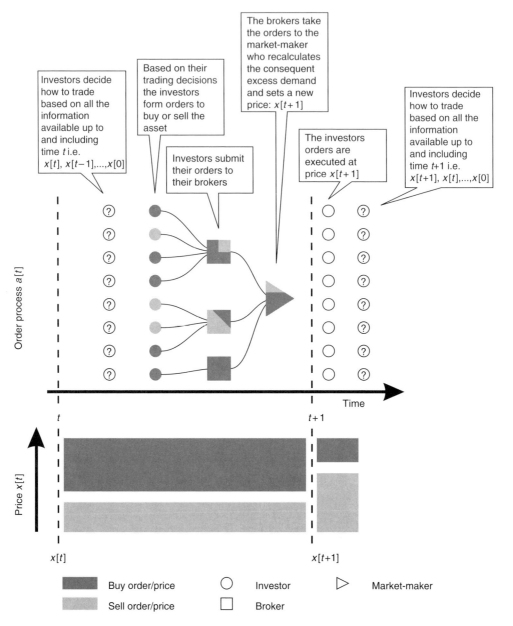

Investors decide how to trade based on all the information available up to and including time $t$ i.e. $x[t], x[t-1],...,x[0]$

Based on their trading decisions the investors form orders to buy or sell the asset

Investors submit their orders to their brokers

The brokers take the orders to the market-maker who recalculates the consequent excess demand and sets a new price: $x[t+1]$

The investors orders are executed at price $x[t+1]$

Investors decide how to trade based on all the information available up to and including time $t+1$ i.e. $x[t+1], x[t],...,x[0]$

Order process $a[t]$

Time

$t$

$t+1$

Price $x[t]$

$x[t]$

$x[t+1]$

Buy order/price     ○ Investor     ▷ Market-maker

Sell order/price     □ Broker

**Fig. 1.2** A schematic representation of the temporal order in which events occur in the trading of financial assets through the investor—broker—market-maker chain. For simplicity, we assume all orders are market orders and thus are all transacted at the new price set by the market-maker. We also have assumed that all orders are placed at the same time; this is purely for clarity, as described in Chapter 4.

with simple limit orders of the form 'buy if the traded price is lower than $y_i$' and 'sell if the traded price is higher than $y_i$'. The market-maker simultaneously defines a bid price $x^-$ and an ask price $x^+$, where of course $x^- < x^+$ to prevent arbitrage. After collecting all the orders $a_i[t]$, re-assessing the excess demand $D[(t+1)^-] = \sum_i a_i[t]$ (where $(t+1)^-$ indicates the time immediately before time $t+1$) and hence moving the bid and ask prices $(x^-[t+1]$ and $x^+[t+1]$, respectively), the market-maker will execute:

- all market orders
- all buy limit orders $(a_i[t, x[t+1]] > 0)$, for which $y_i \geq x^+[t+1]$
- all sell limit orders $(a_i[t, x[t+1]] < 0)$, for which $y_i \leq x^-[t+1]$.

The market-maker's book will then contain buy orders for which $y_i < x^+[t+1]$ and sell orders for which $y_i > x^-[t+1]$. Some of these may lie within the market-maker's spread, that is $x^-[t+1] < y_i < x^+[t+1]$. Although these orders were unacceptable to the market-maker, they can be filled by other agents with opposite orders within the spread. This trading inside the spread tends to remove all orders in this price region, leaving a collection of buy orders for which $y_i < x^-[t+1]$ and sell orders for which $y_i > x^+[t+1]$. An example of such an order book is shown in Fig. 1.3, and graphically in Fig. 1.4.

| Last trade | | | Time | Shares | |
|---|---|---|---|---|---|
| **23.300** | | | 07:31 | 100 | |
| **Buy orders** | | | **Sell orders** | | |
| **Broker** | **Shares** | **Price** | **Broker** | **Shares** | **Price** |
| A | 800 | 23.299 | C | 2900 | 23.300 |
| B | 100 | 23.290 | B | 400 | 23.340 |
| C | 4000 | 23.280 | A | 100 | 23.360 |
| B | 1000 | 23.221 | A | 800 | 23.379 |
| B | 1100 | 23.220 | B | 500 | 23.400 |
| B | 1000 | 23.200 | C | 4000 | 23.410 |
| B | 1000 | 23.200 | B | 4000 | 23.410 |
| A | 500 | 23.120 | A | 2000 | 23.440 |
| B | 100 | 23.110 | B | 100 | 23.590 |
| A | 2100 | 23.040 | B | 500 | 23.600 |
| A | 4900 | 23.040 | B | 100 | 23.690 |
| A | 100 | 23.040 | B | 200 | 23.730 |
| B | 400 | 23.010 | A | 2000 | 23.900 |
| A | 100 | 22.920 | B | 70 | 23.980 |
| B | 100 | 22.910 | B | 54 | 23.990 |
| 12 more | | | 26 more | | |

**Fig. 1.3**  An example of a market-maker's order book showing the (limit) orders remaining after all possible trades have been executed. Data taken from http://www.3Dstockcharts.com shows market activity on the financial index asset QQQ on 13 July 2002.

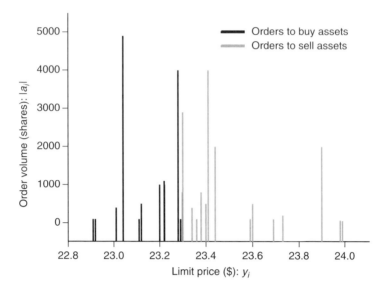

**Fig. 1.4**    A graphical representation of the order book shown in Fig. 1.3.

The (limit) orders which still remain on the market-maker's order book after all possible trades have been executed, will remain there until the investors withdraw them. As such, the orders remaining on the market-maker's order book still contribute to the excess demand. One can therefore look upon charts such as Fig. 1.4 as showing the 'pressure' on an asset price.

So far it has been assumed that the market-maker can, and always will, process all possible orders. This in turn implies that the market-maker may have to assume either a long position (holding assets) or a short position (owing assets). The position held by the market-maker represents an unwanted risk; the market-maker, as a pure liquidity provider, should not seek to take a speculatory position in the asset. It is therefore likely that the market-maker will also take his/her own position in the asset into account when deciding a new price level to set. This effect can further complicate the relationship between excess demand and price change.[7]

### 1.3.7    Chartism vs fundamentalism

Section 1.3.5.2 discussed how demand for assets arises from investors' expectations of either the future earnings of the asset, or the future price movements. It could be argued that the future movements in the price of the asset reflect movements in its value which are in turn determined by its future earnings. Hence the two sources of demand

---

[7] Jefferies, P., Hart, M. L., Hui, P. M., and Johnson, N. F. (2001) *Eur. Phys. J.* B **20**, 493.

might appear to be the same. However, it is an empirical fact that in virtually all cases, the frequency of movements in the price of a financial asset is orders of magnitude greater than the frequency with which news arrives which could relate to the future earnings of that asset. In addition, a large proportion of all asset positions are held for only a short period of time, so short in most cases as to never benefit from the asset's direct earnings (dividends). This seems to indicate instead that the two sources of demand are actually fundamentally different. Furthermore, the changes in investors' expectations of future price movements could indeed generate a demand for assets which fluctuates with the high frequency that is actually observed. It therefore seems reasonable to consider the principal source of demand as the investors' expectations of future price movements. Broadly speaking, expectations of future price movements can be generated through two distinct schools of thought: chartist principles and fundamentalist principles. A chartist bases his/her expectations of future price movements on the past states of a series of 'technical indicators'. These technical indicators[8] are usually functions of the past series of asset prices $x[0]$, ..., $x[t]$, and sometimes also the volumes $V[0]$, ..., $V[t]$. A fundamentalist on the other hand bases his/her expectations of future price movements on the past states of a series of 'fundamentals'. The fundamentals of an asset are usually parameters relating to the asset's earnings and the economic strength of the institution issuing the asset. Most investors belong to either the chartist or the fundamentalist school of thought with very few employing both principles. It is an ongoing question, and often the cause of much angst, as to whether an investor should trust chartist principles or fundamentalist principles in any given market. A principle of economics known as the Efficient Market Hypothesis (EMH) (e.g. see Campbell *et al.* 1997) claims that all the information concerning an asset—technical and fundamental, public and private—is already incorporated into the current price of the asset. If this principle were true, it would imply that it is theoretically impossible for any investor from any school of thought to make a risk-free profit by following their own trading principles. What one can, however, say in the debate of chartism vs fundamentalism, is that fundamentalism is considered the 'old' school of thought and chartism the 'new'. Consequently, the more modern, liquid, markets seem to be dominated by chartist investors.[9] This is largely due to a belief amongst investors that the more modern, liquid, and speculative markets are the most fertile grounds for applying chartist principles. This clearly leads to a vicious circle which draws more and more chartists into the market as the degree of liquidity and speculation grows. There then arises the following interesting question: if there is a population of traders *looking* for patterns in past prices, *believing* they see such

---

[8] See, for example, Blair, A. (1996) *Investors Chronicle Guide to Charting*, Pitman.
[9] Research in collaboration with Dr J. James of Bank One, London.

patterns,[10] and then *acting* as though those patterns were real, will this process itself induce patterns into the market? Since there is no unique interpretation of such price series in terms of pattern identification, the market of chartists becomes a heterogeneous one. Will some patterns therefore survive, hidden away safely since no chartist happens to be around who could identify them? And what happens in the opposite case where too many chartists are identifying, and acting on, the same apparent pattern? These questions provide the motivation for much of the discussion of market models in Chapter 4.

## 1.4    Observing the market

Having given an overview of the inner workings of financial markets, we now step back and assume the position of an outsider who is observing the 'output' of a particular market. Despite the large number of variables driving the market itself, as discussed in this chapter, the outside observer has a very limited number of output variables at his disposition. Hence he may be forced to regard the market as a 'black box'. For the stock market, the output variables are prices and possibly volumes of trades. In recent years, the frequency of the available data has increased enormously: whereas previously only daily prices were disclosed, now it is possible to get trade-by-trade price data (so-called *tick-data*) albeit with a finite delay time if one does not subscribe to a data provider. Since the price as a function of time $x[t]$ is the primary experimental output variable, or 'observable', it is worth discussing it in some detail.[11]

Consider the typical situation in which we, as outsiders, are provided with a set of high-frequency price data $\{x\}$ over a given, finite time period. Even though the major markets are very liquid, each transaction occurs at a specific moment in time. Hence, the time-series will be a set of data points at discrete times $x[t_1], x[t_2], x[t_3], \ldots$ typically separated by irregular clock-time intervals (e.g. 1 s, 5 s, 2 s, . . .). To add to the complication, many exchanges are not open 24 h per day—plus there are holidays and weekends. Even the ones that do remain open will possibly change their 'character'

---

[10]  Even a purely random price series may appear to have patterns, if one is only observing a finite segment of it. The analogy in a coin-tossing game is as follows: what is the next outcome in the sequence . . . HHHHHHHH? The answer is of course H (heads) or T (tails) with equal probability if the coin is fair. But it is very tempting, and arguably part of human nature, to believe that it will definitely be H (i.e. trend-following behaviour), or definitely be T (i.e. contrarian behaviour).

[11]  We tend to use $y[t]$ or equivalently $y_t$ to denote a financial variable which is defined at discrete times: for example, the closing price or total trading volume each day. We tend to use $y(t)$ to denote the special case in which the financial variable is treated as a function of continuous time. Note that $y[t]$ may not be smooth and differentiable, and hence may need to be described by mapping equations (see Chapters 4–7) as opposed to the typical differential equation approach of standard finance for $y(t)$ (see Chapter 2). The uses of $y[t]$, $y_t$, and $y(t)$ will be made clear from their context throughout the book.

(and hence characteristic price distributions) when one time-zone shuts down and the other opens up, for example, when New York closes or London opens. This is not only very awkward to handle in practical terms, it also raises some tricky conceptual questions regarding a priori assumptions of stationarity, and opens up the possibility of picking up spurious dynamical trends. Even within one single geographic zone, it is unclear how we should 'connect' the value from 4 p.m. on Friday and 8 a.m. the following Monday. Should they be considered to be truly consecutive in the same way as 2:15 p.m. and 2:16 p.m. are on a given day? Unfortunately, there is no unique solution to this time-related problem, and any empirical investigation must be careful to ensure that unintentional correlations are not introduced by whichever approach is chosen.

Another difficult question relates to which *function* of the price we, as observers, should use in order to perform statistical tests. In particular, we wish to extract maximum meaningful information and, possibly more importantly, introduce the minimum amount of spurious correlations or bias by this choice. The following choices are typically the most common when looking at price fluctuations:

1. *Linear price-change*

$$\Delta x[t, t - \Delta t] = x[t] - x[t - \Delta t] \tag{1.1}$$

   or equivalently, using shorthand notation in order to reduce the number of parentheses[12]

$$\Delta x_{t, t-\Delta t} = x_t - x_{t-\Delta t}.$$

2. *Discounted or de-trended price-change.* This attempts to remove the effects of inflation or supposedly deterministic bias etc. by introducing a factor $F[t]$

$$\Delta x^{(F)}[t, t - \Delta t] = F[t]x[t] - F[t - \Delta t]x[t - \Delta t]. \tag{1.2}$$

   The problem then arises as to what form $F[t]$ should take. Fortunately, if $F[t]$ is slowly varying as compared to the time window over which the data is collected, then we can usually assume

$$\Delta x^{(F)}[t, t - \Delta t] \propto \Delta x[t, t - \Delta t].$$

3. *Return.* This focuses on the fractional change in price in order to distinguish the relative importance of a given absolute price-change, for example, in order to

---

[12]  See note 11.

distinguish between the cases of a $1 change in price for a $400 stock as compared to a $1 change for a $10 stock.

$$R[t, t - \Delta t] = \frac{\Delta x[t, t - \Delta t]}{x[t - \Delta t]} = \frac{x[t] - x[t - \Delta t]}{x[t - \Delta t]} \qquad (1.3)$$

or, using our shorthand equivalent,

$$R_{t, t-\Delta t} = \frac{\Delta x_{t, t-\Delta t}}{x_{t-\Delta t}} = \frac{x_t - x_{t-\Delta t}}{x_{t-\Delta t}}.$$

In the typical case that the change in price is much smaller than the price itself, that is, $\Delta x[t, t - \Delta t] \ll x[t - \Delta t]$, we can assume $R[t, t - \Delta t] \propto \Delta x[t, t - \Delta t]$.

4. *Log-return*

$$z[t, t - \Delta t] = \ln \frac{x[t]}{x[t - \Delta t]} = \ln x[t] - \ln x[t - \Delta t] \qquad (1.4)$$

or, using our shorthand equivalent,

$$z_{t, t-\Delta t} = \ln (x_t / x_{t-\Delta t}) = \ln x_t - \ln x_{t-\Delta t}.$$

Depending on the dataset, it may be more convenient to use base-10 logarithms when plotting log-returns. The values using natural and base-10 logarithms just differ by a constant factor. In the limit that $\Delta x[t, t - \Delta t] \ll x[t - \Delta t]$, we have

$$z[t, t - \Delta t] = \ln \frac{x[t]}{x[t - \Delta t]} = \ln \left( 1 + \frac{\Delta x[t, t - \Delta t]}{x[t - \Delta t]} \right)$$

$$\sim \frac{\Delta x[t, t - \Delta t]}{x[t - \Delta t]} = R[t, t - \Delta t].$$

Hence we can again assume $z[t, t - \Delta t] \propto \Delta x[t, t - \Delta t]$.

Each of these price-related definitions has its advantages and disadvantages. Any particular choice may or may not bias a given dataset, hence confusing the usefulness of the conclusions. Again this is a practical problem and there is no easy way out, nor is there any 'right' and 'wrong' answer. Throughout this book we will switch between these quantities according to the data available, and the problem under consideration. Fortunately these quantities all have similar statistical properties in practice, since the change in price $\Delta x[t, t - \Delta t]$ is typically small compared to the absolute values $x[t - \Delta t]$, $x[t]$. This reason, combined with the fact that we do not focus on specific stock data, means that *we will not tend to worry about the distinction between these various price-change measures in this book.*

# 2. Standard finance theory

## 2.1 The problem for standard finance theory

The problem facing *any* theory for managing risk, portfolios, hedging, and derivative pricing, is that the theory's applicability will always be limited by the accuracy of the description employed for the underlying market movements. In standard finance theory,[1] such market movements are typically described by a stochastic process, which then allows one to employ the powerful machinery of stochastic calculus by assuming the continuous-time limit. However, the assumption of a continuous-time limit often yields misleading results as will be discussed in Chapter 6. Furthermore the parameterization and structuring of such stochastic processes is typically very difficult, leading to the creation of *ad hoc* market models through a process resembling alchemy rather than deductive science. Indeed, it is unclear whether one would ever be able to adapt these standard stochastic prescriptions to include the *full* range of 'stylized facts' exhibited by financial market time-series (see Chapter 3). Having said this, we admit that it is easy to criticize. However these criticisms will help guide our discussion of more generalized approaches later in this book.[2] First though, we need to understand the basics behind standard finance theory.

There is no free lunch in finance. At least, this is what the Efficient Market Hypothesis (EMH) claims (e.g. see Campbell *et al.* 1997). The EMH says that the entire history of information regarding an asset is reflected in its price and that the market responds instantaneously to new information. Thus the EMH implies that if any patterns (such as temporal correlations) do exist, they must be so small that no systematic trading strategy can have a better risk/return profile than the market portfolio. Hence according to the EMH, no profitable information about future movements can

---

[1] As in the rest of this book, we use an all-encompassing term 'standard finance theory'. Although convenient for the present purpose, such labels are always dangerous since they lay one open to criticism about exceptions to the rule. However we would claim that standard finance theory tends to adopt particular classes of assumption concerning, for example, temporal correlations. It is these assumptions, and in particular how one might avoid them, which interest us.

[2] For example, if models which are *differential* with respect to time seem limited, one might think about whether models which involve the *integral* of time will work better. This is indeed the approach adopted in Chapter 6 in order to address the question of risk minimization and hedging in real-world markets.

be obtained by studying the past price series. Given the no-free-lunch hypothesis, it makes sense that believers in the EMH would choose a model of asset prices that constitutes a 'random walk' in price-space. The theoretical descriptions used in standard finance theory, are typically built around this assumption that asset prices follow some form of random walk. We therefore need to understand the details, and hence limitations, of a random walk.

## 2.2 Taking a random walk

### 2.2.1 Back to basics

We start by revisiting some fairly well-known probability results. Suppose we are tossing a fair coin. Heads (H) and tails (T) have equal probability of occurring, hence $p[\text{heads}] = p[\text{tails}] = 0.5$. We can think of this coin-toss experiment as drawing a random value $\Delta x$ from a probability distribution function (PDF) $p[\Delta x]$. Let's denote $\Delta x = +d$ as outcome H and $\Delta x = -d$ as outcome T. The PDF $p[\Delta x]$ has the form shown in Fig. 2.1.

We can use the outcomes of this coin-toss experiment to generate a price series for a simple 'coin-toss' market. The price-change at timestep $i$ is given by the coin-toss outcome at that timestep. In accordance with the shorthand notation of Section 1.4, the price-change at timestep $i$ is $\Delta x_{i,i-1} = x_i - x_{i-1}$. We will henceforth use the further abbreviation $\Delta x_{i,i-1} \equiv \Delta x_i$ to denote this price-change at timestep $i$. The price-change over $n$ timesteps is given by $\Delta x_{i,i-n} = x_i - x_{i-n} = \sum_{j=i+1-n}^{i} \Delta x_j$. Consider, for example, a series of outcomes HHTH, which generates a price series that moves up-up-down-up with step-size $d$. The corresponding price series is shown in Fig. 2.2 (thick line) together with the 'tree' formed by all possible such walks.

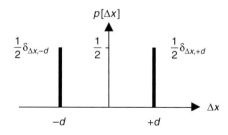

**Fig. 2.1**  Probability distribution function $p[\Delta x]$ for outcomes of a coin-toss experiment or, equivalently, for price-changes in a 'coin-toss' market where up and down price-changes of magnitude $d$ occur with probability 0.5 at each timestep. The Kronecker-delta $\delta_{ij}$ is equal to 1 if $i = j$, otherwise it is zero.

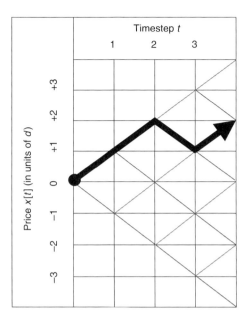

**Fig. 2.2**   Price series in a 'coin-toss' market where up and down price-changes of magnitude $d$ occur with probability 0.5 at each timestep. Thick black line corresponds to the sequence of coin-tosses HHTH. All other possible paths form a 'tree' as shown. The price at timestep 0 is defined as the price-origin $x_0 = 0$.

Broadly speaking, we can think of this simple random-walk model as representing the foundation upon which standard finance theory is built. We say 'broadly' since some finance models are more sophisticated than others. On the other hand, we say 'represents' since the statistical properties related to the correlations between outcomes are indeed quite similar.[3] In particular, this coin-toss price model assumes that the successive outcomes $\{\Delta x_i\}$ are i.i.d. variables, which means *independent and identically distributed*. This makes sense for a coin-toss price mechanism: successive coin-toss outcomes are indeed independent, and since we are using the same coin at each timestep then the PDF $p[\Delta x]$ is identical at every timestep. The coin-toss price model is also consistent with the EMH in that it is impossible to forecast the next outcome based on the past outcomes. In other words, if we were betting on future outcomes, we would not be able to gain systematically over time. In short, we have no 'edge' in the coin-toss market because the price series is random.

To be fair, standard finance theory is not quite that simplistic. It does not necessarily assume that each timestep is a simple coin-toss with two outcomes, up and down of identical step-size. On the other hand, it does assume that the price-process is

---

[3]  See note 1.

random—or so close to random that no systematic profit can be made based on know-ledge of past outcomes. Moreover, it does often make the i.i.d. assumption concerning price-changes. So let's explore this i.i.d. property further for a more general situation. Consider the price-changes[4] in a real market at different timesteps—obviously we should not assume a priori that such price-changes are i.i.d. variables. The PDF for the price-change $\Delta x_i$ at timestep $i$ is $p_i[\Delta x_i]$. Consider a set of such price-changes[5] measured at different timesteps: $\Delta x_1, \Delta x_2, \ldots, \Delta x_i, \ldots, \Delta x_j, \ldots$. Standard finance theory then makes one, or invariably both, of the i.i.d. assumptions below:

**Assumption (i)** *The variables* $\{\Delta x_i\} \equiv \Delta x_1, \Delta x_2, \ldots, \Delta x_i, \ldots, \Delta x_j, \ldots$ *are independent.*

Consider the joint probability distribution $p[\Delta x_i, \Delta x_j]$ which gives the probability of obtaining the values $\Delta x_i$ and $\Delta x_j$ at two particular timesteps $i$ and $j$. These price-changes at timesteps $i$ and $j$ are *independent* if $p[\Delta x_i, \Delta x_j] = p_i[\Delta x_i]p_j[\Delta x_j]$ where $p_i[\Delta x_i]$ and $p_j[\Delta x_j]$ are the individual PDFs for timesteps $i$ and $j$. In other words, the joint probability distribution function can be written as a product of the individual probability distribution functions for the price-changes at timesteps $i$ and $j$. The mean value of any product function of $\Delta x_i$ and $\Delta x_j$, for example, $f[\Delta x_i]g[\Delta x_j]$, then becomes:

$$\langle f[\Delta x_i]g[\Delta x_j]\rangle = \sum_{\Delta x_i, \Delta x_j} f[\Delta x_i]g[\Delta x_j]p[\Delta x_i, \Delta x_j]$$

$$= \left\{\sum_{\Delta x_i} f[\Delta x_i]p_i[\Delta x_i]\right\}\left\{\sum_{\Delta x_j} g[\Delta x_j]p_j[\Delta x_j]\right\}$$

$$= \langle f[\Delta x_i]\rangle\langle g[\Delta x_j]\rangle. \tag{2.1}$$

---

[4] Apart from the suggested scenario in which the variables $\{\Delta x_i\}$ represent price-changes at timesteps $1, 2, \ldots, i$ etc., we could instead take $\{\Delta x_i\}$ to represent any number of other financial data-series, e.g. price-changes for different assets at a given timestep ($i$ becomes an asset label rather than a timestep label); price-changes for different assets at different timesteps; a set of changes in monthly volatilities; daily changes in exchange-rate between different currencies and the US dollar, etc. We just refer to $\Delta x_i$ as a 'price-change' for simplicity. Note that even 'price-change' itself could represent one of many possibilities, for example, the detrended price-change, the return, the log-return using either natural or base-10 logarithms (see Section 1.4). Which of these financial variables is actually closest to being i.i.d. will depend on the financial market itself: there is no way of knowing a priori without performing statistical tests.

[5] See note 4.

One important consequence of this independence arises for $f[\Delta x_i] = \Delta x_i$ and $g[\Delta x_j] = \Delta x_j$, in which case Equation (2.1) gives

$$\langle \Delta x_i \Delta x_j \rangle = \langle \Delta x_i \rangle \langle \Delta x_j \rangle. \tag{2.2}$$

If Equation (2.2) holds, we say $\Delta x_i$ and $\Delta x_j$ are *uncorrelated*. However this is just one particular statistical property of the variables $\Delta x_i$ and $\Delta x_j$, out of the infinite number of possible choices for $f[\Delta x_i]$ and $g[\Delta x_j]$. In particular, Equation (2.2) can be satisfied for a particular dataset without Equation (2.1) being satisfied. Hence we conclude that *independent variables are always uncorrelated*, while *uncorrelated variables are not necessarily independent*. In a real market it is not clear a priori whether the price-changes are truly independent. Most statistical testing, particularly using standard software packages, will just report on the following correlation measure:[6]

$$c_{ij} = \langle \Delta x_i \Delta x_j \rangle - \langle \Delta x_i \rangle \langle \Delta x_j \rangle \equiv \left\langle \left( \Delta x_i - \langle \Delta x_i \rangle \right) \left( \Delta x_j - \langle \Delta x_j \rangle \right) \right\rangle. \tag{2.3}$$

If $c_{ij} = 0$, then the variables are uncorrelated (see Equation (2.2)). However, this leaves wide open the question of whether *higher order* correlations[7] exist. Since we have in mind the example where $i$ and $j$ label individual timesteps, these higher order correlations will represent higher order *temporal* correlations. If on the other hand $i$ and $j$ labelled different assets at the same timestep, for example, these higher order correlations would be higher order *inter-asset* correlations.[8] The correlation measure $c_{ij} = \langle \Delta x_i \Delta x_j \rangle - \langle \Delta x_i \rangle \langle \Delta x_j \rangle$ derived from Equation (2.2), is associated with the $m = 1$ power of $\Delta x_i$ and $\Delta x_j$ (i.e. we have effectively taken $f[\Delta x_i]$ and $g[\Delta x_j]$ proportional to $\Delta x_i$ and $\Delta x_j$ respectively in Equation (2.1)). Higher order correlations are associated with higher powers of $\Delta x_i$ and $\Delta x_j$ (e.g. $f[\Delta x_i]$ and $g[\Delta x_j]$ proportional to $(\Delta x_i)^m$ and $(\Delta x_j)^m$ respectively with $m > 1$) *or* non-analytic functions[9] of $\Delta x_i$ and $\Delta x_j$ (e.g. $f[\Delta x_i]$ and $g[\Delta x_j]$ proportional to $|\Delta x_i|$ and $|\Delta x_j|$, respectively). In principle, one would have to check *all* such higher order correlations in order to provide convincing evidence for independence.

**Assumption (ii)** *The variables* $\{\Delta x_i\} \equiv \Delta x_1, \Delta x_2, \ldots, \Delta x_i, \ldots, \Delta x_j, \ldots$ *are identically distributed.*

---

[6] $c_{ij}$ is often called the *covariance*. Dividing by the standard deviation of $\Delta x_i$ and $\Delta x_j$ yields the *correlation coefficient*. If $i, j$ refer to timesteps of the same data-series, then the correlation coefficient is also known as the *autocorrelation coefficient*.

[7] *Higher order* correlations can also be referred to as *nonlinear* correlations. In this sense, the correlation measure $c_{ij}$ in Equation (2.3) and hence the autocorrelation coefficient, measure *linear* correlations between $\Delta x_i$ and $\Delta x_j$.

[8] Such higher order inter-asset correlations could have important consequences for assessing the risk in a portfolio. Standard finance theory focuses on assessing the risk associated with the linear correlation $c_{ij}$ between assets.

[9] See note 7.

If the individual PDFs $p_i$ and $p_j$ are identical functions, then the variables $\Delta x_i$ and $\Delta x_j$ are *identically distributed*. In a real market, this will not generally be true—for example, the PDF of price-changes on Mondays is not exactly the same as that for Fridays.

All market price-processes are therefore classifiable as one of the following four cases. Standard finance theory tends to consider Case I, which is the easiest to deal with mathematically.

*Case I.* Assumptions (i) and (ii) hold. Hence the price-process is one with i.i.d. price-changes,[10] for example, the coin-toss market.

*Case II.* Only assumption (i) holds. The price-changes are independent, but are not identically distributed. This would be the case for the coin-toss market if different timesteps had different step-sizes and/or a different number of possible outcomes.

*Case III.* Only assumption (ii) holds. The price-changes are not independent, but are identically distributed. This would be the case for the coin-toss market if we were to make the coin-toss outcome at a given timestep conditional on the outcome of previous timesteps. A priori, the unconditional PDFs describing the outcome at each timestep are identical—however the outcomes in a given run will not be independent. An example of such dependence is created by the following rule: *if* we obtain five successive tails TTTTT (i.e. five successive price-changes downwards) *then* we will bias the coin-toss outcome in such a way that there is a very high probability of obtaining T at the next timestep as well (i.e. another price-change downwards). Such a 'memory' effect can, in principle, lead to systematic profit. Believers in the EMH would however claim that such dependence between price-changes must be very small—in fact so small as to be wiped out by transaction costs.

*Case IV.* Neither assumption holds. This is the most mathematically complicated case. However it is also the one which seems closest to reality.

### 2.2.2   Price-changes over one timestep

Let's assume for the moment that we do have i.i.d. price-changes, hence we can focus on the properties of the PDF for the single variable $\Delta x_i \equiv \Delta x$ describing the price-change between any two successive timesteps. The *mean, average,* or *expectation*

---

[10] Recall from Section 1.4 that 'price-change' could mean actual price-change $x_i - x_{i-1}$, fractional price-change or return $[x_i - x_{i-1}]/x_{i-1}$, or log-return $\ln x_i/x_{i-1}$.

value of a function $f[\Delta x]$ is defined as[11]:

$$\langle f[\Delta x]\rangle \equiv \overline{f[\Delta x]} \equiv E\big[f[\Delta x]\big]$$

$$= \sum_{\Delta x} f[\Delta x]p[\Delta x] \equiv \int_{-\infty}^{+\infty} f[\Delta x]p[\Delta x]\,\mathrm{d}(\Delta x). \qquad (2.4)$$

If $\Delta x$ takes discrete values, the mean can be calculated using the summation with $p[\Delta x]$ being a *discrete* PDF; if $\Delta x$ takes continuous values, the mean can be calculated using the integral with $p[\Delta x]$ being a *continuous* PDF (also known as a probability density function). For both discrete and continuous cases, we refer to the associated probability distribution function simply as 'PDF'. Depending on the context, either of them may be more useful.[12] To help in discussing the ideas from general probability theory, we will tend to assume discrete $\Delta x$ since the coin-toss example is itself discrete—however, the conclusions are the same for both discrete and continuous $\Delta x$.[13]

Choosing $f[\Delta x] = \Delta x$ in Equation (2.4) yields the mean value $\langle \Delta x \rangle$ which represents the $m = 1$ 'moment' of $p[\Delta x]$. The $m$th 'central' moment is given by $\langle (\Delta x - \langle \Delta x \rangle)^m \rangle$. Some of these higher order moments have specific names. For example the 'skewness' of $p[\Delta x]$ is given by $\langle (\Delta x - \langle \Delta x \rangle)^3 \rangle / \sigma^3$ where $\sigma$ is the standard deviation of $\Delta x$ over a single timestep, as defined below. The skewness is equal to zero if $p[\Delta x]$ is symmetric. The 'kurtosis' of $p[\Delta x]$ is given by $\kappa \equiv \langle (\Delta x - \langle \Delta x \rangle)^4 \rangle / \sigma^4$ and gives $\kappa = 3$ if $p[\Delta x]$ is Gaussian. We note that the mean $\langle \Delta x \rangle$ may *not* necessarily correspond to a possible experimental outcome. For the coin-toss market, $\langle \Delta x \rangle = \frac{1}{2}(-d) + \frac{1}{2}(+d) = 0$ yet '0' is not a possible outcome. So using mean values to represent 'typical' future behaviour may be misleading. In addition, the mean tells us nothing about the *fluctuations* in $\Delta x$. The common measure of such fluctuations in standard finance theory is the *variance*:

$$\sigma_{i,i-1}^2 \equiv \sigma^2 = \big\langle (\Delta x - \langle \Delta x \rangle)^2 \big\rangle. \qquad (2.5)$$

In the case that the price-process is unbiased, as was the case for the coin-toss market, then $\langle \Delta x \rangle = 0$ and hence $\sigma^2 \equiv \langle (\Delta x)^2 \rangle$. For the coin-toss market, $\sigma^2 \equiv \langle (\Delta x)^2 \rangle = \frac{1}{2}(+d)^2 + \frac{1}{2}(-d)^2 = d^2$. Taking the square root gives the *standard deviation* of

---

[11] We will use the words 'mean', 'average', and 'expectation' value interchangeably. We will also tend to use $\langle f[y]\rangle \equiv \overline{f[y]} \equiv E[f[y]]$ interchangeably.

[12] Prices are, strictly speaking, discrete in terms of the way they are quoted on the exchanges. In addition, any numerical modelling and analysis will necessitate discretizing both the price *and* time. For our purposes, it makes no real difference whether we deal with continuous or discrete values of the price-change $\Delta x$. For the time variable, however, it is very convenient for us to consider *discrete* time in order to go beyond the approximations of standard finance theory. In particular, standard finance theory assumes that an investor can trade continuously (see Section 2.4). The microscopic models of Chapter 4 and 5, and the risk analysis in Chapter 6, focus on discrete time: the connection to continuous-time finance can then be examined by setting the actual interval between timesteps to zero.

[13] See note 12.

the price-change $\Delta x$ over a single timestep. This quantity $\sigma$ is arguably the most important quantity in standard finance theory, and is also known as the *volatility*. It is the volatility that is used in standard finance calculations of risk and option pricing, as we will see later in this chapter. Note that the calculation of the volatility $\sigma$ only involves *two* moments of the PDF $p[\Delta x]$ even though there are an *infinite* number of such moments available. In general, all of these moments will contain new and possibly important information concerning $p[\Delta x]$. Since large price-changes generally happen less frequently than smaller price-changes, the PDF $p[\Delta x]$ of price-changes will generally decrease monotonically to zero as $|\Delta x| \to \infty$. However there are no universal laws about how rapidly this function will decay to zero as $|\Delta x| \to \infty$ in a real market. Hence $p[\Delta x]$ may have significant 'weight' in the tails. In other words, the value of $p[\Delta x]$ may only decay very slowly to 0 as $|\Delta x|$ becomes large, thereby producing so-called *fat tails* in the distribution. Hence the moments for large $m$ may actually be very large. Since information about the market dynamics comes from knowledge of $p[\Delta x]$ for *all* $\Delta x$ (i.e. small and large), we may be missing significant information about the probability of large price-changes if we don't account for this extra weight in the tails somewhere in our calculations. In short, *standard risk calculations based solely on the standard deviation of price-changes, and hence on the first two moments* $m = 1$ *and* 2, *may give misleading results.* Why is this a fundamental worry as opposed to a minor detail? Well, in contrast to most scientific theory where the behaviour around the mean is usually good enough to describe the system, finance theory is supposed to accurately answer questions about risk. And almost by definition, 'risk' has to mean the risk of large losses and hence *large deviations* in price-change away from the mean. As an example, consider the following two model PDFs for the price-change $\Delta x$, a Lorentzian and a Gaussian:

$$p[\Delta x] = \frac{C}{(\Delta x)^2 + C^2 \pi^2} \text{ (Lorentzian)}, \quad p[\Delta x] = \frac{1}{\sqrt{2\pi\sigma^2}} e^{-(\Delta x)^2/2\sigma^2} \text{ (Gaussian)},$$

$$(2.6)$$

where $C$ is a constant. To the eye, they look fairly similar, as can be seen in Fig. 2.3. Both are peaked at $\Delta x = 0$ and die off to zero fairly quickly for large $|\Delta x|$, with the Lorentzian having a narrower but higher peak and fatter tails. If one were to produce the histogram of price-changes $p[\Delta x]$ for many real-world price series on a reasonably short timescale (e.g. minutes, hours, or days) it would be very hard to tell whether the shape was more Gaussian-like or more Lorentzian-like. But surely it cannot make that much difference to financial calculations whether our data is more Gaussian-like or more Lorentzian-like? Well, here is the bombshell: Equation (2.6) shows that those fatter tails for the Lorentzian yield a $p[\Delta x] \sim (\Delta x)^{-2}$ dependence

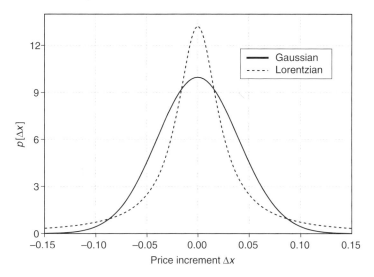

**Fig. 2.3** Comparison between a Gaussian PDF for the price-change $\Delta x$ (solid line) and a Lorentzian PDF (dotted line).

for large $|\Delta x|$. Hence while the variance $\sigma^2$ is finite for a Gaussian, the variance is *infinite* for the Lorentzian. This is worrying, since plugging $\sigma^2 = \infty$ into standard finance formulae (e.g. option pricing formulae) gives nonsensical answers. So as far as standard risk calculations which depend on $\sigma$ are concerned, there is a world of difference between a Gaussian distribution for price-changes and a Lorentzian one, despite the fact that both can be reasonable candidates for fitting real-world price-data. Herein lies a problem: any realistic description of financial risk must account correctly for the tails of the distribution of price-changes $p[\Delta x]$. Hence we need to have maximum possible information about the form of $p[\Delta x]$ which most accurately describes the tails. However, the tails correspond to large deviations $|\Delta x|$ and these deviations become increasingly rare as $|\Delta x|$ increases. Hence the tails are where we have least empirical data points, and therefore least statistical information. To summarize, risk deals with atypical price-changes, yet the volatility measures typical fluctuations around the mean. Hence the volatility is not sufficient to classify risk— more information is required about $p[\Delta x]$, either through higher order moments or detailed knowledge of the functional form of the tails.

### 2.2.3 Price-changes over multiple timesteps

**2.2.3.1 Implications for risk.** As we will now discuss, the problems for standard finance theory do not end with the need for a good characterization of the PDF $p[\Delta x]$ for all $\Delta x$. Section 2.2.2 considered the special case where the price-changes are i.i.d.

Continuing with i.i.d. price-changes for the moment, the probability of observing a particular sequence of price-changes $\{\Delta x_i\} \equiv \Delta x_1, \Delta x_2, \ldots, \Delta x_i, \ldots, \Delta x_n$ given by $p[\{\Delta x_i\} \equiv \Delta x_1, \Delta x_2, \ldots, \Delta x_i, \ldots, \Delta x_n]$, simplifies exactly to:

$$p\big[\{\Delta x_i\} \equiv \Delta x_1, \Delta x_2, \ldots, \Delta x_i, \ldots, \Delta x_n\big] = p[\Delta x_1]p[\Delta x_2]\ldots p[\Delta x_i]\ldots p[\Delta x_n].$$
(2.7)

This is why it was worth studying the properties of $p[\Delta x]$ in some detail. However for anything other than i.i.d. variables, Equation (2.7) does not hold. For the case of independent but not identically distributed price-changes (Case II) we have instead:

$$p\big[\{\Delta x_i\} \equiv \Delta x_1, \Delta x_2, \ldots, \Delta x_i, \ldots, \Delta x_n\big]$$
$$= p_1[\Delta x_1]p_2[\Delta x_2]\ldots p_i[\Delta x_i]\ldots p_n[\Delta x_n].$$
(2.8)

Since the $p$-functions are not identical at consecutive time-steps, this process is effectively *non-stationary*. For dependent variables (Cases III and IV) we cannot split $p[\{\Delta x_i\}]$ up into *any* simple product of single-step PDFs. But why should we be worried about such properties of $p[\{\Delta x_i\}]$? When one considers 'risk' in practice, one typically thinks of the risk of losing money. Suppose we are trading in a market, and because of our positions, any future drop in price of 20 per cent will make us go bankrupt. What is the probability that we will go bankrupt in this market? Suppose we know the PDF for daily price-changes $p[\Delta x]$ and we assume that the daily price-increments are i.i.d. We could then use our knowledge of $p[\Delta x]$ to calculate the probability of the market dropping 20 per cent or more in a given day. We need to add to this the probabilities for the market to drop 20 per cent or more over a period of two days, three days and so on. Note that this could arise in many ways, for example, it could fall 10 per cent each day, or 15 per cent on one day, and 5 per cent on the next, etc. We need to add up all these possible combinations in order to calculate the probability of the market dropping 20 per cent or more over any timescale. This is a straightforward calculation, as we have outlined it. However, it is wrong—at least, it will be wrong if successive price-changes are actually dependent (i.e. not i.i.d.). To illustrate this, let's return to the coin-toss example from Case III in Section 2.2.1, and consider the following scenario. Suppose the dependence of outcomes is such that *if* a sequence of five tails TTTTT arises (i.e. five consecutive price-changes downward) *then* the probability that the next outcome is T becomes unity (i.e., another price-change downward). The consequence would be that the price series would evolve in a seemingly random way until it hit five consecutive downward price-changes. The price would then *continue* to move down indefinitely, producing an enormous crash.

Hence instead of just multiplying the probabilities for independent events that lead to a net loss of 20 per cent or more, we need to consider the *conditional* probabilities along each of the paths that could lead to a loss of 20 per cent or more.

**2.2.3.2   Statistical properties of the moments.** We next consider the statistical properties of the moments of price-changes measured over several timesteps. Our notation for the price-change at timestep $i$ was $\Delta x_i = x_i - x_{i-1}$. Hence the price-change between timestep $0$ and $n$ is given by $\Delta x_{n,0} = \sum_{j=1}^{n} \Delta x_j = x_n - x_0$. The *mean* price-change between timestep $0$ and $n$ is:

$$\langle \Delta x_{n,0} \rangle = \sum_{j=1}^{n} \langle \Delta x_j \rangle, \tag{2.9}$$

which is the well-known result that the *average of the sum is equal to the sum of the averages*. Equation (2.9) holds *irrespective* of whether the price-changes $\Delta x_j$ are i.i.d. or not. For the special case in which each mean is the same $\langle \Delta x_j \rangle \equiv \langle \Delta x \rangle$ (e.g. for i.i.d. variables) then we have:

$$\langle \Delta x_{n,0} \rangle = \sum_{j=1}^{n} \langle \Delta x_j \rangle = n \langle \Delta x \rangle. \tag{2.10}$$

For the very special case of our coin-toss market, we have $\langle \Delta x \rangle = 0$ and hence $\langle \Delta x_{n,0} \rangle = 0$ for an arbitrary time-increment $n$. The *variance* of the price-change between timestep $0$ and $n$ can be calculated as follows:

$$\sigma_{n,0}^2 \equiv \left\langle (\Delta x_{n,0} - \langle \Delta x_{n,0} \rangle)^2 \right\rangle = \left\langle (\Delta x_{n,0})^2 \right\rangle - \langle \Delta x_{n,0} \rangle^2$$

$$= \left\langle \left( \sum_{j=1}^{n} \Delta x_j \right)^2 \right\rangle - \left\langle \sum_{j=1}^{n} \Delta x_j \right\rangle^2$$

$$= \underbrace{\left\langle \sum_{i=1}^{n} \sum_{j=1}^{n} \Delta x_i \, \Delta x_j \right\rangle}_{\Downarrow} - \underbrace{\left\{ \sum_{j=1}^{n} \langle \Delta x_j \rangle \right\}^2}_{\Downarrow}.$$

$$\sum_{i=1}^{n} \left\langle (\Delta x_i)^2 \right\rangle + \sum_{i \neq j} \langle \Delta x_i \, \Delta x_j \rangle \qquad \sum_{i=1}^{n} \langle \Delta x_i \rangle^2 + \sum_{i \neq j} \langle \Delta x_i \rangle \langle \Delta x_j \rangle \tag{2.11}$$

If the price-changes $\Delta x_i$ are *uncorrelated*, then $\langle \Delta x_i \Delta x_j \rangle = \langle \Delta x_i \rangle \langle \Delta x_j \rangle$ for $i \neq j$ and hence Equation (2.11) simplifies exactly to:

$$\sigma_{n,0}^2 = \sum_{i=1}^{n} \langle (\Delta x_i)^2 \rangle - \sum_{i=1}^{n} \langle \Delta x_i \rangle^2 = \sum_{i=1}^{n} \left\{ \langle (\Delta x_i)^2 \rangle - \langle \Delta x_i \rangle^2 \right\} = \sum_{i=1}^{n} \sigma_{i,i-1}^2,$$

(2.12)

hence the well-known result for *uncorrelated* variables that the *variance of the sum is equal to the sum of the variances*. For the special case in which each variance is the same for each timestep (e.g. for i.i.d. variables), $\sigma_{i,i-1}^2 \equiv \sigma^2$ and we have:

$$\sigma_{i,i-n}^2 \equiv \sum_{i=1}^{n} \sigma_{i,i-1}^2 = n\sigma^2,$$

(2.13)

where $\sigma_{i,i-n}^2 = \sigma_{n,0}^2$ since the price-changes at each timestep have the same variance. Equation (2.13) is the result used often by standard finance theory that the standard deviation (i.e. the volatility) of the price-change over an interval of $n$ timesteps increases as

$$\sigma_{i,i-n} = n^{1/2}\sigma.$$

(2.14)

In other words, *the volatility of price-changes over a time-increment n increases as the square-root of the time-increment n*. For the very special case of our coin-toss market, we have $\sigma = d$ and hence $\sigma_{i,i-n} = n^{1/2}d$. Equation (2.14) will reappear in various guises throughout this book. Note that in the *opposite* limit where all the price-changes $\Delta x_i$ are *so correlated* that they all have the same value and sign, $\Delta x$, it then follows that

$$\sigma_{i,i-n}^2 \equiv \langle (\Delta x_{n,0} - \langle \Delta x_{n,0} \rangle)^2 \rangle = \langle (\Delta x_{n,0})^2 \rangle - \langle \Delta x_{n,0} \rangle^2$$

$$= \left\langle \left( \sum_{j=1}^{n} \Delta x_j \right)^2 \right\rangle - \left\langle \sum_{j=1}^{n} \Delta x_j \right\rangle^2$$

$$= \langle (n\Delta x)^2 \rangle - \langle n\Delta x \rangle^2 = n^2 \left( \langle (\Delta x)^2 \rangle - \langle \Delta x \rangle^2 \right)$$

$$= n^2\sigma^2,$$

(2.15)

and hence the volatility of the price-change after $n$ timesteps now increases as

$$\sigma_{i,i-n} = n\sigma.$$

(2.16)

This makes sense: think of walking purposely in a straight line at constant velocity, as opposed to random walking. The distance moved, and hence your standard deviation, is now proportional to the number of timesteps $n$ as opposed to $n^{1/2}$. In the more general case of some *limited* but *non-zero* level of positive correlation, the corresponding expression for the standard deviation will therefore lie between the uncorrelated case of $n^{1/2}$, and the correlated case of $n^1$. If the price-changes $\Delta x_i$ are *anti-correlated* (i.e. their correlation is negative), then the dependence will be more like $n^0$. It turns out that real price series will have the property that the volatility of the price-change after $n$ time-steps increases as $\sigma_{i,i-n} \sim n^{1/\mu}\sigma$ where $\mu$ is some value to be determined by empirical analysis of the price series. A 'persistent walk' implies $1 \leq \mu \leq 2$ while an 'anti-persistent walk' corresponds to $\mu > 2$.

Notice that for the mean (which contains the $m = 1$ moment of the PDF) and the variance (which contains the $m = 2$ moment of the PDF) we have made the following statement: '*the M of the sum is equal to the sum of the M*' where $M$ represents the mean or variance. For the mean this statement was always true, while for the variance it required uncorrelated variables. It turns out that this statement will also apply to higher order moments via the so-called cumulants (which are functions of these moments, as shown in Gershenfeld (1999) and Bouchaud and Potters (2000)). However, the higher the moment, the higher the level of independence required for the statement to hold. This makes sense since, as mentioned earlier, the higher order moments are picking up higher levels of dependence lying buried in the system.

### 2.2.3.3   Probability distribution function.

In Section 2.2.3.2, we obtained results for the moments of the PDF describing the price-change during the time-increment between 0 and $n$, that is, $\Delta x_{n,0} = x_n - x_0$. However, our goal is now to say something about the functional form of the PDF itself, that is, $p[\Delta x_{n,0}]$. Let's start by considering the first non-trivial case, that of $n = 2$. By definition $\Delta x_{n=2,0} = \sum_{j=1}^{2} \Delta x_j = \Delta x_1 + \Delta x_2$, hence there may be various combinations of $\Delta x_1$ and $\Delta x_2$ which add to achieve a given value of $\Delta x_{n=2,0}$. This can be seen easily by referring back to Fig. 2.2. Hence we can write:

$$p[\Delta x_{n=2,0}] = \sum_{\substack{\Delta x_1, \Delta x_2 \\ \text{such that} \\ \Delta x_{2,0} = \Delta x_1 + \Delta x_2}} p[\Delta x_1, \Delta x_2] = \sum_{\Delta x_1} p[\Delta x_1, \Delta x_{n=2,0} - \Delta x_1], \quad (2.17)$$

where $p[\Delta x_1, \Delta x_2]$ is the joint probability distribution of $\Delta x_1$ and $\Delta x_2$. *If* the two price-changes $\Delta x_1$ and $\Delta x_2$ are i.i.d., then we can factorize the joint probability

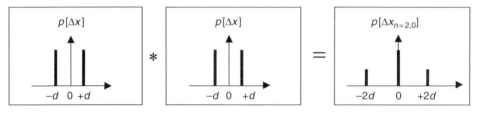

**Fig. 2.4**    Schematic diagram showing convolution of $p[\Delta x]$ with itself, to form $p[\Delta x_{n=2,0}]$.

distribution to obtain:

$$p[\Delta x_{n=2,0}] = \sum_{\Delta x_1} p[\Delta x_1, \Delta x_{n=2,0} - \Delta x_1]$$

$$= \sum_{\Delta x_1} p[\Delta x_1] p[\Delta x_{n=2,0} - \Delta x_1] \equiv p[\Delta x] * p[\Delta x], \qquad (2.18)$$

where $p[\Delta x] * p[\Delta x]$ is a (discrete) convolution of the two PDFs. Repeating this for $n = 3$, we obtain the PDF $p[\Delta x_{n=3,0}]$ as $p[\Delta x_{n=2,0}]$ convoluted with $p[\Delta x]$. This can be repeated for arbitrary $n$. But what does $p[\Delta x_{n,0}]$ look like? We can see this by thinking back to our coin-toss market, described by the single-timestep PDF $p[\Delta x]$ in Fig. 2.1. The convolution will have the effect of 'blurring' the double-peaked function $p[\Delta x]$. For $n = 2$, the convolution is shown in Fig. 2.4.

Referring back to Fig. 2.2, this figure for $p[\Delta x_{n=2,0}]$ makes sense since there are *two* possible ways of obtaining $\Delta x_{n=2,0} = 0$ and *one* possible way of obtaining $\Delta x_{n=2,0} = +2d$ and $\Delta x_{n=2,0} = -2d$. As $n$ increases, the repeated convolutions will increase this 'blurring' effect, and $p[\Delta x_{n,0}]$ will eventually start to look like a bell-shape (i.e. Gaussian). This can even be seen in a crude sense in Fig. 2.4 for $n = 2$. It turns out that we are seeing the *Central Limit Theorem* (CLT) in action. This theorem plays a crucial role in standard finance theory, so we will discuss it in more detail.

**2.2.3.4    Central Limit Theorem.** The price-change during the time-increment between 0 and $n$, is given by $\Delta x_{n,0} = \sum_{j=1}^{n} \Delta x_j$. Let us assume that the price-change variables $\{\Delta x_j\}$ are i.i.d. Given the relation demonstrated in Section 2.2.3.3 between probabilities and convolutions, and the connection between convolutions and Fourier transforms, we will exploit the Fourier transform of the PDF $p[y]$. We start with the identity

$$\langle e^{iqy} \rangle = \int_{-\infty}^{+\infty} e^{iqy} p[y] \, dy. \qquad (2.19)$$

Consider the quantity $\left(\Delta x_{n,0} - n\overline{\Delta x}\right)/n \equiv \left(\Delta x_{n,0} - \overline{\Delta x_{n,0}}\right)/n$, recalling that $\overline{\Delta x_{n,0}}$ is identical to $n$ times the mean price-change per timestep $\overline{\Delta x}$. We perform the following calculation:

$$
\begin{aligned}
\left\langle e^{ik(\Delta x_{n,0} - n\overline{\Delta x})/n} \right\rangle &= \left\langle e^{ik(\Delta x_1 + \Delta x_2 + \Delta x_3 + \cdots + \Delta x_n - n\overline{\Delta x})/n} \right\rangle \\
&= \left\langle e^{ik([\Delta x_1 - \overline{\Delta x}] + [\Delta x_2 - \overline{\Delta x}] + \cdots + [\Delta x_n - \overline{\Delta x}])/n} \right\rangle \\
&= \left[ \left\langle e^{ik(\Delta x - \overline{\Delta x})/n} \right\rangle \right]^n \\
&= \left\langle 1 + \frac{ik}{n}(\Delta x - \overline{\Delta x}) - \frac{k^2}{2n^2}(\Delta x - \overline{\Delta x})^2 + \cdots \right\rangle^n \\
&= \left[ 1 + 0 - \frac{k^2 \sigma^2}{2n^2} + \cdots \right]^n \\
&\approx e^{-k^2 \sigma^2/2n}, \qquad \text{as } n \to \infty. 
\end{aligned}
\tag{2.20}
$$

This calculation requires the assumptions that the price-changes per timestep $\Delta x_j$ are i.i.d., in order to go from the second to the third line, and that we can perform a Taylor expansion around $\overline{\Delta x}$ (fourth line). We have also used the result $e^y = \lim_{n \to \infty}[1 + y/n]^n$. The PDF is obtained by taking the inverse Fourier transform of Equation (2.19), using $q = k/n$:

$$
\begin{aligned}
p\left[\Delta x_{n,0} - \overline{\Delta x_{n,0}}\right] &= \frac{1}{2\pi} \int_{-\infty}^{+\infty} e^{-q^2 n \sigma^2/2} \exp\left[-iq(\Delta x_{n,0} - \overline{\Delta x_{n,0}})\right] dq \\
&= \left[\frac{1}{2\pi n \sigma^2}\right]^{1/2} \exp\left[-\frac{(\Delta x_{n,0} - \overline{\Delta x_{n,0}})^2}{2n\sigma^2}\right].
\end{aligned}
\tag{2.21}
$$

In the limit that $n \to \infty$, we therefore have that the PDF approaches a Gaussian[14] distribution, independent of the specific form of the distribution $p[\Delta x]$ of the price-changes over one timestep. This is the CLT. Equation (2.21) can be rewritten as

$$
p\left[\Delta x_{n,0} - \overline{\Delta x_{n,0}}\right] = \left[\frac{1}{2\pi \sigma_{n,0}^2}\right]^{1/2} \exp\left[-\frac{(\Delta x_{n,0} - \overline{\Delta x_{n,0}})^2}{2\sigma_{n,0}^2}\right],
\tag{2.22}
$$

---

[14] The Gaussian distribution is also known as the normal distribution.

where $\sigma_{n,0} = n^{1/2}\sigma$. In other words, the PDF of price-changes $\Delta x_{n,0}$ has the following Gaussian form:

$$p[\Delta x_{n,0}] = \left[\frac{1}{2\pi\sigma_{n,0}^2}\right]^{1/2} \exp\left[-\frac{(\Delta x_{n,0} - \overline{\Delta x_{n,0}})^2}{2\sigma_{n,0}^2}\right], \qquad (2.23)$$

where $\sigma_{n,0}$ is the standard deviation. Therefore, for $n \to \infty$, the PDF of price-changes over time-increment $n$ becomes Gaussian with a corresponding volatility (i.e. standard deviation) given by $\sigma_{n,0} = n^{1/2}\sigma$. In Section 2.2.3.2, we found that the relation $\sigma_{n,0} = n^{1/2}\sigma$ is true if the variables are uncorrelated and identically distributed. In the present case the variables are i.i.d., and hence by necessity are also uncorrelated: hence we recover the same result. This eventual convergence of the PDF to a Gaussian explains why the Gaussian distribution is used throughout standard finance theory as a model for price-changes.

The implications of the CLT for finance seem remarkable. It seems that the Gaussian distribution, which is arguably the simplest function to manipulate in mathematical terms, is also completely justifiable. However, this whole statement needs to be looked at in more detail. To summarize the CLT story, we have shown that the PDF for price-changes over increments of $n$ timesteps (or equivalently, over a real time-increment $\Delta t = n\tau$ where $\tau$ is the time-interval for one timestep) will approach Gaussian if:

(1) the individual price-changes $\Delta x_1, \Delta x_2, \ldots, \Delta x_n$ over a single timestep (or equivalently, over a real time-interval $\tau$) are i.i.d. variables, and
(2) the PDF $p[\Delta x]$ for price-changes over a single timestep (or equivalently, over a real time-interval $\tau$) has a finite variance[15] $\sigma^2$, and
(3) $n$ is so large that the limit $n \to \infty$ has effectively been reached (or equivalently, $\Delta t$ is so large that the limit $\Delta t/\tau \to \infty$ has effectively been reached).

Unfortunately, it turns out that these three conditions are *not* typically met on the timescales of interest in real markets (e.g. hourly, daily, and possibly even weekly). *Hence it cannot be assumed that the PDF of price-changes over the time-increments $\Delta t$ of interest, will be Gaussian.* Let us take (1), (2), and (3) one at a time, starting with (1). As will be shown in Chapters 3 and 6, there is strong evidence that the price-changes over a time-interval $\tau$—where $\tau$ may be of the order of minutes, hours, days, or even possibly weeks—are not i.i.d. Although the low-order temporal correlations

---

[15] This is because of the necessity to expand in a Taylor series during the derivation (see Equation (2.20)).

such as $c_{ij}$ defined in Equation (2.3) are usually zero, higher order temporal correlations typically survive. Hence the price-changes are not i.i.d., and (1) does not hold. Now we turn to (2). We have already seen that there are distributions (e.g. Lorentzian) that might look reasonable as models for the PDF of price-changes $p[\Delta x]$, and yet have infinite variance. As will be demonstrated in Chapter 3, the PDFs of price-changes in real markets can look quite similar to a Lorentzian over small time-increments—in particular, they seem to have inverse power-law tails that yield very large higher moments. These large higher moments of $p[\Delta x]$ lead consequently to a very slow convergence to Gaussian. Finally let us consider (3). In major markets, the timescale on which trades occur is quite short. However time-increments of at least $\tau = 60$ min are typically needed for real price series in order that conditions (1) and (2) will hold to a reasonable approximation. The standard financial machinery used in practice tends to assume that the PDF of daily price-changes is Gaussian. However, it is clear that a timescale of $\Delta t = 1$ day corresponds to less than $10\tau$ and hence does *not* correspond to the $n \to \infty$ limit. There is a related point concerning risk calculations. The CLT was derived by performing a Taylor expansion, and for this reason strictly only applies in the limit $n \to \infty$. What happens in practice is that as $n$ increases, the Gaussian form grows in the central portion of the PDF around the mean $\overline{\Delta x_{n,0}}$. However the CLT makes no guarantees about the convergence to a Gaussian in the tails of the PDF $p[\Delta x_{n,0}]$, that is, we cannot guarantee that $p[\Delta x_{n,0}]$ will have Gaussian form for *large* deviations $\Delta x_{n,0}$. Given that the probability of having a large price-change is determined by the functional form of $p[\Delta x_{n,0}]$ at large $\Delta x_{n,0}$, there is therefore no guarantee that the Gaussian form can be used at all for risk calculations.

Before leaving the discussion of PDFs of price-changes, we note a special case of the above CLT discussion, in which the PDF of price-changes for single timesteps $p[\Delta x]$ is Gaussian, that is,

$$p[\Delta x] = \left[\frac{1}{2\pi\sigma^2}\right]^{1/2} \exp\left[-\frac{(\Delta x - \overline{\Delta x})^2}{2\sigma^2}\right] \qquad (2.24)$$

as in Fig. 2.3, with a standard deviation $\sigma$. We also assume that the price-changes are i.i.d., which means that we can generate the PDF for $n = 2$ timesteps by just convolving $p[\Delta x]$ with itself (recall Section 2.2.3.3). However, we know from Fourier Transform theory that a Gaussian convolved with itself also yields a Gaussian. Hence the PDF $p[\Delta x_{2,0}]$ for price-changes over two timesteps is also a Gaussian, with $\sigma_{n=2,0} = 2^{1/2}\sigma$. We can repeat this for any $n$, yielding

$$p[\Delta x_{n,0}] = \left[\frac{1}{2\pi \sigma_{n,0}^2}\right]^{1/2} \exp\left[-\frac{(\Delta x_{n,0} - \overline{\Delta x_{n,0}})^2}{2\sigma_{n,0}^2}\right] \qquad (2.25)$$

as in Equation (2.23) with a standard deviation $\sigma_{n,0} = n^{1/2}\sigma$. In this sense, the Gaussian distribution is said to be *stable*. Another way of saying the same thing is that the resulting Gaussian is *self-similar* on all scales: it has the same functional form on all time scales $n$, that is, for all values of $n$ as can be seen from Equations (2.24) and (2.25). This self-similarity can also be seen by eye if we use Equation (2.24) to generate a price-change at each timestep, as shown in Fig. 2.5.

We can make this self-similarity more obvious by defining a new variable $w_n = n^{-1/2}\Delta x_{n,0}$, and hence $\overline{w_n} = n^{-1/2}\overline{\Delta x_{n,0}}$. Using $\sigma_{n,0} = n^{1/2}\sigma$ and Equation (2.25),

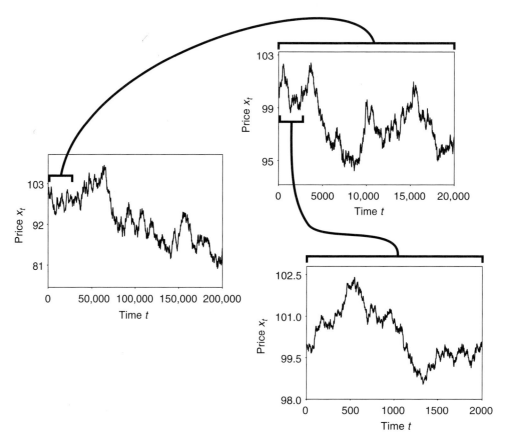

**Fig. 2.5**   A random-walk price series created by generating a price-change at each timestep using the Gaussian PDF of Equation (2.24). The price series looks similar over different time windows.

we can write the normalization condition for $p[\Delta x_{n,0}]$ as

$$\int_{-\infty}^{+\infty} p[\Delta x_{n,0}]\,d(\Delta x_{n,0})$$

$$= \left[\frac{1}{2\pi n\sigma^2}\right]^{1/2} \int_{-\infty}^{+\infty} \exp\left[-\frac{(n^{1/2}w_n - n^{1/2}\overline{w_n})^2}{2n\sigma^2}\right] d(n^{1/2}w_n) = 1, \qquad (2.26)$$

and hence

$$\left[\frac{1}{2\pi\sigma^2}\right]^{1/2} \int_{-\infty}^{+\infty} \exp\left[-\frac{(w_n - \overline{w_n})^2}{2\sigma^2}\right] dw_n = 1. \qquad (2.27)$$

This means that by *scaling* $\Delta x_{n,0}$, which is the price-change over an increment of $n$ timesteps, we have produced a PDF $p[w_n = n^{-1/2}\Delta x_{n,0}]$, which is *invariant* under changes in $n$. This PDF is given by

$$p[w_n = n^{-1/2}\Delta x_{n,0}] = \left[\frac{1}{2\pi\sigma^2}\right]^{1/2} \exp\left[-\frac{(w_n - \overline{w_n})^2}{2\sigma^2}\right]. \qquad (2.28)$$

We will return to this point in Chapter 3 when we look at self-similarity for real price-change distributions.

### 2.2.4 Continuous-time evolution equation for the probability distribution function of price-changes

We have discussed the PDF of price-changes used in standard finance theory, that is, the Gaussian distribution. Using this distribution, one can easily generate a price series by randomly picking values of the price-change variables from the PDF. The resulting price series constitutes a random walk. This is also commonly referred to as a *Wiener process*, or *Brownian motion*. We had focused on discrete time, in order to properly understand the underlying assumptions behind the Gaussian PDF for price-changes. Now we will bring our discussion closer to standard finance theory, by moving over to *continuous-time* analysis in order to obtain the *same* result of a Gaussian functional form.

Suppose that we are at some particular timestep during the random walk generated by the coin-toss price model of Fig. 2.2. Let us define $p[x_t = md]$ to be the probability that the price at time $t$ is $x[t] \equiv x_t = md$. The probability of a positive/negative price-change is $p[\Delta x_{t,t-1} = \pm d] = 1/2$. We can thus obtain the probability $p[x_t = md]$

in the following manner:

$$p[x_t = md] = p[x_{t-1} = (m+1)d]p[\Delta x_{t,t-1} = -d]$$
$$+ p[x_{t-1} = (m-1)d]p[\Delta x_{t,t-1} = +d]$$
$$= \tfrac{1}{2}(p[x_{t-1} = (m+1)d] + p[x_{t-1} = (m-1)d]). \qquad (2.29)$$

Now we can subtract $p[x_{t-1} = md]$ from both sides of Equation (2.29) to get

$$p[x_t = md] - p[x_{t-1} = md]$$
$$= \tfrac{1}{2}(p[x_{t-1} = (m+1)d] + p[x_{t-1} = (m-1)d]) - p[x_{t-1} = md]$$
$$= \tfrac{1}{2}((p[x_{t-1} = (m+1)d] - p[x_{t-1} = md])$$
$$+ (p[x_{t-1} = (m-1)d] - p[x_{t-1} = md])),$$

and hence

$$\frac{(p[x_t = md] - p[x_{t-1} = md])}{\delta_t}$$

$$= \frac{\delta_x^2}{2\delta_t}((p[x_{t-1} = (m+1)d] - p[x_{t-1} = md])$$

$$+ (p[x_{t-1} = (m-1)d] - p[x_{t-1} = md]))/\delta_x^2, \qquad (2.30)$$

where $\delta_t$, $\delta_x$ are the 'mesh-sizes' in time and price. In the coin-toss price model we took these as 1 and $d$ respectively. Equation (2.30) contains the discrete approximation of several partial derivatives. If we take the limit of the 'mesh' of price and time going to zero, that is, $\delta_t$, $\delta_x \to 0$ but keep $\delta_x^2/2\delta_t$ finite, we get

$$\frac{\partial p(x,t)}{\partial t} = D\frac{\partial^2 p(x,t)}{\partial x^2}, \qquad (2.31)$$

where $D \equiv \delta_x^2/2\delta_t$ is a 'diffusion constant'. Note that because we have taken the continuous limit of price as well as time, $p(x,t)$ is a continuous PDF for the price $x$ at time $t$. Equation (2.31) is the *diffusion equation*, and its solution gives the probability $p(x,t)dx$ that the price has a value in the infinitesimal range $x \to x + dx$ at time $t$. It can also be called a *Wiener process*, or a *Fokker–Planck* partial differential equation which governs the evolution of a probability density for an underlying *Markov process*.[16] Physicists also call this *Brownian motion* and use it to describe

---

[16] A Markov process is characterized by the property that the outcome at the *next* timestep (i.e. the next price-change) does not depend on past outcomes (i.e. the past price-changes). Hence the value of the price at the next timestep only depends on the present value of the price. Hence our coin-toss price model corresponds to a Markov process.

the random-walk dynamics of particles diffusing in a gas. Implicit in the derivation of Equation (2.31) was the Markov property used in Equation (2.29) whereby the next price-change is independent of all previous price-changes. This Markov property is the *same* as that assumed in Section 2.2.1 for the coin-toss price model in discrete time. Hence it is no surprise that the solution of this diffusion equation is the familiar Gaussian function, that is,

$$p(x, t) = \frac{1}{\sqrt{4\pi Dt}} \exp\left[-\frac{(x - x_0)^2}{4Dt}\right], \tag{2.32}$$

where the standard deviation is given by $t^{1/2}(2D)^{1/2}$. This represents the PDF for the price $x$ at time $t$ given the price level $x_0$ at time $t = 0$. Hence we immediately see the correspondence with the Gaussian form of Equation (2.23) in which the standard deviation was given by $n^{1/2}\sigma$, with $n$ being the number of discrete timesteps as opposed to $t$ which is the continuous time-interval. Note that if we had included a bias term in this model, Equation (2.31) would pick up a drift term, hence yielding a generalized diffusion, or Fokker–Planck, equation.

### 2.2.5   Stochastic differential equations for the evolution of the price

We have looked at the derivation of standard finance theory's Gaussian PDF for price-changes. In particular we obtained a description of how this PDF evolved as the time interval $t$—or equivalently the number of timesteps $n$—increased. One can present an equivalent view of this same process using *stochastic differential equations*, in which a stochastic equation of motion is obtained for the price in continuous time $x(t)$. We will look at this methodology, and then use it later in this Chapter to derive standard option pricing theory.

We start with our coin-toss price model, where the price-change at timestep $i$ is given by $\Delta x_i = x_i - x_{i-1}$. We will denote $\sigma \Delta X_i$ as this price-change, where $\sigma$ controls the step-size and $\Delta X_i$ is a stochastic variable describing the coin-toss outcome at timestep $i$. Since we assume i.i.d. price-changes, we can drop the subscripts, hence $\Delta x = \sigma \Delta X$. We then assume that the increment in $x$ is so small that we can replace $\Delta x \to dx$, and similarly $\Delta X \to dX$. Hence we have a stochastic differential equation for the price:

$$dx = \sigma\, dX. \tag{2.33}$$

Standard finance theory makes the assumption that $dX$ is a random variable taken from a Gaussian PDF, with zero mean and a standard deviation equal to $(dt)^{1/2}$. In so doing, standard finance theory is basically assuming that $dt$ corresponds to a *small* time-increment which is however sufficiently *large* that the CLT is valid; that is, it is saying that d$t$ is somehow large enough to consist of $n \rightarrow \infty$ individual timesteps with associated price-changes per timestep which are i.i.d. and which have finite variance. Hence d$t$ is assumed to be large enough that the PDF for single-step price-changes (e.g. the coin-toss PDF of Fig. 2.1) has convolved with itself an 'infinite' number of times. If all this were true, then the CLT would be valid and the PDF for price-changes over the time-increment d$t$ would indeed be Gaussian. Of course if time were truly continuous, then there would indeed exist $n = \infty$ infinitesimal timesteps in any finite time and hence the assumption of Gaussianity would be true. However we know that the actual duration of each timestep cannot realistically be made smaller than the time interval between trades. This time interval is always finite and sometimes quite large, hence explaining why non-Gaussianity can be observed in real financial data in contrast to the predictions of standard finance (see Chapter 3).

We have so far considered price-change processes that comprise a stochastic (i.e. random) term such as a coin-toss, hence our probabilistic description. In standard finance theory, a deterministic *drift* term is often added to account for a possible overall trend in the market. The reasons for a priori inclusion of such a term are debatable—after all by symmetry, both directions (up and down) are equally 'available'. Despite this, such drift terms are included—hence we will also include them in our discussion. Therefore, Equation (2.33) becomes

$$\mathrm{d}x = \sigma\,\mathrm{d}X + \mu\,\mathrm{d}t, \tag{2.34}$$

where $\mu$ is a deterministic bias term, that is, a deterministic rate-of-change of the price. We can integrate Equation (2.34) to give

$$x(t) = x(0) + \mu t + \phi\sigma\sqrt{t}, \tag{2.35}$$

where $\phi$ is a random variable drawn from a Gaussian distribution with mean zero and unit variance, that is, $\phi \sim N[0, 1]$. Strictly speaking, Equation (2.35) allows $x$ to become negative. Hence it is standard practice to consider the price-change to be the *fractional* change in price, that is, the return (see Section 1.4)

$$\frac{\mathrm{d}x}{x} = \sigma\,\mathrm{d}X + \mu\,\mathrm{d}t, \tag{2.36}$$

which integrates to give

$$x(t) = x(0)\exp\left[\left(\mu - \frac{\sigma^2}{2}\right)t + \phi\sigma\sqrt{t}\right]. \tag{2.37}$$

In order to give more examples of stochastic differential equations, we now briefly mention two further models used in finance, for example, for modelling interest rates. The first includes the effect that interest-rates often seem to have of 'returning to the mean'. This process is

$$dx = \sigma \, dX + (v - \mu x) \, dt, \tag{2.38}$$

which is called a *mean-reverting random walk*. If $x$ is small such that $v > \mu x$, the positive coefficient in front of $dt$ means that $x$ will move up on average. If $x$ is large such that $v < \mu x$, $x$ will move down on average. Equation (2.38) therefore includes a phenomenological description of a type of temporal correlation which restores $x$ to its mean, and hence lies beyond the basic random walk described in Section 2.2.1. Note however that our earlier claims that such stochastic differential equations can at best only include a limited subset of the actual higher order temporal correlations exhibited by real market data, still holds. With $r$ instead of $x$, this type of random walk is the so-called Vasicek model for the short-term interest rate. The second model that we will mention has an additional factor in the random part:

$$dx = \sigma \sqrt{x} \, dX + (v - \mu x) \, dt. \tag{2.39}$$

This is the Cox, Ingersoll, and Ross model for the short-term interest rate. Obviously an infinite number of such stochastic differential equations can be introduced by making the drift and/or fluctuating parts increasingly complicated. However, in our opinion such an approach lacks a good microscopic understanding, and sometimes even empirical justification in terms of actual data. Nevertheless, the connection between the finance world and the field of stochastic calculus has drawn many applied mathematicians into the study of quantitative finance. This in turn has had a positive feedback effect in terms of generating increasing numbers of modifications to the basic stochastic differential equation for a random walk. However at their heart, these models all make a priori assumptions concerning the type of temporal dynamics in the asset price process. It is precisely *because* of such simplifying assumptions that it is possible to write down stochastic differential equations. Despite this shortcoming, the field of stochastic calculus with application to finance, can and does fill courses and books all by itself, many times over. The standard pricing theory for options, the so-called Black–Scholes theory, arguably provides the showcase for this stochastic calculus (see Section 2.4.3). For more details on the machinery of stochastic calculus, we refer to the excellent discussions in Wilmott *et al.* (1996) and Wilmott (1998).

## 2.3    Risk: tails of the unexpected

There are many possible measures that one might use to quantify the risk in a given market. As mentioned earlier in Chapter 2, the standard measure of risk in the finance industry is the volatility $\sigma$. A numerical value for $\sigma$ can be obtained empirically by calculating the standard deviation of the distribution of empirical price-changes, obtained over a given time-increment $\Delta t$. *If* the PDF of these empirical price-changes was indeed Gaussian, then the use of $\sigma$ as the sole risk measure would make some sense: in an unbiased market where the mean price-change is zero, then $\sigma$ is the only parameter which defines the shape of the Gaussian PDF. However, there are several problems with the methodology of quantifying risk using this one parameter $\sigma$:

1. The parameter $\sigma$ is obtained from the empirical price-change distribution for a fixed time-increment $\Delta t$ (e.g. one day). It therefore only measures the risk associated with this fixed, pre-determined time-interval $\Delta t$. As mentioned earlier in Section 2.2.3.1, this ignores the risk of losses accumulated over consecutive time-increments $\Delta t$. To an investor, however, such risks are clearly just as important. Whether you lose your money all in one day *or* over a period of three days, you will still be bankrupt. In the case where price-changes have higher order temporal correlations, the risk due to accumulated losses over several consecutive time-increments can be significantly different from that calculated assuming i.i.d. price-changes with a fixed value of $\sigma$ for time-increment $\Delta t$. Furthermore, draw-downs and crashes cannot be captured by any a priori, fixed timescale. We return to this discussion in Section 3.6 where we investigate a price series with higher order temporal correlations, and in Chapter 7 where we look at crashes using a microscopic market model.
2. The parameter $\sigma$ does not take into account the value of the maximal loss *inside* the time-interval $\Delta t$. Consider an example whereby the price-change measured over the whole day would have been just about acceptable to an investor: however in reality he was made bankrupt at 12.15 p.m. when the price plunged by twice that amount. The price then recovered later that afternoon giving a relatively small change on the daily scale—but this was too late for our investor.
3. The parameter $\sigma$ treats both upward price movements (i.e. 'market gains') and downward price movements (i.e. 'market losses') equally from the point of view of risk, whereas they should be distinguished. After all, large gains do not represent a risk.
4. Empirical price-change PDFs which approximate to a Lorentzian distribution—or more generally to the Levy distribution to be introduced in Chapter 3—will yield

a very large numerical value for the standard deviation $\sigma$. While $\sigma$ is finite for a Gaussian PDF, it is strictly infinite for a Lorentzian PDF despite the fact that the two functions look similar. Hence it may be difficult to determine $\sigma$ accurately in practice for such a price series.

5. A strict Gaussian functional form is not justified for the tails of the PDF of price-changes regardless of the value chosen for the time-increment $\Delta t$. This is because the CLT only applies near the centre of the distribution. Hence the parameter $\sigma$ does not tell us much about the tails of the PDF, where significant risk actually lies.

A more general theoretical approach to risk will be presented in Chapter 6. For now we pursue the standard theory approach, and look briefly at an alternative measure of risk which is sometimes used in the finance industry in an attempt to avoid these problems with $\sigma$. This alternative measure of risk concerns the probability of extreme losses or the so-called Value-at-Risk (VaR). It takes the view that one should choose a measure of risk that focuses on the possibility of large, unexpected downward movements of the market. In particular, the focus is on the probability of large *negative* price-changes. Imagine that we have $n$ samples of a random variable $y$. For example, these could correspond to price-changes over successive days, or weeks. We will label these as $\{y_i\} = \{y_1, y_2, \ldots, y_n\}$. We assume that they all correspond to the same PDF $p[y]$ *and* we assume that the drawings are independent (i.i.d.). Of course such assumptions are *not* a priori true, however we will continue. Following the VaR philosophy, the risk can be associated with the minimum value contained in $\{y_i\} = \{y_1, y_2, \ldots, y_n\}$, that is, the largest negative price-change. Making the i.i.d. assumption, the probability that $y_{min} < -\Omega$, where $\Omega$ is the magnitude of the largest negative price-change that our portfolio can withstand, can be calculated as follows:

$$p[y_{min} < -\Omega] = 1 - [p_>[-\Omega]]^n = 1 - [1 - p_<[-\Omega]]^n$$
$$\approx 1 - \exp[-np_<[-\Omega]], \quad \text{for } p_<[-\Omega] \ll 1, \tag{2.40}$$

where we have defined the cumulative probability distributions as

$$p_<[-\Omega] = \int_{-\infty}^{-\Omega} p[y] \, dy \quad \text{and} \quad p_>[-\Omega] = \int_{-\Omega}^{\infty} p[y] \, dy, \tag{2.41}$$

with $p_<[-\Omega] + p_>[-\Omega] = 1$. Hence $p[y_{min} < -\Omega] \approx 1 - \exp[-np_<[-\Omega]]$ gives us the required probability that $y_{min} < -\Omega$ for a series of $n$ trials. For the Gaussian PDF $p[y] = (1/\sqrt{2\pi\sigma^2})e^{-y^2/2\sigma^2}$,

$$p_<[-\Omega] = \frac{1}{2}\text{erfc}\left[\frac{\Omega}{\sqrt{2}\sigma}\right], \tag{2.42}$$

where $\text{erfc}[y]$ is the complementary error function. Therefore $\Omega = \sqrt{2}\sigma\,\text{erfc}^{-1}[2p_<[-\Omega]] \propto \sigma$. This shows us that even in the VaR methodology, which supposedly focuses on the tails of the distribution, the resulting risk measure may still end up relying indirectly on the estimated volatility $\sigma$.

## 2.4    Eliminating risk within the Black–Scholes option pricing theory

### 2.4.1    Introducing derivatives

Having taken a look at aspects of financial risk, we now turn to look at the *hedging* of risk within standard finance theory using derivatives. This forms the core of much of standard quantitative finance. It is clever stuff—in fact, the theory of option pricing won Merton and Scholes a Nobel prize. However despite its mathematical beauty, there can be some serious pitfalls when trying to implement it in practice. In Chapter 6 we look at how one might go beyond this standard finance theory, or so-called Black–Scholes, treatment. But for now, we content ourselves to sit back, and enjoy the maths. Our treatment borrows heavily from the masters in the field: Wilmott *et al.* (1996). We start with a brief review of what derivatives actually are.

**2.4.1.1    Futures and forwards.** A *forward* contract is a contract entered into by two parties where they *must* fulfil the contract on expiry. This usually means exchanging assets for a pre-determined price. It is particularly popular in the currency markets where the asset is a given amount of currency of a given denomination, and the pre-determined price is the discounted exchange rate for that currency. A *future* contract is essentially the same as a forward contract, though traded in a slightly different way (as discussed in Chapter 1). The forward or future contract must be exercised at expiry. The expiry $T$ (also called the delivery date or maturity date) of the contract is determined at the time of the writing of the contract, as is the exercise price $X$ (also called the forward price or future price). We denote $V_T[x_T, X]$ as the contract value at expiry $T$ given that the asset price at expiry is $x_T$. Since there is no element of choice, it costs nothing to enter into a forward or futures contract. The payoff diagrams at expiry for the purchaser of a call contract (a contract to buy the asset) and a put contract (a contract to sell the asset) are as follows:

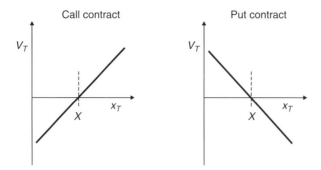

Hence the payoff is given by $(x_T - X)$ for the call contract and $(X - x_T)$ for the put contract. For the other party in this contract, this diagram represents the losses at expiry.

**2.4.1.2   Options.** An *option* is like a car insurance. It is a contract that you enter into with another party, for example, an insuring institution or bank, which writes the contract. In the case of car insurance, this would be the insurance company. You purchase the contract for a relatively small amount of money, typically some fraction of the underlying asset. In the case of car insurance, this is a small fraction of the actual worth of the car. The contract is of fixed term (e.g. a few months). The insurance can be against all manner of conditions involving the underlying asset. If the conditions regarding the underlying asset (at the expiry of the contract for a 'European option' or at any time for an 'American option') are unfavourable to you (e.g. the car is wrecked; the stock you're holding is worthless), you exercise the option, that is, you demand that the option writer fulfill his part of the contract by paying out to you. The payoff you would then receive could far exceed the cost of the option, the premium. If the conditions regarding the underlying are favourable to you (e.g. the car is fine; the stock you are holding has appreciated in value), you would not exercise the option. You would then lose the initial option cost, corrected by the underlying interest rate to allow for the loss-of-interest during the lifetime of the option contract. The insuring institution, on the other hand, pockets this amount. Of course, they are entering into many of these types of contracts and are hoping that the net profit from a large number of relatively low-cost option contracts will compensate (or maybe even exceed) the possible outlays in the case of options being exercised. Central to the pricing of options, therefore, is an estimate of the underlying risk of the option being exercised. Hence any option pricing model necessarily needs a suitable stochastic/probabilistic model of the behaviour of the underlying asset price during the lifetime of the option.

Things are obviously far from simple due to the fact that the underlying asset has a fluctuating value and can vary quite considerably over the lifetime of the option. It is said that a week is a long time in politics—it can be a very long time in the financial markets as well. How can one therefore go about building a model to give a 'price' to such contracts? Clearly one could leave it to 'market forces' to decide the price—the expectation would be that after some trial and error, the market participants would collectively arrive at some agreed prices for these contracts. But how would one then put a price on new forms of contract? And what happens if the market does not seem to be behaving 'normally'?

We will look at the standard finance theory approach to pricing such options. This approach is 'standard' in the sense that it rests on the standard models of financial asset price variations that we have been looking at earlier in this chapter. It is also 'standard' in that it treats time as a continuous variable. A crucial quantity in the pricing of options is a measure of the fluctuations expected during the lifetime of the option. In a Gaussian world, and hence standard finance theory, this is given by the volatility (i.e. standard deviation of price-changes) $\sigma$.

### 2.4.2  Types of options

Options come in many different forms. Loosely speaking, a wide class of these are considered by standard finance theory as being describable by the same formalism. In particular, the prices of these options are obtained by solving the same partial differential equation: the so-called *Black–Scholes equation*. How can so many different option prices be obtained as solutions of the same partial differential equation? The answer lies in the fact that the different characteristics of these options appear as different constraints/boundary conditions on the allowed solutions of this equation. We will take a brief look at some of these options, and hence boundary conditions, and their respective payoffs.

Options are either 'calls' or 'puts'. A *call option* is one where the option-buyer (i.e. holder) is acquiring the option of purchasing a prescribed asset from the option writer, for a prescribed amount (i.e. exercise price or strike price, $X$). A *put option* is one where the option-buyer is acquiring the option of selling the asset under the same set of pre-defined conditions. Since the option affords the holder a right, but not an obligation, then clearly an option should cost something.

A 'European option' is one which may *only* be exercised at expiry. The expiry $T$ of the option is determined at the time of writing the contract, and we denote $V_T[x_T, X]$ as the option payoff at expiry $T$ given that the asset price at expiry is $x_T$. The strike price $X$ is determined at the time of writing of the contract. The simplest type of

European option is known as a 'vanilla' option. The payoff diagrams at expiry for the purchaser of a vanilla European call option and vanilla European put option are as follows:

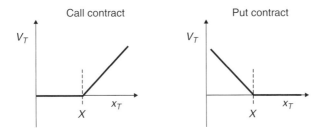

Hence the payoff for a call option is given by $\max[x_T - X, 0]$ and for a put option by $\max[X - x_T, 0]$. For the option-writer, these diagrams represent the losses at expiry. Both the above payoff diagrams represent truncated versions of the payoff diagrams for the futures contracts given in Section 2.4.1.1. From the point of view of the option-writer, these payoff diagrams obviously have a considerable potential loss. So how much should the option-writer charge the option-buyer to compensate for this. In short, how much should an option cost? In the next section, we answer this within the standard finance framework, which relies on random walks. In Chapter 6, we take a more general point of view, relaxing the assumptions of standard finance theory.

Apart from the vanilla option, European options come in other flavours. For example, a cash-or-nothing call is an example of a 'digital' or 'binary' option, and has the following payoff:

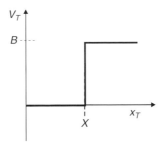

Here the payoff is $BH[x_T - X]$ where $H[\cdots]$ is the Heaviside function. We can combine calls and puts with various strike prices to give portfolios with a variety of payoffs, for example, a 'bullish vertical spread' as shown below. 'Bullish', because the investor profits from a rise in the asset price; 'vertical' because there are two strike prices involved; 'spread' because it is made up of the same type of option (i.e. calls).

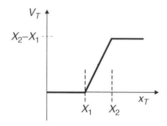

The payoff is given by: $\max[x_T - X_1, 0] - \max[x_T - X_2, 0]$. The payoff is achieved by buying one call option, and writing one call option with the same expiry date but larger strike price. This is a way of redirecting risk, and that is what portfolio management is all about. An American option may be exercised at *any* time prior to expiry, in contrast to the European option. Not only must a value be assigned to it, but one would also need to determine *when* it is best to exercise the option. These types of option are some of the hardest to price. Another type of option is the path-dependent (e.g. 'Asian' or lookback) option. For these options the payoff depends on a function of the asset price during the lifetime of the option.

### 2.4.3   Going, going, gone: the magic of zero risk

We now give the derivation, and solution, of the Black–Scholes equation for option pricing. Our starting point is the stochastic differential equation, Equation (2.36) that describes the asset-price movement comprising a random variable and a drift term:

$$\frac{dx}{x} = \sigma \, dX + \mu \, dt, \tag{2.43}$$

where the random variable $dX$ is taken from a Gaussian PDF with mean 0 and variance $dt$. As has been the message throughout this chapter, this equation can only ever be a coarse approximation to the discrete-time, non-Gaussian, temporally correlated movement of asset prices observed in the real financial markets. We accept this for now, but return to the consequences of deviations from these assumptions in Chapter 6.

   Assume that at time $t$, the current value of the option is $V$ and the current value of the asset is $x$. We do not need to specify whether this is a call or put option at this stage. The important point is that $V$ is a function of $x$ and $t$, that is, $V(x, t)$. So here we have an example of a function of a stochastic variable $x$. If these were *usual* functions, then we would use our *usual* calculus expansion

$$dV(x, t) = \frac{\partial V}{\partial x} \, dx + \frac{\partial V}{\partial t} \, dt + \cdots \tag{2.44}$$

where the dots denote higher order terms which we would *usually* neglect in the limit of very small $dx$ and $dt$. We know that even without the higher order terms,

Equation (2.44) works fine for deterministic functions—that is, we plug in values for the partial derivatives, and out pops a value of $dV$. That is what we all learn in undergraduate calculus, and that is what we *usually* use. However in the case of *stochastic* functions, things are more complicated. Given a value of $t$, we can only make a *probabilistic* statement about the value of $x$ and hence $V$. In this case we had better hang on to these higher order terms in Equation (2.44) until we can work out what terms are negligible in the limit of small time-intervals $dt$. In so doing, we will be implicitly using a type of calculus that is the engine behind all standard, modern financial engineering: *Ito calculus*. In fact we only need one particular result of this Ito calculus, which is the so-called *Ito's lemma*. This is also basically all that is used in the financial world. According to Ito's lemma, the correct form of Equation (2.44) given that $x$ is a stochastic variable, is

$$dV(x, t) = \frac{\partial V}{\partial x} dx + \frac{\partial V}{\partial t} dt + \frac{1}{2} \frac{\partial^2 V}{\partial x^2} dx^2 + \cdots, \qquad (2.45)$$

where the dots denote higher order terms. If we plug Equation (2.43) into (2.45), we get

$$dV(x, t) = \frac{\partial V}{\partial x} (x\sigma\, dX + x\mu\, dt) + \frac{\partial V}{\partial t} dt + \frac{1}{2} \frac{\partial^2 V}{\partial x^2} (x\sigma\, dX + x\mu\, dt)^2, \qquad (2.46)$$

where we have dropped the dots denoting higher order terms. We now have to expand out the terms in Equation (2.46). The last bracket is where we need to do some work:

$$(x\sigma\, dX + x\mu\, dt)^2 = \underbrace{x^2\sigma^2 (dX)^2}_{\text{Term 1}} + \underbrace{2x^2\sigma\mu (dX)(dt)}_{\text{Term 2}} + \underbrace{x^2\mu^2 (dt)^2}_{\text{Term 3}} \qquad (2.47)$$

*Term 1.* As discussed throughout this chapter, the standard finance theory model is to assume that the stochastic process $dX$ is a random walk with an associated PDF whose standard deviation is equal to $(dt)^{1/2}$. Hence $(dX)^2$ is of the order $dt$.

*Term 2.* We wish to keep terms of the order $dt$, hence our specific interest in Term 1. However Term 2 clearly has a higher order dependence: heuristically we can think of it as something like $(dt)^{1/2}(dt)$ which is hence a higher order term than $dt$. Hence we will neglect it.

*Term 3.* This clearly has a higher order dependence than $dt$. Hence we will neglect it.

This yields a simplified form of Equation (2.47):

$$(x\sigma\, dX + x\mu\, dt)^2 = x^2\sigma^2\, dt \ldots \qquad (2.48)$$

Putting Equation (2.48) into (2.46) and doing a little bit of tidying up gives

$$dV(x, t) = \left[\sigma x \frac{\partial V}{\partial x}\right] dX + \left[\mu x \frac{\partial V}{\partial x} + \frac{1}{2}\sigma^2 x^2 \frac{\partial^2 V}{\partial x^2} + \frac{\partial V}{\partial t}\right] dt. \qquad (2.49)$$

So far so good, but we still have a stochastic equation for the option price $V(x, t)$, that is, given the time $t$ and the current asset price we still cannot get a unique value for the option price $V$. Our goal is to obtain a unique price for the option. For this, we need to consider a strategy for holding the option and the asset. This is the process of 'hedging', which will be discussed in detail in Chapter 6. Ideally we would do this in a way that gives minimum, or even zero, risk. The magic of the Black–Scholes approach to option pricing gives us exactly that—and here is how. Suppose we have a portfolio comprising one option and a quantity $-\Delta$ of the underlying asset (note here that we are thus considering the position of the option contract holder). The value of our portfolio at time $t$ is

$$\Pi(x, t) = V(x, t) - \Delta(x, t)x(t), \qquad (2.50)$$

where so far we have shown the implicit dependence on $x$ and $t$ just to keep things formally correct. So as not to make things too messy, we now drop these dependences—let us just remember they are still there. At any given time $t$, the underlying asset price will more than likely change, hence so should the value of the option $V$ and hence the value of the portfolio. Hence the change in the value of the portfolio between time $t$ and $t + dt$ is given by

$$d\Pi = dV - \Delta \, dx \qquad (2.51)$$

Notice that the amount of the asset that we hold at time $t$ *does not* change between time $t$ and $t + dt$ since we do not a priori know what will happen to the asset price $x(t)$. So while $\Delta$ stays constant in the time-interval $t \to t + dt$, the asset price changes by $dx$, hence the option price changes by $dV$, hence the value of our portfolio changes by $d\Pi$. We can now substitute Equation (2.49) into (2.51) to give

$$d\Pi = \sigma x \left[\frac{\partial V}{\partial x}\right] dX + \left[\mu x \frac{\partial V}{\partial x} + \frac{1}{2}\sigma^2 x^2 \frac{\partial^2 V}{\partial x^2} + \frac{\partial V}{\partial t}\right] dt - \Delta \, dx \qquad (2.52)$$

and Equation (2.43) into (2.52) to give

$$d\Pi = \sigma x \left[\frac{\partial V}{\partial x}\right] dX + \left[\mu x \frac{\partial V}{\partial x} + \frac{1}{2}\sigma^2 x^2 \frac{\partial^2 V}{\partial x^2} + \frac{\partial V}{\partial t}\right] dt - \Delta x[\sigma \, dX + \mu \, dt]. \qquad (2.53)$$

Collecting up terms gives

$$d\Pi = \sigma x \left[\frac{\partial V}{\partial x} - \Delta\right] dX + \left[\mu x \frac{\partial V}{\partial x} + \frac{1}{2}\sigma^2 x^2 \frac{\partial^2 V}{\partial x^2} + \frac{\partial V}{\partial t} - \mu \Delta x\right] dt. \qquad (2.54)$$

The factor $[\partial V/\partial x - \Delta]$ is a **very important term**! This is because it controls the stochastic element in the portfolio variation $\mathrm{d}\Pi$ and hence the portfolio risk. Even though Equation (2.54) appears to still be stochastic, we can *remove* the stochastic term *if* we can engineer the following condition at each time $t$:

$$\Delta = \frac{\partial V}{\partial x} \tag{2.55}$$

Now, there is a lot that one could say about the practical complications of implementing this seemingly harmless mathematical trick. We will leave this for Chapter 6, and instead just move on to the final answer for the option price in standard finance theory. We assume that the condition in Equation (2.55) holds exactly at every value of $t$ (N.B. $t$ is continuous, hence it needs to hold at an infinite number of points!). Then Equation (2.54) becomes

$$\mathrm{d}\Pi = \left[ \mu x \frac{\partial V}{\partial x} + \frac{1}{2}\sigma^2 x^2 \frac{\partial^2 V}{\partial x^2} + \frac{\partial V}{\partial t} - \mu \Delta x \right] \mathrm{d}t. \tag{2.56}$$

Substituting in from Equation (2.55), (2.56) becomes

$$\mathrm{d}\Pi = \left[ \frac{1}{2}\sigma^2 x^2 \frac{\partial^2 V}{\partial x^2} + \frac{\partial V}{\partial t} \right] \mathrm{d}t, \tag{2.57}$$

which is a completely *deterministic* equation for the change in the value of the portfolio at each time $t$. In other words, there is no longer a random $\mathrm{d}X$ term affecting the value of the portfolio. In short, **the risk has been eliminated, yielding a zero-risk portfolio**.

Now, imagine that we had not purchased the option or underlying asset. Instead we had chosen the risk-free option of putting our capital in a reputable bank with fixed, guaranteed interest rate of value $r$. In this case our portfolio would instead have consisted entirely of cash and would have increased in value over the same time period $t \to t + \mathrm{d}t$, by an amount $\mathrm{d}\Pi = r\Pi \mathrm{d}t$. Since we presumably have no way of making either a profit or loss systematically in our random-walk market, these two gains should be equal, that is, from Equation (2.57) we obtain

$$r\Pi \mathrm{d}t = \left[ \frac{1}{2}\sigma^2 x^2 \frac{\partial^2 V}{\partial x^2} + \frac{\partial V}{\partial t} \right] \mathrm{d}t. \tag{2.58}$$

Substituting from Equations (2.50) and (2.55) into (2.58) gives

$$r\left[ V - x\frac{\partial V}{\partial x} \right] \mathrm{d}t = \left[ \frac{1}{2}\sigma^2 x^2 \frac{\partial^2 V}{\partial x^2} + \frac{\partial V}{\partial t} \right] \mathrm{d}t. \tag{2.59}$$

We want our results to hold for *all* times $t$ during the life of the option, hence the factors multiplying $dt$ on both sides of Equation (2.59) can be equated, that is, we can effectively cancel out the terms $dt$. This gives the equation

$$r\left[V - x\frac{\partial V}{\partial x}\right] = \left[\frac{1}{2}\sigma^2 x^2 \frac{\partial^2 V}{\partial x^2} + \frac{\partial V}{\partial t}\right]$$

(2.60)

or, rearranging slightly, the final equation,

$$\frac{\partial V}{\partial t} + \frac{1}{2}\sigma^2 x^2 \frac{\partial^2 V}{\partial x^2} + rx\frac{\partial V}{\partial x} - rV = 0$$

(2.61)

which is the famous **'Black–Scholes equation'**. As long as the implicit assumptions made in its derivation are satisfied, any derivative security whose price depends only on the current value of $x$ and $t$, and which is paid for up-front, must satisfy this equation. Notice the amazing property that this equation is *independent* of the drift term $\mu$. Hence two people can disagree on the value of the drift but obtain the same option price. Of course, to solve this equation we need to know the boundary conditions. These boundary conditions define what type of option we are considering, as we will now discuss. For a European call option, the boundary conditions are

$$V(x, T) = \max(x - X, 0), \quad V(0, t) = 0, \quad V(x, t) \xrightarrow{x \to \infty} x.$$

If $x = 0$, it remains zero since $dx$ is also now zero. For a European put option, the boundary conditions are

$$V(x, T) = \max(X - x, 0), \quad V(0, t) = X e^{-r(T-t)}, \quad V(x, t) \xrightarrow{x \to \infty} 0.$$

If $x = 0$, it remains zero since $dx$ is also now zero, hence the value of the put becomes the discounted strike price. The solutions of the Black–Scholes equation are as follows.

### 2.4.3.1   European call option

$$V(x, t) = x\,\Phi[d_1] - X e^{-r(T-t)}\Phi[d_2], \text{ where}$$

$$\Phi[z] = \frac{1}{\sqrt{2\pi}}\int_{-\infty}^{z} e^{-\frac{1}{2}y^2}dy, \quad d_1 = \frac{\ln(x/X) + \left(r + \frac{1}{2}\sigma^2\right)(T-t)}{\sigma\sqrt{T-t}},$$

$$d_2 = \frac{\ln(x/X) + \left(r - \frac{1}{2}\sigma^2\right)(T-t)}{\sigma\sqrt{T-t}}.$$

(2.62)

The European call value solution $V(x, t)$ as a function of $x$ has the following form:

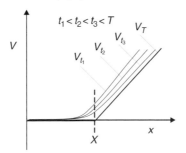

### 2.4.3.2   European put option

$$V(x, t) = X e^{-r(T-t)} \Phi[-d_2] - x\, \Phi[-d_1]  \tag{2.63}$$

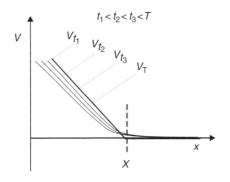

The **hedging strategy** for the European call option $\Delta = \partial V/\partial x = \Phi[d_1]$ has the following form:

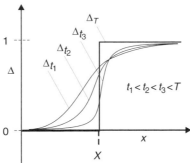

For the European put option, the corresponding hedge is given by $\Delta = \partial V/\partial x = \Phi[d_1] - 1$. We note that these solutions can be checked by direct substitution into the Black–Scholes equation. If the values of the asset just before expiry are close to $X$

then the hedge may change from approximately 0 to 1 *many times*. But what about the effect of the associated transaction costs? Yes, that is a problem with this formalism. There is no obvious place to include the effect of transaction costs which, of course, could be enormous if you have to hedge continuously.

The Black–Scholes theory is a mathematical marvel. However even though it is widely used, and indeed has changed the whole face of derivatives trading, we have no guarantee that it really works in practice. Why? Well, it is built upon some strong implicit assumptions concerning random-walk models of asset prices, in addition to the use of continuous-time calculus. It *only* works out so neatly in mathematical terms because these assumptions have been made. As a prelude to Chapter 3, we therefore end with the following summary. If the statistics of the real market and the ideal random-walk market disagree, then standard finance theory may not apply to the market in question. Worse still, standard finance theory may even give misleading answers to important questions of investment, hedging, risk management, etc. The extent of this error will depend on the type of financial calculation in question. Even if the actual PDF for price-changes is not too different from a Gaussian, the missing temporal correlations may be strong enough to throw quantitative calculations regarding hedging strategies, risk, and portfolio management wildly off-track. Worse still, the 'missing features' may not be treatable within a perturbation-type treatment. In short: one cannot quantify the limitations of standard finance theory until it is compared to a more general theory that *does not* make the same approximations.

# 3.   A complex walk down Wall Street

## 3.1   Facing the stylized facts

We have discussed the random-walk model, which underpins standard theoretical treatments of asset-price movements. But how different is the real world, and what are the consequences of these differences? In this Chapter we set out to explore real-world market dynamics by analysing data from two quite distinct markets. In both cases, the linear (i.e. low-order) correlation of price-changes is essentially zero implying that the associated price series would be judged to be a 'random walk' by many industry-standard statistical packages. However we show that this data actually exhibits significant non-linear (i.e. higher order) temporal correlations across a range of timescales, together with non-Gaussian price distributions. Our findings illustrate the general results reported in the Econophysics literature[1] that real markets tend to deviate from the standard random-walk paradigm in a fundamental way. These empirical features form part of the so-called *stylized facts* of financial markets. Any candidate market models or financial calculations concerning risk or derivative pricing, clearly ought to be made consistent with these stylized facts—hence the motivation for the present empirical study.

Let's return for a moment to our dot-com company *risk-e.com* whose price-history is shown in Fig. 1.1. Suppose we are trying to uncover what 'extra' information might be hidden in the past behaviour of the stock price $x[t]$, by analysing the statistics of $x[t]$ over recent history. In trying to specify 'recent history' we immediately face a problem. How much recent history should be included? From a statistical analysis point of view, it is usually the case of 'the more the merrier' in that the data-tests will be less susceptible to problems of finite size. However just because the data is available for the past 5 years, should we really be placing equal weight on its behaviour in 1996–97 and 2000–01? We have no guarantee that the price-process $x[t]$ is stationary on any timescale; indeed the probability distribution function (PDF) of price-changes

---

[1]  See the numerous data analysis papers on www.unifr.ch/econophysics, which report studies on price series taken from a wide range of financial markets. See also Mantegna and Stanley (2000) and Bouchaud and Potters (2000).

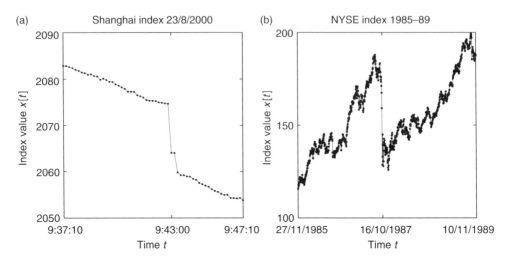

**Fig. 3.1**   Periods of arguably atypical behaviour, arising in the (a) Shanghai stock exchange index and (b) NYSE daily composite index.

and its associated statistics may be strongly time-dependent. Even if we assume that it is reasonably stationary, maybe we should treat the period of the 1999–2000 'bubble' as atypical, that is, a special case. However in true complex systems style, it could be claimed that *every* case is a special case. One can always find reasons for excluding or including particular periods, particularly in hindsight having already seen the data. Herein lies one of the major problems with analysing financial data. All such data seem to have atypical periods at some stage or another. Figure 3.1 shows two such examples of arguably atypical behaviour, arising in the markets to be analysed in this chapter.

So should such atypical periods be included when calculating the statistics? This is a crucially important question, given our interest in calculating risk. After all, risk is concerned with large deviations in the tails of the distribution. However the frequency of occurrence of such deviations decreases as the size of the deviation increases, hence the decision to exclude or include a few such data-points can have a profound effect on the estimation of the best-fit distribution for the tails. One could try to base this decision to exclude or include the rare events by classifying them as exogenous (i.e. generated by external effects) or endogenous (i.e. self-generated by the internal dynamics). However it is not easy to make such a distinction when considering real data, and mixtures of the two will certainly arise. In our opinion, all data points should be included when forming the statistics. Even if the stimulus was completely external, the response of the market is controlled by its own internal feedback mechanisms; hence this response carries some information about the market's internal dynamics. In short it is all part of the same complex system. However, many readers may not agree. In fact, different people looking at the same dataset could come to somewhat different conclusions as to the exact functional form of the PDF of price-changes, depending on how they decided to process the dataset.

## 3.2    Statistical tools and datasets

There are many statistical packages available commercially for analysing time-series data. However, such standard packages only tend to investigate the more obvious, low-order correlations (e.g. autocorrelation of price-changes). In fact it would be really surprising if such tests were to show anything significant, not least because a lot of people with access to these packages would then trade based on such correlations. Such trading would then distort or diminish the correlations themselves. Therefore it is not surprising that, as far as standard statistical tests based on these lower-order correlations are concerned, financial market data appears essentially 'random'. However as we discussed in Chapter 2, this implies nothing about the existence of higher order temporal correlations, or deviations from Gaussian behaviour. Our goal is not to list the results of such standard tests here, but rather to exploit the points raised in Chapter 2 in order to look beyond the standard analysis. In particular we wish to see if higher order temporal correlations can be detected over a range of different timescales, and the degree to which the resulting distributions of price-increments deviate from the Gaussian form. The appearance of such higher order correlations and deviations from Gaussian behaviour would sound the warning bell against automatic application of results from standard finance theory.

There are thousands of possible price series we could look at, and hundreds of different markets. One of the significant contributions of Econophysics has been to establish that the price statistics across a wide range of supposedly different financial markets worldwide, exhibit certain universal properties.[2] It seems that despite the differences in detail between these markets in terms of how trades are registered, trading hours, etc., there is something that they hold in common which is driving the market price-dynamics. Our viewpoint is that this common element is the presence of traders who are buying and selling, moving into the market or staying out, and taking actions based in part on the past behaviour of the market. In Chapters 4 and 5 we will

---

[2] Given the limited space, we cannot carry out a thorough statistical analysis over many different markets. Nor can we provide a detailed discussion of the datasets themselves. Instead the results presented here provide a flavour of the many similar ones already present in the Econophysics literature. In particular, we refer to Mantegna and Stanley (2000), Bouchaud and Potters (2000) and www.unifr.ch/econophysics.

see how this common feature can indeed give rise to the stylized facts observed across financial markets. But first, we will illustrate these common features by focusing on two market datasets, which one might initially believe were quite different. These two datasets are the NYSE composite index recorded on a daily basis between 1966 and 2000[3] and the Shanghai stock exchange index recorded at 10-s intervals during a period of eight months in 2001–02. Apart from the fact that the two markets are in distinct geographical and temporal zones, they also differ in their history and level of liquidity. The NYSE composite index reflects the long-running, well-established and highly liquid US stock market. By contrast, the Shanghai stock exchange is essentially an emerging market that is relatively young in terms of global trading. Despite these structural differences, we will show that there are in fact surprising similarities between the dynamics observed in these two markets. This observation is therefore consistent with claims being made within the Econophysics community that apparently distinct financial markets can exhibit universal dynamical features.[4]

Our discussion will also illustrate the common situation in practice whereby one is given either a long but low-frequency dataset such as the daily NYSE composite index,[5] or a short but high-frequency dataset such as the Shanghai stock index data. Choices therefore have to be made about the best way to analyse this data in order to minimize any bias. This type of problem is fine in academia where one can spend all day building and cleaning datasets. Practitioners on the other hand regularly face a much tougher situation: they may be handed a low-frequency dataset measured over a relatively short period and yet be expected to produce realistic calculations of derivatives prices and hedging strategies. For this reason we will return to the data analysis problem in Chapter 6, where we look at the practical implementation of a generalized derivatives theory using a much shorter version of the NYSE daily data, in order to reflect this common situation.[6] For the time being, we will stick with our large NYSE daily dataset, and our high-frequency Shanghai dataset, in order to pin down their statistical and dynamical features.

## 3.3    Empirical analysis

Figure 3.2 shows the Shanghai price series represented by our dataset. Even by eye, one can see that the index undergoes frequent large movements by contrast to the

---

[3] At the time of writing, this data is freely available on www.unifr.ch/econophysics.

[4] See note 2.      [5] See note 3.

[6] The conclusions reached in Chapter 6 regarding non-Gaussian behaviour and higher-order temporal correlations, are consistent with those in the present Chapter. This suggests that the stylized facts are reasonably robust to changes in size of dataset.

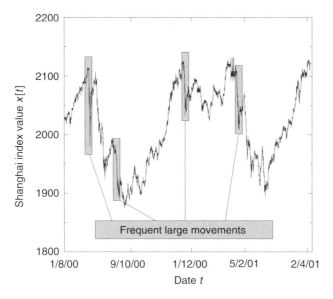

**Fig. 3.2**    Shanghai stock market index measured at 10-s intervals over the period 1/8/00–2/4/01.

Gaussian random walk shown in Fig. 2.5. A close-up of one such large change was shown in Fig. 3.1. Such large changes will tend to increase the magnitude of the PDF in the tails of the distribution, hence generating fat-tailed distributions. The pioneering study of empirical data within the Econophysics field was performed by Mantegna and Stanley[7] who studied minute-by-minute data for the S&P500 index over the 6-year period 1984–90. Our study is similar to their original analysis.[8] We form a series of log-returns (see Section 1.4) of index changes[9] for each of the two market indices:

$$z[t, t - \Delta t] \equiv z[t] = \log \frac{x[t]}{x[t - \Delta t]}, \tag{3.1}$$

where $\Delta t$ is a given time-interval separating the index records, and $x[t]$ is the index value at time $t$. It is known from empirical studies that there exists an intra-day pattern of market activity in large financial markets.[10] A possible explanation for this

[7] Mantegna, R. N. and Stanley, H. E. (1995) *Nature* **376**, 46. See also Mantegna and Stanley (2000) for further discussions.                                                                                                       [8] See note 7.

[9] We drop the explicit $\Delta t$ from the log-return $z[t, t - \Delta t]$: Mantegna and Stanley's original paper is written in terms of the index-change variable $Z$ and we want to facilitate any comparison by the reader to their original paper.

[10] Gopikrishnan, P., Meyer, M., Amaral, L. A. N., and Stanley, H. E. (1998) *Eur. Phys. J.* B **3**, 139; Gopikrishnan, P., Plerou, V., Amaral, L. A. N., Meyer, M., and Stanley, H. E. (1999) *Phys. Rev.* E **60**, 5305; Wood, R. A., McInish, T. H., and Ord, J. K. (1985) *J. Fin.* **40**, 723; Harris, L. (1986) *J. Fin. Econ.* **16**, 99; Admati, A. R. and Pfleiderer, P. (1988) *Rev. Fin. Stud.* **1**, 3; Ekman, P. D. (1992) *J. Futures Markets* **12**, 365.

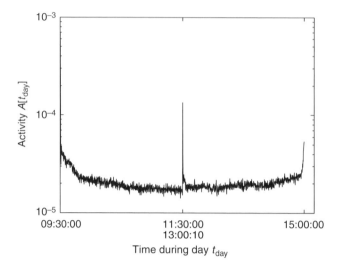

**Fig. 3.3**  Daily (i.e. intra-day) pattern for the absolute changes of the Shanghai index.

intra-day pattern is the reaction to the information gathered during the hours when the market is closed, together with the fact that many liquidity traders are active near the closing hours. There is a similar intra-day pattern in the absolute changes in the Shanghai index $|z[t]|$, which we wish to remove before proceeding. The intra-day activity pattern $A[t_{\text{day}}]$, where $t_{\text{day}}$ denotes the time during the day, can be defined as

$$A[t_{\text{day}}] = \langle |z[\text{daytime}[t] = t_{\text{day}}]| \rangle, \tag{3.2}$$

where the operator daytime$[t]$ returns the time during the day corresponding to an absolute time of $t$. The intra-day pattern $A[t_{\text{day}}]$ for the Shanghai index is shown in Fig. 3.3.

Similar intra-day patterns have been observed in other markets, such as the Hang Seng. In order to remove the systematic effect of this intra-day pattern, we re-define the returns for the Shanghai index as follows: $z[\text{daytime}[t]] \rightarrow z[\text{daytime}[t]]/A[t_{\text{day}}]$. Such a re-definition is obviously not applied to the NYSE composite index, since the dataset is daily and hence has no intra-day pattern. We are now ready for the analysis. We start by looking at the standard linear (i.e. low-order) correlations between returns. In particular we look at the autocorrelation of returns, which is essentially just the correlation measure $c_{ij}$ defined in Equation (2.3). Specifically we use the following normalized definition of the autocorrelation:

$$\rho[\{z[t]\}, \{z[t - \Delta t]\}] = \langle (z[t] - \overline{z[t]})(z[t - \Delta t] - \overline{z[t - \Delta t]}) \rangle / \sigma^2, \tag{3.3}$$

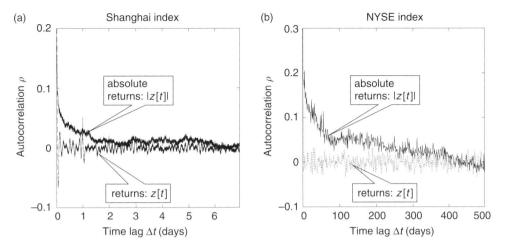

**Fig. 3.4** Autocorrelation of returns and absolute returns for the (a) Shanghai index and (b) NYSE as a function of the time-lag $\Delta t$.

where $\sigma^2$ is the variance of $z[t]$ and $\Delta t$ is a given time lag. Hence if the returns $z[t]$ and $z[t - \Delta t]$ are uncorrelated, then

$$\langle (z[t] - \overline{z[t]})(z[t - \Delta t] - \overline{z[t - \Delta t]}) \rangle = \langle (z[t] - \overline{z[t]}) \rangle \langle (z[t - \Delta t] - \overline{z[t - \Delta t]}) \rangle = 0.$$
$$(3.4)$$

Figure 3.4 shows the autocorrelation of returns for both markets.

As can be seen, the autocorrelation function of returns is essentially zero for all time-lags $\Delta t \neq 0$. This behaviour is consistent with the standard finance theory model of uncorrelated price-increments. We therefore turn to look at non-linear (i.e. higher order) temporal correlations. As mentioned in Section 2.2.1, one such measure is given by the autocorrelation of the *absolute* value of returns $|z[t]|$. Since this removes the sign from the returns, it is a measure of the temporal correlations in the *size* of the return fluctuations. This correlation measure can be obtained from Equation (3.3) simply by inserting moduli around every $z$-dependent term, that is, $z[t] \rightarrow |z[t]|$ and so on. Figure 3.4 confirms that this autocorrelation measure is non-zero over a wide range of time lags $\Delta t$. We can conclude that *the non-linear (i.e. higher order) temporal correlations in the returns $z[t]$ survive over a surprisingly long period.* In fact for the NYSE, these correlations last for several months. To understand better why there is such a long decay of the autocorrelation of absolute returns, we examine a 'time-dependent' or 'local' volatility from the returns' series. This quantity can be determined by calculating the standard deviation of the fluctuation in returns over a small time-window taken in the vicinity of a given time $t$. Figure 3.5 shows how this local volatility then varies as a function of time $t$ for the NYSE.

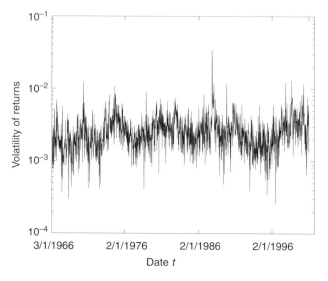

**Fig. 3.5**  Local volatility as a function of time for the NYSE index.

This local volatility is far from constant.[11] It exhibits frequent large deviations and a bursty structure associated with clustering. This clustering reflects the tendency for volatile periods in the market to generate further volatility in the immediate future: volatility breeds volatility. This finding is therefore consistent with the long decay in the autocorrelation of absolute returns in Fig. 3.4. On a microscopic level, one could relate this volatility clustering to market-activity as reflected by the number of trades, etc. Such market activity therefore appears to be a highly non-stationary process.

Next we look at the full distribution of returns using the methodology of Mantegna and Stanley. Mantegna and Stanley proposed that a so-called truncated Levy distribution represents a good model for the PDF of price-changes, in contrast to the Gaussian paradigm. The truncated Levy distribution comprises a Levy distribution over the main central portion of the PDF, with an approximately exponential truncation in the outer tails. A Levy distribution is the name given to a general class of fat-tailed distributions of which the Lorentzian is a particular example. The characteristic feature of a stable symmetric Levy distribution is that it has power-law tails for large deviations:

$$p[z] \equiv p_{L,\alpha}[z] \sim |z|^{-(1+\alpha)}, \quad \text{for } |z| \to \infty, \tag{3.5}$$

---

[11] We note that even the intra-day volatility can vary significantly.

where the parameter $\alpha$ satisfies $0 < \alpha < 2$ in order to guarantee that the PDF is stable under convolution. It follows that the second moment, and hence the variance and standard deviation, are *infinite*. There is no simple analytic expression for $p_{L,\alpha}[z]$, except when $\alpha = 1$ which corresponds to the Lorentzian distribution shown in Fig. 2.3:

$$p_{L,\alpha=1}[z] = \frac{C}{z^2 + C^2\pi^2} \xrightarrow{|z|\to\infty} C|z|^{-2}. \tag{3.6}$$

Although it is not so easy to see, the case $\alpha = 2$ yields the Gaussian. In this limit, the tails are no longer power-law, but are instead exponential—equivalently one can say that the region over which power-law behaviour appears goes to zero for $\alpha \to 2$. Like the Gaussian and the Lorentzian, the Levy distribution is also stable under convolution for $0 < \alpha < 2$. The consequence of this stability is the following. Suppose that the PDF for price-changes over a given time-increment is truly Levy, and that these price-changes are independent and identically distributed (i.i.d). When we then produce the price-change PDF over any larger time-increment by convoluting the PDF with itself as discussed in Chapter 2, the PDF of price-changes will remain Levy on *all* timescales. Hence we *never* achieve convergence to a Gaussian. Looking back at the conditions for the Central Limit Theorem (CLT) to hold as discussed in Section 2.2.3.4, we can see why this arises: although the price-changes might be i.i.d. and we put ourselves in the limit of $n \to \infty$, the variance of single-step price changes is *infinite*, hence the conditions of the CLT for convergence to a Gaussian are not met. This is simply a consequence of the fact that the power law in the tail of $p_{L,\alpha}[z]$ corresponds to $\alpha < 2$, yielding an infinite variance. Hence although the Levy distribution is appealing as a model PDF for price-changes because of the empirical evidence for power-law tails, this feature of non-convergence to a Gaussian is less attractive. For this reason, the *truncated* Levy distribution was introduced: it retains power-law tails out to large $z$, but then becomes exponential,[12] hence guaranteeing a *finite* variance and an *eventual* convergence to Gaussian under convolution.

We will first summarize our conclusions concerning the PDF of price-change returns, before showing the numerical results themselves. For *both* the NYSE and the Shanghai market, the following statements hold: the distribution of returns shows

---

[12] There is no unique definition of a truncated Levy distribution regarding the exact value of $z$ at which the power-law behaviour stops. Nor is there a rule concerning the precise form of the PDF once it has stopped, other than saying that it should then have a faster decay. The defining feature is just that the variance is now finite and eventual convergence to the CLT result of Gaussian is therefore guaranteed. In practice, additional parameters are introduced to parametrize the truncated Levy distribution. We refer to Mantegna and Stanley (2000) and Bouchaud and Potters (2000) for a more detailed discussion of these distributions.

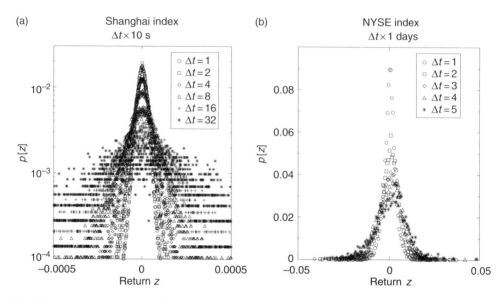

**Fig. 3.6** PDF of returns over different time-increments $\Delta t$, for the (a) Shanghai market index and (b) NYSE composite index. For the Shanghai market, $\Delta t$ is in units of 10-s intervals, while for NYSE $\Delta t$ is in units of days.

apparent scaling behaviour which cannot be modelled by a Gaussian distribution. The non-Gaussian dynamics of the stochastic process underlying the time-series of returns, can be modelled quite well using a truncated Levy distribution. A power-law behaviour is observed for the probability of zero returns. The power-law behaviour in the tails (i.e. large $z$) drops slower than Gaussian, but faster than a Levy stable distribution. This ensures the existence of a large but finite standard deviation (i.e. volatility) for these markets.

Now we turn to the numerical results themselves. For each market, we use the original time-series to generate a new time-series of returns, where each return is calculated for a fixed time-increment $\Delta t$. Since we are interested in how the markets behave over different timescales, we then repeat this procedure for various $\Delta t$. We then plot the PDF of these returns for each timescale $\Delta t$. These are shown in Fig. 3.6. The sets of PDFs look quite different for each market, and for different timescales $\Delta t$ within each market. As expected, the distributions are roughly symmetrical with a wider spread for increasing $\Delta t$. However, the positive and negative tails of the distributions are larger than that of a Gaussian process.[13] Since larger $\Delta t$ implies less

---

[13] In addition to the visual appearance, this statement can be checked by trying to fit Gaussians to these PDFs. Despite the different possible criteria that one could use to fit such a Gaussian, the central peak in the data always tends to be narrower and higher while the tails in the data are always fatter. This is shown, for example, in Fig. 3.9.

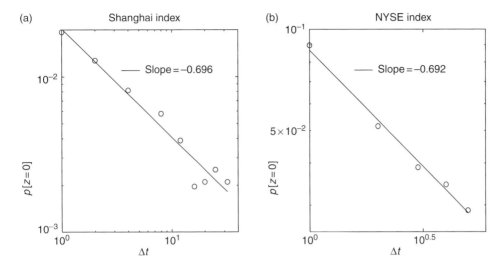

**Fig. 3.7**  A log–log plot showing the central peak of the PDF $p[z = 0]$ as a function of the time-increment $\Delta t$ for the (a) Shanghai market index and (b) NYSE composite index.

data points, it is difficult to determine the parameters characterizing the distributions just by investigating the spreads. Hence we will study the peak values at the centre of the distribution $p[z = 0]$, that is, the probability that the return is zero, as a function of $\Delta t$. In this way, we can investigate the point in each probability distribution with the largest amount of associated data. Graphs of these peak heights as a function of $\Delta t$ are shown in Fig. 3.7. The data are fit well by a straight line on the log–log plot in each case, and hence exhibit a power-law behaviour. The slopes are $-0.6957$ (Shanghai) and $-0.6922$ (NYSE), which are very close in value.[14] In particular, both are different from the value expected for a Gaussian PDF, as we now show. From Equation (2.25) we know that the PDF for a Gaussian would have the form:

$$ p_G[z] = \left[ \frac{1}{2\pi \Delta t \sigma^2} \right]^{1/2} e^{-z^2/(2\Delta t \sigma^2)}, \tag{3.7} $$

where $\sigma^2$ is the variance for a single timestep and $\Delta t$ is the number of timesteps per time-increment. Hence $\log p_G[z = 0] = -0.5 \log \Delta t + \text{constant}$, yielding a slope of

In Chapter 6, we report values of the excess kurtosis for the NYSE data which further confirms its non-Gaussian nature.

[14]  A very similar value of $-0.712 \pm 0.025$ was observed by Mantegna and Stanley for the S&P500.

value $-0.5$. Hence *both* markets give slopes that are similar to each other, but *neither* gives a value close to the Gaussian result.

The scaling behaviour of the associated non-Gaussian process in both markets can be seen from Fig. 3.7 to survive over a wide range of $\Delta t$. Let us assume for the moment that the main central portion of the distribution of returns can be described by a Levy stable distribution. The Levy distribution, while not known in closed form, can be expressed as the following exact integral, in terms of the index $\alpha$ and an extra parameter $\gamma$:

$$p_{L,\alpha}[z] \equiv \frac{1}{\pi} \int_0^\infty e^{-\gamma \Delta t |q|^\alpha} \cos(qz) \, dq, \qquad (3.8)$$

where $e^{-\gamma \Delta t |q|^\alpha}$ is the so-called characteristic function of a symmetrical Levy stable process (see Mantegna and Stanley (2000) for more details). The probability of zero-return is hence given by

$$p[z = 0] = p_{L,\alpha}[0] \equiv \frac{\Gamma[1/\alpha]}{\pi \alpha (\gamma \Delta t)^{1/\alpha}} \qquad (3.9)$$

where $\Gamma$ is the Gamma function. Hence $\log p[z = 0] = -(1/\alpha) \log \Delta t + \text{constant}$ which has a slope $-(1/\alpha)$. Taking the reciprocal of the empirical slope values found above, we obtain $\alpha = 1.44$ for Shanghai and $\alpha = 1.44$ for NYSE (both to three significant figures). This is to be compared to $\alpha = 2$ for a Gaussian. We note that in the original scaling study of the S&P500, Mantegna and Stanley found essentially the same value of $\alpha = 1.40 \pm 0.05$.

We now investigate whether this Levy scaling can be extended across the entire PDF of returns for both markets and for all timescales $\Delta t$. To do this, we perform the transformations

$$z_s \equiv z/[(\Delta t)^{1/\alpha}], \quad \text{and} \qquad (3.10)$$

$$p_s[z_s] \equiv (\Delta t)^{1/\alpha} p_{L,\alpha}[z] = (\Delta t)^{1/\alpha} p_{L,\alpha}[(\Delta t)^{1/\alpha} z_s]. \qquad (3.11)$$

*If* the PDFs were Gaussian and hence $\alpha = 2$, it is easy to see that Equations (3.10) and (3.11) become

$$z_s \equiv z/[(\Delta t)^{1/2}], \quad \text{and} \qquad (3.12)$$

$$p_s[z_s] \equiv (\Delta t)^{1/2} p_G[(\Delta t)^{1/2} z_s] = (\Delta t)^{1/2} \left[ \frac{1}{2\pi \Delta t \sigma^2} \right]^{1/2} \exp - \frac{\left[ (\Delta t)^{1/2} z_s \right]^2}{2 \Delta t \sigma^2}$$

$$= \left[ \frac{1}{2\pi \sigma^2} \right]^{1/2} e^{-z_s^2/(2\sigma^2)}, \qquad (3.13)$$

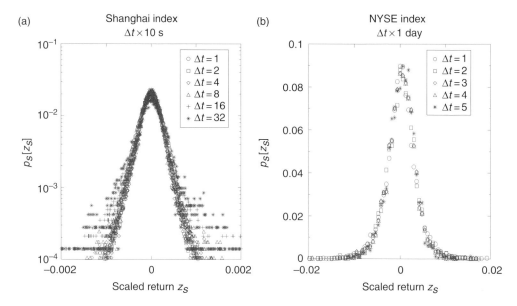

**Fig. 3.8**   Re-scaled plot of Fig. 3.6 using the transformations in Equations (3.10) and (3.11). For both the (a) Shanghai market index and (b) NYSE composite index, we use $\alpha = 1.44$ to three significant figures. This value of $\alpha$ comes from the slopes in Fig. 3.7.

which is *independent* of the time-increment $\Delta t$. Hence all curves would then appear identical when plotted in the transformed variable $z_s$. This is exactly the property of self-similarity that we mentioned in Section 2.2.3.4 of Chapter 2. This Gaussian scaling is a special case of the Levy scaling result in Equations (3.10) and (3.11), and suggests that *if* the PDFs were approximately Gaussian, then they should appear to collapse onto a single curve under the transformations of Equations (3.10) and (3.11) with $\alpha \approx 2$. Since we have already found evidence that $\alpha = 1.44$ for both markets,[15] we will instead use this value to perform the scaling in Equations (3.10) and (3.11). The rescaled PDFs are shown in Fig. 3.8 that is, $p_s[z_s]$ vs $z_s$ for different $\Delta t$. We emphasize that they correspond to the same data as in Fig. 3.6. The data-collapse for $\alpha = 1.44$ is quite impressive, and reasonably complete[16] apart from some data points in the tails of the Shanghai dataset. The closer one looks to the central point

---

[15] Of course, all markets will not necessarily have this same value of $\alpha$. However research studies to date suggest that all markets show similar scaling properties, with values of $\alpha$ deviating from the Gaussian value of 2.

[16] In order to be consistent, we have performed this re-scaling using the same value of $\alpha$ as that deduced from Fig. 3.7. We note however that the data-collapse can be improved by choosing $\alpha$ close, but not exactly equal, to 1.44. This makes sense, because of the natural error in estimating the slope in Fig. 3.7.

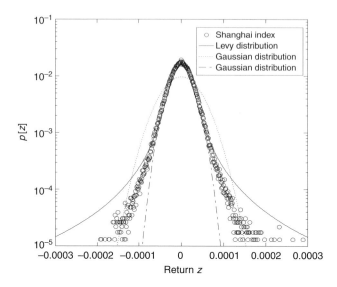

**Fig. 3.9** PDF of returns for the Shanghai market data with $\Delta t = 1$. This plot is compared to a stable symmetric Levy distribution using the value $\alpha = 1.44$ determined from the slope in Fig. 3.7. The agreement is very good over the main central portion, with deviations for large $z$. Two attempts to fit a Gaussian are also shown. The wider Gaussian is chosen to have the same standard deviation as the empirical data. However, the peak in the data is much narrower and higher than this Gaussian, and the tails are fatter. The narrower Gaussian is chosen to fit the central portion, however the standard deviation is now too small. It can be seen that the data has tails which are much fatter and furthermore have a non-Gaussian functional dependence.

$z_s = 0$, the stronger is the extent of this data-collapse. These observations imply that the Levy distribution is a better description than the Gaussian to describe the dynamics of the price-process for small-to-medium sized returns. Figure 3.9 shows the Shanghai data, together with the Levy distribution corresponding to $\alpha = 1.44$, and a 'best-fit' Gaussian chosen to have the same standard deviation as the experimental data. Also shown is a narrower Gaussian whose standard deviation was chosen to be significantly smaller than that of the experimental data in order to fit the central portion of the data curve.

One can extend this investigation in order to determine if a truncated Levy distribution can be used to describe the stochastic process for larger returns that are outside the Levy stable region. Since one would in this case like an accurate representation of the tails, it is better to work with the cumulative distribution $p[z < Z]$ for each timescale $\Delta t$, where $p[z < Z]$ is the probability that the return $z$ is less than a given value $Z$. While we will not go through the specific analysis here, we make the comments that the tails generally decay to zero with an exponent $\alpha > 2$ which is therefore outside the Levy stable regime.[17] Hence the earlier claim that the variance will be large but finite.

Finally we comment on one further simple test. We saw earlier that the autocorrelation function of returns is zero for anything but the smallest timescales in both markets. This implies that the returns are essentially uncorrelated. If we assume they are also identically distributed, then the results of Chapter 2 suggest that the standard deviation $\sigma_{\Delta t}$ should increase as $\sigma_{\Delta t} \propto (\Delta t)^{1/2}$. However, non-zero residual correlations or non-stationarity of the price-process could alter this relationship. In Chapter 6 we investigate this further for the NYSE dataset. The numerical results show that the $(\Delta t)^{1/2}$ scaling is not followed for all $\Delta t$. This again provides evidence for a price-process which is beyond standard finance theory. In order to further explore the presence of higher order correlations using such scaling ideas, Bouchaud and Potters (2000) suggested investigating the scaling relationship $\langle z_{t,t-\Delta t}^{q} \rangle \sim (\Delta t)^{\varsigma_q}$, where $z_{t,t-\Delta t}$ are the returns for a given time-increment $\Delta t$ and $q$ is an arbitrary power. The case $q = 2$ represents the scaling of the variance. The use of a function $\varsigma_q$ allows the $\Delta t$-dependence to change exponent over different timescales. This enables an investigation of so-called multiscaling by mapping out $\varsigma_q$ as a function of $q$.

## 3.4   Challenging the standard theory

We have uncovered various empirical facts associated with real markets. Our particular examples concerned two structurally and historically different markets, and yet similar statistical results were obtained for each of these markets. In particular these results lie outside the usual paradigm adopted by standard finance theory. We stress that these results are just an illustration of the large number of such studies that have appeared in the Econophysics field. Taking these statistical studies as a whole, the evidence strongly suggests that despite the nuances that different markets seem to have, there is a basic set of qualitative *stylized facts* which markets across the world seem to exhibit. Although there is as yet no complete list of such facts, the following features, which we illustrated in Section 3.3, do appear:

- fat-tailed PDF of price-changes, with non-trivial scaling properties
- slow decay of the autocorrelation of absolute value of price-changes
- volatility clustering
- fast decay of the autocorrelation of price-changes.

---

[17] See, for example, the original paper of Mantegna and Stanley for the S&P500. For similar analysis applied to the Hang Seng index, see Wang, B. H. and Hui, P. M. (2001) *Eur. Phys. J.* B **20**, 573.

The ability to reproduce these features represents an important test for any candidate market model. However the Gaussian random-walk paradigm does not include the first three of these features. The standard model is therefore an approximation to the truth. It may not be a bad approximation in terms of giving the general form of the distribution of a given financial variable, but the 'devil is in the details'.

The conceptual argument against any non-random walk behaviour of markets is related to arbitrage, that is, the idea that there should be 'no-free lunch' in the financial markets. In short the argument goes like this: 'Surely if there was an opportunity for predicting the future behaviour with any certainty at all, then someone would have found it and traded on it—hence they would have traded away this opportunity'. The same argument is also applied to propose that no such opportunities can exist between markets, for example, it should not be possible to buy futures contracts at the same time as assets, and then reverse the trade in some way in order to make money. If that opportunity existed, someone would find it—and the opportunity would gradually disappear as the person traded on it. However there are various practical arguments that one can make against this theoretical hypothesis:

1. In order to exploit an opportunity, you have to find it in the first place. In other words, in order that no such opportunity exists, somebody somewhere would have to find it, and then trade on it. After all, you can only pick up a 'free' $20 bill off the ground if you happen to stumble across it. In order to guarantee exploitation, such opportunities should therefore be somewhat 'obvious'. However, higher order temporal correlations are, almost by definition, extremely well hidden and hence non-obvious.

2. Even assuming such an opportunity has been found, and someone has started trading on it, the timescale over which this opportunity then dies away may not be that small. This is particularly true if the person trades in small amounts (which he/she is likely to do if they do not want anyone else to notice). Alternatively, the transaction costs may be too large to take full advantage. For example, in emerging markets, it may need an insider within the country to make the trade in order to avoid various tax penalties and legal barriers.

3. Suppose that the markets *are* effectively random at some instant in time. The fact that there are chartists who *think* they see patterns in this randomness, and seem to have a set toolbox for interpreting the next movements, means that patterns could be introduced into the subsequent market dynamics merely by the collective actions of these traders. This issue is the subject of Chapters 4 and 5.

In short, we feel that one could justifiably turn the arbitrage question around and ask: 'why *shouldn't* there be some form of arbitrage opportunity, albeit limited?'

## 3.5   Towards a general stochastic process framework

In Chapter 2 we discussed i.i.d. variables using probability theory. However we saw in Section 3.3 that real price-changes do not seem to have this i.i.d. property. For completeness, we will therefore give a brief discussion of how probability theory can be extended to discuss non-i.i.d. variables. Suppose that $y_1$ and $y_2$, measured at times $t_1$ and $t_2$, respectively, correspond to two market variables. Some possibilities include the following:

- $y_1$ and $y_2$ are prices for the same asset, or increments in that asset price.
- $y_1$ and $y_2$ are volumes of trade, or increments in volume of trade.
- $y_1$ is a price or increment in the price, while $y_2$ is a volume or increment in the volume.
- $y_1$ and $y_2$ are measurements of the daily volatility, or increments in the daily volatility.

In addition, $y_1$ and $y_2$ could represent an infinite number of functions (both linear, and non-linear) of these prices, volumes, volatilities, etc. Equally, $y_1$ and $y_2$ could refer to different assets or markets. Given the global nature of today's markets and common news sources, there could be any number of financial variables which are non-i.i.d., or which have become non-i.i.d. over time.

The joint probability distribution for having an outcome (e.g. a price) $y_1$ at time $t_1$, and an outcome (e.g. a price) $y_2$ at time $t_2$, is given by $p[y_2, t_2; y_1, t_1]$. If we consider a string of variables (e.g. prices) obtained at a sequence of times, we have

$$p[y_N, t_N; y_{N-1}, t_{N-1}; \ldots; y_1, t_1] \equiv p[\{y, t\}] \tag{3.14}$$

A priori, we do not know whether there are any hidden correlations, nor do we know the probability distribution of the individual variables (e.g. prices) at each time. We can rewrite this expression exactly in terms of conditional probabilities as

$$
\begin{aligned}
&p[y_N, t_N; y_{N-1}, t_{N-1}; \ldots; y_1, t_1] \\
&\quad = p[y_N, t_N | y_{N-1}, t_{N-1}; \ldots; y_1, t_1] p[y_{N-1}, t_{N-1}; \ldots; y_1, t_1] \\
&\quad = p[y_N, t_N | y_{N-1}, t_{N-1}; \ldots] p[y_{N-1}, t_{N-1} | y_{N-2}, t_{N-2}; \ldots] \\
&\quad\quad \times p[y_{N-2}, t_{N-2}; y_{N-3}, t_{N-3}; \ldots] \\
&\quad = \prod_{i=2}^{N} p[y_i, t_i | y_{i-1}, t_{i-1}; y_{i-2}, t_{i-2}; \ldots; y_1, t_1] p[y_1, t_1], \tag{3.15}
\end{aligned}
$$

where $p[y_i, t_i | y_{i-1}, t_{i-1}; \ldots; y_1, t_1]$ is the conditional probability to see an outcome $y_i$ at time $t_i$ given a history of earlier values $y_{i-1}, t_{i-1}; y_{i-2}, t_{i-2}; \ldots; y_1, t_1$. If we know the conditional probabilities, and we know the past history, then we can determine the probability distribution of future values. In the simplifying case that the distribution in Equation (3.14) is invariant under an arbitrary translation of the origin of time for all $N$, the process is said to be stationary. (Note that if only the means and covariances are independent of time, then the process is called weak or wide-sense stationary.) We can then rewrite each term in Equation (3.15) as follows:

$$p[y_i, t_i | y_{i-1}, t_{i-1}; y_{i-2}, t_{i-2}; \ldots; y_1, t_1]$$
$$= p[y_i, t | y_{i-1}, t - T_1; y_{i-2}, t - T_2; \ldots; y_1, t - T_{i-1}]. \tag{3.16}$$

If this conditional probability can be limited to a finite history for all $t$, we can write

$$p[y_i, t | y_{i-1}, t - T_1; y_{i-2}, t - T_2; \ldots; y_1, t - T_{i-1}]$$
$$= p\left[ y_i, t | \underbrace{y_{i-1}, t - T_1; y_{i-2}, t - T_2; \ldots; y_{i-n}, t - T_n}_{n \text{ terms}} \right]. \tag{3.17}$$

We will now simplify the notation by writing $y_i, t \to y_t$, hence the above equation becomes

$$p[y_t | y_{t-T_1}, y_{t-T_2}, \ldots] = p\left[ y_t | \underbrace{y_{t-T_1}, y_{t-T_2}, \ldots, y_{t-T_n}}_{n \text{ terms}} \right], \tag{3.18}$$

which describes an $n$th order Markov process. In the simplifying case that $n = 1$, $p[y_t | y_{t-T_1}, y_{t-T_2}, \ldots]$ is equivalent to $p[y_t | y_{t-T}]$ which is usually referred to simply as a Markov process. This is the case of the coin-toss price model of Chapter 2, and hence the random-walk price model in standard finance theory, with $y_{t-T}$ representing the price at time $t - T$ and $y_t$ representing the price at time $t$. If $y$ and $t$ are both discrete variables, then we can simply replace $p[y_t | y_{t-T}] \to p[y_t | y_{t-1}]$ and we hence have a Markov chain (see Feller (1968) and Gershenfeld (1999)). Note that we can always convert an $n$th order Markov process for a scalar variable $y$ into a first-order Markov process in an $n$-dimensional variable, for example, by converting

$$y_t, y_{t-1} \to \underline{w}_t = \begin{pmatrix} y_t \\ y_{t-1} \end{pmatrix}. \tag{3.19}$$

For a simple Markov chain with $M$ possible values of $y_t$ (i.e. $M$ possible 'states' $y_{t,\alpha}$ where $\alpha = 1, 2, \ldots, M$) we have

$$p[y_{t+1,\beta}] = \sum_{\alpha=1}^{M} p[y_{t+1,\beta} | y_{t,\alpha}] p[y_{t,\alpha}] \tag{3.20}$$

Defining an $M$-component vector of the state probabilities $\underline{p}_t = \{p[y_{t,1}], p[y_{t,2}], \ldots,$ $p[y_{t,M}]\}$ and a matrix of transition probabilities $[\underline{\underline{P}}]_{\alpha\beta} = p[y_{t+1,\alpha}|y_{t,\beta}]$, the update for all states can be written:

$$\underline{p}_{t+1} = \underline{\underline{P}} \cdot \underline{p}_t. \tag{3.21}$$

Applying this repeatedly in the case that $\underline{\underline{P}}$ is time-independent, gives

$$\underline{p}_{t+n} = \left[\underline{\underline{P}}\right]^n \cdot \underline{p}_t. \tag{3.22}$$

The powers of the matrix $\underline{\underline{P}}$ therefore determine the temporal evolution of the system. If it is possible to get from every state to every other state of the system, then the system is said to be ergodic. In a steady state whereby $\underline{p}_{t+1} = \underline{p}_t = \underline{p}$, we have that $\underline{p} = [\underline{\underline{P}}] \cdot \underline{p}$. In this way we can find the stationary probabilities for occupying each of the $M$ states. The continuous-time analogue of this Markov chain equation follows a similar derivation.

We have presented a brief methodology for describing the stochastic properties of price-models which go beyond the coin-toss price model of Chapter 2. The use of $n > 1$ Markov models will allow a degree of temporal correlation and dependence to be incorporated, in addition to the possibility of non-identical distributions at different times. In the next section, we will explicitly use an $n = 2$ (i.e. second-order) Markov chain calculation to look at the effect of temporal correlations on earnings in a model market setting. Although the market scenario itself is quite artificial, it illustrates very well how counter-intuitive the investment process can be in the presence of temporal correlations.

## 3.6 Effects of temporal correlations in a market

### 3.6.1 Winning by losing

We have seen empirically that subtle temporal correlations can lie hidden in financial time-series. There is no quick recipe to say how one might exploit such correlations. However we would like to demonstrate, using a simple example, how the presence of correlations can produce counter-intuitive effects in terms of trading and investment.

Suppose you are a day-trader who focuses on two particular markets, call them A and B. At the beginning of each day, you have to decide whether to invest in market A or B. Having decided, you invest a fixed amount to open up a position in your chosen market. At the end of the day you close out that position. You therefore either win or lose on that day according to whether you made a profit or a loss. To keep things simple, we imagine that you receive one unit of reward if you win, and are fined one unit of reward if you lose. We will also assume that the subtleties of your position can be subsumed into a simple probability of winning. Let's start with market A. In the absence of transaction costs and the market-maker's spread, we will take[18] your probability of winning in market A to be $p_{win,A} = 0.5$. You would therefore neither win nor lose on average. If we include the effect of transaction costs and the market-maker's spread, your probability of winning is effectively lowered to $p_{win,A} < 0.5$. Now consider market B. Again your probability of winning in the presence of transaction costs and the market-maker's spread, is $p_{win,B} < 0.5$. Hence in both markets you will lose on average.

Now comes the remarkable result which we will subsequently prove. In the presence of certain types of temporal correlation in either market A or B or both, you can actually *win* on average by switching between A and B, even though you would lose if you played repeatedly in just one of the two markets. Hence the phrase: *winning by losing*. Moreover you do not have to have a complicated investment plan for switching— random switching between A and B will work fine, as will periodic switching.[19] This remarkable effect, which is known as the Parrondo effect,[20] is a completely alien notion within standard finance theory. The Parrondo effect sounds wonderful for the investor, however there is a catch. Just as you can systematically win on average by switching between two particular types of losing markets, you can also systematically lose on average if you switch between two particular types of winning markets. It all depends on the temporal correlations and associated dynamics in these two markets, as we will now show.

For simplicity we will assume the particular scenario in which the probability $p_{win,A}$ of winning in market A is independent of past outcomes, just like the coin-toss of standard finance theory. However we assume that in market B, the trader's investment strategy is such that the probability $p_{win,B}$ of him winning now depends on his past success. We will denote $X[t]$ as the trader's capital at the beginning of day $t$, or equivalently at the end of day $t - 1$. If he wins on day $t$, his capital becomes $X[t+1] = X[t] + 1$. If he loses, it becomes $X[t + 1] = X[t] - 1$. Since his success in market B depends on his previous success, his capital $X[t]$ is no longer an $n = 1$ Markov process. We will consider the specific case where his success in market B depends on his success in the previous two timesteps. Following Section 3.5, we can form a Markov chain in terms of the state $\{X[t - 1] - X[t - 2], X[t] - X[t - 1]\}$ whose components are the change in capital during day $t - 2$ and the change in capital during

---

[18] This is consistent with the standard finance idea of random-walk markets.

[19] An example of periodic switching would be: Monday and Tuesday, market A; Wednesday and Thursday, market B; Friday and Monday, market A etc.

[20] Parrondo, J. M. R., Harmer, G. P., and Abbott, D. (2000) *Phys. Rev. Lett.* **85**, 5226.

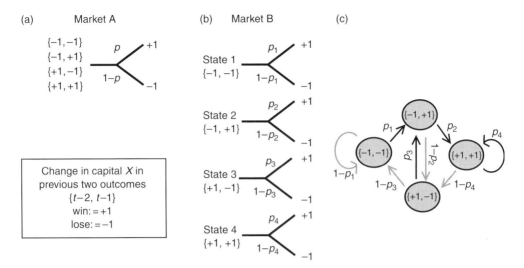

**Fig. 3.10** (a) and (b) Markets A and B and the respective probabilities of winning ($+1$) and losing ($-1$) based on the present state of the vector describing the change in capital in the two previous outcomes. (c) Diagram showing the four possible states and the transition probabilities between these states for market B.

day $t - 1$, respectively. We summarize the probabilities for winning and losing in Fig. 3.10.

We start the analysis by considering market B, which contains the non-trivial temporal correlations. For the moment we assume that the trader is only playing in market B. Hence we can define the following vector state that is written in terms of his capital $X_B$ at timesteps $t - 2$, $t - 1$, and $t$ from playing market B:

$$Y_B[t] = \begin{pmatrix} X_B[t] - X_B[t-1] \\ X_B[t-1] - X_B[t-2] \end{pmatrix}. \tag{3.23}$$

Clearly this vector can only take four distinct states:

$$Y_B[t]: \underset{\text{state 1}}{\begin{pmatrix} -1 \\ -1 \end{pmatrix} \begin{pmatrix} \text{lose} \\ \text{lose} \end{pmatrix}} \quad \underset{\text{state 2}}{\begin{pmatrix} +1 \\ -1 \end{pmatrix} \begin{pmatrix} \text{win} \\ \text{lose} \end{pmatrix}} \quad \underset{\text{state 3}}{\begin{pmatrix} -1 \\ +1 \end{pmatrix} \begin{pmatrix} \text{lose} \\ \text{win} \end{pmatrix}} \quad \underset{\text{state 4}}{\begin{pmatrix} +1 \\ +1 \end{pmatrix} \begin{pmatrix} \text{win} \\ \text{win} \end{pmatrix}}. \tag{3.24}$$

We now define $\pi_i[t]$ *as the probability that the agent is in state $i$ at time $t$.* The probabilities $\pi_i[t]$ form a vector $\underline{\pi}[t]$ with four components, since there are four possible values of $i$

$$\underline{\pi}[t] = \begin{pmatrix} \pi_1[t] \\ \pi_2[t] \\ \pi_3[t] \\ \pi_4[t] \end{pmatrix}. \tag{3.25}$$

Referring back to the possible probabilities for winning in market B given a particular state, we can write a dynamical matrix equation for the evolution of this probability vector:

$$\underline{\pi}[t+1] = \underline{\underline{A}}\,\underline{\pi}[t], \tag{3.26}$$

where

$$\underline{\underline{A}} = \begin{pmatrix} 1-p_1 & 0 & 1-p_3 & 0 \\ p_1 & 0 & p_3 & 0 \\ 0 & 1-p_2 & 0 & 1-p_4 \\ 0 & p_2 & 0 & p_4 \end{pmatrix}. \tag{3.27}$$

Hence we have formed a Markov chain, as discussed in Section 3.5. We are interested in the steady-state behaviour, hence we are interested in the solutions in the long time limit $t \to \infty$. In particular, we would like to know if there are any solutions of $\underline{\pi}[t+1] = \underline{\underline{A}}\,\underline{\pi}[t] \equiv \underline{\pi}$, hence

$$(\underline{\underline{A}} - \underline{\underline{I}})\underline{\pi} = 0, \tag{3.28}$$

which represents four coupled equations for the individual components. Solving these equations yields

$$\underline{\pi} = \begin{pmatrix} \pi_1 \\ \pi_2 \\ \pi_3 \\ \pi_4 \end{pmatrix} = \frac{1}{N} \begin{pmatrix} (1-p_3)(1-p_4) \\ p_1(1-p_4) \\ p_1(1-p_4) \\ p_1 p_2 \end{pmatrix}, \tag{3.29}$$

where $N = (1-p_3)(1-p_4) + 2p_1(1-p_4) + p_1 p_2$. Notice that while $\pi_1 + \pi_2 + \pi_3 + \pi_4 = 1$, $p_1 + p_2 + p_3 + p_4 \neq 1$ in general. The probability of winning in a generic run in market B in this stationary regime is therefore given by

$$p_{\text{win,B}} = \sum_{i=1}^{4} \pi_i p_i = \frac{p_1(p_2 + 1 - p_4)}{(1-p_4)(1-p_3+2p_1) + p_1 p_2} = \frac{1}{2+c/s}, \tag{3.30}$$

where $c = (1-p_4)(1-p_3) - p_1 p_2$ and $s = p_1(p_2 + 1 - p_4)$. Since $s$ is always positive, it is $c$ that controls whether the trader is winning on average in market B, that is, $c < 0$ and hence $p_{\text{win,B}} > 1/2$, or losing, that is, $c > 0$ and hence $p_{\text{win,B}} < 1/2$. The criterion that the trader is losing in market B is therefore $c > 0$ and hence

$$(1-p_4)(1-p_3) > p_1 p_2. \tag{3.31}$$

The criterion that the trader is losing when playing in market A is

$$(1 - p) > p. \tag{3.32}$$

Now we consider the situation in which the trader randomly switches between markets A and B. Since he chooses markets A and B at random by flipping an unbiased coin, then the same analysis follows as for market B, as long as we make the replacement

$$p_i \rightarrow p_i' = \frac{p_i + p}{2}. \tag{3.33}$$

Hence the criterion that he loses in the random-switching scenario is given by

$$(1 - p_4')(1 - p_3') > p_1' p_2',$$

$$\left(1 - \frac{p_4 + p}{2}\right)\left(1 - \frac{p_3 + p}{2}\right) > \left(\frac{p_1 + p}{2}\right)\left(\frac{p_2 + p}{2}\right). \tag{3.34}$$

Hence the criteria that he would lose in either market A or B, but wins by randomly switching between them, are given by the following inequalities:

$$(1 - p) > p,$$

$$(1 - p_4)(1 - p_3) > p_1 p_2, \tag{3.35}$$

$$(2 - p_4 - p)(2 - p_3 - p) < (p + p_1)(p + p_2).$$

If we make the following choice of probabilities

$$p = \tfrac{1}{2}, \quad p_1 = \tfrac{9}{10}, \quad p_2 = p_3 = \tfrac{1}{4}, \quad p_4 = \tfrac{7}{10}, \tag{3.36}$$

then markets A and B are both fair, that is, $p_{\text{win,A}} = p_{\text{win,B}} = 1/2$. In order to make markets A and B losing, we will now choose

$$p = \tfrac{1}{2} - \varepsilon, \quad p_1 = \tfrac{9}{10} - \varepsilon, \quad p_2 = p_3 = \tfrac{1}{4} - \varepsilon, \quad p_4 = \tfrac{7}{10} - \varepsilon, \tag{3.37}$$

and ask: for what range of $\varepsilon$ are the three criteria in Equation (3.35) satisfied? Setting these probabilities into the inequalities, yields the answer

$$0 < \varepsilon < \tfrac{1}{168}. \tag{3.38}$$

This is the range of $\varepsilon$ such that markets A and B are each losing on average, while switching randomly between them results in winning on average. This effect is counter-intuitive, and originates entirely from the nature of the temporal correlations. It has no analogue in the random-walk world assumed by standard finance theory.

### 3.6.2    Drawdowns and crashes

In this section we explore another consequence of the existence of higher order temporal correlations, related to the properties of potential 'drawdowns' or crashes.[21] Such drawdowns represent moments when the market undergoes a set of downward moves over consecutive timesteps. There is no fixed timescale over which a drawdown will last—both this, and the magnitude of the drawdown, will depend on the precise nature of the temporal correlations. Here we provide a toy model of a price-process which exhibits such higher order temporal correlations while appearing 'random' from the point of view of lower order correlations. The model was discussed by Johansen and Sornette[22] and serves as an illustration of the practical importance of higher order temporal correlations.

Suppose we have a price-process $x[t]$ such that the price-change at timestep $t$ can be written

$$\Delta x[t, t-1] \equiv \Delta x[t] = x[t] - x[t-1] = \varepsilon[t] + \varepsilon[t-1]\varepsilon[t-2], \qquad (3.39)$$

where $\varepsilon[t]$ is a white-noise process with zero mean and unit variance, and we have used the shorthand notation $\Delta x[t] \equiv \Delta x[t, t-1]$. In particular, we will take the following simple form:

$$\varepsilon[t] = \begin{cases} +1 \\ -1 \end{cases} \quad \text{with probability } 0.5 \qquad (3.40)$$

The mean value of the price-change $\Delta x[t]$ becomes

$$\langle \Delta x[t] \rangle = \langle \varepsilon[t] \rangle + \langle \varepsilon[t-1]\varepsilon[t-2] \rangle. \qquad (3.41)$$

The term $\langle \varepsilon[t-1]\varepsilon[t-2] \rangle$ can be either positive or negative with equal probability, hence the mean value of the price-change is zero. Next consider the mean of the product of price-changes at different times, that is, the autocorrelation function $\langle \Delta x[t] \Delta x[t'] \rangle$. Again by writing out the various cases, it is straightforward to show that $\langle \Delta x[t] \Delta x[t'] \rangle = 0$. Hence the price series produced looks 'random' since its mean and autocorrelation are both zero. In other words, passing the resulting price series $x[t]$ through standard statistical software packages that just look at low-order correlations such as the autocorrelation, would conclude that the price series is a random walk.

---

[21] 'Drawdown' is the term typically used to describe gentler crashes.
[22] Johansen, A. and Sornette, D., preprint xxx.lanl.gov/cond-mat/0010050. See also Johansen, A. and Sornette, D. (2001) *J. Risk* **4**, No. 2, p. 69.

However this is not the case. If we look at higher-order correlation functions, we begin to find that non-zero correlations appear which should be absent in a strict random walk. In other words, there are temporal correlations in the resulting price series $x[t]$ which are buried from sight of any standard linear statistical analysis tools. Consider for example the three-point correlation function $\langle \Delta x[t-2]\Delta x[t-1]\Delta x[t]\rangle$. In a random-walk model, this should be zero—but in the present case it is non-zero. Furthermore the conditional mean $\langle \Delta x[t]|\Delta x[t-2], \Delta x[t-1]\rangle$, that is, the mean of $\Delta x[t]$ given the values of $\Delta x[t-2]$ and $\Delta x[t-1]$, is not always zero. In particular,

$$\langle \Delta x[t]|\Delta x[t-2], \Delta x[t-1]\rangle \propto \Delta x[t-2]\Delta x[t-1] \neq \langle \Delta x[t]\rangle = 0. \qquad (3.42)$$

Since this conditional quantity is not always zero, the price series $x[t]$ has some level of predictability. This is a consequence of the market having memory: the expected value of its next movement depends on the product of the past two movements.

We now illustrate the dramatic effect that such higher order temporal correlations can have on the size and duration of a drawdown, defined as a drop in the price $x[t]$ from a local maximum in $x[t]$ to a local minimum in $x[t]$. Using Equation (3.39), we can generate the possible price-changes at each timestep. These are shown in the following table:

| $\varepsilon[t-2]$ | $\varepsilon[t-1]$ | $\varepsilon[t]$ | $\Delta x[t]$ |
|---|---|---|---|
| +1 | +1 | +1 | +2 |
| +1 | +1 | −1 | 0 |
| +1 | −1 | +1 | 0 |
| +1 | −1 | −1 | −2 |
| −1 | +1 | +1 | 0 |
| −1 | +1 | −1 | −2 |
| −1 | −1 | +1 | +2 |
| −1 | −1 | −1 | 0 |

The largest price-change per timestep is +2 or −2. More importantly, we can also say something about the largest drawdown and its duration. Looking at the table, it can be seen that the sequence of coin-tosses $\varepsilon[t]$ giving the largest drawdown is $\pm 1, -1, +1, -1, -1, \pm 1$ which leads to a series of price-changes $0/+2$, $-2, -2, +2/0$. Hence the longest drawdown has duration of two timesteps and magnitude of four units. The temporal correlations, which were buried in the price series and which showed up in an indirect way within higher order correlation functions, have now surfaced very clearly in the drawdowns. To see this explicitly, imagine what the corresponding answer would be for the usual random coin-toss price model where

$$\Delta x[t] \equiv x[t] - x[t-1] = \varepsilon[t]. \tag{3.43}$$

Again the mean and autocorrelation are both zero, so Equation (3.43) appears indistinguishable from the price-model of Equation (3.39). However the truth is quite different: in particular, the coin-toss price series in Equation (3.43) can generate drawdowns of unlimited length and size, corresponding to an infinite string of tails (T) which generates a string of $-1$s. In particular, a drawdown of length at least $n$ (i.e. a sequence of at least $n$ outcomes $-1$) has a probability $(0.5)^n$ of occurring. Hence there is a small but finite probability of obtaining drawdowns of any length and hence any size. This is in sharp contrast to the model with temporal correlations given by Equation (3.39) which can never generate drawdowns larger than four or longer than two timesteps. Hence we have seen that the presence of higher order temporal correlations in a price series can have dramatic effects on the price dynamics, yielding results that are quite different from the standard finance random-walk model. We note that while the effect of the higher order correlations in the present model was to *limit* the size of the drawdowns, the opposite can of course occur. A priori it is impossible to say what will happen without knowing the correlation details, hence the importance of accounting for such higher order temporal correlations in any theoretical finance model.

# 4. Financial market models with global interactions

## 4.1 A bottom-up approach

So far we have talked about stochastic processes, and have criticized the standard model of finance. The common theme of this criticism has been that standard finance theory has an Achilles heel, which is the limited applicability of the stochastic models typically employed to describe the underlying market movements. No matter how sophisticated one's model for portfolio management, derivatives pricing, risk analysis, etc., it is limited by the reliability and accuracy of the underlying model describing the market dynamics. It goes without saying that many modifications to these standard stochastic models have been suggested in the academic literature. How does one decide which modification will work best in a given market? Or how might we systematically create a new, stochastic supermodel? One way might be to make a detailed empirical comparison between the resulting statistics for various candidate stochastic models, and the stylized facts discussed in Chapter 3. However, this would necessarily involve a detailed comparison to past data for that particular market. The basic question then arises: will history actually repeat itself in this market?

A related problem arises if we are interested in understanding the evolution of a new market. By definition, there is now no history available. A recent example is that of the Euro prior to its launch—perhaps we would have liked to get a feel for the possible future evolution of its exchange rate against other major currencies. Is there any way to understand, at least in a general qualitative way, what will happen following such a launch? Alternatively, we might be regulators trying to work out what will happen when some global rules concerning the market we are monitoring or controlling, are changed. Again, we would like to get a feel for likely scenarios. An example of this would be the lifting of constraints on a given currency's exchange rate vs the US dollar—for example, the case of the Colombian Peso in the late 1990s. What will be the effect? Is there any way that we can say, at least in general terms, whether volatility is likely to increase, decrease, or stay the same? Maybe instead we are trying to work out what will happen following a particularly significant market event, or a given piece of bad news (e.g. the 2001–02 Enron scandal, or the 11 September tragedy in the United States). Is there any way we can foresee the likely extent of any resulting downturn, or the expected recovery time, or the volatility evolution in the immediate future?

These are all important practical questions, but obviously very hard to answer. Certainly no stochastic model of the type we have seen is ever going to answer these questions for us. After all, such stochastic models would require the model-builder to decide a priori which modifications are likely to be important in the future for that particular market. The model-builder is therefore forced to include his own forecast of how he believes the market will behave—in particular, he must make implicit assumptions about future trader activity. Going further, we can ask the following: no matter how sophisticated any stochastic supermodel that we develop, would we really be any closer to understanding how the markets are going to behave?

A science-motivated approach would suggest that we need instead to develop a microscopic understanding of what goes on in a market, in order to work out the best way to extend standard finance theory to address such questions. If it ain't broke don't fix it—but if it is broke, then fix it in a way that you understand. Looking to physics, we recall that thermodynamics—which studies the macroscopic behaviour of gases—lacked a firm foundation and understanding until the development of an atomistic theory based on statistical mechanics. So can we do the same as was done with the understanding of gases? In other words, can we hope to model the microscopic structure of markets based on how we think traders behave, and then use this to understand the observed macroscopic price dynamics? It seems like a hopeless task. But just as you do not need to know the detailed quantum properties of atoms in order to model the macroscopic average properties of a gas, so in the same way we would hope that one could develop a macroscopically realistic model of the market even though the microscopic details are grossly over-simplified. In short, maybe we can build market models which can be used to answer the above questions, but without having to include the characteristics of each individual trader. We do know that traders are a diverse bunch of people, with diverse opinions, time horizons, profit margins, trading capital, etc.—so maybe we can get away with a model which incorporates this diversity or heterogeneity, but without worrying about individual traders' preferences, likes, and dislikes. As we show in this chapter and Chapter 5, we can indeed get a significant distance towards reproducing the so-called stylized facts of Chapter 3 using very simple models of a population of heterogeneous agents (traders). Such models, in our opinion, open the way to next-generation finance. In addition, these models offer something significant in return to the scientific community: they are generic models of a complex system. As discussed in Chapter 1, the successful development of a theory to describe the dynamics of a complex system represents a fundamental outstanding problem within the sciences. For these reasons, we are going to spend some time discussing such models.

## 4.2    Two's company, but three's a crowd

It is clear that the fluctuations observed in financial time-series should, at some level, reflect the interactions, feedback, frustration, and adaptation of the markets' many and diverse participants. Using the analogy between markets and casinos, the trader becomes a gambler and the market becomes the game.[1] Since there are many market agents, this game is a multi-agent (multi-trader) game. The possible actions in this game become 'buy', 'sell', or 'do nothing'. The goal? This could be to win, or at least not to lose. In particular, this real-world market game will incorporate the following features.[2]

*Limited, primarily global information.*    In a 2-player game we can usually work out what the decision of the other player was, just by looking at the pay-off we receive. However, in a game with 3 or more players, where we each receive just global information, it will not in general be possible to work out exactly what each agent did.[3] This leaves each player with an inherent uncertainty as to the strategies that each of the others used. In short, it is practically impossible for you to infer the microscopic strategies played by each of the other players, based only on global information concerning the winning outcome. In a market where there is no private exchange of information, the players see the price move—they then either win or lose based on their own decision to buy, sell, or do nothing, and the actual move- ment of the price. Any one trader can never work out exactly what another particular trader did.[4]

The IT infrastructure and communications in place in most of today's main financial centres is such that every large investor has access to essentially all the information that is available regarding any financial asset they are trading. In short, a good starting approximation is that all such information is public as opposed to private. This implies that all the agents base their investment decisions on the same information[5]: we refer to this information as 'global information' and assign it the variable $\mu[t]$.

---

[1]  The interesting twist is that the spin of the roulette wheel, or deal of the cards, is actually determined by the aggregate action of the population of gamblers (agents) themselves.
[2]  These features are consistent with the features of a complex system (see Chapter 1).
[3]  If the players are competing, they are unlikely to phone each other to report on what they are doing. Even if they did, there would be no guarantees that such information was reliable.    [4] See note 3.
[5]  In Chapter 5, we will look at the effect of imitation, which implies some degree of local information as to what other groups of agents are doing.

*Many participants.*    Classical game theory tends to focus on games with $N = 2$ players. It then aims to deduce the equilibrium properties under which pay-offs are maximized. Since there are few players, and few strategies, there are a small number of such equilibria. It is therefore reasonable to expect that the players would recognize, and be able to evaluate, the details of such equilibria, and would act accordingly. However, when there are many players, this is not possible practically. For a simple $N$-player game, where each player has only $s = 2$ strategies, the pay-off diagram which must be analysed to deduce these equilibria has $2^N$ entries. For $N = 2$, it is just a $2 \times 2$ matrix and hence the equilibria are easy to compute: however, the complexity of this computation increases rapidly as $N$ increases. No human player would be able to perform this computation for large $N$. It is therefore impossible for a financial market agent $i$ to deduce his best investment strategy at any given time $t$ (and hence his optimal order $a_i[t]$) without a complete knowledge of what orders $a_j[t]$ all the other agents $j \neq i$ will place. For this reason, agents will attempt to keep their orders secret from the other agents to avoid giving away any advantage. This has the result that the agents act independently of each other and must come to their own, inductive, conclusions about what their optimal order should be.

Although the market has many participants, it is not 'many' in the usual sense of statistical physics. For example, in a gas, there are of order $10^{23}$ atoms or molecules— however, there are probably of order only $10^2$ market agents (traders) whose effect on the market is significant. It is these traders that we wish to model, since it is the aggregate of their actions which moves the price. The $10^2$ traders in question include large banks, pension funds, institutions, and hedge funds.

*Dynamical, as opposed to static.*    Financial markets are continually evolving, and one can in principle trade on very short timescales. Hence, a market represents a *repeated* game at the very least. The research on repeated $N$-player games that exists tends to focus on randomly picking out 2 players at each timestep and making them play a particular game. The system is then updated, a new pair of players chosen, and so on. Hence, there is no sense in which all $N$ players are all playing at the same time, unlike in an actual market.

As stressed in Chapter 1, the issue of time and timing in markets is a crucial one. Time underlies the dynamics, introduces causality and hence produces a strict flow of events, that is, the action $A[t_A]$ cannot affect the action $B[t_B]$ if $t_A > t_B$. Even though individual agents may place their orders at slightly different times, the rate-limiting step is the market-maker. The market-maker can only work at a finite speed (even if the job is done electronically) and so will batch together all the orders which have been submitted since the order book was last cleared. This makes the system inherently discrete in time, and hence we can use the simplifying step

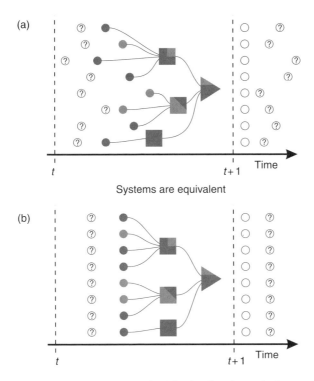

**Fig. 4.1**    Schematic diagram, with key as per Fig. 1.2, showing the equivalence of (a) the real market wherein orders can be placed by agents at different times, and (b) the simplified system wherein all agents place orders simultaneously.

of assuming that the agents all submit their orders at the same time. This assumption is *not* an approximation since the two systems are equivalent, as shown in the schematic diagram of Fig. 4.1. We do however propose making an approximation to the real market in the way that the orders are executed. Specifically, we would like to impose the tight temporal framework of decision–order–price update–order execution, shown in the schematic diagram of Fig. 1.2. The imposition of this framework is equivalent to asserting that all orders are market orders, since they are executed immediately after the asset price has been updated by the market-maker. This approximation simplifies the model framework greatly and is likely to be a reasonable approximation for high frequency trading where agents form an opinion as to which way the asset price will move over the next few trades. Consequently, the only thing that is important to these agents is that their trade be immediate in order to benefit from the movement. We will therefore only consider orders of the form $a_i[t, x[t + 1]] = a_i[t]$.

*Adaptation.*   A simple framework for an inductive agent is to allocate to that agent a number $s$ of 'strategies' $R$, which map the available global information $\mu[t]$ at time $t$ to an investment decision or 'action' $a_R^{\mu[t]}$. The provision of a set of $s$ strategies allows the agents to inductively reason what will be the best order to make at time $t$, by looking at how well the strategies have performed previously. This also gives an agent scope for being able to adapt his behaviour to the current market conditions. A strategy that performed well at one stage in the past can become superseded by another as the nature of the market's behaviour changes.

*Feedback.*   The global information $\mu[t]$, which contains all relevant information about the asset being traded, must contain variables such as the previous traded prices of the asset and the previous traded volumes. However, these variables are themselves generated by the system as output, so we have the situation that the system output is subsequently being used as part of the system input. This is feedback. If the approximation is made that the population of agents is dominated by chartists—who typically only consider patterns in previous asset prices and volumes to be relevant information—then the feedback in the system is perfect in the sense that there are no external factors influencing the agents' orders. The market therefore just feeds off itself. Not only is this a particularly interesting type of system to investigate, but also one of increasing relevance to the real financial markets. As discussed in Chapter 1, the more modern, liquid, and speculatory markets are precisely the ones that are becoming dominated by chartists.

*Competition.*   One would expect the nature of the market to be one of outright competition. However, whether the agents might be cooperating with each other at some level, is a subtle point. The aim of each and every agent is to make a profit from their speculatory trading. However, it is not necessarily the case that profit earned by one agent will have the consequence of a direct loss for another; the system is not closed. This is mainly due to the freedom of the market-maker to manipulate the price of the asset at will. This process requires no flow of capital in the system and yet can generate or diminish the collective wealth of the population of agents with positions in the asset. Agents who are buying assets will tend to be pleased if the traded price for their order is lower than the asset price at the time they ordered. Similarly, agents who are selling will tend to be pleased if the traded price for their order is higher than the asset price at the time they ordered. However, an excess of buyers/sellers moves the asset price up/down, therefore the group of agents who 'wins' is the sellers/buyers as they get to sell/buy at a higher/lower price. At the point of trading, therefore, there will be competition to be in the minority group of 'winners'. However, the agents could also cooperate in order to manipulate the market-maker and so increase the value of their positions. We will be looking at these aspects related to how agents 'win', throughout this chapter.

## 4.3   'To bar, or not to bar . . .'

The economist Brian Arthur proposed the following problem[6] to embody why the economy, and in particular, a financial market, is so 'complex'. It incorporates the necessary ingredients mentioned in Section 4.2, which are characteristic of the financial market 'game', and was specifically designed to illustrate the shortcomings of standard economic theory. In particular, it shows the importance of out-of-equilibrium behaviour in a financial system, where agents behave inductively rather than deductively since they only have limited information available. It goes beyond the standard rational expectations model of how traders should (in theory) behave. It will serve as our launch-point into the development of a multi-trader model for describing financial markets, hence we will discuss it in some detail.

Suppose there is a popular bar—which Arthur envisaged as the El Farol bar in Santa Fe (United States)—and that you have to decide whether to show up on a given night each week. This could be a Friday night, say, when your favourite band is playing. Your goal is to attend *provided* you can get a seat. The trouble is, there are about $N = 100$ other people all trying to decide the same thing—there is only limited seating (say for $L_{bar} = 60$ people) and we assume that all potential attendees wish to sit down. Hence, it will not be worth the effort of showing up if the bar is overcrowded. But you do not know whether it will be overcrowded without phoning the other 100 people and asking them what they plan to do. And there are two problems with such phoning around: you may not know how many other people are potential customers, or their names or telephone numbers, and even if they told you, should you believe them? Let us imagine that, each week, the bar manager publishes the actual number of attendees, $N_{attend}$ in the local paper the following day. Hence, everyone knows the previous outcomes. Based on this, you each try to predict whether the bar is likely to be *overcrowded* the following week (implying you should stay at home, running the risk that the bar is actually undercrowded) or *undercrowded* (implying you should make the effort to show up, running the risk that the bar is actually overcrowded). The $N = 101$ potential customers (including you) quickly realize that predictions of how many will attend depend on others' predictions of how many will attend (since this determines the actual attendance). But others' predictions in turn depend on their predictions of others' predictions. And so on. Hence, there is no correct expectational model—if everybody made the same decision, it would automatically be the wrong decision since everyone would either stay away (in which case you should have turned up) or they all show up (in which case you should have stayed away). A so-called mean-field theory describing a 'typical' agent will not work.

---

[6] See Arthur, W. B. (1999) *Science* **284**, 107.

This situation can be simulated on a computer choosing a pool of possible prediction methods given a particular set of recent outcomes, and randomly assigning a few such prediction methods to each agent. In this way, we capture the idea that the market of customers is heterogeneous, and that the quality of a given strategy depends on the strategies being used by all other agents. The practical problem with such a simulation is that it is difficult to define a suitable pool of strategies. Since the actual attendance numbers range from $0$ up to $N$, the number of possible patterns of past attendances is enormous and hence so is the number of possible strategies. We will therefore abstract the basic features of this model using a binary approach, as described in more general terms in Section 4.4.

## 4.4   From the bar to the market

The El Farol bar problem of Section 4.3 alluded to a system where agents compete against each other for a limited resource: seating in a crowded bar. Each agent used only global information concerning past attendance numbers to work out whether to attend or not. Since the crucial ideas of competition, limited resources, adaptivity, etc., are well represented in the El Farol bar problem, we will explore it as a simplistic analogy to the action of traders in a financial marketplace. However, in making this analogy, we have to ask ourselves the following questions:

- What is the global information in a financial market?
- How do financial market agents (i.e. traders) decide how to trade?
- How do financial market agents 'win'?
- What other important properties do real financial market agents possess, that is, what else is missing?

We will discuss each of these questions in turn with the aim of forming a model of the behaviour of financial market traders in the spirit of the El Farol bar problem.

### 4.4.1   What is the global information in a financial market?

There are clearly many types of information available to traders: for example, the price histories of assets, histories of traded volumes, dividend yields, market capitalization, recent news, company reports. In reality all, some, or none of these information sources may actually be useful in making an investment decision for a particular asset. However, it is not our interest here to work out which of these information sources is *actually* useful; we simply need to know which sources financial market agents tend to use most. This question is easier to answer, and underlies the attractiveness of modelling the traders rather than attacking the market dynamics head-on. If we think about what we *ourselves* see most of, in relation to financial market assets such as stock, the answer has to be its price. The media is full of reports on recent price behaviour. Similarly, charts of prices occupy the majority of traders' screens on trading floors. It thus seems reasonable to take the source of global information upon which the traders act, to be based on the past history of prices for the financial asset of interest.

We now have to decide on a method of 'encoding' this past history of price movements in a simple yet representative way. The simplest alphabet we can use to describe the past history of an asset's price, is the binary alphabet of 0s and 1s. The simplest encoding would then be to assign one letter of this alphabet to each timestep.[7] For example, in the El Farol bar problem, one could assign a '0' to the state where the bar was undercrowded (more seats than customers) and a '1' to the overcrowded state. In this way, an agent in the El Farol bar problem could look at the string of recent outcomes (e.g. .... 101110) and work out which nights it would have been best to attend. In a similar vein, the past history of asset prices $x[t]$ can be encoded by assigning a '0' to a price movement $\Delta x[t, t-1] = x[t] - x[t-1]$, which is smaller than a given value $L[t]$ (i.e. $\Delta x[t, t-1] < L[t]$) and a '1' for $\Delta x[t, t-1] > L[t]$. In this way the global information represents a caricature of the past history of asset prices with relation to the quantity $L[t]$. In the El Farol bar problem, the resource level $L[t]$ is related to the seating capacity of the bar against which attendance is judged. In the case of a financial market, $L[t]$ could represent a number of financial or economic variables, which could be either endogenous to the market or exogenous. An endogenous example could be the movement of a second financial product against which the movement of the asset of interest is judged, for example, the market index. An exogenous example could be the arrival of external news. Changing $L[t]$ affects the system's quasi-equilibrium, hence $L[t]$ could also be used to mimic a changing external environment due to some macroeconomic effect: for example, if interest rates are low, people may be tempted to put their money into the stock market. Conversely, if interest rates become high, then people may seek the risk-free choice of a high-interest bank account. In short, $L[t]$ indicates some measure of the attractiveness of the stock, or stock market as a whole, just as it indicates the attractiveness of the bar in the El Farol bar problem.

Since we wish to consider agents with limited capabilities, or equivalently agents who only deem recent information relevant, we shall build our source of global information from only the $m$ most recent outcomes (0s and 1s). This has the immediate

---

[7] The idea of encoding global outcomes in multi-agent games as binary digits, and the subsequent discussion of the resulting strategy space, is due to Challet, D. and Zhang, Y. C. (1998) *Physica A* **256**, 514. See www.unifr.ch/econophysics/minority for a complete bibliography.

consequence that the number of possible states for the global information is finite and equal to $P = 2^m$. For $m = 2$, the only possible patterns in price are: up–up, up–down, down–up, and down–down (where 'up' and 'down' are with reference to $L[t]$). We can thus think of the different possible states of the global information variable forming a 'space' with one state for each unique asset price history (e.g. 11, 10, 01, and 00 for $m = 2$). We refer to this space as the 'history space' and denote the state at time $t$ as the decimal equivalent of the string of $m$ 0s and 1s: $\mu[t] \in \{0 \ldots P - 1\}$. For example, the history bit-string 00 corresponds to $\mu = 0$ while 11 corresponds to $\mu = 2^2 - 1 = 3$. The dynamics of the model within this history space can be represented on a directed graph. The particular form of directed graph relevant to this model is called a de Bruijn graph. Examples are shown in Fig. 4.2.

We have addressed what represents global information, but we have not discussed how it is generated. This amounts to the question 'what makes an asset price rise or fall in a financial market?' It is commonly believed that excess demand—that is,

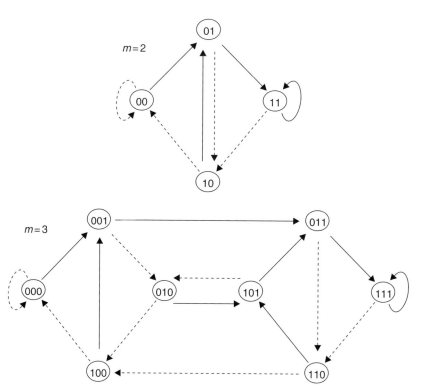

**Fig. 4.2**   History space for $m = 2$ and 3, showing the states available and transitions possible in the global information variable $\mu[t]$. Dotted line transitions imply negative price increments with respect to $L[t]$ (i.e. most recent outcome is '0'), whereas solid line transitions imply positive price increments with respect to $L[t]$ (i.e. most recent outcome is '1').

the difference between the number of assets sought and the number offered—exerts a force on the price of the asset. Furthermore, it is believed that a positive excess demand will force the price up and a negative demand will force the price down. A reasonable first-order approximation to the price formation process would then be:

$$\ln(x[t]) - \ln(x[t-1]) = D[t^-]/\lambda \qquad (4.1)$$

or

$$x[t] - x[t-1] = D[t^-]/\lambda, \qquad (4.2)$$

where $D[t^-]$ represents the excess demand in the market just *prior* to time $t$, while time $t$ represents the time when the new price $x[t]$ is set and the buy/sell orders are executed.[8] The scale parameter $\lambda$ represents the 'market depth', that is, how sensitive a market is to an order imbalance. In general, we would expect $\lambda$ to be some increasing function of the number of traders $N$ trading in that asset. If there are only a few agents trading the asset, the impact of each of them on the price is likely to be higher than if there are many agents, since the market-maker will then attempt to make the same amount of money off fewer agents. Numerical studies of several markets have shown a linear relationship between order imbalance and price-change to be broadly appropriate.

To summarize, we will take the global information upon which agents (traders) base their investment decisions to be the past history of the $m$ most recent price movements $\Delta x[t, t-1]$ relative to $L[t]$. Each price movement $\Delta x[t, t-1] = x[t] - x[t-1]$ is taken to be a function of the excess demand in the market just prior to $t$ (i.e. the demand which has built up between $t-1$ and $t$). This excess demand is determined by the aggregate of the agents' individual investment decisions. We thus have a feedback process: global information dictates investment decisions, investment decisions create a demand, total demand then generates new global information, and so on. This strong feedback is an essential feature of financial markets and as such should be considered as one of the essential ingredients for a market model.

### 4.4.2 How do financial market agents decide how to trade?

Our financial market agents act inductively[9] in order to make their investment decisions, just as in the El Farol bar problem. The only information an agent has available is the global information variable $\mu[t]$ and any parameters internal to the agent himself, such as his own wealth or investment track record. Real financial market

---

[8] Typically the price-changes at each timestep will be small compared to the price. Hence, $\ln(x[t]) - \ln(x[t-1])$ is approximately proportional to $x[t] - x[t-1]$ implying Equations (4.1) and (4.2) have the same basic form.
[9] There is no a priori 'correct' action that they can deduce.

agents operate on similar grounds. A reasonable representative model of a financial market agent might be someone with preconceived ideas of which way to trade given a particular set of circumstances. The agent may modify which of these preconceived ideas he trusts most, based on its previous successes or failures at predicting which investment decision should be made. Let us therefore imagine that each agent owns a small library of $s$ strategy books. A strategy book details what investment decision the agent should make, based on the observed recent price pattern which is represented by the global information $\mu[t]$. As such, the book details chartist principles. We denote the suggested action (investment decision) of strategy book $R$, given global information (previous price pattern) $\mu[t]$, to be $a_R^{\mu[t]}$. If a strategy book is 'full', then it will have a suggested action for each possible state of the global information. Thus, each of these strategy books has $2^m$ pages, one for each pattern. If there are only two possible suggested actions (e.g. 'buy' and 'sell') there will be $2^{2^m}$ possible books an agent can buy, and subsequently use as guidelines on how to trade. In other words, an agent in possession of one of these strategy books, whichever he chooses to buy, can find a page giving guidelines on how to trade in every possible market state. It seems unlikely however, that in reality such a complete book exists for any general value of $m$. Indeed, even if such a book did exist, it is unlikely that a given market participant would consider all the pages to be useful. For example, page one of a strategy book may say that if the asset price has fallen three days running one should sell on the fourth day. Page three may say that if the asset price has fallen, then recovered and then fallen again, one should buy. The agent holding this book may well believe in page one but think that the guidelines of page three are useless; he himself considers the pattern down–up–down to be no trading signal at all. This agent would therefore continue to hold any previous position he had if he saw the pattern down–up–down. Nevertheless, the *set* of strategy books is complete. By this we mean that every possible (binary) response to every possible (binary) price history is represented. Agents may seek to trade in completely different ways to each other, but as long as the behaviour of the agents is characterized by taking a binary action based on binary global information, then every possible set of beliefs and preconceptions that an agent could have can be ascribed to holding[10] a certain (limited) library of these $2^{2^m}$ strategy books. Of course, agents will in general have quite different libraries—equivalently, they will

---

[10] An agent does not necessarily have to 'buy' such strategy books. These books could also represent a set of innate rules that an agent may already carry in his head, resulting from his individual character and temperament or background, or resulting from the trading restrictions placed on him by the financial institution for which he works. Hence, instead of 'buying' certain strategies, the agent can be thought of as 'buying into' certain strategies. The effect is the same. As a by-product of this approach, we note that we are indirectly incorporating the basic notion of 'behavioural finance'.

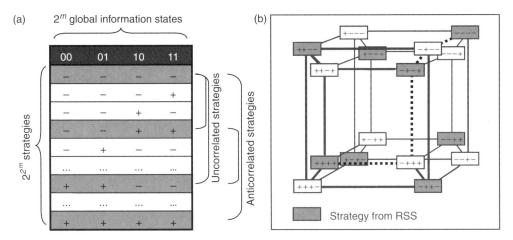

**Fig. 4.3** 'Strategy space' for $m = 2$. (a) Schematic representation of the $2^{2^m} = 16$ different strategies (i.e. strategy books). The greyed strategies belong to the Reduced Strategy Space (RSS) and are either totally uncorrelated or anticorrelated with respect to each other. There are $2^{m+1} = 8$ strategies in the RSS. (b) Representation of a $2^m = 4$ dimensional hypercube, which demonstrates the Hamming distance between strategies. The minimum number of edges linking strategies is the Hamming distance; for example, the dotted line shows a Hamming distance of 4 between strategies $----$ and $++++$.

have bought different books[11]—hence they will *not* take the same actions in the same circumstances. In other words, agents are heterogeneous—just what is expected from real life, but just what is *not* included in standard economic models.

The beauty of dealing with a complete set of binary strategy books (i.e. strategies) is that the 'space' of strategies can be broken down in a logical and useful manner. In Fig. 4.3, we show a picture of the strategy space for the case $m = 2$, using $\{-,+\}$ to denote the two possible actions $\{-1,+1\}$ for each global information state $\mu[t]$.

Strategies within the subset which is shaded grey, possess particularly simple inter-relationships.[12] In particular, pairs of strategies taken from this subset have one of the following types of correlation:

*Anticorrelated.* For example, any two agents using the strategies $----$ and $++++$, respectively, would take the opposite action irrespective of the sequence of previous outcomes, that is, irrespective of the global information state. Hence, one agent will *always* do the opposite of the other agent. For example, if one agent buys at a given timestep, the other agent will sell. Their net effect on the excess demand $D[t]$ therefore cancels out at each timestep. Hence, together they will not contribute to fluctuations in $D[t]$ and hence the price. In short, *they do not contribute to the volatility*.

---

[11] See note 10.   [12] See note 7.

This is a crucial observation for understanding the behaviour of the volatility in this system, as we discuss later.

*Uncorrelated.* For example, any two agents using the strategies $----$ and $--++$, respectively, would take the opposite action for two of the four histories, while they would take the same action for the remaining two histories. Assuming that the $m = 2$ histories occur equally often, the actions of the two agents will be uncorrelated on average.

Although there are $2^P \equiv 2^{2^{m=2}} = 16$ strategies (i.e. strategy books) in the strategy space, there are subsets of strategies that can, therefore, be classed as either purely anticorrelated or uncorrelated.[13] Consider, for example, the two groups:

$$U_{m=2} \equiv \{----, \; ++--, \; +-+-, \; -++-\},$$

$$\overline{U_{m=2}} \equiv \{++++, \; --++, \; -+-+, \; +--+\}.$$

Any two strategies within $U_{m=2}$ are uncorrelated since they have a relative Hamming distance[14] of $P/2$. Likewise, any two strategies within $\overline{U_{m=2}}$ are uncorrelated since they have a relative Hamming distance of $P/2$. However, each strategy in $U_{m=2}$ has an anticorrelated strategy in $\overline{U_{m=2}}$: for example, $----$ is anticorrelated to $++++$, $++--$ is anticorrelated to $--++$, etc. This subset of strategies comprising $U_{m=2}$ and $\overline{U_{m=2}}$, forms a Reduced Strategy Space (RSS).[15] Since it contains the essential correlations of the Full Strategy Space (FSS), it turns out that running a simulation within the RSS reproduces the main features of the full model. The RSS has a reduced number of strategies, $2.2^m = 2P \equiv 2^{m+1}$, as compared to the FSS which has $2^P \equiv 2^{2^m}$. For $m = 2$, there are 8 strategies in the RSS as compared to 16 in the FSS. The choice of RSS is not unique, that is, a given FSS can have many possible choices for RSS.

### 4.4.3   How do financial market agents 'win'?

Each agent holds a library of $s$ strategy books, which map the present available global information $\mu[t]$ to an action $a_R^{\mu[t]} \in \{-1, +1\}$. Let $-1$ indicate a sell decision and $+1$ indicate a buy decision. It is essential that the agents should hold $s > 1$ strategy books in their library in order that they may adapt their behaviour to the current market conditions. An agent with only one strategy book available would have no other choice

---

[13] There is the additional, trivial case of 'fully correlated' which represents the correlation of a given strategy with itself.

[14] A convenient measure of the distance (i.e. closeness) between any two strategies is the 'Hamming distance', defined as the number of bits that need to be changed in going from one strategy to another. For example, the Hamming distance between $----$ and $++++$ is $P = 4$, while the Hamming distance between $----$ and $--++$ is just $P/2 = 2$.

[15] See note 7.

than to follow blindly the only investment suggestion available, that is, follow his one strategy book. An agent with $s = 1$, therefore, does not have the opportunity to learn how to trade most effectively. The crucial question is then 'How do the agents choose which of their $s$ strategy books to use in order to trade effectively?'. One physically realistic answer is as follows: each agent uses the strategy book (i.e. strategy) which would have been the most successful in the past, judging from the past history of the market. To work this out, each agent needs to keep a tally of the success rate $S_R[t]$ for each of his strategies ($R$ is the strategy label). Hence, different agents holding the same strategy book will agree on its relative merit. This is a key feature of the model design: it can lead to large groups of agents agreeing which is the best strategy book in their separate libraries and thus *independently* making the same investment decision. The consequence of this is that agents might rush to the market in groups (crowds) even in the absence of any direct communication between each other.

We still need to define exactly how the agents will judge the success of, and hence reward, their strategy books. In the El Farol bar problem, there are $N$ regular bar-goers but only $L_{bar} < N$ seats. The reward scheme is therefore simple: bar-goers are successful if they attend *and* they manage to obtain a seat. Thus, any strategy book that suggests the agent go to the bar at time $t$ ($a_R^{\mu[t]} = 1$) when it turns out the bar is undercrowded ($N_{attend}[t] < L_{bar}$), should be rewarded positively. A suitable strategy reward structure could thus be proposed as:

$$S_R[t + 1] = S_R[t] - a_R^{\mu[t]}(N_{attend}[t] - L_{bar}),\qquad(4.3)$$

where $N_{attend}[t]$ is the number of attendees at time $t$. This reward system gives the strategy books a pay-off proportional to how under/overcrowded the bar actually was. The reward structure of Equation (4.3) can be generalized to:

$$S_R[t + 1] = (1 - 1/T)S_R[t] - a_R^{\mu[t]}\chi[N_{attend}[t] - L_{bar}],\qquad(4.4)$$

where $T$ represents a timescale over which the previous successes or failures of the predictions of strategy book $R$ are 'forgotten'. The function $\chi[x]$ in the second term is an odd, increasing function of $x$, which is typically taken to be either $\chi[x] = x$ or $\chi[x] = \text{sgn}[x]$. We emphasize that this reward scheme implicitly assumes that the bar-goers value sitting down above other criteria. While this makes sense for many situations, it is not universal. For example, customers of college-based bars do not seem to view seating as a necessary requirement for a successful evening. The motto 'the more the merrier' often seems more appropriate. In more general and realistic situations, the correct reward scheme is likely to be less simple than in Arthur's El Farol bar problem. Until a specific reward scheme is defined, the bar model remains ill-specified. Putting this another way, the precise reward scheme chosen is a fundamental property of the resulting system and directly determines the resulting dynamical evolution.

As we have discussed, the El Farol bar problem can be seen as being somewhat analogous to a financial market where the bar-goers are replaced by traders. In the same way that a general bar problem requires a non-trivial reward scheme, any realistic agent-based market model will need a non-trivial reward scheme in order to avoid inconsistencies with financial market microstructure. With this in mind, we will now pursue a more concrete connection between the bar problem and a market model, in terms of the strategy reward structure. Earlier we suggested an analogy between the attendance of bar-goers to El Farol, $N_{\text{attend}}[t]$, and the financial asset price change. These quantities provide the global information variables in each case. Taking Equation (4.4) and using this analogy, we can write down a strategy book pay-off $g_R[t+1]$ such that $S_R[t+1] = (1 - 1/T)S_R[t] + g_R[t+1]$. This implies $g_R[t+1] = -a_R^{\mu[t]}\chi[\Delta x[t+1, t] - L[t+1]]$. Using our price formation process from Equation (4.2), we then obtain:[16]

$$g_R[t+1] = -a_R^{\mu[t]}\chi[D[(t+1)^-]/\lambda - L[t+1]]. \qquad (4.5)$$

The actions $a_R^{\mu[t]}$, when followed by the agents, represent buy or sell orders in the market. Hence the total demand is given by:

$$D[(t+1)^-] = \sum_{R=1}^{2^P} n_R[t] a_R^{\mu[t]}, \qquad (4.6)$$

where $n_R[t]$ is the number of agents who are using strategy book $R$ at time $t$ in order to make their investment decisions. Strategy $R$ is the most successful strategy book that these $n_R[t]$ agents hold.

We can see that timing is becoming important, with some quantities evaluated at $t+1$ and others at $t$, etc. So let us look more closely at these timings. Equation (4.6) is for the excess demand at time $(t+1)^-$, that is, just prior to time $t+1$. Thus, $D[(t+1)^-]$ can only result from all the information that is available at time $t$, that is, the global information $\mu[t]$ and the set of strategy book scores $\{S_R[t]\}$. From this information, the agents take actions $a^{\mu[t]}$ producing a total demand $D[(t+1)^-]$. The agents' actions (i.e. orders) however do not get realized (i.e. executed) until time $t+1$, when the new price $x[t+1]$ is known. The pay-off function Equation (4.5) rewards agents positively for deciding to sell (buy) assets, $a^{\mu[t]} = -1$ (1), when the number of buyers (sellers) minus sellers (buyers) exceeds $\lambda L[t+1]$. If we take the reference

---

[16]  The seating capacity $L_{\text{bar}}$ in the bar problem, and the resource level $L[t]$ in the market model, are not numerically equivalent. This is because $\langle D[t]\rangle \approx 0$ for an unbiased market, while $\langle N_{\text{attend}}[t]\rangle \approx L_{\text{bar}}$ for the bar.

asset (e.g. a bond) to have a zero return, that is, $L[t + 1] = 0$, we can see that the strategy reward structure of Equation (4.5) rewards strategy books for suggesting the *minority* trading decision, that is, to sell (buy) when there is a majority of buyers (sellers). The binary model with this assumption of $L[t] = 0$ for all $t$, is thus referred to as the 'Minority Game', which was originally proposed by Challet and Zhang. The structure of the Minority Game was further generalized by Johnson *et al.* to incorporate a variable number of active agents.[17] The agents in this generalized model, known as the 'Grand Canonical Minority Game' (GCMG),[18] each has a 'confidence level' $r$ and will only participate in the game if the score of their best strategy book $S_{R^*}$ is higher than this level (i.e. $S_{R^*} > r$). This feature whereby traders only participate (i.e. trade) when they are sufficiently confident of success, is a crucial ingredient for building a successful multi-agent market model.

Let us investigate why the goal of trading in the minority group could be a physically reasonable ambition for the agents. We introduce a notional wealth $W_i$ of an agent $i$ as follows:

$$W_i[t] = \phi_i[t]x[t] + C_i[t], \qquad (4.7)$$

where $\phi_i$ is the number of assets held and $C_i$ is the amount of cash held. It is clear from Equation (4.7) that an exchange of cash for assets at any price does not in any way affect the agents' notional wealth. However, the point is in the terminology: the wealth $W_i[t]$ is only *notional* and not real in any sense. The only *real* measure of wealth is $C_i$, the amount of capital the agent has available to spend. Thus, it is evident that an agent has to do a 'round trip' (i.e. buy (sell) an asset then sell (buy) it back) to discover whether a *real* profit has been made. Let us consider two examples of such a round trip: in the first case, the agent trades with the minority decision, and in the second he trades with the majority decision.

- trading with the minority decision

| $t$ | Action $a[t]$ | $C_i[t]$ | $\phi_i[t]$ | $x[t]$ | $W_i[t]$ |
|---|---|---|---|---|---|
| 1 | submit buy order | 100 | 0 | 10 | 100 |
| 2 | buy..., submit sell order | 91 | 1 | 9 | 100 |
| 3 | sell | 101 | 0 | 10 | 101 |

---

[17] Johnson, N. F., Hart, M., Hui P. M., and Zheng, D., (2000) *Int. J. Theo. Appl. Fin.* **3**, 443; Jefferies, P., Johnson, N. F., Hart, M., and Hui, P. M., (2001) *Eur. Phys. J. B* **20**, 493.  [18] See note 17.

- trading with the majority decision

| $t$ | Action $a[t]$ | $C_i[t]$ | $\phi_i[t]$ | $x[t]$ | $W_i[t]$ |
|---|---|---|---|---|---|
| 1 | submit buy order | 100 | 0 | 10 | 100 |
| 2 | buy..., submit sell order | 89 | 1 | 11 | 100 |
| 3 | sell | 99 | 0 | 10 | 99 |

As can be seen, trading with the minority decision creates wealth for the agent on performing the necessary round trip, whereas trading with the majority decision loses wealth. However, if the agent had held the asset for a length of time between buying it and selling it back, his wealth would also depend on the rise and fall of the asset price over the holding period. So, although the Minority Game strategy-book reward mechanism seems perfectly reasonable for a collection of traders who simply buy/sell on one timestep and sell/buy back on the next, this is *not* of course what real financial traders do in general. This is the main criticism of the Minority Game as a market model.

To keep consistency with the real financial market, it seems that we need a more subtle reward mechanism than simply rewarding strategy books which suggest trading with the minority decision. We have identified that whilst trading with the minority decision can be beneficial, the minority pay-off structure makes no consideration of the rise or fall in the value of the agent's portfolio $\phi_i$ of assets. Let us try to rectify this by examining the form of the agent's notional wealth, Equation (4.7). If we differentiate the notional wealth, we get an expression for $\Delta W_i[t+1, t] = W_i[t+1] - W_i[t]$:

$$\Delta W_i[t+1,\, t] = \Delta C_i[t+1,\, t] + x[t+1]\Delta\phi_i[t+1,\, t] + \phi_i[t]\Delta x[t+1,\, t].$$

The first two terms cancel because the amount of cash lost $-\Delta C_i[t+1,\, t]$ is used to buy the extra $\Delta\phi_i[t+1,\, t]$ assets at price $x[t+1]$. This leaves us with:

$$\Delta W_i[t+1,\, t] = \phi_i[t]\Delta x[t+1,\, t]. \tag{4.8}$$

We can then use Equation (4.8) to work out an appropriate reward $g_R[t+1]$ for each strategy based on whether its investment suggestion $a_R^{\mu[t]}$ would have induced a positive or negative increase in notional wealth. Let us first use the fact that the price change $\Delta x[t+1,\, t]$ is roughly proportional to the excess demand $D[(t+1)^-]$: this can be seen explicitly from our earlier equation for the price formation, Equation (4.2). We therefore obtain from Equation (4.8):

$$\Delta W_R[t+1,\, t] \propto \phi_R[t]D[(t+1)^-].$$

We then identify the accumulated position in the asset for strategy $R$ at time $t$ to be $\phi_R[t]$: this represents the sum of all the actions (investment suggestions) made by that strategy, which would have been executed between time $0$ and $t$ had the strategy been used. Remembering that at time $t$ the action (order) $a_R^{\mu[t]}$ has not yet been executed (it gets executed at $t + 1$), this gives $\phi_R[t] = \sum_{i=0}^{t-1} a_R^{\mu[i]}$. Let us then set the pay-off $g_R[t + 1]$ given to a strategy book $R$, to be an increasing (odd) function $\chi$ of the notional wealth increase $\Delta W_R[t + 1, t]$ for that strategy. We thus arrive at:

$$g_R[t + 1] = \chi \left[ \sum_{i=0}^{t-1} a_R^{\mu[i]} D \left[ (t + 1)^- \right] \right].$$

Note that if agents were comparing this notional wealth increase with the wealth increase available through investment in another asset (e.g. a bond) with return $L[t + 1] \neq 0$, then we would have instead

$$g_R[t + 1] = \chi \left[ \sum_{i=0}^{t-1} a_R^{\mu[i]} \left[ D \left[ (t + 1)^- \right] / \lambda - L[t + 1] \right] \right]. \tag{4.9}$$

We could also propose a locally weighted equivalent of Equation (4.9) where the reward given to a strategy is more heavily weighted on the result of its recent actions, rather than the actions it made further in the past. This gives:

$$g_R[t + 1] = \chi \left[ \sum_{i=0}^{t-1} (1 - 1/T)^{t-1-i} a_R^{\mu[i]} \left[ D \left[ (t + 1)^- \right] / \lambda - L[t + 1] \right] \right], \tag{4.10}$$

where $T$ again represents a characteristic timescale over which the position accumulated by the strategy is 'forgotten'. In the limit $T = 1$, Equation (4.10) becomes $g_R[t + 1] = \chi[a_R^{\mu[t-1]} \left[ D \left[ (t + 1)^- \right] / \lambda - L[t + 1] \right]$: that is, only the position resulting from the most recently executed trade is taken into account. With $T = 1$, this pay-off structure essentially rewards a strategy at time $t + 1$ based on whether the notional wealth change $\Delta W_R[t + 1, t]$ was more positive than it would have been if action $a_R^{\mu[t-1]}$ had not been taken.

If Equation (4.10) is used in an agent-based market model, the agents play the strategy they hold which has collected the highest 'virtual' notional wealth. We mean 'virtual' in the sense that the strategy itself will not have actually collected this notional wealth, unless it has been played incessantly since time $t = 0$. The agents in this model are hence all striving to increase their notional wealth, and are allowed to do so by taking arbitrarily large positions $\phi_i$. This suggests that the agents of a realistic market model need more attributes than simply a library of strategy books in order to function in a realistic manner: after all, real financial agents have finite resources and cannot take such arbitrarily large positions.

### 4.4.4    What else is missing?

In the El Farol bar problem, the agents have to make the simple decision as to whether or not attend the bar. In reality, such decisions may also be influenced by an agent's available funds, or maybe even whether they are still hung-over from the last time they visited. While such complications could be incorporated, this would deviate from our quest for a minimal model, that is, a model that explains the observed market behaviour yet employs a minimal number of physical characteristics. However, in order to generate stable and realistic market dynamics, we will see that *some* additional properties of 'real' traders do indeed need to be incorporated. Let us start by looking at the dynamical behaviour of the GCMG: this is the case of the El Farol bar problem with $L_{bar} = N/2$ (which corresponds to $L[t] = 0$) but generalized such that agents only participate if the score of their perceived best strategy book is greater than the confidence level $r$. We will compare the GCMG's dynamical behaviour with that of the corresponding financial market model (MM) constructed with a strategy pay-off structure given by Equation (4.10) with $L[t] = 0$. We have simulated each with the same parameters: $N = 501$ agents, $s = 2$ strategies per agent, $T = 100$ time horizon beyond which strategy scores 'forget' past performance, an $r = 4$ pay-off point confidence-to-trade threshold, and the $\chi = $ sgn strategy pay-off $(+1/-1$ point for a good/bad investment suggestion). Each simulation was run for agents with low memory $m = 3$ and for agents with high memory $m = 10$. The resultant price $x[t]$ and number of active agents $V[t] = \sum_{R=1}^{2^P} n_R[t-1]$ are displayed in Fig. 4.4. Note that both the price-change and volume at time $t$ depend on the agents' actions at time $t - 1$.

The two different values of the agent's global information memory length $m$ (or more formally the ratio $P/N$) in Fig. 4.4, describe markets in two distinctly different 'phases'. Arguably one of the most important features of these types of model is that there is a common perception of a given strategy $R$'s (virtual) success. For example, $S_{R=1}[t]$ for one agent is the same as $S_{R=1}[t]$ for another agent. This implies that the number of agents adopting the same action is dependent on the number which hold each strategy. At low memory (low $P/N$) there are relatively few strategies available but many agents; consequently many agents will hold the same strategy. This implies that in this 'crowded phase', there will be a large group of agents using a successful strategy $R^*$ and hence adopting the same action $a_{R^*}^{\mu[t]}$ (i.e. a *crowd*). However, there will only be a small group using a strategy such as the anticorrelated strategy $\overline{R^*}$ and hence adopting the opposite action $a_{\overline{R^*}}^{\mu[t]} = -a_{R^*}^{\mu[t]}$ (i.e. an *anticrowd*). The result of this high agent coordination is a volatile market with large asset price movements. Conversely for high $m$ (high $P/N$), hardly any agents hold the same strategy and so the crowds and anticrowds are small and of similar size. This results in a market with low agent coordination and consequently lower volatility and fewer large changes in

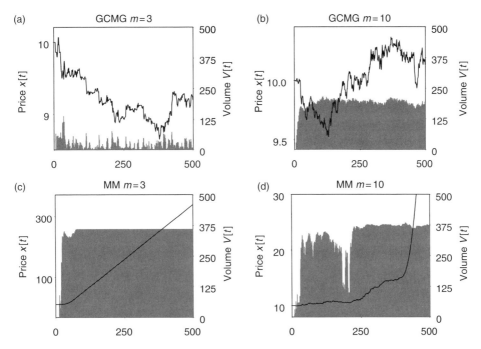

**Fig. 4.4**   Temporal evolution of the price $x[t]$ and 'volume' (i.e. number) of active agents $V[t]$ in the (a and b) GCMG and the (c and d) Market Model (MM) for two different values of the global information memory length $m$. Parameters for the simulations were: $N = 501, s = 2, T = 100$, and $r = 4$ with binary (i.e. $\chi = \text{sgn}$) strategy pay-off.

the price. With this distinction between low and high $m$ regimes in mind, let us briefly describe the dynamics in each model.

*GCMG.*   At low $m$ and with a sufficiently high confidence-to-trade threshold, the GCMG is able to reproduce many of the stylized facts of real markets. It can be seen from Fig. 4.4 that the number of active agents (volume) is generally low and bursty. The asset price series is thus characterized by frequent large movements, giving fat-tailed distributions of returns, and clustered volatility. The autocorrelation of the GCMG asset price movements is essentially zero: as soon as lots of agents start taking the same action, the strategies which produce that action are penalized as can be seen from Equation (4.5). At high $m$, the absence of agent coordination leads to a lack of activity clustering, hence the series of asset prices appears more random.

*MM.*   At low $m$, the MM asset price very quickly acquires a steady trend. Any agent with at least one trend-following strategy (i.e. price changes $\ldots \Delta x[t - 2] > 0$, $\Delta x[t-1] > 0$, $\Delta x[t] > 0 \Rightarrow a_R = 1$) will join the trend and hence benefit, notionally, from the consequent asset price movement. Because the strategies and hence agents are allowed to accrue limitless positions, the trend is self-reinforcing since $\Delta W_R$ just keeps getting bigger for the trend-following strategies. At high $m$, the lack of agent coordination means that it is harder for the model to find this attractor—however, sooner or later a majority of trend-following strategies will have collected sufficiently large scores $S_R$ and positions $|\phi_R|$ to be traded successfully. From then on, the pattern of success is self-reinforcing and again the steady trend is created. This result is the natural consequence of wanting the agents to maximize notional wealth at the same time as being allowed arbitrarily large positions.

So it seems that whilst the dynamics of the adapted El Farol bar problem, the GCMG, are stable and market-like, the dynamics of the so-called MM are unstable and un-market-like. By trying to develop a strategy reward structure which more realistically models the actions of a financial market agent, as opposed to a bar attendee, we have introduced an instability into the model. This shows all too clearly how the strategy book reward structure defines the nature of the model itself. This instability in the MM seems to arise from the potential for the agents to take up arbitrarily large positions in the financial asset. This is clearly not a physically realistic situation: after all, nobody is infinitely rich, and only a finite amount of the asset is available. Even if the MM agents cannot *actually* buy (sell) more assets because the market has become illiquid, as long as there is still a positive (negative) *demand* for the asset then the MM price will keep rising (falling). Therefore, even by pretending to want to buy (sell) more assets, the agents can manipulate the price up (down) to profit their long (short) position. Therefore, the MM should have a mechanism which stops the agents from demanding to buy (sell) more assets. Perhaps the most obvious contender for this mechanism is the finite resources of the agents: an agent cannot place an order to buy (sell) assets if he does not have the required funds (assets) to complete the transaction. Let us then investigate whether adding the property of finite resources to the agents of our model, helps stabilize the dynamical behaviour.

**4.4.4.1   Agent wealth.** Financial market agents only have finite resources. The amount of resources available to the agents will depend on how wealthy they are, or how tight the regulations imposed by their risk managers are. For example, some institutions will not allow themselves to be over-exposed to the risky movements of a particular asset and so will insist that positions in this asset are limited to a certain number of quanta. This limitation has the effect of putting a ceiling on the demand to buy or sell assets in the marketplace: the hard limit of the agents' resources thus in turn imposes a hard limit on the magnitude of price trends. We can include the effect of limited agent resources in our market model (MM) by allocating agent $i$ an initial capital $C_i[0]$, and position $\phi_i[0]$, and then updating this capital using:

$$C_i[t] = C_i[t-1] - \Delta\phi_i[t, t-1]x[t]. \tag{4.11}$$

We can then further impose the limitations to trading based on the agents' inventory of cash and assets. Specifically, an agent is not permitted to trade at time $t$ if:

$$a_R^{\mu[t]} = 1 \cap C_i[t] < x[t],$$

$$a_R^{\mu[t]} = -1 \cap \phi_i[t] < 0.$$

In words, the first condition states that an agent cannot submit a buy order unless he has at least enough capital to buy the asset at the quoted price. The second condition states that he cannot submit an order to short-sell if he already holds a short position. If we imposed no limit on short-selling, an unstable state of the system would exist wherein all agents short-sell indefinitely. We initialize this generalized MM market model (we will call it MM(W) where W represents 'wealth') with agent resources such that the agents' initial buying power is equal to their initial selling power, that is, $\{C_i[0], \phi_i[0]\} = \{n\, x[0], n-1\}$. Hence, each agent starts off with the power to buy or sell $n$ assets (he is allowed up to one short-sell). If we then increase $n$ from $n = 1$, we see a qualitative change in the dynamical behaviour of this market model with the periods of trending grow longer as $n$ increases. We investigate this behaviour by fixing $n$ and running the model for 1500 timesteps, recording the value of the global information $\mu[t]$ in the last 500 timesteps $t$. We then count the number of times within these last 500 timesteps when either $\mu = 0$ occurs (implying negative price movements over the last $m$ timesteps) or $\mu = P - 1$ occurs (implying positive price movements). We denote the frequency with which these states occur as $f_{trend}$. If the model visited all states of the global information $\mu[t]$ equally, we would expect $f_{trend} = 1/P + 1/P = 2/P$: in particular, this would arise if the states were visited randomly.

Figure 4.5 shows the variation of $f_{trend}$ with $n$, and has several interesting features. First it can be seen that as $n$ is increased, and the consequent wealth available to the agents grows, the tendency of the model to be dominated by price trending increases dramatically. Also, we see that at low $n$, $f_{trend}$ is below the limit of equally visited (e.g. randomly visited) $\mu$ states. This is due to the high degree of anti-persistence in the system, which arises because the demand is so tightly bounded by the agents' limited resources. The large spread in the results arises from the tendency of the model to exhibit clustering of states of activity: persistence follows persistence and anti-persistence follows anti-persistence. This activity clustering in turn arises because an agent's strategy book will be penalized for suggesting that an agent join a trend, since this corresponds to trading with the majority group. However, once the trend has been joined, the strategy book will be rewarded as the notional value of its position grows.

The major source of agent diversity in the market models so far, has been the heterogeneity in the allocation of strategy books in the agents' libraries. However, the

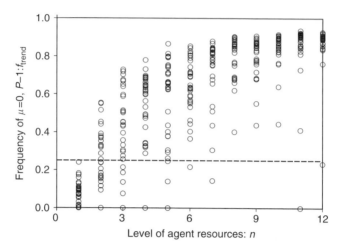

**Fig. 4.5**   The frequency of occurrence, $f_{\text{trend}}$, of the global information states $\mu = 0$, $P-1$ as a function of each agent's capital resource level $n$. The results were taken from the last 500 timesteps of a 1500 timestep simulation. The market model used was the MM(W) model with evolving agent wealth. The model parameters were $N = 501$, $m = 3$, $s = 2$, $T = 100$, and $r = 4$, with a binary ($\chi = $ sgn) strategy reward scheme. The dashed line represents equally visited $\mu$-states, hence $f_{\text{trend}} = 2/P = 2/2^3 = 0.25$.

introduction of an agent wealth brings about a secondary source of diversity. Even if we initiate the model with all agents having an equal allocation of wealth in the form of cash plus assets, the wealth of the agents $W_i$ will soon become heterogeneous as a direct result of their heterogeneous strategies. Figure 4.6 shows the heterogeneity of agents' wealth growing with time during a MM(W) simulation. After many timesteps have elapsed, the distribution of agents' wealth seems to reach an equilibrium in which many agents have lost the majority of their wealth to a minority of agents—this minority now holds significant wealth. In other words, we are witnessing the spontaneous creation of a wealth-based hierarchy within the multi-agent society.

The heterogeneity of agents' wealth in the MM(W) model is fed back into the system through the buying power of the agents. However, although wealthier agents have the potential to buy and sell more assets, they still only trade in single quanta of the asset at any given timestep, just like the poorer agents. Therefore, it may be more reasonable to propose that the agents trade in sizes proportional to their individual wealth, that is,

$$\Delta\phi_i[t, t-1] = \gamma \frac{C_i[t-1]}{x[t-1]}, \quad \text{for} \quad a_{R_i^*}^{\mu[t-1]} = 1,$$

$$\Delta\phi_i[t, t-1] = \gamma \phi_i[t-1], \quad \text{for} \quad a_{R_i^*}^{\mu[t-1]} = -1,$$

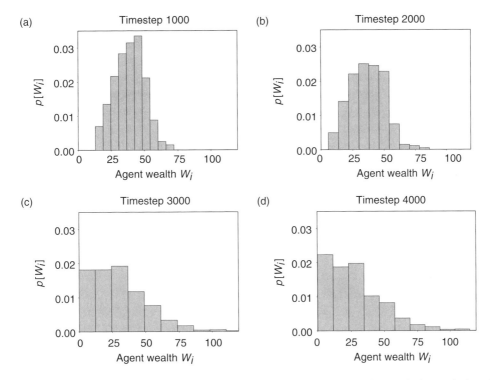

**Fig. 4.6** Probability distribution of the agents' wealth $W_i$ at four different times $t$ during evolution of the MM(W) model. Initially all agents were allocated the same resources $\{C_i[0], \phi_i[0]\} = \{3x[0], 2\}$ with the initial price $x[0] = 10$. Parameters for the simulation were $N = 1001, m = 3, s = 2, T = 100$, and $r = 4$, with a binary $(\chi = \text{sgn})$ strategy reward scheme.

where $R_i^*$ is the highest scoring strategy of agent $i$. The factor $\gamma$ then enumerates what fraction of an agent's resources (i.e. cash for buying, assets for selling) he is willing to transact at any given time. In general, assets need to be divisible in this system, that is, the sense of agents buying and selling a quanta of the asset as in MM(W) is lost. This in turn means that instead of the degree of trending being controlled by the level of initial resource allocation $n$, it is instead determined by $n/\gamma$ since this effectively determines the number of trades agents can make in any trending period before hitting the boundary of their capital resources. Also, with this system of trading in proportion to wealth, trends will start steep and end shallow as agents run out of resources and thus make smaller and smaller trades. Apart from these qualitative differences, the system has a very similar dynamical behaviour to the more straightforward MM(W) model.

Diversity in strategies and wealth are the two big sources of agent heterogeneity that we have covered so far. This agent heterogeneity has led to a market model

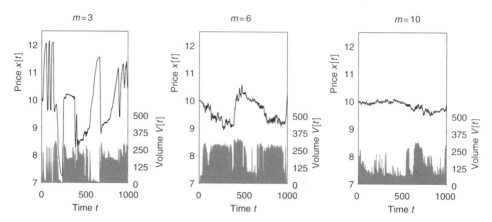

**Fig. 4.7**   Examples of the dynamical behaviour of the price $x[t]$ and volume $V[t] = \sum_{R=1}^{2^P} n_R[t-1]$ of the MM(W) model for three different levels of crowding, as determined by the memory length. The parameters for the simulation are $N = 501$, $m = 3$, $s = 2$, $T = 100$, and $r = 4$, with a binary ($\chi = \text{sgn}$) strategy reward scheme.

with dynamical behaviour that is interesting and diverse over a large parameter range. However, the typical price/volume output only starts to become representative of a real financial market at higher $m$, as can be seen in Fig. 4.7. As discussed earlier, the high $m$ regime represents a 'dilute' market where very few traders act in a coordinated fashion. However, we would expect that a real financial market is *not* in a dilute phase at all, but instead has large groups of agents forming crowds which rush to the market together creating a bursty pattern of activity. Why then do these models, when pushed into the smaller $m$ regime as shown in Fig. 4.7, produce endless bubbles of positive followed by negative speculation?

**4.4.4.2   Trading timescales.** To answer the above question, we investigate further the subject of agent diversity. Although our agents have differing sets of strategies and consequently different wealth, they all act on the same timescale. When we ourselves look at charts such as Fig. 4.7, we see patterns not only on a small point-to-point scale but also on a much larger scale. In short, we try to identify patterns over a wide range of timescales, all the way up to the 'macro' scale of the boom–bust speculative bubbles. From a knowledge of these patterns, we tend to form opinions about what will happen next. We would then trade accordingly in an attempt to maximize our wealth. However, the agents we have modelled *cannot* view the past price series in this way: instead they are forced to consider patterns of length $m$ timesteps, where $m$ is a single, fixed number. Patterns of any greater length than this go unnoticed by the agents and hence are not traded upon. This is why these patterns exist in our model. Now, we already know from the concept of arbitrage that when a real pattern is traded upon, it should slowly be removed from the price series. Consider the following pattern:

| Time $t$ | 1 | 2 | 3 | 4 | 5 | 6 | 7 | 8 | 9 | 10 | 11 | 12 | 13 | 14 |
|---|---|---|---|---|---|---|---|---|---|---|---|---|---|---|
| Price $x[t]$ | 14 | 10 | 11 | 12 | 13 | 15 | 14 | 10 | 11 | 12 | 13 | 15 | 14 | 10 |

If we were able to identify this pattern repeating, our best course of action would be to submit a buy order between times $t = 1$ and $t = 2$, that is, $a[1] = 1$. We could then buy the asset at $x[2] = 10$. Between times $t = 5$ and 6, we would submit an order to sell $a[5] = -1$, and sell the asset at $x[6] = 15$. We then continue: $a[7] = 1$, $a[11] = -1$, and so on. This ensures that we always buy at the bottom price and sell at the top. Trading in this way is against the trend since $a[t]D[(t + 1)^-] < 0$: it is in effect minority trading. Thus, trading to maximize our wealth with respect to this pattern leads to the weakening of the pattern itself, just as in the Minority Game. We conclude therefore that the *presence* of strong patterns in the MM(W) and other similar market models at low $m$, is simply due to the *absence* of agents within the model who can identify these patterns and hence arbitrage them out.

From the above discussion, it is clear that in a realistic market model, we should have agents who can analyse the past series of asset price movements over *different* timescales. One possible way of achieving this is to include a heterogeneity in the strategy book pattern length (i.e. memory) $m$. Within such a framework, agents would look at patterns not only of differing length but also of differing complexity. However, it is more straightforward to propose a generalization to the way the agents interpret the global information of past price movements, in such a way as to allow observation of patterns which occur over different timescales but which have the same complexity ($m$). This can be easily achieved by allowing the agents to have a natural information bit-length $\tau$ such that the global information available to them, $\mu_\tau[t]$, is updated according to the sign of $\Delta x[t + 1, t + 1 - \tau] - L[t + 1]$ as opposed to being based simply on $\Delta x[t + 1, t] - L[t + 1]$. The following example table shows how the above pattern would be encoded for $L[t] = 0$ by agents having $\tau = 1, 2, 3, 4$.

| Time $t$ | | 1 | 2 | 3 | 4 | 5 | 6 | 7 | 8 | 9 | 10 | 11 | 12 | 13 | 14 |
|---|---|---|---|---|---|---|---|---|---|---|---|---|---|---|---|
| Price $x[t]$ | | 14 | 10 | 11 | 12 | 13 | 15 | 14 | 10 | 11 | 12 | 13 | 15 | 14 | 10 |
| 'Best' action $a^*[t]$ | | 1 | 1 | 1 | 1 | $-1$ | $-1$ | 1 | 1 | 1 | 1 | $-1$ | $-1$ | 1 | 1 |
| sgn $[\Delta x[t, t - 1]]$ | | | $-$ | $+$ | $+$ | $+$ | $+$ | $-$ | $-$ | $+$ | $+$ | $+$ | $+$ | $-$ | $-$ |
| sgn $[\Delta x[t, t - 2]]$ | | | | $-$ | $+$ | $+$ | $+$ | $+$ | $-$ | $-$ | $+$ | $+$ | $+$ | $+$ | $-$ |
| sgn $[\Delta x[t, t - 3]]$ | | | | | $-$ | $+$ | $+$ | $+$ | $-$ | $-$ | $-$ | $+$ | $+$ | $+$ | $-$ |
| sgn $[\Delta x[t, t - 4]]$ | | | | | | $-$ | $+$ | $+$ | $-$ | $-$ | $-$ | $-$ | $+$ | $+$ | $-$ |

If each agent only considered the past two bits of information, that is, $m = 2$, then the 'best' strategies for different values of the information bit-length $\tau$ would be as shown in the table below. These 'best' strategies have been obtained from inspection of the example table above: specifically, by looking at timesteps where the different $m = 2$ bit-strings $\{--, -+, +-, ++\}$ occur, and then seeing the respective 'best' action $a^*[t]$ given this bit string.

| $\mu[t]$ | Bit-length $\tau$ | | | |
|---|---|---|---|---|
| | 1 | 2 | 3 | 4 |
| $--$ | 1 | 1 | 1 | ? |
| $-+$ | 1 | 1 | $-1$ | $-1$ |
| $+-$ | 1 | 1 | 1 | 1 |
| $++$ | ? | ? | ? | 1 |

A question mark next to a particular value of the global information $\mu[t]$ denotes that, for this state, the best action is sometimes $a_{R*}^{\mu[t]} = 1$ and sometimes $a_{R*}^{\mu[t]} = -1$. We can, therefore, see that it is only when we include longer timescale patterns $\tau > 2$, that we get a clear signal of when the optimal time to sell occurs ($a_{R*}^{\mu[t]} = -1$): shorter timeframe patterns give no such clear indication. This then demonstrates that an agent holding strategies of different bit-length $\tau$ could identify optimal times to buy and sell, and hence arbitrage patterns of length very much greater than the memory length $m$.

## 4.5   Choosing a model

Section 4.4 discussed how a realistic market model could be built from the framework of the El Farol bar problem, by successive adaptation of the model's features to the real-life scenario of financial market trading. This involved not only modifying the strategy book reward structure, which fundamentally changes the style of game, but also changing the subtleties of the agents' composition. We discussed how the inclusion of finite agent resources, and diversity in trading timescales, can yield a model which is free from instabilities and atypical market patterns. There are also subtleties of the market itself which we have not addressed, that is, the presence and actions of a market-maker together with all other possible market-moving influences such as news arrival. However, our original goal was to understand what lies behind some of the more interesting dynamical properties observed in a market. For example, what gives rise to the observed high volatility in today's crowded markets? It will be impossible to answer these types of questions if the model we use to simulate the market is of comparable complexity to the market itself. Instead, we need to focus on a minimal set of underlying assumptions in order to make sense of what is, after all, a very 'complex' system.

In the following sections, we will present and analyse a *minimal* market model in order to address the question concerning the origins of market volatility. We will choose the most basic model we have, which reflects at least *some* major aspects of financial trading and yet also reproduces the stylized facts observed in real financial market data. In particular, we shall investigate the *direct* application of the El Farol bar problem to a financial market. By this we mean that we will preserve the structure of 'complete' strategy books, and the global information given by the past series of price increments relative to $L[t]$. We will then construct a demand for assets using Equation (4.6) and will reward strategy books using Equation (4.5). As discussed earlier, this structure captures the essence of what is important at the time of trading but neglects to take full account of the agents' accumulated positions. Despite this shortcoming, the model may well prove to be an adequate model of trading on short (intra-day) timescales where agents seek to make money on the immediate, per-trade basis.

## 4.6  The 'El Farol Market Model'

### 4.6.1  Specifying the model

Let us begin by summarizing how this minimal market model is specified. The model has six parameters:

- $N$ = the number of agents
- $m$ = the 'memory' of the agents
- $s$ = the number of strategy books (i.e. strategies) held by each agent
- $r$ = the minimum score that an agent's best strategy book $R^*$ must have in order for him to participate
- $T$ = the time horizon over which strategy book scores are 'forgotten'
- $L[t]$ = the size of increment against which the asset's movement is judged.

A schematic diagram of the model is shown in Fig. 4.8. The agents all observe a common binary source of information representing recent price movements, of which they only remember the previous $m$ bits. Hence, the global information available to each agent at time $t$ is given by $\mu[t]$, where in decimal notation $\mu[t] \in \{0 \ldots P - 1\}$ with $P = 2^m$. Each strategy book $\underline{a}_R$ contains as its elements $a_R^\mu$. These elements

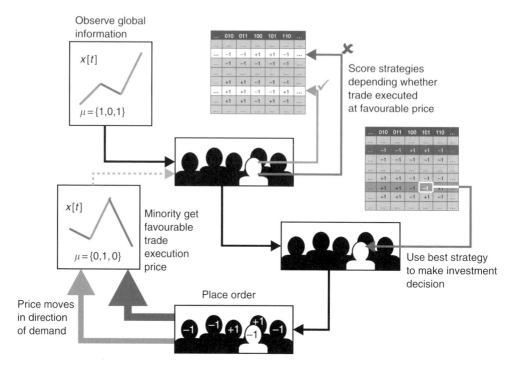

**Fig. 4.8** Schematic diagram of the El Farol Market Model, which is a binary multi-agent game. This model represents our minimal market model.

provide an action $\{-1, +1\}$ representing $\{\text{sell}, \text{buy}\}$, for each of the possible $P$ values of the global information $\mu$. There are hence $2^P$ possible strategy books. The agents are allocated randomly a subset $s$ of these strategy books at the outset of the game: they are not allowed to replace these during the game. The agents keep the score $S_R[t]$ of each of their strategy books' previous successes, regardless of whether the strategy book's investment suggestion was used or not. Following Equation (4.5), success is defined by the reward structure:

$$S_R[t+1] = (1 - 1/T)S_R[t] - a_R^{\mu[t]}\text{sgn}\left[D\left[(t+1)^-\right]/\lambda - L[t+1]\right], \quad (4.12)$$

where the demand for assets immediately prior to the deal execution time $t + 1$, is given by

$$D[(t+1)^-] = n_{\text{buy\_orders}}[t] - n_{\text{sell\_orders}}[t] = \sum_{R=1}^{2^P} n_R[t]a_R^{\mu[t]}. \quad (4.13)$$

Here $n_R[t]$ is the number of agents choosing to follow the investment suggestion of strategy book $R$ at time $t$. The agents always use their highest performing strategy book $R^*$, that is, $S_{R^*} = \max[\{S_R\}_s]$, but only participate at a given timestep if this performance has exceeded the confidence-to-trade threshold of $r$. If $S_{R^*} < r$, then the agents do not participate. The feedback in this market model arises through the updating of the global information $\mu[t]$, where the most recent bit of binary information is defined by the sign of the price movement $\Delta x[t, t-1]$ relative to $L[t]$. Hence, we can calculate the update of the decimal global information variable $\mu[t]$ according to the following expression:

$$\mu[t+1] = 2\mu[t] - PH[\mu[t] - P/2] + H\left[D\left[(t+1)^-\right]/\lambda - L[t+1]\right], \quad (4.14)$$

where $H[x]$ is the Heaviside function. This makes sense because the increment in the asset price is generally an increasing function of the demand, for example

$$x[t] - x[t-1] = D[t^-]/\lambda. \quad (4.15)$$

Despite its unfamiliar appearance, Equation (4.14) for the update of $\mu[t]$ is easy to evaluate. For example, consider the case of $m = 2$ and $L[t] = 0$ for all $t$. Suppose the recent outcome bit-string is 00 and hence $\mu[t] = 0$: a negative excess demand will give $\mu[t+1] = 2 \cdot 0 - 2^2 \cdot H[0 - (2^2/2)] + 0 = 0$ corresponding to an updated recent outcome bit-string 00, while a positive excess demand will give $\mu[t+1] = 2 \cdot 0 - 2^2 \cdot H[0 - (2^2/2)] + 1 = 1$ corresponding to an updated recent outcome bit-string 01. Now suppose the recent outcome bit-string is 01 and hence $\mu[t] = 1$: a negative excess demand will give $\mu[t+1] = 2 \cdot 1 - 2^2 \cdot H[1 - (2^2/2)] + 0 = 2$ corresponding to an updated recent outcome bit-string 10, while a positive excess demand will give $\mu[t+1] = 2 \cdot 1 - 2^2 \cdot H[1 - (2^2/2)] + 1 = 3$ corresponding to an updated recent outcome bit-string 11.

### 4.6.2 Parameterizing the El Farol Market Model

We now examine the price $x[t]$ and 'volume' of orders $V[t] = \sum_{R=1}^{2^P} n_R[t-1]$. Let us start by deciding on the parameter set $\{N, m, s, r, T, L[t]\}$. The agents in our model represent financial individuals or institutions which are capable of moving the market with their orders. We are thus not considering the actions of small home investors in these models. Consequently, we expect there to be of order $10^2 \rightarrow 10^3$ of these market-moving agents. It thus seems reasonable to set $N = 500$. We have discussed previously that the financial market is likely to be in a 'crowded' phase wherein large groups of agents agree on the same course of action and rush to the market together. In the context of the binary model structure, this necessitates us having many agents holding similar strategy books. This condition requires that $N s \gg 2P = 2^{m+1}$ (recall that there are $2P$ strategy books in the RSS). We can satisfy this condition by setting $m = 3$ and $s = 2$. Hence the agents are adaptive because they can change which strategy book they use, and the set of global information states is small, but not trivially so. The parameters $r$ and $T$ together define the number of strategy books which will have a success rate above the confidence-to-trade threshold. If the demand generated by the agents were a zero-mean random variable, we would expect the strategy book reward structure of Equation (4.12) to give success scores $S_R[t]$ with a variance $\sigma^2[S_R]$ given by $\sigma^2[S_R] = 1/(1 - \alpha^2)$, where $\alpha = 1 - 1/T$. If we then said that a reasonable characteristic timescale over which strategy book scores are forgotten was of order $T = 100$ timesteps, this would give $\sigma[S_R] \approx 7$. In reality of course, the demand is not a random variable and we find that the variance of strategy book success scores is smaller than this value due to competition between the strategy books. We thus pick a value of $r = 4$ as a reasonable confidence-to-trade threshold, since it will represent approximately a one-sigma deviation from the random coin-toss success rate of $S_R = 0$. Finally, we note that the parameter $L[t]$—which represents the increment in value of a reference asset (the asset to which the traded asset is being compared)—can in general be time dependent. However, the role of $L[t]$ is simply to shift the reference frame of the model, hence it is not particularly instructive to consider its time dependence here. We do, however, note that if the value of $L[t]$ is changing on a timescale comparable to the timestep size of the model itself, we expect this extra source of dynamical behaviour to be important.[19] For our purposes, we will take $L[t] = L$, that is, the increment in value of the reference asset is a constant.

### 4.6.3   Reproducing the stylized facts

Having formalized and parameterized the El Farol Market Model, we are ready to run the simulations. Every new simulation of the market will be unique due to the random initial allocation of strategy books among agents. We do not wish here to analyse specific run-dependent anomalies in the output, but will instead focus on general behavioural patterns and statistical features. Specifically we are interested to see whether this model, with the given physically motivated parameterization, reproduces the stylized facts of a financial market. First, let us inspect by eye the model's output.

Figure 4.9 shows the typical evolution of the El Farol Market Model, for different fixed increments in value of the reference asset. For a reference asset which appreciates in value ($L > 0$), the market price of the traded financial asset also appreciates and vice versa. For $L = 0$ we observe an apparently unbiased movement in price for the traded

---

[19] For example, if $L[t]$ reflects news arrival, and significant news arrives very frequently, then this news-arrival process is likely to be a major factor in determining the dynamics of the market.

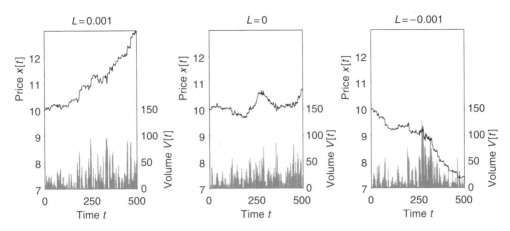

**Fig. 4.9**  Typical price and volume charts produced by the El Farol Market Model as specified in Section 4.6.1 and parameterized in Section 4.6.2. Each chart represents a different fixed value $L[t] = L$, which corresponds to the constant increment in value of the reference asset.

asset. These results make sense: Equation (4.12) tells us that for $L > 0$, agents tend to reward buying strategies ($a_R^{\mu[t]} = 1$) over selling strategies (and vice versa for $L < 0$). This creates a bias in the demand and consequently the price increment. This mirrors what we observe for financial indices where the reference asset is typically taken to be the rate of interest *and* inflation combined. Historically, during periods of inflation and positive interest, market indices have tended to appreciate in value. The activity pattern of trading in the asset looks from Fig. 4.9 to be interesting and non-random. Activity seems to be clustered, with periods of high volume trading following other similar periods. Large movements in the asset value, compared with the average volatility, also seem to be common. We will now investigate these properties by looking into the statistics of the series of asset price-changes $\Delta x[t + 1, t]$ with $L = 0$.

Figure 4.10 shows that the distribution of asset price increments, produced by the El Farol Market Model, deviates significantly from the random case (i.e. Gaussian or so-called 'normal' distribution). The high probability of large movements is reflected in the high kurtosis (peakedness) of the PDF and the deviation of the QQ plot from the diagonal line. Figure 4.11 shows graphically that the linear (i.e. low-order) correlations between the price increments are small and short-ranged: however, the autocorrelation in the local volatility is of much longer range and has large magnitude. The autocorrelation of the local volatility represents a non-linear (i.e. higher order) correlation measure for the price increments, and is practically equivalent to the auto-correlation of absolute returns. Comparing Figs 3.4 and 4.11, we hence see that the El Farol Market Model is capable of capturing both the low-order *and* higher order correlations which are observed in real market data (see Chapter 3).

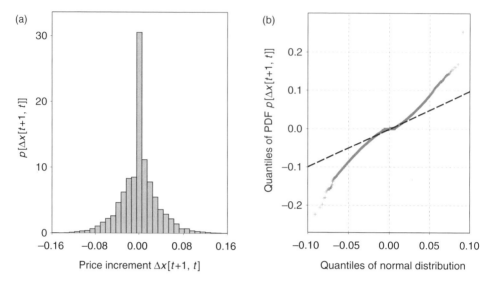

**Fig. 4.10** Properties of the series of asset price increments $\Delta x[t+1, t]$ produced by the El Farol Market Model as specified in Section 4.6.1 and parameterized in Section 4.6.2. Here $L = 0$. (a) The histogram represents the probability distribution function (PDF) of the asset price-changes, and exhibits extremely high kurtosis (fat tails). (b) A QQ plot which demonstrates the deviation of this distribution from the random (i.e. Gaussian or so-called 'normal') case. The dashed line is that expected for a Gaussian (i.e. normal) distribution.

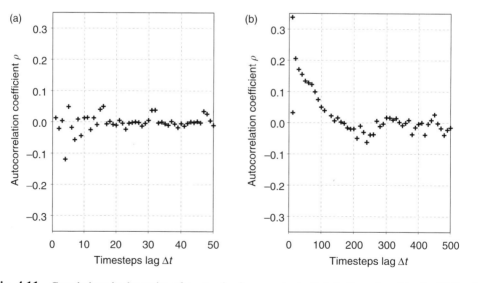

**Fig. 4.11** Correlations in the series of asset price increments $\Delta x[t + 1, t]$ produced by the El Farol Market Model as specified in Section 4.6.1 and parameterized in Section 4.6.2, with $L = 0$. (a) The autocorrelation of the price increments and (b) the autocorrelation of the local volatility as measured over 10 timesteps.

To summarize, *the statistical features of the El Farol Market Model are consistent with the stylized facts observed in real financial markets.* Of course, this does not mean that the market model we have simulated is either 'correct and unique' or even just 'correct'. However, it does show that the model is capable of exhibiting the kind of rich behaviour that is observed in real financial markets, despite the minimal set of assumptions and parameters.

## 4.7  Dynamics of the 'El Farol Market Model'

The El Farol Market Model described in Section 4.6, seems to be an easily specifiable system. However, there are subtle choices to be made when writing a computer program to implement the game. These can lead to different results for the time evolution of the game from any two programs, even though the programs are 'identical'. Despite the fact that the market model is exactly as stated earlier, and even though we might use exactly the same parameter set for any two simulations, the numerical results will differ in their specific time evolution because of:

1. Different initial conditions. These initial conditions come in three forms:

    (a) Initial strategy book allocation among the agents. This initial strategy book assignment is random and yet fixed from the outset, hence providing a systematic 'disorder' which is built into each run. In technical terms, different runs will generally have different realizations of this 'quenched disorder'. The strategy book allocation can be represented as a matrix $\underline{\underline{\Omega}}$ for the case $s = 2$ strategies per agent. This $2P \times 2P$ (in the RSS) quenched disorder matrix has as its elements $\Omega_{R,R'}$, where $\Omega_{R,R'}$ is the number of agents who have first been allocated strategy book $R$ and then $R'$. Since the order of allocation is irrelevant, we can without loss of generality consider a symmetrical matrix $\underline{\underline{\Psi}} = \frac{1}{2}\left(\underline{\underline{\Omega}} + \underline{\underline{\Omega}}^{\mathrm{T}}\right)$ to describe the quenched disorder in the system. An example matrix is shown below:

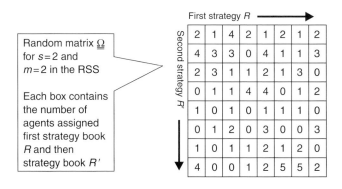

(b) Initial success score of the strategy books. If this initial score distribution is not 'typical', then a bias can be introduced into the game which never disappears. In short, the system never recovers from this bias. We will assume that no such initial bias exists, that is, we assume that the initial score-vector distribution is 'typical' and does not introduce any long-term bias. In practice this is achieved, for example, by setting all the initial scores to zero.

(c) Initial history used to seed the simulation. This is not in general an important effect. We assume that any transient effects resulting from the particular history seed will disappear quickly, that is, we assume that the initial history seed does not introduce any long-term bias.

2. Each run has an intrinsic stochasticity because of accidental ties in strategy books' success scores. These ties are typically rare. When they do occur, the rules of the game are such that an unbiased coin-toss will determine which strategy book is used. In the event that the total demand from the agents is equal to $\lambda L$ and hence $\Delta x[t + 1, t] = L$, the global information state $\mu[t]$ must also be updated by a coin-toss. Hence, even if two runs have the same initial conditions, as defined above, they will eventually differ in their time evolution due to this stochasticity.

In the rest of this chapter, we will focus on the static (i.e. time-averaged) quantities of the multi-agent game. We note, however, that a fuller treatment which includes the dynamics can also be carried out. The secret to this dynamical description is as follows. The simulation uses coin-tosses to resolve ties in strategy book success scores and to update the global information in the situation where $\Delta x[t + 1, t] = L$. These events inject stochasticity into the game's evolution. However, one can average over this stochasticity to yield a description of the game's deterministic dynamics via mapping equations[20]: these mapping equations just involve the vector of all the strategy books' success scores $\underline{S}[t]$, and the global information $\mu[t]$. We note that this can be done generally, *without* making the simplifications necessary to obtain the Minority Game, that is, it can be done for time dependent $L[t]$, general confidence level $r$, and general time horizon $T$.

## 4.8    Statics of the 'El Farol Market Model': the origins of volatility

We will now explore the El Farol Market Model specified in Section 4.6.1 and parameterized in Section 4.6.2. Because of the important role that volatility plays in

[20] For the simpler case of the Minority Game, see Jefferies, P., Hart, M., and Johnson, N. F. (2002) *Phys. Rev. E* **65**, 016105.

the financial world, we have set ourselves the goal of understanding the origins of volatility in our market model, and quantifying this volatility based on the model's parameters. We are aiming at a pedagogical presentation of an analytic derivation of this volatility, hence we will make some further simplifications for the purpose of clarity. Specifically, we set the reference asset to have a zero return, that is, $L[t] = 0$. We will also force all agents to participate in trading at every timestep, that is, the 'volume' $V[t] = N$ for all $t$. This is achieved by taking the limits $T \to \infty$ and $r \to -\infty$. In this regime, the model we recover is the basic Minority Game of Challet and Zhang.[21] Thus, we have reduced the parameter set to the three parameters $\{N, m, s\}$.

### 4.8.1  Numerical results for the volatility

The asset price is defined by Equation (4.2). Thus, the volatility of the asset price increments is simply a function of the volatility of the agents' total demand for assets. We denote this volatility in demand simply by $\sigma[D[t^-]] = \sigma$. The volatility $\sigma$ is then a time-averaged quantity given by the equation

$$\sigma^2 = \frac{1}{n} \sum_{t=1}^{n} D[t^-]^2 - \left( \frac{1}{n} \sum_{t=1}^{n} D[t^-] \right)^2. \qquad (4.16)$$

We are thus assuming that the distribution of price increments is stationary over the period $1 \leq t \leq n$, such that the volatility is a time-independent property of the time-series. This is one reason why we use a simplified model wherein all the agents must participate at each timestep: if the number of active agents was instead a function of time, we would expect that the volatility would become highly time dependent (recall our discussion of volatility clustering in Section 4.6.3). We must also keep this stationarity in mind when we produce a numerical value for $\sigma$ from the market model simulations: the model takes a while ($n \gg 2^m$ timesteps) to settle into a dynamical steady state, hence it is necessary to discard the initial timesteps of the simulation when making a numerical measurement of the steady-state volatility. For simplicity, we shall also consider the model to have strategy books drawn from the RSS as discussed in Section 4.4.2. It turns out that many of the time-averaged features of the model obtained using the RSS, such as the volatility, are almost identical to those produced by the model using the FSS. The reason for this is that all the important *types* of correlations between strategies (i.e. fully correlated, uncorrelated and anticorrelated)

---

[21] See note 7.

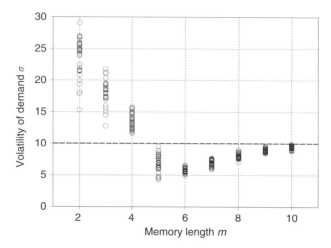

**Fig. 4.12**  Numerical results for the volatility of total demand $\sigma$ in a simplified version of the El Farol Market Model (i.e. Minority Game) as a function of 'memory' $m$. Model parameters are $N = 101$ and $s = 2$. The dashed line at $\sigma = \sqrt{N} = 10.0$ represents the 'random limit', where all the agents simply toss a coin to decide on an investment action.

are present in the RSS. Therefore, the $2^{m+1}$ strategy books in the RSS provide an adequate representation of the $2^{2^m}$ strategy books in the FSS.

We now look at some numerical results for this simplifed El Farol Market Model (i.e. Minority Game). Following our earlier discussion, we choose $V[t] = N = 101$ active agents each having $s = 2$ strategy books (i.e. strategies). We then examine the volatility of the model's output as a function of $m$, the 'memory' or global information bit-string length that the agents use. We run the simulation 32 times for each value of $m$. Each run of the model corresponds to a different realization of the quenched disorder (i.e. different realization of the disorder in strategy book selection, as discussed in Section 4.7).

Figure 4.12 suggests that there are two distinct 'phases' of the model market, according to the value of $m$. The low-$m$ phase is characterized by a decrease in $\sigma$ as $m$ increases: this is the 'crowded' phase we discussed earlier where the number of strategies $2^{m+1}$ (in the RSS) is small compared to the number of agents $N$. The high-$m$ phase is characterized by a slow increase in $\sigma$ towards some limiting value as $m$ increases. This phase is called the 'dilute' phase since the number of strategies $2^{m+1}$ (in the RSS) is now large compared to the number of agents $N$.

### 4.8.2   Qualitative explanation for the variation of volatility

Before looking at a detailed quantitative theory, we first give a simple qualitative picture to explain what is happening. It all relates back to the correlation between strategies, discussed in Section 4.4.2. In the 'crowded' phase, that is, at small $m$, there will at any one time be a large number of agents who are using the same (e.g. the perceived best) strategy and so will flood into the market as large groups or *crowds*, producing large swings in demand and hence a high volatility as shown. If the memory $m$ of the agents is larger, then the crowd of agents using the same strategy will be smaller simply because many may not hold the best strategy—the chances of a given agent holding the instantaneous best strategy decrease as $m$ increases. There will also be groups of agents who are forced to use the anticorrelated (e.g. the perceived worst) strategy: these can be thought of as *anticrowds* since they cancel out the market action of the crowds at every timestep $t$ *regardless* of the particular history bit-string at that timestep. This cancellation effect causes a reduction in the size of the market volatility. In the dilute phase of very large memory $m$, it is very unlikely that any two agents will hold the same strategy and so the market can be modelled as a group of independent coin-tossing agents.

Let us make this a bit more quantitative. Consider the oversimplified case of $N$ independent agents each deciding on an investment decision by tossing a coin. Each agent, therefore, provides a random-walk process in terms of increasing or decreasing the demand $D[t^-]$ by 1 asset. Assume for the moment that these coin-tosses are uncorrelated. Then the results of Chapter 2 tell us that the total variance $\sigma^2$ for this random walk in excess demand $D[t^-]$, is given by the *sum* of the individual variances produced by each of the $N$ agents. If the agent decides $a^{\mu[t-1]} = 1$, then he contributes 1 to the excess demand $D[t^-]$. If, by contrast, the agent decides $a^{\mu[t-1]} = -1$, then he contributes $-1$ to the excess demand. In both cases the random-walk 'step-size' is $d = 1$. This coin-tossing agent chooses $a^{\mu[t-1]} = 1$ with probability $p = \frac{1}{2}$, and $a^{\mu[t-1]} = -1$ with probability $q = \frac{1}{2}$. The variance contributed to $\sigma^2$ by this agent is therefore given by $4\,pqd^2 = 1$ since $d = 1$ (see *Background Math box*). Summing over all $N$ agents, the total variance in the excess demand $\sigma^2$ is given by $4Npqd^2 = N$. Hence the standard deviation (i.e. volatility) of demand is given by $\sigma = \sqrt{N}$ which, for $N = 101$, gives $\sigma = 10.0$ which is the dashed 'coin-toss' line of Fig. 4.12.

In reality, on any given turn of the game, there will be a number of agents using the same, or similar, strategies. Consider the subset of agents $n_R$ using a particular strategy $R$. Although there is no information available to a given agent about other individual agents, nor is any direct communication allowed between agents, this subset of agents $n_R$ using a particular strategy $R$ will all make the same investment decision at each timestep *irrespective* of the particular history bit-string for that timestep. Hence, they will act as a *crowd*. Since the corresponding random-walk 'step-size' that this crowd contributes is $d \equiv n_R$, this crowd should contribute a variance $4pqd^2 = 4\frac{1}{2}\frac{1}{2}n_R^2 = n_R^2$ to the total variance. However, because of the initial strategy allocation, there may also be a subset of agents $n_{\bar{R}}$ who are using the anticorrelated strategy to $R$,

> **Background Math**
> The expressions below follow directly from the results in Chapter 2, but are summarized here for clarity. Consider a random walk along the $y$-axis, with step-size $= d$ and number of steps $= N$.
>
> The probability of moving in a positive (negative) direction at each step $= p$, $(q)$, where $p + q = 1$.
>
> The mean displacement $y_{N=1}$ for $N = 1$ is given by:
>
> $$\langle y_{N=1} \rangle = pd + q(-d) = (p - q)d; \quad \text{hence} \quad \langle y_{N=1} \rangle = 0 \text{ if } p = q = \tfrac{1}{2}.$$
>
> To calculate the variance $\sigma_{N=1}^2$ for $N = 1$, we start with $\langle y_{N=1}^2 \rangle = pd^2 + q(-d)^2 = (p+q)d^2 = d^2$; hence $\sigma_{N=1}^2 \equiv \langle y_{N=1}^2 \rangle - \langle y_{N=1} \rangle^2 = d^2 - (p-q)^2 d^2 = d^2[1 - (2p - 1)^2] = 4\,pqd^2$.
>
> For uncorrelated steps, the **variance (or average) of the sum = sum of the variances (or averages)**. The mean displacement $y_N$ for $N \geq 1$ is, therefore, given by:
>
> $$\langle y_N \rangle = N\langle y_{N=1} \rangle = N(p - q)d \quad \text{and hence} \quad \langle y_N \rangle = 0, \text{ if } p = q = \tfrac{1}{2}.$$
>
> The variance $\sigma_N^2$ for $N \geq 1$ is, therefore, given by $\sigma_N^2 = N\sigma_{N=1}^2 = 4Npqd^2 \equiv \sigma^2$.
>
> Hence $\sigma_N^2 \equiv \sigma^2 = Nd^2$, if $p = q = \tfrac{1}{2}$. Note that $\sigma_N^2 \equiv \sigma^2 = N$, if $p = q = \tfrac{1}{2}$ and $d = 1$.

that is, $\bar{R}$. This second group, the *anticrowd*, makes the *opposite* investment decision to the crowd at each timestep *irrespective* of the particular history bit-string for that timestep. Over the timescale during which these two opposing strategies $R$ and $\bar{R}$ are being played, the fluctuations are determined only by the net crowd-size $n_R^{\text{eff}} = n_R - n_{\bar{R}}$, which constitutes the net step-size of the crowd–anticrowd pair. Hence, the net contribution by this crowd–anticrowd pair to the random-walk variance, is given by $4pqd^2 = \left[ n_R^{\text{eff}} \right]^2$. We will now use this result. Suppose strategy $R^*$ is the highest scoring at a particular moment: the anticorrelated strategy $\overline{R^*}$ is, therefore, the lowest scoring at that same moment. In the limit of small $m$, the size of the strategy space is small. Each agent hence carries a considerable fraction of all possible strategies. Therefore, even if an agent picks $\overline{R^*}$ among his $s$ strategies, he is also likely to have a high scoring strategy. Therefore, many agents will choose to use either $R^*$ itself (if they hold it) or a similar one. Very few agents will have such a poor set of strategies that they are forced to use a strategy similar to $\overline{R^*}$. In this regime, there are practically no anticrowds, and the crowds dominate. Therefore, $n_R \approx N \delta_{R,R^*}$ and hence $n_R^{\text{eff}} \approx N \delta_{R,R^*}$. Hence, the variance varies as $\sigma^2 \approx N^2$ and is larger than the independent agent limit of $N$, in agreement with Fig. 4.12. In the limit of large $m$, the strategy space is very large and agents will have a low chance of holding the same strategy. Even if an agent has several low-scoring strategies, the probability of his best strategy being strictly anticorrelated to another agent's best strategy (hence forming a crowd–anticrowd pair) is small. All the crowds and anticrowds will tend to be of size 0 or 1, implying that the agents act independently. This yields the coin-toss limit discussed above. In the intermediate $m$ region where the minimum in the observed volatility exists, the size of the strategy space is relatively large. Hence some agents may get stuck with $s$ strategies which are all low scoring at a particular timestep. They hence form anticrowds. Considering the extreme case where the crowd and anticrowd are of similar size, we have $n_R^{\text{eff}} \sim 0$ and hence the volatility is essentially zero. This is again consistent with the numerical results. The regime of small volatility will arise for small $s$ since, in this case, the number of strategies available to each agent is small—hence some of the agents may indeed be forced to use a strategy which is little better than the worst-performing strategy $\overline{R^*}$. In other words, the cancellation effect of the crowd and anticrowd becomes most effective in this intermediate $m$ region for small $s$. Increasing $s$ should make this minimum less marked, as again observed numerically. We can summarize this crowd–anticrowd argument by Fig. 4.13.

### 4.8.3   Quantitative explanation for the variation of volatility

Consider a given realization of the quenched disorder $\underline{\underline{\Psi}}$. At a timestep $t$ in a given run for this given $\underline{\underline{\Psi}}$, there is a current score-vector $\underline{S}[t]$ and a current history $\mu[t]$, which together define the state of the game. The excess demand $D[(t+1)^-]$ is given by:

$$D[(t+1)^-] \equiv D[\underline{S}[t], \mu[t]]. \tag{4.17}$$

The volatility for a given run corresponds to a *time average* for a given realization of the quenched disorder $\underline{\underline{\Psi}}$ and a given set of initial conditions. We will eventually average over many runs, hence effectively average over all realizations of the quenched disorder $\underline{\underline{\Psi}}$ and all sets of initial conditions. However, first we focus on a given realization of the quenched disorder $\underline{\underline{\Psi}}$.

   We assume that the quantities of interest, that is, the mean and standard deviation of the demand, 'self-average' for the given realization of the quenched disorder $\underline{\underline{\Psi}}$. In other words, we assume that the average over time is equivalent to an average over

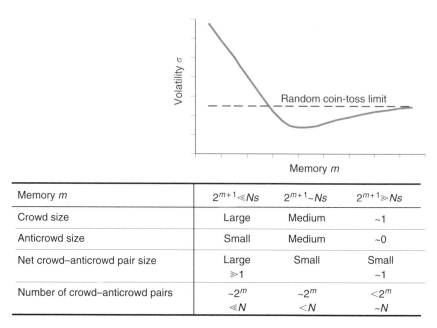

| Memory $m$ | $2^{m+1} \ll Ns$ | $2^{m+1} \sim Ns$ | $2^{m+1} \gg Ns$ |
|---|---|---|---|
| Crowd size | Large | Medium | $\sim 1$ |
| Anticrowd size | Small | Medium | $\sim 0$ |
| Net crowd–anticrowd pair size | Large $\gg 1$ | Small | Small $\sim 1$ |
| Number of crowd–anticrowd pairs | $\sim 2^m$ $\ll N$ | $\sim 2^m$ $< N$ | $< 2^m$ $\sim N$ |

**Fig. 4.13**   Diagram explaining the qualitatively different behaviour of the volatility in demand for low, intermediate, and high memory $m$ regimes in terms of crowd and anticrowd sizes.

initial conditions, for the given realization of the quenched disorder $\underline{\underline{\Psi}}$. Such self-averaging in which time averages are taken to be equal to ensemble averages is very common in science, especially physics. For example, when describing the statistical properties of a gas of molecules, there are so many collisions between these molecules that we are guaranteed to explore all the possible microstates of the system either by looking at a time average for a particular system, or an ensemble average over many systems. In the present system, as long as we have (a) 'typical' initial conditions as discussed earlier, plus (b) the stochasticity as a result of coin-tosses to resolve ties, plus (c) the small memory $m$ limit, then the system is indeed self-averaging to a good approximation for a given $\underline{\underline{\Psi}}$. (By 'typical' we mean representative of the set of possible configurations.) Let us rewrite the expression for the demand (Equation (4.13)) using the RSS:

$$D[\underline{S}[t], \mu[t]] = \sum_{R=1}^{2P} n_R^{S[t]} a_R^{\mu[t]}. \tag{4.18}$$

In Equation (4.18) above, we have denoted the explicit dependence of $n_R[t]$, which is the number of agents following the investment suggestion of strategy $R$, on the vector of strategy success scores $\underline{S}[t]$. Now we calculate the average demand, where the average is over time for a given realization of the quenched disorder $\underline{\underline{\Psi}}$. We define $\langle X[t] \rangle_t$ as a time average over the variable $X[t]$ for a given $\underline{\underline{\Psi}}$. By assuming the self-averaging property for a given $\underline{\underline{\Psi}}$, we are essentially assuming that the system is ergodic for a given $\underline{\underline{\Psi}}$: hence all histories are visited with equal frequency in a given run. Hence,

$$
\begin{aligned}
\langle D[\underline{S}[t], \mu[t]] \rangle_t &= \sum_{R=1}^{2P} \left\langle a_R^{\mu[t]} n_R^{\frac{S[t]}{R}} \right\rangle_t \\
&= \sum_{R=1}^{2P} \left\langle a_R^{\mu[t]} \right\rangle_t \left\langle n_R^{\frac{S[t]}{R}} \right\rangle_t \\
&= \sum_{R=1}^{2P} \left( \frac{1}{P} \sum_{\mu=0}^{P-1} a_R^{\mu[t]} \right) \left\langle n_R^{\frac{S[t]}{R}} \right\rangle_t \\
&= \sum_{R=1}^{2P} 0 \cdot \left\langle n_R^{\frac{S[t]}{R}} \right\rangle_t = 0.
\end{aligned}
\tag{4.19}
$$

Notice that we have averaged over all values of the global information $\mu[t]$ separately, because of our ergodic assumption. We are interested in the fluctuations of the demand about this average value. Hence we move on to consider the volatility of the demand. The variance $\sigma_\Psi$ of the demand for a particular quenched disorder $\underline{\underline{\Psi}}$, is given from Equations (4.16) and (4.19) by:

$$
\begin{aligned}
\sigma_\Psi^2 &= \langle D[\underline{S}[t], \mu[t]]^2 \rangle_t - \langle D[\underline{S}[t], \mu[t]] \rangle_t^2 \\
&= \langle D[\underline{S}[t], \mu[t]]^2 \rangle_t \\
&= \sum_{R,R'=1}^{2P} \left\langle a_R^{\mu[t]} n_R^{\frac{S[t]}{R}} a_{R'}^{\mu[t]} n_{R'}^{\frac{S[t]}{R'}} \right\rangle_t .
\end{aligned}
\tag{4.20}
$$

Now we break this double sum into three parts: $\underline{a_R} \cdot \underline{a_{R'}} = P$ (fully correlated), $\underline{a_R} \cdot \underline{a_{R'}} = -P$ (anticorrelated), and $\underline{a_R} \cdot \underline{a_{R'}} = 0$ (uncorrelated). Note that we can only do this decomposition in the RSS. Hence,

$$
\sigma_\Psi^2 = \sum_{R=1}^{2P} \left\langle \left(a_R^{\mu[t]}\right)^2 \left(n_R^{\frac{S[t]}{R}}\right)^2 \right\rangle_t + \sum_{R=1}^{2P} \left\langle a_R^{\mu[t]} a_{\bar{R}}^{\mu[t]} n_R^{\frac{S[t]}{R}} n_{\bar{R}}^{\frac{S[t]}{R}} \right\rangle_t
$$

$$
+ \sum_{R \neq R' \neq \bar{R}}^{2P} \left\langle a_R^{\mu[t]} a_{R'}^{\mu[t]} n_R^{\frac{S[t]}{R}} n_{R'}^{\frac{S[t]}{R'}} \right\rangle_t
$$

$$
= \sum_{R=1}^{2P} \left\langle \left(n_R^{\frac{S[t]}{R}}\right)^2 - n_R^{\frac{S[t]}{R}} n_{\bar{R}}^{\frac{S[t]}{R}} \right\rangle_t + \sum_{R \neq R' \neq \bar{R}}^{2P} \left\langle a_R^{\mu[t]} a_{R'}^{\mu[t]} \right\rangle_t \left\langle n_R^{\frac{S[t]}{R}} n_{R'}^{\frac{S[t]}{R'}} \right\rangle_t
$$

$$
= \sum_{R=1}^{2P} \left\langle \left(n_R^{\frac{S[t]}{R}}\right)^2 - n_R^{\frac{S[t]}{R}} n_{\bar{R}}^{\frac{S[t]}{R}} \right\rangle_t + \sum_{R \neq R' \neq \bar{R}}^{2P} \left( \frac{1}{P} \sum_{\mu=0}^{P-1} a_R^{\mu[t]} a_{R'}^{\mu[t]} \right) \left\langle n_R^{\frac{S[t]}{R}} n_{R'}^{\frac{S[t]}{R'}} \right\rangle_t
$$

$$
= \sum_{R=1}^{2P} \left\langle \left(n_R^{\frac{S[t]}{R}}\right)^2 - n_R^{\frac{S[t]}{R}} n_{\bar{R}}^{\frac{S[t]}{R}} \right\rangle_t , \tag{4.21}
$$

where strategy $\bar{R}$ is anticorrelated to strategy $R$. We can write this sum over $2P$ terms as a sum over $P$ terms as follows:

$$
\sigma_\Psi^2 = \sum_{R=1}^{2P} \left\langle \left(n_R^{\frac{S[t]}{R}}\right)^2 - n_R^{\frac{S[t]}{R}} n_{\bar{R}}^{\frac{S[t]}{R}} \right\rangle_t
$$

$$
= \sum_{R=1}^{P} \left\langle \left(n_R^{\frac{S[t]}{R}}\right)^2 - n_R^{\frac{S[t]}{R}} n_{\bar{R}}^{\frac{S[t]}{R}} + \left(n_{\bar{R}}^{\frac{S[t]}{R}}\right)^2 - n_{\bar{R}}^{\frac{S[t]}{R}} n_R^{\frac{S[t]}{R}} \right\rangle_t
$$

$$
= \sum_{R=1}^{P} \left\langle \left(n_R^{\frac{S[t]}{R}}\right)^2 - 2 n_R^{\frac{S[t]}{R}} n_{\bar{R}}^{\frac{S[t]}{R}} + \left(n_{\bar{R}}^{\frac{S[t]}{R}}\right)^2 \right\rangle_t
$$

$$
= \sum_{R=1}^{P} \left\langle \left(n_R^{\frac{S[t]}{R}} - n_{\bar{R}}^{\frac{S[t]}{R}}\right)^2 \right\rangle_t . \tag{4.22}
$$

This provides a key general result:

$$
\sigma_\Psi^2 = \sum_{R=1}^{P} \left\langle \left(n_R^{\frac{S[t]}{R}} - n_{\bar{R}}^{\frac{S[t]}{R}}\right)^2 \right\rangle_t .
$$

The problem is: how do we work out how many people $n_R^{S[t]}$ are using a given strategy $R$ at a given timestep $t$? The technique for calculating $n_R^{S[t]}$ will depend greatly on the quenched disorder in the system. A different calculation technique is needed for large, sparsely filled quenched disorder matrices as compared to small densely filled matrices since, for example, the discreteness of agents becomes important in the former case. We will present an analytical treatment of the volatility in these two different regimes.

**4.8.3.1 Analytic form for volatility in the crowded regime.** We will look at the limiting case where the averaging over the quenched disorder only includes distributions of the matrix $\underline{\underline{\Psi}}$ which are almost flat, that is, we assume that this ensemble averaging is dominated by the matrices $\underline{\underline{\Psi}}$ which are nearly flat. This will be a good approximation for small $m$ since in this limit the standard deviations of the entries $\Psi_{R,R'}$ are much smaller than their means. This result holds because in the crowded low-$m$ regime, there are many more agents than there are available strategies and hence $N$ is greater than the number of entries. The technique for calculating $n_R^{S[t]}$ will involve, in both $m$-regimes, a re-labelling operation on the strategies. In the crowded regime we will re-label the strategies according to their score. This involves re-writing the sum in Equation (4.22), this time using a strategy label based on a score ranking $K$ as opposed to the decimal form $R$. Label $K$ is used to denote the rank in terms of strategy score, that is, $K = 1$ is the highest scoring strategy position, $K = 2$ is the second-highest scoring strategy position etc.:

$$S_{K=1} > S_{K=2} > S_{K=3} > S_{K=4} > \cdots \tag{4.23}$$

A given strategy $R$ may at a given timestep have label $K = 1$, while a few timesteps later have label $K = 5$. Because we know that $S_R = -S_{\bar{R}}$ (since all strategy scores start off at zero), we have that $S_K = -S_{\bar{K}}$ where $\bar{K} = 2P + 1 - K$. Rewriting Equation (4.22) gives:

$$\sigma_\Psi^2 = \sum_{K=1}^{P} \left\langle \left( n_K^{S[t]} - n_{\bar{K}}^{S[t]} \right)^2 \right\rangle_t . \tag{4.24}$$

Consider a typical graph of strategy scores as a function of time for a given realization of the quenched disorder $\underline{\underline{\Psi}}$. This graph is represented by Fig. 4.14 (recall we are focusing on the regime of small $m$).

The ranking (i.e. label) of a given strategy in terms of success score is changing all the time, since the individual strategies have a variation in score which fluctuates rapidly (see e.g. $S_{R=1}[t]$ in Fig. 4.14). This implies that the specific identity of the $K$th highest scoring strategy is changing all the time. It also implies that $n_R^{S[t]}$ is changing

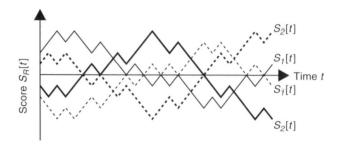

**Fig. 4.14**  Schematic representation of the variation of strategy success score $S_R[t]$ for two uncorrelated strategies (thick and thin solid lines) and their respective anticorrelated partners (thick and thin dashed lines).

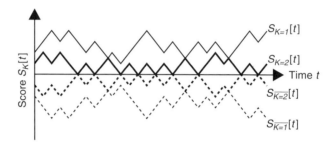

**Fig. 4.15**  Schematic representation of the strategy success scores from Fig. 4.14, now displayed in terms of $S_K[t]$ where $K$ labels the strategies from highest success score to lowest.

rapidly in time. In order to proceed, we therefore shift our focus to considering the time evolution of the highest scoring strategy, second highest scoring strategy, etc. This has a much smoother time evolution than the time evolution for a given strategy $S_R[t]$. In short, we shift focus from the time evolution of the success score of a given strategy (i.e. from $S_R[t]$) to the time evolution of the success score of the $K$th highest scoring strategy (i.e. to $S_K[t]$). From this point of view, Fig. 4.14 is transformed into Fig. 4.15.

We make the assumption that the spread of agents across the strategy space is fairly uniform, that is, $\underline{\underline{\Psi}}$ is a fairly uniform matrix. (This is where we appeal to the model being in the crowded, i.e. low-$m$, regime.) It therefore makes sense that there will be more agents playing the highest scoring strategy than the second highest scoring etc., that is, it follows from Equation (4.23) and our understanding of the system that we now have:

$$n_{K=1} > n_{K=2} > n_{K=3} > n_{K=4} > \cdots$$

Hence the rankings in terms of highest score and popularity are identical. (Note that the ordering in terms of the labels $\{R\}$ would not be sequential, i.e. it is *not* true that $n_{R=1} > n_{R=2} > n_{R=3} > n_{R=4} > \cdots$.) As shown in Fig. 4.15, the time evolution of the strategy scores is such that the score for a given $K$ tends to fluctuate around a mean value. Hence we expect that the number of traders playing the strategy in position $K$ at any timestep $t$, will also fluctuate around some mean value. In short, the quantities $n_K^{S[t]}$ and $n_{\bar{K}}^{S[t]}$ will, therefore, fluctuate in time but far less so than the individual strategy quantities $n_R^{S[t]}$ and $n_{\bar{R}}^{S[t]}$. Thus, we can make the approximation that:

$$n_K^{S[t]} = n_K + \varepsilon_K[t],$$

where $\varepsilon_K[t]$ is assumed to be a white noise term with zero mean and small variance. Here $n_K$ is the mean value. Hence from Equation (4.24), we get:

$$\sigma_\psi^2 = \sum_{K=1}^{P} \left\langle (n_K + \varepsilon_K(t) - n_{\bar{K}} - \varepsilon_{\bar{K}}(t))^2 \right\rangle_t$$

$$= \sum_{K=1}^{P} \left\langle ((n_K - n_{\bar{K}}) + (\varepsilon_K(t) - \varepsilon_{\bar{K}}(t)))^2 \right\rangle_t$$

$$= \sum_{K=1}^{P} \left\langle (n_K - n_{\bar{K}})^2 + (\varepsilon_K(t) - \varepsilon_{\bar{K}}(t))^2 + 2(n_K - n_{\bar{K}})(\varepsilon_K(t) - \varepsilon_{\bar{K}}(t)) \right\rangle_t$$

$$\simeq \sum_{K=1}^{P} \left\langle (n_K - n_{\bar{K}})^2 \right\rangle_t = \sum_{K=1}^{P} (n_K - n_{\bar{K}})^2, \tag{4.25}$$

since the latter two terms involving noise will average out to be small. The resulting expression involves no time dependence.

This entire discussion has been for a given realization of the quenched disorder $\underline{\underline{\Psi}}$. We now wish to perform an ensemble average over the various possible realizations of quenched disorder. The values of $n_K$ and $n_{\bar{K}}$ for each $K$ will depend on the precise form of $\underline{\underline{\Psi}}$. Let us denote the ensemble average as $\langle \ldots \rangle_\Psi$, and define for simplicity the notation $\langle \sigma_\psi^2 \rangle_\psi = \sigma^2$. We perform this ensemble average on either side of Equation (4.25). Since $\langle (n_K - n_{\bar{K}})^2 \rangle_\psi$ is just an expectation value of a function of two variables $n_K$ and $n_{\bar{K}}$, we can rewrite it exactly using the joint probability distribution for having $n_K$ and $n_{\bar{K}}$, which we call $p[n_K, n_{\bar{K}}]$. Hence:

$$\sigma^2 = \sum_{K=1}^{P} \left\langle (n_K - n_{\bar{K}})^2 \right\rangle_\psi$$

$$= \sum_{K=1}^{P} \sum_{n_K=0}^{N} \sum_{n_{\bar{K}}=0}^{N} (n_K - n_{\bar{K}})^2 p[n_K, n_{\bar{K}}]. \tag{4.26}$$

So how do we evaluate this? Well, in general it will depend on the joint probability function $p[n_K, n_{\bar{K}}]$ which in turn will depend on the ensemble of quenched disorders $\{\underline{\underline{\Psi}}\}$ which are being averaged over. We will now assume that the probability distribution $p[n_K, n_{\bar{K}}]$ will be sharply peaked around the $n_K$ and $n_{\bar{K}}$ values given by the expected values for a flat quenched-disorder matrix $\underline{\underline{\Psi}}$. Let us call these values $n_K^{\text{flat}}$ and $n_{\bar{K}}^{\text{flat}}$. Hence $p[n_K, n_{\bar{K}}] = \delta_{n_K, n_K^{\text{flat}}} \delta_{n_{\bar{K}}, n_{\bar{K}}^{\text{flat}}}$ and so:

$$\sigma^2 = \sum_{K=1}^{P} \sum_{n_K=0}^{N} \sum_{n_{\bar{K}}=0}^{N} (n_K - n_{\bar{K}})^2 p[n_K, n_{\bar{K}}] \simeq \sum_{K=1}^{P} \left( n_K^{\text{flat}} - n_{\bar{K}}^{\text{flat}} \right)^2.$$

This represents our main result for the crowded regime:

$$\sigma^2 = \sum_{K=1}^{P} \left( n_K^{\text{flat}} - n_{\bar{K}}^{\text{flat}} \right)^2. \tag{4.27}$$

We now calculate explicit expressions for the case of a flat quenched disorder matrix $\underline{\underline{\Psi}}$. Each entry of the matrix will have a mean of $N(1/2P)^s$ agents, for general $s$. We can use this to then calculate the expected number of agents who are playing strategy $K$, that is, $n_K^{\text{flat}}$. In particular, for $s = 2$, we can count the number of agents $n_K^{\text{flat}}$ by adding up elements in a reshuffled version of the (flat) quenched disorder matrix, $\Psi_{K,K'}$. Agents will only play strategy $K = \kappa$ if they do not hold any better strategy $K < \kappa$. Thus, the contributing elements of $\Psi_{K,K'}$ to $n_K^{\text{flat}}$ are those with $\{K, K'\} = \{\kappa, K \geq \kappa\}$ and $\{K, K'\} = \{K \geq \kappa, \kappa\}$. This is illustrated in the diagram below for $m = 2$:

Consider, for example, the expected number of agents using the strategy occupying position $K = 3$ in the list ordered by strategy scores, for $m = 2$. Any agent *using* the strategy in position $K = 3$ cannot have any strategy with a higher position, by definition of the rules of the game (the agents use their highest scoring strategy). Hence, the agents using the strategy in position $K = 3$ are represented by the shaded bins. Since we are assuming that the occupation of the bins is uniform ($\Psi_{K,K'} = N(1/2P)^{s=2}$), the expected number of agents using the strategy in position $K = 3$ is given by:

$$n_K^{\text{flat}} = N\left(\frac{1}{8}\right)^2 \sum_{\text{filled elements}} \Psi_{K,K'} = N\left(\frac{1}{64}\right)((8-3) + (8-3) + 1) = \frac{11N}{64}.$$

For more general $m$ and $K$ values, this becomes:

$$n_K^{\text{flat}} = N\left(\frac{1}{2P}\right)^2((2P-K) + (2P-K) + 1) \equiv \frac{(2^{m+2} - 2K + 1)N}{2^{2(m+1)}}, \qquad (4.28)$$

where we have used $P \equiv 2^m$. Likewise, we have that

$$n_{\bar{K}}^{\text{flat}} = N\left(\frac{1}{2P}\right)^2((2P - \bar{K}) + (2P - \bar{K}) + 1) \equiv \frac{(2^{m+2} - 2\bar{K} + 1)N}{2^{2(m+1)}}$$

$$= \frac{(2^{m+2} - 2(2^{m+1} - K + 1) + 1)N}{2^{2(m+1)}} = \frac{(2K - 1)N}{2^{2(m+1)}},$$

where we have used the identity $\bar{K} = 2P + 1 - K \equiv 2^{m+1} + 1 - K$. We emphasize that the above results depend on the assumption that the averages are dominated by the effects of flat distributions for the quenched disorder matrix $\underline{\underline{\Psi}}$, and hence will only be quantitatively valid for low $m$. Using Equation (4.27), we therefore have that:

$$\sigma^2 = \sum_{K=1}^{P}\left(n_K^{\text{flat}} - n_{\bar{K}}^{\text{flat}}\right)^2$$

$$= \sum_{K=1}^{P}\left(\frac{(2^{m+2} - 2K + 1)N}{2^{2(m+1)}} - \frac{(2K-1)N}{2^{2(m+1)}}\right)^2 = \frac{N^2}{2^{4m+2}}\sum_{K=1}^{P}(2^{m+1} - 2K + 1)^2.$$

Expanding out the bracket and using the standard relations:

$$\sum_{r=1}^{n} 1 = n, \quad \sum_{r=1}^{n} r = \frac{1}{2}n(n+1), \quad \sum_{r=1}^{n} r^2 = \frac{1}{6}n(n+1)(2n+1),$$

we obtain:

$$\sigma^2 = \frac{N^2}{2^{4m+2}}\sum_{K=1}^{P}(2^{m+1} - 2K + 1)^2 = \frac{N^2}{3 \cdot 2^m}(1 - 2^{-2(m+1)}).$$

Hence

$$\sigma = \frac{N}{\sqrt{3}\, 2^{m/2}}(1 - 2^{-2(m+1)})^{1/2}, \tag{4.29}$$

which should be valid for small $m$. Figure 4.16 shows the analytical result of Equation (4.29) together with the numerical results for the volatility for different realizations of the quenched disorder $\underline{\underline{\Psi}}$. It can be seen that with our simple treatment of the system, we have managed to capture the dependence of the volatility on

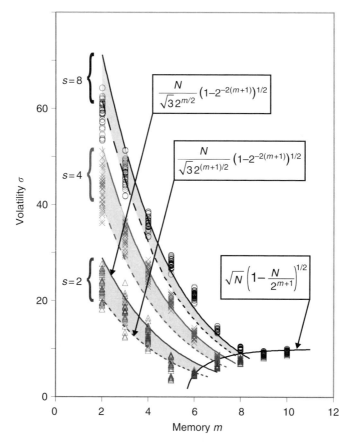

**Fig. 4.16** Analytical approximations to the volatility in demand for a simplified version of the El Farol Market Model (known as the Minority Game) as a function of agent memory $m$. Symbols represent numerical results. Plot corresponds to $N = 101$ active agents. Displayed are results for $s = 2, 4$, and 8 strategies per agent. Separate analytical approximations are made for the crowded (low-$m$) and dilute (high-$m$) regimes. In the crowded regime, the upper/lower analytical estimates (solid/dashed lines) represent entirely ordered/disordered rankings of strategies. (Entirely ordered would be $n_{K=1} > n_{K=2} > \cdots n_{K=2^P}$).

the model parameters in the low-$m$ regime. We note that the analytical approximation of Equation (4.29) gives a volatility which is slightly higher than the numerical ensemble-averaged result. The main reason for this is the effect of non-zero disorder in $\underline{\underline{\Psi}}$ (i.e. non-flat matrices). Whilst our calculation here assumed an ensemble of quenched disorder matrices $\{\underline{\underline{\Psi}}\}$ which were essentially flat, this will only be the case in practice for $N \to \infty$. As will be shown in Section 4.8.3.2, the effect of finite disorder will be to destroy the ordered ranking of strategies $n_{K=1} > n_{K=2} > \cdots n_{K=2P}$. Without this clear ranking of strategies, the assumptions leading to Equation (4.29) are inappropriate. Section 4.8.3.2 shows that an alternative form of Equation (4.26) (i.e. Equation (4.34)) can then be used. Using Equation (4.34) and assuming no strategy ordering (i.e. $f_{Q',\bar{Q}} = 1/(2P)$) we then arrive at:

$$\sigma = \frac{N}{\sqrt{3}\, 2^{(m+1)/2}}(1 - 2^{-2(m+1)})^{1/2}. \tag{4.30}$$

Equations (4.29) and (4.30) shown in Fig. 4.16 thus represent upper and lower analytical estimates for the volatility corresponding to entirely ordered and entirely disordered strategy rankings, respectively. In general, one would expect that the numerical results would lie within these bounds; this is borne out in Fig. 4.16. Note that the low-$m$ analytic curves can be obtained for any $s \geq 2$ using the generalized form of Equation (4.28):

$$n_K^{\text{flat}} = N(1/2P)^s[(2P - K + 1)^s - (2P - K)^s]. \tag{4.31}$$

We show the analytical approximation and numerical results for $s = 2, 4$, and $8$ strategies per agent in Fig. 4.16.

Equation (4.27) has a very simple interpretation in terms of the crowd–anticrowd idea presented in Section 4.8.2, since it represents the sum of the variances for each crowd–anticrowd pair. For a given strategy $K$, there is an anticorrelated strategy $\bar{K}$. The $n_K$ agents using strategy $K$ are doing the opposite to the $n_{\bar{K}}$ agents using strategy $\bar{K}$ irrespective of the global information bit-string. Hence the average effective group-size for each crowd–anticrowd pair is $n_K^{\text{eff}} = n_K^{\text{flat}} - n_{\bar{K}}^{\text{flat}}$: this represents the net step-size of this crowd–anticrowd pair's random walk. Hence the net contribution by this crowd–anticrowd pair to the variance is given by

$$(\sigma^2)_{K\bar{K}} = 4pqd^2 = \left(n_K^{\text{eff}}\right)^2 = \left(n_K^{\text{flat}} - n_{\bar{K}}^{\text{flat}}\right)^2. \tag{4.32}$$

Since these crowd–anticrowd pairs incorporate all the strong correlations, we can safely assume that the separate crowd–anticrowd pairs execute random walks which are uncorrelated with respect to each other.[22] Hence, the total variance is given by the sum of the individual variances:

$$\sigma^2 = \sum_{K=1}^{P}(\sigma^2)_{K\bar{K}} = \sum_{K=1}^{P}\left(n_K^{\text{flat}} - n_{\bar{K}}^{\text{flat}}\right)^2$$

in agreement with Equation (4.27).

### 4.8.3.2    Analytic form for the volatility in the dilute regime.

If the ensemble of quenched disorder matrices $\{\underline{\underline{\Psi}}\}$ contains a large proportion of non-flat member matrices,[23] we have to approach the averaging over this ensemble of quenched disorders in a different manner than in Section 4.8.3.1. The reason is that the PDF of the number of agents using the $K$th most successful strategy, is no longer well approximated by $p[n_K, n_{\bar{K}}] = \delta_{n_K, n_K^{\text{flat}}} \delta_{n_{\bar{K}}, n_{\bar{K}}^{\text{flat}}}$. As $m$ increases, the quenched disorder matrix $\underline{\underline{\Psi}}$ will become increasingly sparse. All the (integer/half-integer) entries $\Psi_{R,R'}$ must add up to give $N$, the total number of agents: hence as the number of entries $2^{m+1} \times 2^{m+1}$ grows, the matrix becomes filled with an increasing number of zeros. The number of agents using each strategy then tends towards either being zero or one. Hence, $n_R[t]$ is dominated by the disorder rather than the success of the strategy. Furthermore, due to the minority nature of the model, strategies being used will tend to perform less well than strategies which are not used. Thus, strategies which are held by more agents will be less successful than those which are held by few (or no) agents. This leads to a 'market impact force' on $n_K$. In the low-$m$ crowded regime, the more successful a strategy was, the more agents would play it. The market impact effect was less important there since the number of agents holding each strategy was roughly equal (flat $\underline{\underline{\Psi}}$). In the high-$m$ dilute regime, the opposite is true and the market impact dominates. Hence, the more agents that hold a given strategy, the less successful that strategy is on average. This effect can be seen clearly in Fig. 4.17.

Figure 4.17 shows that the form $p[n_K, n_{\bar{K}}] = \delta_{n_K, n_K^{\text{flat}}} \delta_{n_{\bar{K}}, n_{\bar{K}}^{\text{flat}}}$ calculated as in Section 4.8.3.1 neglecting market impact, is not a good approximation for the high-$m$ regime. In this case, the general analysis is more complicated, and should incorporate the dynamical 'market impact' behaviour of the model. However, we will now develop an approximate theory along slightly different lines which gives good agreement with the numerical results.

---

[22]  In the RSS, strategies are either completely anticorrelated or completely uncorrelated to each other.
[23]  The term non-flat quenched disorder matrix $\underline{\underline{\Psi}}$ refers to a case where the standard deviation of each entry $\Psi_{R,R'}$ is large in comparison with the mean value of the entry. This will become increasingly likely as $m$ increases.

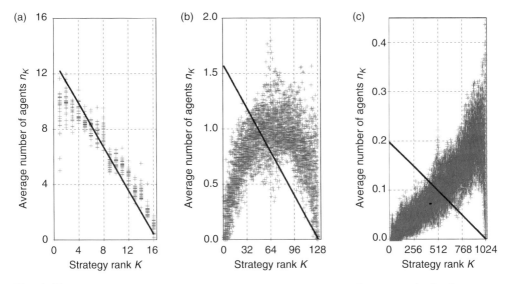

**Fig. 4.17** Average number of agents $n_K$ using the $K$th most successful strategy book. The crosses represent time averages for 32 different runs. The model parameters were $N = 101$ and $s = 2$ with the memory $m$ equal to (a) 3, (b) 6, and (c) 9. The lines correspond to $n_K^{\text{flat}}$ calculated for the low-$m$ regime as described in Section 4.8.3.1.

For the case of ensembles containing a significant number of non-flat quenched disorder matrices $\underline{\underline{\Psi}}$, we can make the following statements:

1. By definition of the labels $\{K\}$, we retain the ranking in terms of success score, that is, it is always true that $S_{K=1} > S_{K=2} > S_{K=3} > S_{K=4} > \cdots$
2. However, the disorder in the matrix $\underline{\underline{\Psi}}$ distorts the number of traders playing a given strategy away from the flat-matrix results. Hence, we *do not* in general have
$$n_{K=1} > n_{K=2} > n_{K=3} > n_{K=4} > \cdots$$

Hence the rankings in terms of highest success score and popularity are no longer identical. In general, we have instead:

$$n_{K'} > n_{K''} > n_{K'''} > \cdots$$

where the label $K' \neq 1$, $K'' \neq 2, \ldots$. However, we can introduce a new label $\{Q\}$ which will rank the strategies in terms of popularity, that is,

$$n_{Q=1} > n_{Q=2} > n_{Q=3} > \cdots$$

where $Q = 1$ represents $K'$, $Q = 2$ represents $K''$, etc. We now return to the original general form for the volatility, averaged over time, initial conditions and quenched disorder (Equation (4.26)), and rewrite it slightly:

$$\sigma^2 = \sum_{K=1}^{P} \sum_{n_K=0}^{N} \sum_{n_{\bar{K}}=0}^{N} (n_K - n_{\bar{K}})^2 p[n_K, n_{\bar{K}}]$$

$$= \frac{1}{2} \sum_{K=1}^{2P} \sum_{n_K=0}^{N} \sum_{n_{\bar{K}}=0}^{N} (n_K - n_{\bar{K}})^2 p[n_K, n_{\bar{K}}]$$

$$= \frac{1}{2} \sum_{K=1}^{2P} \sum_{K'=1}^{2P} \left( \sum_{n_K=0}^{N} \sum_{n_{K'}=0}^{N} (n_K - n_{K'})^2 p[n_K, n_{K'}] \right) f_{K',\bar{K}}, \qquad (4.33)$$

where $f_{K',\bar{K}}$ is the probability that $K'$ is the anticorrelated strategy to $K$ (i.e. $\bar{K}$) and is hence given by $f_{K',\bar{K}} = \delta_{K',2P+1-K}$. This manipulation is exact so far. We now switch to the popularity labels $\{Q\}$ to give:

$$\sigma^2 = \frac{1}{2} \sum_{Q=1}^{2P} \sum_{Q'=1}^{2P} \left( \sum_{n_Q=0}^{N} \sum_{n_{Q'}=0}^{N} (n_Q - n_{Q'})^2 p[n_Q, n_{Q'}] \right) f_{Q',\bar{Q}}. \qquad (4.34)$$

Consider any particular strategy which was labelled previously by $K$ and is now labelled by $Q$. Unlike in our treatment of the flat disorder matrix, we are *not* guaranteed that strategy $Q$s anticorrelated partner $\bar{Q}$ will lie in position $\bar{Q} = 2P+1-Q$. This is because of the relabelling operation: all we can say is that the strategy $R$ has changed label from $K \rightarrow Q[K]$ while the anticorrelated strategy $\bar{R}$ has changed label from $\bar{K} \rightarrow \bar{Q}(\bar{K})$ and that in general $\bar{Q} \neq 2P+1-Q$. We thus have two tasks: first to deduce the probability distribution $p[n_Q, n_{Q'}]$ and second to deduce the probability distribution $f_{Q',\bar{Q}}$. In the high-$m$ regime, the number of available strategies is so much larger than the number of agents, that the number using a given strategy $n_R$ is very likely to be zero, slightly likely to be one and almost never anything greater than one. Thus, when the strategies are ranked in terms of the number of agents using them, we have to a good approximation that $n_{Q=1}, n_{Q=2}, \ldots, n_{Q=N} = 1$ and $n_{Q=N+1}, \ldots, n_{Q=2P} = 0$. This gives us:

$$p[n_Q, n_{Q'}] \simeq \delta_{n_Q, H[N-Q]} \delta_{n_{Q'}, H[N-Q']}. \qquad (4.35)$$

Next we turn our attention to $f_{Q',\bar{Q}}$, the probability that the strategy $Q'$ is anti-correlated to the strategy $Q$. First we note that within the groups $n_{Q=1} \ldots n_{Q=N}$ and $n_{Q=N+1} \ldots n_{Q=2P}$, the number of agents using each strategy is the same, consequently the strategies' rankings within these groups are arbitrary. Second we reiterate that the disorder among strategies, rather than the success, is the main factor in determining whether they are used by agents or not. This implies that there is no particularly strong reason why a strategy in group $n_{Q=1} \ldots n_{Q=N}$ should have its anticorrelated partner in either the same group or group $n_{Q=N+1} \ldots n_{Q=2P}$. These two facts combined, lead us to the conclusion that a good approximation to $f_{Q',\bar{Q}}$ would be to say that there is roughly equal probability of finding the anticorrelated partner of $Q$ *anywhere* in the range $Q' = 1 \ldots 2P$, that is, we have:

$$f_{Q',\bar{Q}} \simeq 1/(2P) \tag{4.36}$$

for all $Q'$, and all $Q$. Now we can substitute the approximate forms from Equations (4.35) and (4.36) into Equation (4.34). This then gives:

$$\sigma^2 = \frac{1}{4P} \sum_{Q=1}^{2P} \sum_{Q'=1}^{2P} (H[N-Q] - H[N-Q'])^2. \tag{4.37}$$

The value of each summand term in Equation (4.37) is either zero or one. If we count the number of times the summand is equal to one, we get:

$$\sigma^2 = (1/4P)2N(2P - N).$$

Hence, we have the following approximate form for the volatility in the high-$m$ regime, which is valid for any $s$:

$$\sigma = \sqrt{N} \left( 1 - \frac{N}{2^{m+1}} \right)^{1/2}. \tag{4.38}$$

Figure 4.16 shows the analytical approximation in Equation (4.38) for the volatility in the high-$m$ regime. Again we seem to have captured the dependence of the volatility on the model parameters. Just as we observed in the numerical simulations, the volatility tends towards the random, coin-toss limit of $\sigma = \sqrt{N}$ as the memory $m \to \infty$. Again we see that our analytical approximation of Equation (4.38) is a little higher than the numerical results. This time the culprit is our analytical approximation for $f_{Q',\bar{Q}}$. It is quite simple to derive a slightly more sophisticated approximation for $f_{Q',\bar{Q}}$ which incorporates the agents' behaviour in picking their most successful strategy. For general $s$, this then yields:

$$\sigma = \sqrt{N} \left( 1 - \frac{Ns - 1}{2^{m+1}} \right)^{1/2}, \tag{4.39}$$

which gives a better fit to the observed ensemble-averaged volatility.

To summarize, our analytical approach has managed to capture the essential interactions driving the variation in volatility for a simplified version of the El Farol Market Model known as the Minority Game. The present analytic results can be extended to account for different model variations. An example is that of 'stochastic strategy picking'. In this version, agents have $s = 2$ strategies each but choose to use their most successful strategy with a probability less than 1, that is, they have a finite probability of using their worst-scoring strategy. The effect of the stochastic strategy picking is to break up the crowds, hence reducing the volatility in the low-$m$ regime.[24] Similarly, one can treat a population of agents which contains a sub-population of stochastic strategy pickers, while the remainder choose their best strategy with probability 1. More generally these analytic approaches to understanding agent-based models based on crowd–anticrowd interaction, need not be limited to finance-related phenomena. Indeed there is currently much work on agent-based systems in computing science, artificial intelligence studies, and in the biological and social sciences.[25] There is even cause to believe that such models and methodologies may help with the more abstract, science-related Holy Grail of understanding complex systems as a whole. Only time will tell.

---

[24] For discussions and analytic models which we have presented concerning stochastic strategy picking, see Jefferies, P., Hart, M., Johnson, N. F., and Hui, P. M. (2000) *J. Phys. A: Math. Gen.* **33**, L409; Hart, M., Jefferies, P., Johnson, N. F., and Hui, P. M. (2001) *Phys. Rev. E* **63**, 017102. See Johnson, N. F., Hui, P. M., Jonson, R., Lo, T. S. (1999) *Phys. Rev. Lett.* **82**, 3360, for a stochastic model which demonstrates explicitly the spontaneous formation of crowds–anticrowds in a competing population.

[25] See the work of D. Wolpert and K. Tumer at NASA Ames Research Center, www.nasa.arc.gov, on Collectives.

# 5. Financial market models with local interactions

## 5.1 Clustering and herd behaviour

The non-Gaussian empirical results in Chapter 3 suggest that market participants do not behave entirely randomly. Chapter 4 examined the collective behaviour of agents in a market, assuming that these agents do not share any local information. The formation and action of crowds was seen to play a crucial role in determining the price dynamics, in particular the volatility. These crowds were *unintentional* in the sense that an agent became a member of a particular crowd via the strategy he was using, rather than because he decided to join that crowd *per se*. In short, this was a crowding in strategy space.

In this chapter we look at a complementary situation in which agents may interact and share opinions: they may hence imitate each other and thereby act as a crowd. Such crowding has been termed 'herd formation' in the Econophysics literature. As in Chapter 4, our goal is to build minimal yet justifiable models, which are consistent with the stylized facts observed in financial market price data. In the present case of addressing local interactions between agents, the models will not include as much detail as those of Chapter 4 concerning market microstructure. Although this could be added, we will focus instead on the statistical properties of various simple models. In particular, the herding mechanism in these models will be taken as fundamentally stochastic in nature. We will leave the interested reader to explore the intriguing possibility of combining the key elements of the models from this chapter and Chapter 4.

Cont and Bouchaud[1] proposed a simple agent-based model of such herd behaviour, with a demand generating mechanism, which depends on the collective action of the traders in a cluster (i.e. herd or crowd). Unlike the models of Chapter 4 where agents were independent, the agents in a cluster come to a collective decision and then all

[1] Cont, R. and Bouchaud, J. P. (2000) *Macroeconom. Dynam.* **4**, 170.

act in the same way. A cluster of agents may represent, for example, the investors in a mutual fund.

Consider $N$ agents (traders) trading in a single asset. The cluster formation is modelled by establishing links between the agents. Let $q_{ij}$ be the probability that the $i$th agent and the $j$th agent are connected. For simplicity $q_{ij}$ is taken to be independent of $i$ and $j$, that is, $q_{ij} = q$ where $q$ is a constant. An agent therefore has an average of $q(N-1)$ links to the other agents. To ensure that the average number of links per agent is finite in the limit $N \to \infty$, we take $q = c/N$ where $c$ is a constant, which is less than (but close to) unity, that is, $0 < 1 - c \ll 1$. At each timestep of the market's evolution the $N$ agents are partitioned stochastically into clusters of different sizes according to the parameter $c$, which characterizes inter-agent connectivity. The herding behaviour is introduced through the collective action of the agents in these clusters. Each agent $i$ may take one of three possible actions, labelled by $a_i \in \{-1, 0, 1\}$. The action $a_i = +1$ denotes a buy order, $a_i = -1$ denotes a sell order, and $a_i = 0$ denotes not trading.[2] The variable $a_i$ can thus be thought of as combining the roles of the 'investment suggestion' $a^{\mu[t]}$ and the 'confidence level' $r$ from the agent models of Chapter 4. Agents in a given cluster have a common opinion and thus $a_i = a_j$ for $i$ and $j$ belonging to the same cluster. The probability of carrying out a transaction is characterized by a parameter $\nu$, where $0 \le \nu \le 1$. The probabilities of $a_i$ being $+1$ and $-1$ are assumed to be the same, that is, $p[a_i = +1] = p[a_i = -1] = \nu/2$ and hence $p[a_i = 0] = 1 - \nu$. The parameter $\nu$ characterizes how frequently a transaction occurs, and thus represents the *activity* in the market. The model is therefore completely characterized by the two parameters $\nu$ and $c$.

In this simple model the formation of herds (i.e. clusters) is purely geometrical and depends only on the parameter $c$. At each timestep of the market's evolution the herding process divides the $N$ agents into clusters of various sizes. The probability distribution of cluster sizes $p[s]$ can be studied either by numerical simulation, or using probability and random graph theory. Most relevant to our discussion is the functional form of $p[s]$. For $c = 1$, the probability distribution function (PDF) has the form[3]

$$p[s] \sim \frac{A}{s^{5/2}}, \tag{5.1}$$

where $A$ is a constant. For $0 < 1 - c \ll 1$,

$$p[s] \sim \frac{A}{s^{5/2}} \exp\left[\frac{-(1-c)s}{s_0}\right]. \tag{5.2}$$

---

[2] This is the same as the 'Grand Canonical' feature in Chapter 4, whereby agents can decide not to trade.
[3] We use the symbol $\sim$ to denote the functional dependence. For practical purposes, it can be thought of as meaning 'approximately proportional to'.

Equation (5.1) exhibits a pure power-law dependence of the cluster size, whereas Equation (5.2) exhibits a power-law dependence which becomes truncated at a cluster size of order $s_0$, after which an exponential dependence takes over. We will see that the power-law behaviour of $p[s]$ will carry over to the distribution of log-returns of the price when the collective herd behaviour is taken into account in driving price movements. We leave the discussion on determining the exponent of this power-law behaviour to Sections 5.2 and 5.3, where a related model with identical results will be studied. Interestingly, such power-law behaviour for cluster-size distributions also emerges from standard percolation problems (see Section 5.4). The connectivity in the present model is set-up via long-range interactions between the agents, in contrast to the nearest-neighbour interactions usually assumed when studying percolation problems on a lattice. The exponent $-\frac{5}{2}$ in the cluster-size distribution is consistent with that obtained in percolation theory for spatial dimensions higher than the upper critical dimension of the percolation problem. Percolation-type models of markets, which amount to putting the Cont–Bouchaud model onto a spatial lattice, will be discussed in Sections 5.4 and beyond.

Suppose the $N$ participants are divided into a total of $n_c$ clusters at a given point in the model's evolution. All the agents in the $\alpha$th cluster of size $s_\alpha$ have the same demand $a_\alpha$. Clearly then $\sum_{\alpha=1}^{n_c} s_\alpha = N$. Some of these agent-clusters decide to place buy orders ($a_\alpha = +1$), other agent-clusters may decide to place sell orders ($a_\alpha = -1$), and a fraction $(1 - \nu)$ of agent-clusters decide to make any transaction at all ($a_\alpha = 0$). Price movements are small if the excess demand, which is (as before) the difference in the number of buy and sell orders, is small. Just before time $t$, the market-maker gathers all orders $a_i[t-1]$ and calculates an excess demand given by

$$D[t^-] = \sum_{i=1}^{N} a_i[t-1] = \sum_{\alpha=1}^{n_c} s_\alpha[t-1]\,a_\alpha[t-1]. \tag{5.3}$$

Using the argument from Chapter 4 relating excess demand to price change (Equation (4.1)), the single timestep log-return defined in Equation (1.4) is given by

$$z[t] = \ln x[t] - \ln x[t-1] = \frac{D[t^-]}{\lambda} \equiv \frac{1}{\lambda} \sum_{\alpha=1}^{n_c} s_\alpha[t-1]\,a_\alpha[t-1], \tag{5.4}$$

where we have used the shorthand $z[t] \equiv z[t, t-1]$. As in Chapter 4, the parameter $\lambda$ is the market depth. The temporal ordering of this model is thus as follows. At time $t-1$ the $N$ agents form $n_c$ clusters. Within each cluster $\alpha$ the $s_\alpha$ agents each place an identical order $a_i[t-1] = a_\alpha[t-1]$. Just before time $t$ the market maker collects all these orders, which results in an excess demand $D[t^-]$. The market maker then moves the price accordingly to a new level $x[t]$, the orders are executed and new clusters form.

The price is therefore driven by the effect of trading between different clusters of agents. Since a fraction $(1 - \nu)N$ of agents have $a_i = 0$, then $\langle V[t] \rangle = \nu N$ is the average number of active agents and hence the average volume of orders received. Note that the cluster configuration at time $t+1$ is independent of that at time $t$ in this present model, since the topology of agent–agent connections changes randomly at each timestep. Let us now consider how we might simulate this model on a computer: we start off with a randomly generated cluster configuration $\{s_\alpha[t]\}$ for a given parameter $c$. Using the consequent cluster sizes $s_\alpha[t]$ and the randomly generated orders $a_\alpha[t]$ for a given activity probability $\nu$ we form a demand $D[(t+1)^-]$. From this demand we can evaluate the log-return $z[t+1]$. In the next timestep, another random set of orders compatible with $\nu$ and $c$ is generated and $z[t+2]$ is evaluated. Repeating the procedure gives a series of log-returns for which statistical properties can be analysed. Interesting generalizations of the model with a built-in dynamical process for the coagulation and fragmentation of clusters have been proposed. Some of these will be discussed in later sections.

This model readily gives power-law behaviour in the PDF of price returns, together with an exponential cutoff for large cluster sizes and hence large returns. For small values of $\nu$, the net demand is dominated by one or just a few clusters. The PDF of log-returns then follows that of the cluster distribution. An analytic treatment of the excess kurtosis (recall Chapter 2) gives

$$\kappa - 3 = \frac{2c + 1}{V(1 - (c/2))(1 - c)^3 A[c]} \tag{5.5}$$

for $0 < 1 - c \ll 1$, where $A[c]$ is a normalization constant of order unity. The result that the excess kurtosis varies as $1/V$ implies that a small average volume of active agents leads to large price fluctuations. This is consistent with the fact that large price fluctuations occur more often in smaller or less active markets—it is also consistent with the numerical results of Chapter 4 for the Grand Canonical Minority Game (GCMG) in the 'crowded' regime corresponding to small memory $m$ (see Fig. 4.4). Even though the average volume is small, its bursty structure creates large changes in demand and hence large changes in the price.

## 5.2     Transmission of information: the EZ model

The herd-formation model of Cont and Bouchaud is static in that the partition of the agents into clusters at one timestep *is independent* of the partition at an earlier

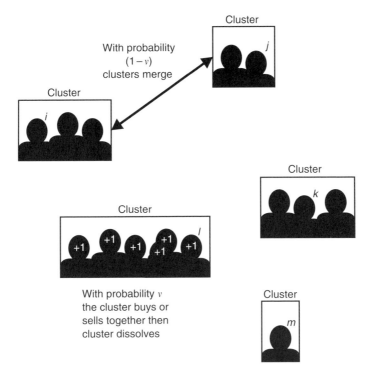

**Fig. 5.1** The dynamical herd formation model, referred to as the EZ model.

timestep. However, we know that one of the reasons for herd formation is the spreading and sharing of opinion. Eguiluz and Zimmermann (EZ) generalized the Cont and Bouchaud model by incorporating a *dynamical* process of herd formation via the spread or transmission of opinion.[4] Consider again our market of $N$ agents, in which agent $i$ can be in one of three possible states represented by $a_i = +1$ for buying, $a_i = -1$ for selling, and $a_i = 0$ for the inactive state. Trading occurs with a probability $v$, as in the previous model. At the beginning of the simulation, all the agents are isolated with their state set to $a_i = 0$. As time evolves, agents may spread their opinion and hence form clusters with a common opinion, as indicated in Fig. 5.1.

At any particular timestep, an agent belongs to a cluster of a certain size. An isolated agent represents a cluster of size one. At each timestep, an agent (e.g. the $i$th agent) is chosen at random. Let $s_i$ be the size of the cluster to which this agent belongs. Since the agents within a given cluster have a common opinion, all agents within the same cluster will act together as a crowd. With probability $v$, the agent and hence the whole cluster

---

[4] Eguiluz, V. M. and Zimmermann, M. G. (2000) *Phys. Rev. Lett.* **85**, 5659.

decides to make a transaction, for example, to buy or to sell with equal probability $v/2$ as in the model of Cont and Bouchaud. This collective action of a cluster of agents creates a price movement that depends on the size of the cluster. After the transaction, the cluster is then broken up into isolated agents all in the inactive ($a_i = 0$) state. With probability $(1 - v)$, the chosen agent decides not to make a transaction: instead he tries to accomplish further transmission of information rather than jumping into a decision to buy or sell. The other agents in the cluster follow. In this case, another agent $j$ is chosen at random. The two clusters of sizes $s_i$ and $s_j$ then combine to form a bigger cluster. The EZ model is thus characterized by a single parameter $v$. The set-up of the model is shown schematically in Fig. 5.1. The connectivity among the agents, characterized by the parameter $c$ in the Cont–Bouchaud model, is now driven by the dynamics of the EZ model. The parameter $v$ can again be interpreted as the *activity* in the market. For small $v$ (i.e. $v \ll 1$), not many transactions take place. Instead, agents tend to spend their time in dispersing information. This leads to the build-up of internal connectivity and hence the formation of larger clusters. When a large cluster of agents eventually trades, the price movement (which is given in terms of the size of the cluster) is large. In the other limit of $v \to 1$, nearly every randomly chosen agent trades and the system consists of mostly isolated agents. The price movements will then be small and random. For intermediate values of $v$, the price should consist of many small movements, with occasional larger ones arising when a cluster of agents submit their orders. For example, a value of $v = 0.01$ corresponds to about one cluster of buy or sell orders in every 100 iterations. The extreme case of forming one giant super-cluster containing all agents—which would be analogous to the phenomenon of Bose–Einstein condensation in physics—is unlikely unless $v$ is very small, that is, $v \ll 1/(N \ln N)$.

Demand in the EZ model is generated in a similar way to the Cont–Bouchaud model as given by Equation (5.3). However, here the total order size corresponds to the size of cluster to which the chosen agent $i$ belongs ($s_i$), thus:

$$D[t^-] = s_i[t-1]\, a_i[t-1]. \tag{5.6}$$

The excess demand therefore has a magnitude given by $|s_i|$ and has equal probability $v/2$ of being positive or negative. Putting the excess demand in Equation (5.4) yields a log-return $z[t]$. We note that the EZ model can be easily implemented numerically.[5]

Figure 5.2 shows a time-series of price movements generated using the EZ model. Evidence of occasional large movements can be identified in the log returns. Since $v$ is small, we have re-scaled the time axis such that a time unit represents the average

---

[5]  See the book-website www.occf.ox.ac.uk/books/fmc for a simple Fortran program, which runs on both UNIX and Windows platforms.

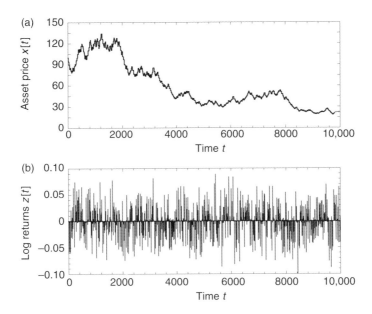

**Fig. 5.2** (a) Price and (b) log-returns as a function of time, generated using the EZ model with $N = 10,000$ agents, $v = 0.01$ and a market depth of $\lambda = 5 \times 10^4$.

time it takes for an order to arrive. The average number of connections per agent measures the connectivity within the EZ model. The connectivity is driven by the dynamics, hence it fluctuates with time. The simulation gives a mean connectivity $\langle c \rangle \approx 0.76$.

Let us now examine the statistics of the distribution of log-returns a little more closely. Figure 5.3 shows the PDF of positive returns $p[z]$ on a log–log plot. A power law is observed over a range of $z$ values, with an exponent of $-1.5$. The width of the range over which the power law is observed, depends on the value of $v$. If the volume of active agents is generally high, or equivalently the order flows are frequent, large returns are rare and hence an exponential tail is manifest in the PDF $p[z]$. For very small values of $v$, large clusters are formed and rare but large returns appear. In between, there is a critical value of $v$ for which the power law is observed[6] over a large range of $z$. It follows from the definition of price returns in terms of excess demand that the distribution of price returns is determined by the distribution of cluster-sizes. This distribution is obtained by counting the number of occurrences $n_s$ of a cluster of size $s$ over time. The cluster size distribution is shown in Fig. 5.4 in terms of $n_s/n_1$, using the same set of parameters as before.

---

[6] There are also finite-size effects in numerical studies, caused by the finite number of agents.

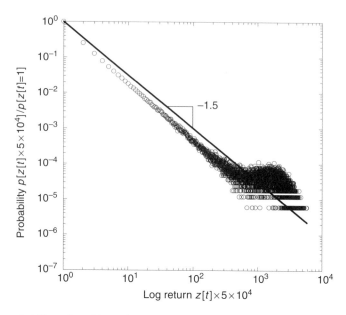

**Fig. 5.3**  The probability of positive price returns within the EZ model with $N = 10,000$ agents, $v = 0.01$ and a market depth of $\lambda = 5 \times 10^4$ as a function of the return on a log–log scale.

The distribution shows power law behaviour with an exponent $-5/2$, identical to the Cont–Bouchaud model and to percolation theory in high dimensions (i.e. $>6$ dimensions). The exponent $-5/2$ is thus independent of the details of the dynamics of herd formation and cluster fragmentation. The two exponents $-3/2$ (Fig. 5.3) and $-5/2$ (Fig. 5.4) are related in that $p[z]$ is determined by the probability of a randomly picked agent belonging to a cluster of size $s = \lambda z$. Hence $p[z]$ is proportional to the number of agents belonging to a cluster of size $s$, that is, $p[z] \sim n_s \times s \sim s^{-5/2} \times s \sim s^{-3/2} \sim z^{-3/2}$ as observed numerically. The EZ model can be generalized to include more elaborate mechanisms for herd formation and decision-making in a cluster of agents. It could also be extended to include feedback mechanisms between the agents' performance and their actions, as for the models of Chapter 4.

## 5.3  Analytic model: generating function approach

One can write a dynamical equation for the evolution of the EZ model at different levels of approximation. For example, one could start with a microscopic description of the system by noting that at any moment in time, the population can be described

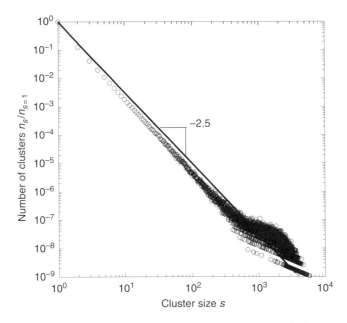

**Fig. 5.4**   Distribution of cluster sizes in the EZ model with $N = 10,000$ agents, $v = 0.01$.

by a partition $\{l_1, l_2, \ldots, l_N\}$ of the $N$ agents into clusters. Here $l_s$ is the number of clusters of size $s$. For example, $\{N, 0, \ldots, 0\}$ and $\{0, 0, \ldots, 1\}$ correspond to the extreme cases in which all agents are isolated and all agents belong to one big cluster, respectively. Clearly, the number of agents must be conserved $\sum_{i=1}^{N} i l_i = N$. The dynamics could then be described by the time-evolution of the probability function $p[l_1, l_2, \ldots, l_N]$: in particular, taking the continuous-time limit would yield an equation for $\mathrm{d}p[l_1, l_2, \ldots, l_N]/\mathrm{d}t$ in terms of transitions between partitions. For example, the fragmentation of a cluster of $s$ agents leads to a transition from the partition $\{l_1, \ldots, l_s, \ldots, l_N\}$ to the partition $\{l_1 + s, \ldots, l_s - 1, \ldots, l_N\}$. For our purposes, however, it is more convenient to work with the *average* number $n_s$ of clusters of size $s$, which can be written as $n_s = \sum_{\{l_1, \ldots, l_N\}} p[l_1, \ldots, l_s, \ldots, l_N] \cdot l_s$. The sum is over all possible partitions of the system into clusters. Since $p[l_1, \ldots, l_N]$ evolves in time, so does $n_s[t]$. After the transients have died away, the system is expected to reach a steady-state in which $p[l_1, \ldots, l_N]$ and $n_s[t]$ become time-independent in the large-$N$ limit. The time-evolution of $n_s[t]$ can be written down for the EZ model either by intuition, or by invoking a mean-field approximation to the equation for $\mathrm{d}p[l_1, l_2, \ldots, l_N]/\mathrm{d}t$. Taking the intuitive route, one can immediately write down the following dynamical equations in the continuous-time limit:

$$\frac{\partial n_s}{\partial t} = -\frac{v s n_s}{N} + \frac{(1-v)}{N^2} \sum_{s'=1}^{s-1} s' n_{s'} (s-s') n_{s-s'}$$

$$- \frac{2(1-v) s n_s}{N^2} \sum_{s'=1}^{\infty} s' n_{s'}, \quad \text{for } s \geq 2 \tag{5.7}$$

$$\frac{\partial n_1}{\partial t} = \frac{v}{N} \sum_{s'=2}^{\infty} (s')^2 n_{s'} - \frac{2(1-v) n_1}{N^2} \sum_{s'=1}^{\infty} s' n_{s'}. \tag{5.8}$$

The terms on the right-hand side of Equation (5.7) represent all the ways in which $n_s$ can change. The first term represents a decrease in $n_s$ due to the dissociation of a cluster of size $s$: this happens only if an agent belonging to a cluster of size $s$ is chosen and that agent decides to make a transaction. The former occurs with probability $s n_s / N$ and the latter with probability $v$. The second term represents an increase in $n_s$ as a result of the merging of a cluster of size $s'$ with a cluster of size $(s - s')$. The third term describes the decrease in $n_s$ due to the merging of a cluster of size $s$ with any other cluster. For the $s = 1$ case described by Equation (5.8), the chosen agent remains isolated after making a transaction; thus Equation (5.8) does not have a contribution like the first term of Equation (5.7). The first term that appears in Equation (5.8) reflects the increase in the number of single agents due to fragmentation of a cluster after a collective transaction is taken. Similarly to Equation (5.7), the last term of Equation (5.8) describes the merging of a single agent cluster with a cluster of any other size. Equations (5.7) and (5.8) are so-called 'master equations' describing the dynamics within the EZ model.

In the steady-state, Equations (5.7) and (5.8) yield:

$$s n_s = \frac{(1-v)}{(2-v)N} \sum_{s'=1}^{s-1} s' n_{s'} (s-s') n_{s-s'}, \quad \text{for } s \geq 2 \tag{5.9}$$

$$n_1 = \frac{v}{2(1-v)} \sum_{s'=2}^{\infty} (s')^2 n_{s'}. \tag{5.10}$$

Equations of this type are most conveniently treated using the general technique of 'generating functions'. As the name suggests, these are functions which can be used to generate a range of useful quantities. Consider

$$G[y] = \sum_{s'=0}^{\infty} s' n_{s'} y^{s'}, \tag{5.11}$$

where $y = e^{-\omega}$ is a parameter. Note that $s \, n_s/N$ is the probability of finding an agent belonging to a cluster of size $s$. If $G[y]$ is known, $s \, n_s$ is then formally given by

$$sn_s = \frac{1}{s!} G^{(s)}[0],$$
(5.12)

where $G^{(s)}[y]$ is the $s$th derivative of $G[y]$ with respect to $y$. $G^{(s)}[y]$ can be decomposed as

$$G[y] = n_1 y + \sum_{s'=2}^{\infty} s' n_{s'} y^{s'} \equiv n_1 y + g[y],$$
(5.13)

where the function $g[y]$ governs the cluster size distribution $n_s$ for $s \geq 2$. The next task is to obtain an equation for $g[y]$. This can be done in two ways. One could either write down the terms in $(g[y])^2$ explicitly and then make use of Equation (5.9), or one could construct $g[y]$ by multiplying Equation (5.9) by $e^{-\omega s}$ and then summing over $s$. The resulting equation is:

$$(g[y])^2 - \left(\frac{2-v}{1-v}N - 2n_1 y\right) g[y] + n_1^2 y^2 = 0.$$
(5.14)

First we solve for $n_1$. From Equation (5.13), $g[1] = G[1] - n_1 = N - n_1$. Substituting $n_1 = N - g[1]$ into Equation (5.14) and setting $y = 1$, yields

$$g[1] = \frac{1-v}{2-v}N.$$
(5.15)

Hence

$$n_1 = N - g[1] = \frac{1}{2-v}N.$$
(5.16)

To obtain $n_s$ with $s \geq 2$, we need to solve for $g[y]$. Substituting Equation (5.16) for $n_1$, Equation (5.14) becomes

$$(g[y])^2 - \left(\frac{2-v}{1-v}N - \frac{2N}{2-v}y\right) g[y] + \frac{N^2}{(2-v)^2} y^2 = 0.$$
(5.17)

Equation (5.17) is a quadratic equation for $g[y]$ which can be solved to obtain

$$g[y] = \frac{(2-v)N}{4(1-v)} \left(1 - \sqrt{1 - \frac{4(1-v)}{(2-v)^2} y}\right)^2$$

$$= \frac{(2-v)N}{4(1-v)} \left(2 - \frac{4(1-v)}{(2-v)^2} y - 2\sqrt{1 - \frac{4(1-v)}{(2-v)^2} y}\right).$$
(5.18)

Some undergraduate mathematics now becomes useful: using the expansion[7]

$$(1-x)^{1/2} = 1 - \frac{1}{2}x - \sum_{k=2}^{\infty} \frac{(2k-3)!!}{(2k)!!} x^k, \tag{5.19}$$

we have

$$g[y] = \frac{(2-v)N}{2(1-v)} \sum_{k=2}^{\infty} \frac{(2k-3)!!}{(2k)!!} \left( \frac{4(1-v)}{(2-v)^2} y \right)^k. \tag{5.20}$$

Comparing the coefficients in Equation (5.20) with the definition of $g[y]$ in Equation (5.13), the probability of finding an agent belonging to a cluster of size $s$ is given by:

$$\frac{sn_s}{N} = \frac{(2-v)}{2(1-v)} \frac{(2s-3)!!}{(2s)!!} \left( \frac{4(1-v)}{(2-v)^2} \right)^s. \tag{5.21}$$

It hence follows that the average number of clusters of size $s$ is

$$n_s = \frac{(2-v)}{2(1-v)} \frac{(2s-3)!!}{s(2s)!!} \left( \frac{4(1-v)}{(2-v)^2} \right)^s N = \frac{(1-v)^{s-1}(2s-2)!}{(2-v)^{2s-1}(s!)^2} N. \tag{5.22}$$

The $s$-dependence of $n_s$ is implicit in Equation (5.22), with the dominant dependence arising from the factorials. Recall Stirling's series for $\ln[s!]$:

$$\ln[s!] = \frac{1}{2}\ln[2\pi] + \left( s + \frac{1}{2} \right)\ln[s] - s + \frac{1}{12s} - \cdots. \tag{5.23}$$

Retaining the few terms shown in Equation (5.23) is in fact a very good approximation, giving an error of $<0.05$ per cent for $s \geq 2$. It hence follows from Equation (5.22) that

$$n_s \approx \left( \frac{(2-v)e^2}{2^{3/2}\sqrt{2\pi}(1-v)} \right) \left( \frac{4(1-v)}{(2-v)^2} \right)^s \frac{(s-1)^{2s-3/2}}{s^{2s+1}} N. \tag{5.24}$$

The $s$-dependence can be deduced as

$$n_s \sim N \left( \frac{4(1-v)}{(2-v)^2} \right)^s s^{-5/2}. \tag{5.25}$$

For small values of $v$, the dominant dependence on $s$ is found to be

$$n_s \sim s^{-5/2}, \tag{5.26}$$

---

[7] The 'double factorial' operator !! denotes the product: $n!! = n(n-2)(n-4)\cdots$.

which is exactly the behaviour observed numerically for the EZ model (see Fig. 5.4) and is also the behaviour of $n_s$ in the Cont–Bouchaud model. For large $s$, the power law behaviour is masked by the function in parentheses in Equation (5.25). The present results are valid when there is a spread in the size of clusters: for very small values of $v$, transactions are so infrequent that agents tend to crowd into one big cluster. The behaviour will be quite different when such a big cluster dominates. Note that the general technique described here can be applied to other problems. Related to the generating function are other similar functions such as the characteristic function, and the moment-generating function. As a general rule, one should try to work with the function that is most convenient for evaluating the quantity concerned: the general procedure for getting at the solution is then more or less the same.[8]

## 5.4   The percolation problem

The specific value of the exponent characterizing the distribution of cluster sizes (i.e. 5/2) suggests a connection to the percolation problem, which we will now explore. The percolation problem[9] is a geometrical problem related to connectivity. Take, for example, a two-dimensional (2D) square lattice on which a fraction $q$ of the sites are randomly occupied by black dots, as shown in Fig. 5.5. Dots on neighbouring sites are regarded as belonging to the same cluster. For small values of $q$, the dots are mostly isolated and hence form clusters of only one agent, together with a few clusters of larger sizes. As $q$ increases, larger clusters are formed. The 'percolation transition' refers to the occurrence of a connected path of dots from one side of the lattice to another, say from top to bottom. In the limit of large lattices, this occurs at a critical fraction $q_c$ called the 'percolation threshold', the precise value of which depends on the lattice type and geometric dimension. For one-dimensional (1D) systems, $q_c = 1$ since any missing dot in a 1D array interrupts the path from one end to another. For a 2D square lattice, $q_c \simeq 0.593$. At $q_c$, dots in the connected path form an infinitely connected cluster, with the remaining dots forming clusters of various sizes. Right at $q_c$, it has been found that the distribution of cluster sizes $n_s$ follows a power law of the form $n_s \sim s^{-\tau}$, where $\tau$ is the exponent conventionally used in percolation theory to characterize the cluster-size distribution. The value of $\tau$ depends only on the geometric dimension of the system and is independent of other details, for example,

---

[8]  See also D'Hulst, R. and Rodgers, G. J. (2000) *Int. J. Theor. Appl. Finance* **3**, 609; Xie, Y., Wang, B. H., Quan, H. J., Yang, W. S., and Hui, P. M. (2002) *Phys. Rev. E* **65**, 046130.

[9]  See, for example, Stauffer, D. and Aharony, A. (1994) *Introduction to Percolation Theory*. Taylor and Francis, London.

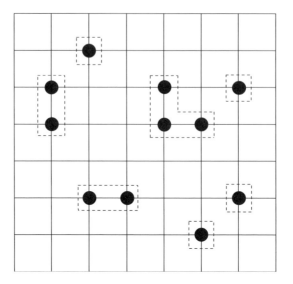

**Fig. 5.5** Schematic diagram showing cluster formation on a 2D lattice. Dots represent agents and the dashed lines grouping these agents represent the extent of clusters.

lattice types. For 2D $\tau \approx 2$, while for dimensions higher than six (which is the 'upper critical dimension' of the percolation problem) we have $\tau = 5/2$.

## 5.5  Cont–Bouchaud model on a lattice

The connection between the Cont–Bouchaud model, the EZ model, and percolation problem now becomes clear. Since there is no underlying lattice in the Cont–Bouchaud and EZ models, each agent has the chance to be connected to any one of the other agents in the population. Therefore, the number of 'neighbouring sites' is large—hence the Cont–Bouchaud and EZ models can be regarded as lattice models in very high spatial dimensions, for which the exponent $\tau = 5/2$ follows immediately. It would be interesting, therefore, to investigate the effects of putting the Cont–Bouchaud and EZ models onto a lower dimensional lattice. Although such a model might seem abstract, the lattice could be thought of as an ordered version of the population of traders standing on a trading floor: traders then can 'connect' to their nearest neighbours by talking, facial gestures, or eye contact in order to pass on an opinion. Stauffer and coworkers studied a series of models based on the percolation problem.[10] The simplest one goes as follows. In a 2D square lattice, a fraction $q$ of the sites is occupied. The occupied sites represent the agents. Agents occupying neighbouring sites form

[10]  See, for example, Stauffer, D., de Oliveira, P. M. C., and Bernardes, A. T. (1999) *Int. J. Theor. Appl. Finance* **2**, 83; Stauffer, D. and Sornette, D. (1999) *Physica A* **271**, 496.

a cluster with a common perception of the market. All agents within a cluster act collectively. They buy with probability $v_{buy} = v/2$, sell with probability $v_{sell} = v/2$, and remain inactive with probability $(1 - v)$. The limit $v \ll 1$ is typically considered. The price movements are again determined by the excess demand (as in Equations (5.3) and (5.4)), with each agent contributing the same amount.

In the simplest form of the model one simply generates a geometric configuration of agents on the lattice (traders on the trading floor) and then lets them trade randomly in accordance with the probabilities $v_{buy}$ and $v_{sell}$. Since $v \ll 1$, only one or a few clusters actually trade at any given timestep. The distribution of price movements is therefore expected to follow that of the cluster sizes. To analyse the statistics of this simple market model one should in practice average over many timesteps for a given geometric configuration, as well as over many independent configurations for given parameters $v$ and $q$. The power law behaviour in the cluster size distribution for the percolation problem near the percolation threshold, naturally leads to a power law in the price-returns with an exponent $\tau'$ equal to the exponent $\tau$ characterizing the cluster size distribution. We have then $p[z] \sim z^{-\tau'=\tau}$, which was also the case in the basic Cont–Bouchaud model. This model has been studied using hypercubic lattices in spatial dimensions from 2 to 7; the corresponding exponent $\tau$ varies from $\tau \approx 2$ in 2D to $\tau = 5/2$ for dimensions higher than or equal to 6. The resulting asset-return distributions are consistent with the fat-tailed behaviour of real financial asset returns as demonstrated in Chapter 3. Besides the fat tails in the price-returns, the percolation model can also be made geometrically dynamical (just as the EZ model is a dynamical version of the Cont–Bouchaud model) in order to reproduce the additional feature of volatility clustering. This can be achieved by allowing for a dynamical correlation between the connectivity of agents from one timestep to the next. The simplest way to do this is to allow a certain percentage of agents, say 1 per cent, to try and move to an empty neighbouring site after each timestep. This models the behaviour of information transport across, for example, a trading floor through the direct movement of traders. With this modification, the distribution of returns shows the same features as in the basic percolation models, with the same value for the exponent. In addition the resulting volatility shows, via its autocorrelation function, the kind of clustering effect seen in real markets (recall Chapter 3).

## 5.6    Variations on a theme

The cluster-size exponent $\tau$ leads to a power law in the distribution of returns $p[z] \sim z^{-\tau'}$ with $\tau' = \tau = 5/2$ in high dimensions (within the Cont-Bouchaud model, with or without an underlying lattice). However several modifications have been made in an effort to make the value of $\tau'$ larger, and hence closer to the values observed in real markets. In addition, the stochastic nature of these models implies that trading is noisy and prices may go up and up (or down and down) without any 'restoring force' to bring the price back to some kind of mean or 'fundamental' level. It is debatable whether such a fundamental price-level really exists in practice, but it could easily be incorporated into the model as follows. Instead of having the probabilities of selling and buying be equal, we may impose a higher (lower) buying probability $v_{buy}$ when the current price $x[t]$ is below (above) this imposed fundamental level $x_0$. Stauffer and coworkers introduced the form

$$v_{buy} = (1 - \varepsilon \log[x/x_0])\frac{v}{2} \quad \text{and} \quad v_{sell} = (1 + \varepsilon \log[x/x_0])\frac{v}{2},$$

where $\varepsilon$ is a parameter characterizing the strength of this fundamental price restoring-force effect. Note that $v_{buy} + v_{sell} = v$, and in the case of $\varepsilon = 0$ the basic model is recovered. Detailed numerical studies show that while the price time-series looks very different for $\varepsilon \neq 0$, the resulting price-return distribution and the autocorrelation of volatility are nearly identical to those with $\varepsilon = 0$ for lattices from 2D to 7D. Thus the stylized facts of this model are unaffected by the addition of this restoring force, even though the price produced is prevented from moving too far away from the imposed fundamental value.

For percolation models operating exactly at $q = q_c$, the exponent $\tau'$ follows the exponent $\tau$. However, there is no a priori reason why a market should know, and hence adjust itself, to behave as a system exactly at $q_c$. For $q \ll q_c$, the price changes will be small since only small clusters exist. As $q$ increases, larger price changes will occasionally arise. Hence sweeping from $q \ll q_c$ to $q = q_c$ can mimic the build-up of a speculative bubble wherein agents start forming larger and larger clusters of the same opinion. Numerical results obtained by sweeping a system from $q = 0.1$ to $q = q_c$ have shown that $p[z] \sim z^{-\tau'}$ over a range of $z$, with $\tau'$ in 2D enhanced by about 0.5 to reach $\tau' \simeq 2.5$, as opposed to $\tau' \simeq 2.0$. Another possible way to change the seemingly robust $\tau'$ value, is to consider a size-dependent activity $v[s]$. This is not unreasonable since, for example, large pension funds would avoid high risk investments, and would trade less often than small professional investors. Size-dependent activity has also been observed in the analysis of other economical data, for example, in the growth dynamics of firms and economies of countries. Stauffer and Sornette have proposed the form $v[s] = 1/\sqrt{s}$. This has the effect of removing the parameter $v$ from the model. With this size-dependent activity incorporated into the percolation model, the effect of sweeping towards $q_c$ gives an exponent of $\tau' \simeq 3$ in 2D. In all the models discussed so far, the change in the logarithm of price is taken to be a linear function of the excess demand as in Equation (5.4). Obviously the relationship need not be linear. In fact a non-linear dependence would also shift the value of $\tau'$.

## 5.7    Modified EZ models

The EZ model is characterized by the activity $\nu$ together with the mechanism for cluster coagulation and fragmentation. A cluster of agents dissolves with 100 per cent certainty after a transaction, and combines with another cluster with 100 per cent certainty if the cluster remains inactive. Under these conditions, the distribution of cluster sizes is then characterized by the same exponent $\tau = 5/2$ as in the percolation problem in high spatial dimensions. We will now demonstrate how the EZ model can be extended to give rise to model-dependent exponents for the cluster-size distribution, and how the generating function approach can be applied to describe the modified model analytically.

We will keep the essential structure of the basic EZ model here but with the modification that a cluster will dissolve after a transaction with a probability depending on cluster size, and it will combine with another cluster with a probability depending on the size of the two clusters involved. At each timestep an agent, say the $i$th one, is chosen at random. Thus, the agent belongs to a cluster of size $s_i$. With probability $\nu$ the agent—and hence the whole cluster since agents in a cluster share the same opinion—decides to make a transaction, that is, to buy or sell with equal probability $\nu/2$. After the transaction, the cluster is then broken up into isolated agents with a probability $f[s_i]$, which depends on $s_i$. With probability $(1 - \nu)$ the agent—and hence the whole cluster—decides not to trade. In this case, another agent $j$ is chosen at random. The $j$th agent belongs to a cluster of size $s_j$. The two clusters of size $s_i$ and $s_j$ then combine to form a bigger cluster with probability $f[s_i]f[s_j]$, but remain separated otherwise. With the choice $f[s] = 1$ the original EZ model is recovered. Analytically, this particular formulation of the fragmentation and coagulation process can be readily treated by the generating function approach discussed earlier.

This probabilistic cluster-formation process may even mimic certain aspects of behaviour in a real financial market. One such aspect is the effect of news arrival. Imagine that one of the agents is in a cluster of size $s_i$, which receives some external news at a given timestep with probability $\nu$. This external news suggests to the members of the cluster that they should immediately trade. Since the news is external, the cluster acts together in this one moment, subsequently the cluster has a finite probability of dissociation. The agents may sense that they are members of a large crowd (e.g. through their effect on the asset price); their probability of dissociation is therefore likely to be a decreasing function of the crowd size. The principle of this is that agents may like to feel the assurance of being part of a large crowd, as opposed to acting alone. By contrast, with probability $(1 - \nu)$ there is no news arrival from outside. The agent in the chosen cluster, uncertain about whether to buy or to sell, makes contact with an agent in another cluster of size $s_j$. The agents share information and

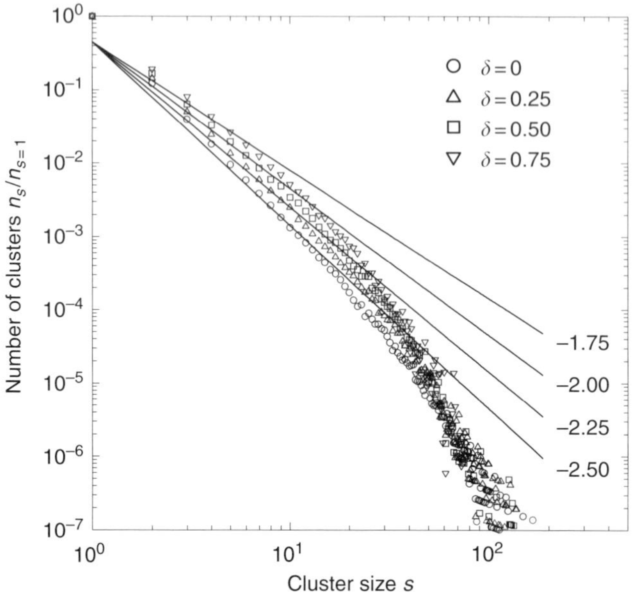

**Fig. 5.6** Cluster-size distribution for the modified EZ model with $N = 10,000$ agents, $v = 0.01$ and with $f[s] = s^{-\delta}$, for different values of $\delta$.

come up with a new opinion. Each of them then separately tries to persuade the other members of their cluster to accept the new opinion. With probability $f[s_i](f[s_j])$ the opinion of cluster $i(j)$ changes to the new opinion. Thus, the two clusters combine with probability $f[s_i]f[s_j]$.

To illustrate how particular forms of $f[s]$ may alter the exponent $\tau$ in the cluster size distribution, we consider the case of $f[s] = s^{-\delta}$. Figure 5.6 shows $n_s$ for several values of $\delta$. The solid lines are guides to the eye indicating that the exponent $\tau$ is described by $\tau = 5/2 - \delta$, and hence is now model-dependent. It follows that the exponent $\tau'$ of the price-returns also becomes model-dependent in this modified EZ model. Analytically, the master equations for the case of $f[s] = s^{-\delta}$ can readily be written as

$$\frac{\partial n_s}{\partial t} = -\frac{vs^{1-\delta}n_s}{N} + \frac{(1-v)}{N^2}\sum_{s'=1}^{s-1}(s')^{1-\delta}n_{s'}(s-s')^{1-\delta}n_{s-s'}$$

$$-\frac{2(1-v)s^{1-\delta}n_s}{N^2}\sum_{s'=1}^{\infty}(s')^{1-\delta}n_{s'}, \quad \text{for } s \geq 2 \tag{5.27}$$

$$\frac{\partial n_1}{\partial t} = \frac{v}{N}\sum_{s'=2}^{\infty}(s')^{2-\delta}n_{s'} - \frac{2(1-v)n_1}{N^2}\sum_{s'=1}^{\infty}(s')^{1-\delta}n_{s'}, \tag{5.28}$$

with the physical meaning of each term being similar to that for Equations (5.7) and (5.8). The steady-state equations become

$$s^{1-\delta}n_s = A \sum_{s'=1}^{s-1}(s')^{1-\delta}n_{s'}(s-s')^{1-\delta}n_{s-s'} \tag{5.29}$$

$$n_1 = B \sum_{s'=2}^{\infty}(s')^{2-\delta}n_{s'}. \tag{5.30}$$

The constant coefficients $A$ and $B$ are given by

$$A = \frac{1-v}{Nv + 2(1-v)\sum_{s'=1}^{\infty}(s')^{1-\delta}n_{s'}} \quad \text{and} \quad B = \frac{Nv}{2(1-v)\sum_{s'=1}^{\infty}(s')^{1-\delta}n_{s'}}.$$

Setting $\delta = 0$ in Equations (5.29) and (5.30) recovers Equations (5.9) and (5.10) for the basic EZ model. A generating function

$$G[y] = \sum_{s'=0}^{\infty}(s')^{1-\delta}n_{s'}y^{s'} = n_1\,y + g[y] \tag{5.31}$$

can be introduced where $g[y] = \sum_{s'=2}^{\infty}(s')^{1-\delta}n_{s'}\,y^{s'}$ and $y = e^{-\omega}$. The function $g[y]$ satisfies a quadratic equation of the form

$$(g[y])^2 - \left(\frac{1}{A} - 2n_1\,y\right)g[y] + n_1^2\,y^2 = 0, \tag{5.32}$$

which is a generalization of Equation (5.14). With $n_1 + g[1] = \sum_{s'=1}^{\infty}(s')^{1-\delta}n_{s'}$ and Equation (5.32), $n_1$ can be obtained as

$$n_1 = \frac{(1-v)^2 - v^2\,A^2\,N^2}{4(1-v)^2 A}. \tag{5.33}$$

Solving Equation (5.32) for $g[y]$ gives

$$g[y] = \frac{1}{4A}\left(1 - \sqrt{1 - 4n_1\,A\,y}\right)^2. \tag{5.34}$$

Following the steps leading to Equation (5.25), we obtain $n_s$ in the modified EZ model:

$$n_s \sim N \left(\frac{4(1-v)\left((1-v) + \left(Nv/\sum_{s'=1}^{\infty}(s')^{1-\delta}n_{s'}\right)\right)}{\left((Nv/\sum_{s'=1}^{\infty}(s')^{1-\delta}n_{s'}) + 2(1-v)\right)^2}\right)^s s^{-(5/2-\delta)}. \tag{5.35}$$

For $\delta = 0$, $\sum_{s'=1}^{\infty}(s')^{1-\delta}n_{s'} = N$ and hence Equation (5.35) reduces to the result in Equation (5.25) for the EZ model. For $\delta \neq 0$, it is difficult to solve explicitly for $n_s$. However, the summation simply gives a constant, and thus for small $v$ the dominant dependence on the cluster size $s$ is $n_s \sim s^{-(5/2-\delta)}$. This dependence on $s$ therefore agrees with the numerical results (see the discussion for Fig. 5.6).

It is interesting to extend the treatment to arbitrary, but properly normalized, forms of $f[s]$. In this case, we start with the master equations for $s \geq 2$ and $s = 1$ respectively:

$$\frac{\partial n_s}{\partial t} = -\frac{v s n_s}{N} f[s] + \frac{(1-v)}{N^2} \sum_{s'=1}^{s-1} s'n_{s'}(s-s')n_{s-s'}f[s']f[s]$$

$$- \frac{2(1-v)s n_s}{N^2} \sum_{s'=1}^{\infty}(s'n_{s'}f[s']f[s] - s(f[s])^2)$$

$$\frac{\partial n_1}{\partial t} = \frac{v}{N}\sum_{s'=2}^{\infty}(s')^2 n_{s'}f[s'] - \frac{2(1-v)n_1}{N^2}\sum_{s'=1}^{\infty}(s'n_{s'}f[s']f[1] - (f[1])^2).$$

The derivations can be carried out in a similar way as before, although the algebra is slightly more complicated. The dominant $s$-dependence turns out to be

$$n_s \sim \frac{s^{-5/2}}{f[s]}. \tag{5.36}$$

This result confirms that the exponent $\tau$, and hence $\tau'$, can be tuned by introducing a size-dependent fragmentation probability $f[s]$. Besides being proposed as a model for trading behaviour in financial markets, such modifications of the EZ model have also been proposed for the study of, for example, different methods for decision-making in a population with herd formation, and for the size distribution of customer groups and businesses.[11]

## 5.8   Other microscopic market models

We close with a brief discussion of two other interesting models which have been proposed in order to understand financial market behaviour.[12]

---

[11] See, for example, Zheng, D., Hui, P. M., Yip, K. F., and Johnson, N. F. (2002) *Eur. Phys. J. B* **27**, 213; Zheng, D., Rodgers, G. J., Hui, P. M., and D'Hulst, R. (2002) *Physica A* **303**, 176; Zheng, D., Rodgers, G. J., and Hui, P. M. (2002) *Physica A* **310**, 480.

[12] In addition, we encourage the reader to investigate the interesting model of Lux, T. and Marchesi, M. (1999) *Nature* **397**, 498, and the article by Farmer, J. D., 'Market force, ecology and evolution', see xxx.lanl.gov, adap–org/9812005.

### 5.8.1    Diffusion-reaction model

Bak and coworkers[13] proposed a model based on a population of $N/2$ sellers, each of which is holding one share of a stock, and $N/2$ buyers, each of which wants to buy a share. The population is a mixture of noise traders and rational traders, thus forming an inhomogeneous population. Each of the rational agents knows his own 'fair' price for selling or buying an asset ($y_i$ in the discussion of limit orders in Chapter 1), the value of which is based on his own perception of the value of the asset and the level of risk acceptable to him. The rational agents only trade when their own fair price is met. A seller sells when a buyer is willing to pay at a price that is equal to (or higher than) the seller's fair price. After a transaction, a buyer becomes a seller of the same character and vice versa. A population with pure rational agents will eventually evolve to a situation in which trading stops, when the range of buying prices becomes separated from the range of selling prices. The noise traders, by contrast, decide their selling price or buying price randomly within some preset range. Of course, they expect to buy within a lower range of prices and to sell within a higher range of prices. When their price is not met, they randomly change their expected price by one unit up or down. This random movement of the expected prices stimulates more transactions. After a transaction, a new noise buyer picks a price randomly within the range $0 \rightarrow x[t]$, where $x[t]$ is the current price, that is, the price of the most recent transaction. A new noise seller picks a price randomly within the range $x[t] \rightarrow x_{max}$, where $x_{max}$ is a preset upper bound on the stock price. The behaviour of a population consisting entirely of noise traders yields a non-trivial time-correlation in the price changes. The problem can be mapped onto a diffusion-reaction problem: the agents' buying and selling prices diffuse, and when the prices coincide a reaction (i.e. a transaction) occurs. The correlations, and hence the tail exponent for the distribution of price returns, can be modified by changing the behaviour of the noise traders in the mixed population. Note that these models describe trading in a financial asset through submission of *limit orders* to the market-maker. These models are thus in contrast to the microscopic market models described so far in this book, which consider trading via *market orders* only. Ideally, a realistic microscopic market model would incorporate the effects of both types of trading.

### 5.8.2    Small-world networks

The potential importance of herd behaviour in a range of human settings, has recently led to intensive investigations concerning the structure of connectivity

---

[13]  Bak, P., Paczuski, M., and Shubik, M. (1997) *Physica A* **246**, 430.

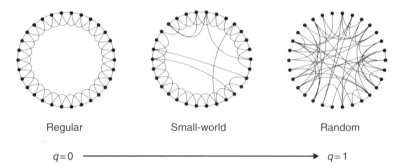

**Fig. 5.7**    A small-world network with $N = 30$ agents and $k = 4$, is obtained by randomly rewiring the connections in a regular world with probability $q$.

between members of a population (agents). One of the most interesting models is the *small-world network*.[14]

The construction of a small world network can be achieved as follows. For a population of $N$ agents, a 'regular world' of $k$ neighbours is first constructed by arranging the agents in a circle, that is, in a 1D chain with periodic boundary conditions. Each agent is then connected to his $k$ neighbours having the shortest possible separations. Figure 5.7 shows a regular world of $N = 30$ agents and $k = 4$. A parameter $q$ is then introduced which characterizes the geometrical features in the small world: in particular, $q$ is the probability that an existing link in the regular world is *replaced* by a link to a randomly picked agent in the population. To construct a small world in practice, we start with the regular world and scan through each of the links, replacing them by a randomly established link with probability $q$. For $q \approx 1$, nearly all the links are replaced and the resulting network is referred to as a random network or random graph (see Fig. 5.7). The parameters are chosen so that $N \gg k \gg \ln N$ hence there is typically no isolated site. For smaller values of $q$, we obtain what is known as a 'small world network'. It is important to note that 'small world' does not mean that the number of agents in the population is small, but instead refers to the particular geometrical connectivity established for $q \ll 1$. A small world network shows several interesting features. We discuss two aspects here. Consider an agent $j$ in the network having $k_j$ neighbours. Among these $k_j$ neighbouring agents, there are at most $k_j(k_j - 1)/2$ links. This is the limiting case where all the agents linked to agent $j$ are also linked among themselves. In a small world network, if we count the actual number of links in the cluster and divide this number by $k_j(k_j - 1)/2$, this will provide us with the fraction of all possible links actually established in the cluster originating

[14] Watts, D. J. and Strogatz, S. H. (1998) *Nature* **393**, 440; Watts, D. J. (1999) *Small Worlds: The Dynamics of Networks between Order and Randomness*, Princeton University Press.

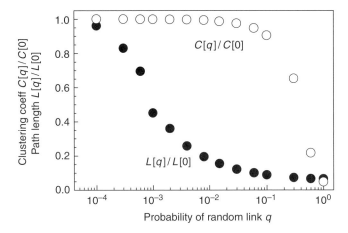

**Fig. 5.8**   The clustering coefficient $C[q]$ and the path length $L[q]$ in a network with $N = 1000$ agents and $k = 4$.

from agent $j$. Taking linked neighours as signifying trusted friends or 'confidantes', this link-fraction then reflects the extent to which friends of agent $j$ are also friends of each other. The clustering coefficient $C[q]$ is the average of this link-fraction over all the agents in a network. For $q \to 0$, $C \sim 3/4$ while for $q \to 1$, $C \sim k/N$ which is *small* in a population with large $N$. The clustering coefficient is a *local* property of the network that measures the 'cliquiness' of a circle of friends.

Figure 5.8 shows $C[q]/C[0]$ for the entire range of $q$ in a network with $N = 1000$ agents and $k = 4$. It is found that for a broad range of $q$, $C[q]$ is substantially higher than $C[q \to 1]$, and that $C[q]$ remains practically unchanged for small $q$ if the network is rewired. By contrast the path length $L[q]$, which is the number of edges in the shortest possible path between two vertices when all possible pairs of vertices are averaged over, shows very different behaviour. For $q \to 0$ we have $L \sim N/2k$, which is large for a big population. For $q \to 1$ we have $L \sim \ln N$. The path length is a *global* property that reflects the average number of friendships in the shortest path connecting two agents. For example, think of someone that you would like to know. It turns out that he or she will be a friend of your friend's friend, and so on. One might expect that the behaviour of $L[q]$ would follow that of $C[q]$. However it turns out that $L[q]$ behaves quite differently (see Fig. 5.8). In the range of small but increasing $q$ for which $C[q]$ remains unchanged, $L[q]$ drops quite rapidly. The network, through probabilistic rewiring, is effective in establishing links between different agents: a few connections could take you to any one you may want to know. It is a small world after all! The difference in the behaviour of $C[q]$ and $L[q]$ indicates that the transition to a small world cannot be detected just by looking at a local property of the network. A small world network is, therefore, characterized by its high clustering coefficient and small characteristic path length. It turns out that real world networks such as the networks of film actors, power grids, and even networks of terrorists, show features that are consistent with a small world, and cannot be explained using either a regular network ($q = 0$) or a random graph ($q = 1$).

The role of such small-world networks in the financial world is yet to be fully explored. For example, one could look at connections between agents, or common shareholders in different companies, or different market sectors and geographical regions, or different financial instruments, or even different financial news sources. Most importantly for the present discussion, the geometrical connection between agents in a small world would be different from that based on percolation models. Since financial markets involve the transmission of information and opinion sharing over a large network of agents, the rich and complicated connectivity among the agents in a small world network could have profound effects on herding behaviour and hence on the resulting financial market dynamics.

As suggested at the beginning of this chapter, the ultimate prize probably lies with joining together the key elements of Chapters 4 and 5, such that agents have access to both global information *and* in addition have the possibility to form local, possibly temporary, networks. Not only would this be of great potential interest for understanding the financial system as a whole, but also for a wide range of other complex system applications. This fascinating prospect awaits future research.

# 6.   Non-zero risk in the real world

## 6.1   The other side of derivatives

In Chapter 2, we looked at how an investor might use derivatives to manage risk. In order for the Black–Scholes pricing theory to work, we needed to make several major assumptions about how financial markets behave. Here we re-visit the whole question of risk and derivatives for real-world markets, without automatically making these assumptions. Consequently, the formalism in this chapter is more complicated than Chapter 2: we therefore present it in a pedagogical manner while emphasizing the practical steps that one needs to take to implement it. The formalism is built upon the landmark work of Bouchaud and Sornette.[1] However, we take things further: in addition to discussing the practical implementation of their inherently non-Black–Scholes scheme, we also address the crucial issue of managing portfolios in the presence of non-zero transaction costs. But we should first start by re-examining the whole topic of derivative pricing and risk. Consider the following example scenario:

> An investor predicts that the price of asset A will increase significantly over the next three months. He therefore buys a large amount of the asset, hoping to sell it back at a profit after that period. The investor can insure his position by also buying an equal quantity of put options dated three months in the future, with a strike price equal to today's asset value. Even if the investor is wrong and asset A falls in value, he will be able to 'unwind' his unfavourable position by selling the assets to the option writer at the same value as he bought them. Hence the investor will only suffer a loss equal to the original put option value, which is essentially his insurance premium on the investment.

Hence the investor holding the portfolio of assets A and the put options, can be sure that his portfolio will not lose more than the original option value. However, the position

[1] Bouchaud, J. P. and Sornette, D. (1994) *Journal de Physique I*, **4**, 863. See also Bouchaud and Potters (2000).

for the *writer* of those options is reversed: the maximum possible achievable profit is the original option value while a large loss could be faced. This can be seen from the payoff function for the put option:[2]

$$\text{payoff} = V_T[x_T, X] = \max[X - x_T, 0]. \tag{6.1}$$

In the event that the price of the underlying asset at expiry is less than the strike price $(x_T < X)$, Fig. 6.1 shows that the writer of the option could be faced with a large payout to the holder. Let us denote $p[x_t | x_0]$ as the conditional probability distribution function (PDF), such that $p[x_t | x_0]\mathrm{d}x_t$ is the probability that the underlying asset price[3] at time $t$ is in the range $x_t \rightarrow x_t + \mathrm{d}x_t$, given that the asset price at the time of writing the contract was $x_0$. We can then calculate the distribution of the option writer's profit or loss on the contract at expiry, that is, his 'variation of wealth' $\Delta W_T$, as follows. We know that the option writer gets to keep the initial option value (the insurance premium) whatever the asset price does. Additionally he has to pay out $V_T[x_T, X]$ if $x_T \leq X$. Hence, using Equation (6.1):

$$\Delta W_T = \begin{matrix} V_0[x_0, X, T], & x_T \geq X; \\ V_0[x_0, X, T] - (X - x_T), & x_T \leq X. \end{matrix} \tag{6.2}$$

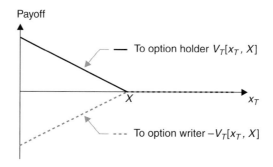

**Fig. 6.1**  Put option payoff at expiry for the option contract holder and writer.

---

[2] Recall from Chapter 2 that we denote the value of an option at time $t$ since the contract was written as $V_t$. Hence, $V_0$ is the option premium and $V_T$ the option payout. Also as before, $X$ is the option 'exercise' or 'strike' price and $T$ is the maturity.

[3] To simplify the appearance of formulae in this chapter, we will use $x_t$ instead of $x[t]$ to denote the asset price at time $t$. Hence $x_t \equiv x[t]$.

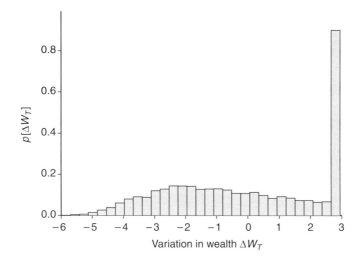

**Fig. 6.2**   Histogram representing the probability distribution function (PDF) of the variation of wealth $p[\Delta W_T]$ resulting from a Monte-Carlo simulation of writing 5000 put options with parameters $x_0 = 8$, $X = 10$, $T = 100$ with an interest rate $r = 0$. The PDF of the underlying asset's price movement[4] $p[R_{t,t-1}]$ was taken to be lognormal with volatility $\sigma = 5\%$.

The PDF for variations of the option writer's wealth is given by:

$$p[\Delta W_T > V_0[x_0, X, T]] = 0,$$

$$p[\Delta W_T = V_0[x_0, X, T]] = \int_X^\infty p[x_T \,|\, x_0] \mathrm{d}x_T, \qquad (6.3)$$

$$p[\Delta W_T = y < V_0[x_0, X, T]] \mathrm{d}\Delta W_T = p[x_T = (y - V_0[x_0, X, T] + X) \,|\, x_0] \mathrm{d}x_T.$$

A histogram showing an example of $p[\Delta W_T]$ is shown in Fig. 6.2.

## 6.2   Hedging to reduce risk

As demonstrated above, the position of an option writer is one in which large potential losses may arise. This is why option writers hedge their position by strategically buying a certain quantity $\phi[x_t, t]$ of the underlying asset. Take the example scenario in which

---

[4]  $p[R_{t,t-1}]$ is the PDF of returns, where the return is defined in Equation (1.3).

the investor buys put options:

---

A bank has sold to an investor a large quantity $n$ of put options on asset A with a strike price equal to the initial asset value $X = x_0 = \$10$. The options were sold at $V_0 = \$1$ each. The asset price falls to $x_{t_1} = \$9$ at time $t_1$, and the bank starts to worry it will have to payout on the option. It thus short-sells $\phi = n$ of asset A as a hedge. By the expiry time of the option, asset A has fallen to a value of $x_T = \$5$ and the payout to the investor is thus $V_T = X - x_T = \$5$. The option writer has made a loss on each of the options of the value minus the payout $V_0 - V_T = -\$4$, but has also made a profit on each of the hedging assets of $-(x_T - x_{t_1}) = \$4$. Overall the option writer has neither made a profit nor a loss: his variation in wealth $\Delta W_T = 0$. If the bank had not hedged, its loss would have been $-\$4$ per option.

---

This demonstrates how hedging can reduce the option writer's potential loss, essentially his risk. In this case, the bank made only one re-hedging at time $t_1$, deciding that they would prepare themselves for what they considered to be a certain payout to the investor at the time of expiry. However, in general, a bank would never be so sure about the outcome of an asset movement, hence it would be more reasonable to accrue the hedging position in smaller chunks, selling and buying the underlying asset when it became more or less likely that the payout would have to be made to the investor.

## 6.3  Zero risk?

By making assumptions about how an underlying financial asset will move, the Black–Scholes analysis of Chapter 2 shows how *in theory* it is possible to *never* lose any capital through writing an option, that is, the variation of the option writer's wealth always remains zero: $\Delta W_T = 0$ and hence 'zero risk'. With the confidence of this outcome behind them, banks are able to justify their exposure to huge derivatives portfolios—and the more derivatives contracts, the more commissions. So what then are the magic ingredients of this theory that guarantee zero risk? Let us recall the main assumptions:

- Continuous time: continuous trading
- Efficient markets: no-arbitrage
- Underlying assets follow a random walk.

These assumptions are questionable for the reasons discussed earlier in this book. However, the one which stands out most in the context of hedging is the first—the assumption of continuous time and hence continuous trading—since it implies the use of a strategy for *continuous* re-hedging. This does not simply mean re-hedging every time the asset price moves: it actually means re-hedging every time *time itself moves*, which is impossible. In addition, the presence of transaction costs gives rise to a financial barrier to high-frequency trading: the greater the number of re-hedgings, the greater the cost to the bank. Presumably there will be a trade-off that banks have to make: the more they re-hedge, the closer they will approach the zero-risk limit—however, the cost of their transactions will imply more expensive options which in turn implies fewer customers. The third assumption—that of a lognormal[5] random walk of the asset price—is closely related to the assumption of continuous time employed in Section 2.4.3. Suppose that in an infinitesimal time $dt$, the asset return $dx/x$ has a PDF $p[dx/x]$ that is highly non-Gaussian. Then in any arbitrarily small but finite time interval $\Delta t$, there will have been an infinite number of trials of $p[dx/x]$. The Central Limit Theorem (CLT) discussed in Section 2.2.3.4 implies that for virtually every choice of $p[dx/x]$, the resulting distribution $p[\Delta x/x]$ should be Gaussian. However, as discussed in Chapter 2 and demonstrated in Chapter 3, the distribution of real asset price returns can be non-Gaussian up to very large time intervals $\Delta t$. Moreover, asset returns can show a non-negligible degree of higher order temporal correlations. The failure of the random walk assumption must therefore also impact on this result of zero-risk derivative portfolios.

## 6.4    Pricing and hedging with real-world asset movements

The fundamental question is: *If we cannot achieve zero risk, then how much risk do we actually have and how can it be minimized?* With news concerning large financial losses and inadequate risk control arriving increasingly often in the media, and the requirements of the international Basel II agreement needing to be implemented, these are questions which banks are increasingly keen to answer. However, it is not obvious *how* to answer such questions. Perhaps adding on corrections to Black–Scholes? Unfortunately it is not easy to do perturbation theory around zero—and zero is the magical value of risk underpinning Black–Scholes. What is clear is that one must avoid making the same implicit initial assumptions as Black–Scholes, by instead going 'back to basics'. In the following sections, we will present such a back-to-basics approach, which focuses on minimizing the option writer's risk.

### 6.4.1    Variation of wealth

We start with the option writer's variation of wealth at the time of the contract expiry:

$$\Delta W_T = \text{value} - \text{payout} + \text{hedging profit.} \qquad (6.4)$$

---

[5] Equation (2.36) which was used to derive the Black–Scholes equation, is a lognormal random walk as opposed to Equation (2.34) which is a random walk. The only difference lies in the variable performing the random walk. In the first case, the variable is $dx/x$ which is the price return (Equation (1.3) in the continuous-time limit). In the second case, the variable is just $dx$. The distinction is unimportant. Typically $dx \ll x$ and hence the price-return $dx/x$ behaves like the price-change $dx$.

The *value* term comes from the cost of the option contract (the premium), which is paid by the holder to the writer at the time of writing, $t = 0$. The option cost is kept by the option writer irrespective of any subsequent underlying asset movement and is thus not a function of $x_{t \neq 0}$. The option cost $V_0$ is banked at the risk-free interest rate $r$ until time of expiry $T$, giving:

$$\text{value} = V_0[x_0, X, T](1 + r)^T. \tag{6.5}$$

The *payout* term comes from the payout which the option writer must give to the option holder at the point of expiry of the option $t = T$, and is thus the final value of the option contract. This *payout* must be paid to the option holder irrespective of any preceding underlying asset movement and is thus not a function of $x_{t \neq T}$.

$$\text{payout} = V_T = V_T[x_T, X]. \tag{6.6}$$

The *hedging profit* term comes from the profit or loss realised on the $\phi_t$ underlying assets, which are held by the option writer at time $t$ for the purposes of hedging. If the writer has not managed to obtain any information about where the asset price will be in the future based on past prices, then the quantity of assets he chooses to hold for hedging will only be a function of time and the current asset price, that is, $\phi_t = \phi_t[x_t]$. Without loss of generality, we formulate the problem in *discrete time* by writing $t = i\tau$ with $i = 1, 2, 3, \ldots$ etc.: later we will comment on the limiting case of $\tau \to 0$ corresponding to the Black–Scholes assumption of continuous time. Between two consecutive times $t - \tau$ and $t$, the option writer holds $\phi_{t-\tau}$ hedging assets: the profit on these assets is therefore $\phi_{t-\tau}(x_t - x_{t-\tau})$. However, the capital $\phi_{t-\tau}x_{t-\tau}$ held in the underlying asset could have been gaining interest at rate $r$. The interest lost in this period is thus $\phi_{t-\tau}x_{t-\tau}(1 + r)^\tau - \phi_{t-\tau}x_{t-\tau}$. Gathering together these contributions, we have the hedging profit from $t - \tau$ to $t$ equal to:

$$\phi_{t-\tau}((x_t - x_{t-\tau}) - x_{t-\tau}((1 + r)^\tau - 1)) = \phi_{t-\tau}(x_t - (1 + r)^\tau x_{t-\tau}).$$

At each timestep $t$, the option writer banks this hedging profit at the risk-free rate until expiry, giving a net variation in wealth due to hedging as:

$$\text{hedging profit} = \sum_{i=1}^{T/\tau} \phi_{(i-1)\tau}(x_{i\tau} - (1 + r)^\tau x_{(i-1)\tau})(1 + r)^{T-i\tau}. \tag{6.7}$$

Combining Equations (6.4)–(6.7) gives us an equation for the variation in the option writer's wealth at expiry:

$$\Delta W_T = V_0(1 + r)^T - V_T + \sum_{i=1}^{T/\tau} \phi_{(i-1)\tau}(x_{i\tau} - (1 + r)^\tau x_{(i-1)\tau})(1 + r)^{T-i\tau}. \tag{6.8}$$

So far we have made *no assumptions* about the actual movement of the underlying asset: $x_t$ could represent any arbitrary process. At the end of this chapter, we will include an additional contribution from the cost of transacting the underlying at each timestep $t = i\tau$. This contribution aside, Equation (6.8) is general. *If* we had made the Black–Scholes assumption of continuous time, which implies taking the limit $\tau \to 0$, then the summation would turn into an integral and Equation (6.8) would become:

$$\Delta W_T = V_0 e^{rT} - V_T + \int_0^T \phi_t \left( \frac{dx_t}{dt} - rx_t \right) e^{r(T-t)} dt. \tag{6.9}$$

However, we do not wish to make this assumption: the formalism does not require it and, amongst other things, we wish to investigate the effects of *discrete hedging* on the risk of writing an option. Discrete hedging simply refers to the process of changing the number of assets held to hedge the option, at discrete time intervals. Note that as written, Equation (6.8) treats the intervals between successive re-hedges as being of equal length $\tau$, but this need not mean the hedge must change at each time $t = i\tau$ because we can easily have $\phi_{i\tau} = \phi_{(i-1)\tau}$. Hence the regularity of the discreteness in time does not limit the applicability of the formalism.

We can now use Equation (6.8) to examine the risk of option writing under different schemes of hedging, different underlying asset movements and different option types (e.g. different payout functions). As an illustration, let us examine the distribution of variation in wealth for different values of the trading time $\tau$. As for Fig. 6.2, we simulate repeatedly the process of writing and (this time) hedging an option on an asset that moves with a random walk. We keep constant the option parameters such as the initial asset value $x_0$, the strike price $X$, the expiry time $T$, and the volatility of the underlying asset's movement $\sigma$. Instead, it is the 'realization' of the underlying asset's price $\{x_t\}|_{t=0 \to T}$, which changes each time we simulate the option writing and hedging process. 'Realization' refers to the specific evolution in time, which in this case is random (lognormal[6]). Figure 6.3 shows an example of five different lognormal asset price realizations.

For each re-hedging time $t = i\tau$ during the asset price realization $x_t$, the hedge $\phi_{i\tau}[x_{i\tau}]$ is calculated using the Black–Scholes delta-hedging recipe (recall Section 2.4.3). At the end of the realization, that is, at $t = T$, we use Equation (6.8) to calculate the overall variation of the option writer's wealth $\Delta W_T$. This process is repeated, and a histogram constructed of all the $\Delta W_T$ values. Figure 6.4 shows an example of such a 'Monte-Carlo' simulation. Each of the histograms was constructed for 5000 realizations of the underlying asset price movement. The four different histograms correspond to four different values for the trading time $\tau$.

---

[6] See note 5.

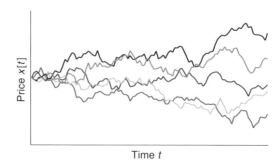

**Fig. 6.3** Five different 'realizations' $\{x_t\}|_{t=0\to T}$ of a random (lognormal) underlying asset price movement.

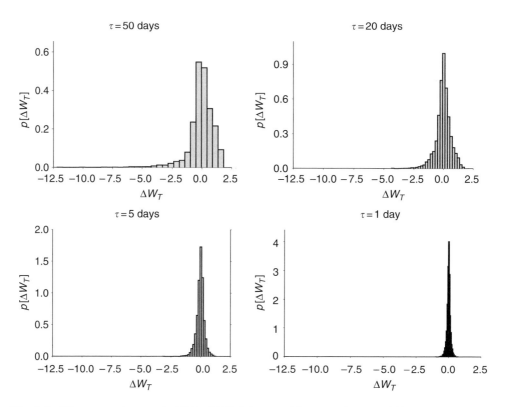

**Fig. 6.4** Histograms showing the PDF $p[\Delta W_T]$ due to writing an option with different frequencies of re-hedging. These results were produced using a Monte-Carlo simulation of 5000 underlying asset price random walks. The option contract considered was a European put with $x_0 = 8$, $X = 10$, $T = 100$ days, and $r = 0$. The option was priced and hedged in accordance with the Black–Scholes theory (Chapter 2). The PDF of the underlying's movement $p[R_{t,t-1}]$ was taken to be lognormal with $\sigma = 5\%$.

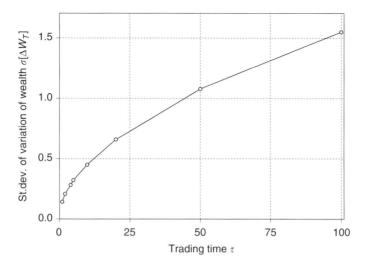

**Fig. 6.5** The standard deviation of the variation of the option writer's wealth $\sigma[\Delta W_T]$ as a function of the trading time $\tau$. The option contract considered was a European put with $x_0 = 8$, $X = 10$, $T = 100$ days, and $r = 0$. The PDF of the underlying's movement $p[R_{t,t-1}]$ was taken to be lognormal with $\sigma = 5\%$.

Figure 6.4 shows that as the trading time decreases (i.e. the frequency of re-hedging increases), the spread in the variation of wealth decreases. This means less risk for the option writer. Let us now examine this dependence of the risk on trading time more closely by constructing a graph of the standard deviation of the distribution for the variation in wealth $\sigma[\Delta W_T]$ as a function of the trading time $\tau$.

Figure 6.5 shows very clearly that as we decrease the trading time (i.e. increase our frequency of re-hedging), the spread in the distribution of $\Delta W_T$ drops markedly. In fact, the dependence of the standard deviation $\sigma[\Delta W_T]$ on trading time $\tau$ essentially follows a square-root dependence:

$$\sigma[\Delta W_T] \propto \sqrt{\tau} \tag{6.10}$$

Equation (6.10) carries the implication that as the trading time reduces to zero (i.e. $\tau \to 0$), the spread in the distribution of wealth variation $\sigma[\Delta W_T]$ also reduces to zero. This essentially recovers the Black–Scholes result, where continuous re-hedging using the delta-hedging strategy removes all of the stochastic variation from the option writer's portfolio, yielding zero risk. This is expected: our Monte-Carlo simulation was consistent with the Black–Scholes theory in that we modelled the underlying asset's price movement as a random walk, with $p[R_{t,t-1}]$ being lognormal.

We know that the random walk model for the underlying asset price movement, is not in general a good one (recall Chapter 3). What would happen if we made another choice for $p[R_{t,t-1}]$? Will the Black–Scholes recipe still work its magic of zero risk with continuous re-hedging? To answer this, we can repeat the Monte-Carlo simulation exactly as before, but this time using a slightly more realistic model for the underlying asset price movement. As a demonstration, we will use a process known as the Hull–White model for the underlying asset price movement. This belongs to a class of models having *stochastic volatility*.[7] Stochastic volatility refers to the fact that in the random evolution of the asset price,

$$dx/x = \mu dt + \sigma dX_1, \tag{6.11}$$

the volatility $\sigma$ *also* undergoes random evolution. In the Hull–White model, the volatility performs a mean-reverting random walk given by:

$$d(\sigma^2) = a(b - \sigma^2)dt + c\sigma^2 dX_2, \tag{6.12}$$

where $a, b, c$ are constants and $dX_1, dX_2$ are observations of uncorrelated Gaussian variables with zero mean and variance proportional to $dt$. Our main concern is not the price process itself, but rather to examine the risk of option writing when $p[R_{t,t-1}]$ incorporates some flavour of the 'stylized facts' observed in empirical price movements (recall Chapter 3). In particular, with suitable choices of $a, b, c$, the PDF $p[R_{t,t-1}]$ has a higher kurtosis (i.e. more peaked, with fatter tails) than the lognormal, as shown in Fig. 6.6.

Figure 6.7 compares the resulting dependence of $\sigma[\Delta W_T]$ on the trading time for the Hull–White model, and the lognormal price process from Fig. 6.5. Figure 6.7 shows a marked *increase* of risk for *all* trading times when using the more realistic Hull–White stochastic volatility model for the underlying. Most importantly, when we extrapolate $\sigma[\Delta W_T]$ back to $\tau = 0$ *we no longer get the zero-risk result of the Black–Scholes continuous delta-hedging recipe*. Followers of the Black–Scholes philosophy might claim that the delta-hedge clearly needs to be modified in light of the new stochastic differential equation governing the asset price movements. In fact, the Black–Scholes formula *can* be re-formulated for stochastic volatility models like the Hull–White model: tricks such as hedging the option not only with a quantity of underlying assets but also a quantity of other options, can be used to *theoretically* reduce the risk for continuous hedging to zero once more. However, here is the big problem for such Black–Scholes followers: in general, there is *no* such differential equation model, like the coupled Equations (6.11) and (6.12), which can adequately reproduce all the

---

[7] For a description of stochastic differential equations like Equations (6.11) and (6.12), see Section 2.2.5 and Wilmott *et al.* (1996). Although stochastic volatility models represent some improvement over a straightforward random walk, they still cannot capture all the higher order temporal correlations and scaling properties found in Chapter 3 for real market data.

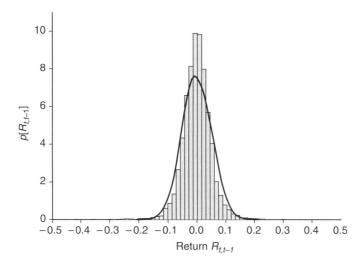

**Fig. 6.6**   PDF of returns $p[R_{t,t-1}]$ for a Hull–White stochastic volatility model and a lognormal model. The histogram represents the Hull–White model with $a = 0.05$, $b = 0.05^2$, $c = 0.25$. The solid line represents the lognormal model with $\sigma = 0.05$.

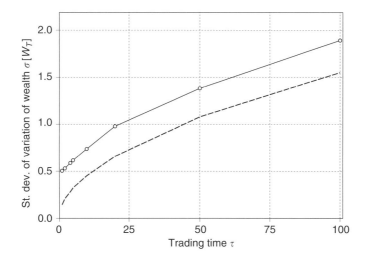

**Fig. 6.7**   The standard deviation of the variation of the option writer's wealth $\sigma[\Delta W_T]$ as a function of the trading time $\tau$ for Hull–White (solid line) and lognormal (dashed line) asset models. The option contract considered was a European put with $x_0 = 8$, $X = 10$, $T = 100$ days, $r = 0$, and $\sigma = 5\%$.

important features of the financial market price-series of interest. So how can one even start to generalize Black–Scholes under these conditions? As suggested by the discussions in Chapters 2 and 3, the 'no model' situation will be the rule rather than the exception. Hence we need to move to the next stage of Bouchaud and Sornette's formalism. We already have a general analytical formula for calculating the variation of the option writer's wealth: now we want to see what happens when we average over all possible *real-world* realizations. This will give us an expression for the *real-world option price*, that is, an option price formula in the absence of a local-time differential model for the asset price evolution.

### 6.4.2    Price for a real-world option

Instead of using a particular model for the underlying, we just consider the financial data itself in order to obtain the option price. We first simplify Equation (6.8) for the variation of the option writer's wealth, by assuming that the risk-free interest rate $r = 0$. This approximation is simply a shift of 'reference frame': we are moving everything to a world where the current value of cash is equal to the future value.[8] We do not *need* to make this approximation here, but the resulting mathematics is made far clearer with it. Hence Equation (6.8) becomes

$$\Delta W_T = V_0 - V_T + \sum_{i=0}^{T/\tau-1} \phi_{i\tau}(x_{(i+1)\tau} - x_{i\tau}), \tag{6.13}$$

where for convenience we have re-defined $i \to i+1$, which changes nothing. Now let us find the mean at $t = 0$ of this variation in wealth over all possible realizations of the underlying asset's price movement $\{x_t\}|_{t=0 \to T}$ during the lifetime of the option, that is, $\langle \Delta W_T \rangle_{x_0,...,x_T}$. We average over Equation (6.13), making the substitution $t = i\tau$ to make the result easier to read:

$$\langle \Delta W_T \rangle_{x_0,...,x_T} = V_0[x_0, X, T] - \langle V_T[x_T, X] \rangle_{x_T} + \sum_{t/\tau=0}^{T/\tau-1} \langle \phi_t[x_t](x_{t+\tau} - x_t) \rangle_{x_{t+\tau} \mid x_t, x_t}.$$

$$\tag{6.14}$$

We have explicitly written out the functional dependencies of $V_0$, $V_T$, and $\phi_t$, to illustrate that the different terms depend on the underlying asset's price at different times: for example, the payoff function $V_T[x_T, X]$ only depends on the asset price at expiry. Equation (6.14) expresses the averaging over realizations $\langle \cdots \rangle_{x_0,...,x_T}$ as an averaging over just the explicit dependence of the term considered (e.g. for the payoff function we have $\langle \cdots \rangle_{x_0,...,x_T} \to \langle \cdots \rangle_{x_T}$). This notation is demonstrated in

---

[8] In fact at the time of writing, interest rates are low across the industrialized world, hence making this a very good approximation. We remove this approximation in Section 6.5.1.

Equation (6.15):

$$\langle f[x_t] \rangle_{x_0,\dots,x_T} = \int f[x_t] p[x_T, x_{T-\tau}, \dots, x_\tau \mid x_0] dx_T dx_{T-\tau}, \dots, dx_\tau$$

$$= \int f[x_t] p[x_t \mid x_0] dx_t$$

$$\equiv \langle f[x_t] \rangle_{x_t} \tag{6.15}$$

given that the asset price starts off from $x_0$ at time $t = 0$ with probability unity. For a term that depends on the underlying asset's price at more than one time, for example, $f[x_{t_1}, x_{t_2}]$ with $t_2 > t_1$, the averaging process of Equation (6.15) is expressed as:

$$\langle f[x_{t_1}, x_{t_2}] \rangle_{x_0,\dots,x_T} = \int f[x_{t_1}, x_{t_2}] p[x_T, x_{T-\tau}, \dots, x_\tau \mid x_0] dx_T dx_{T-\tau} \cdots dx_\tau$$

$$= \int f[x_{t_1}, x_{t_2}] p[x_{t_2} \mid x_{t_1}, x_0] p[x_{t_1} \mid x_0] dx_{t_2} dx_{t_1}$$

$$\equiv \langle f[x_{t_1}, x_{t_2}] \rangle_{x_{t_2} \mid x_{t_1}, x_{t_1}}. \tag{6.16}$$

We are able to express the averaging as in Equations (6.15) and (6.16), since the value of the function $f[x_t]$ cannot be conditional on the value of the underlying asset at any *future* time $t' > t$. Note that we have *not* yet made any assumptions regarding statistical independence. Unless otherwise stated, we will drop the explicit dependence of $p[x_{t+\tau} \mid x_t, x_0]$ on $x_0$, since $x_0$ is fixed throughout. The option cost $V_0$ is not a function of the underlying asset price at any point except $t = 0$. Since we assume that all asset price realizations $\{x_t\} \mid_{t=0 \to T}$ start at the same fixed price $x_0$, a function of $x_0$ alone is constant under the averaging process. Let us now expand the summand of Equation (6.14):

$$\langle \phi_t[x_t](x_{t+\tau} - x_t) \rangle_{x_{t+\tau} \mid x_t, x_t} = \langle \phi_t[x_t] \langle x_{t+\tau} \rangle_{x_{t+\tau} \mid x_t} \rangle_{x_t} - \langle \phi_t[x_t] x_t \rangle_{x_t}$$

$$= \langle \phi_t[x_t](x_t + \mu_t) \rangle_{x_t} - \langle \phi_t[x_t] x_t \rangle_{x_t}$$

$$= \langle \phi_t[x_t] \mu_t \rangle_{x_t}. \tag{6.17}$$

In the second line of Equation (6.17), we equate the average value of the underlying price at time $t + \tau$ (i.e. $\langle x_{t+\tau} \rangle_{x_{t+\tau} \mid x_t}$) to the asset price at time $t$ (i.e. $x_t$) plus a conditional drift term $\mu_t$. Figure 6.8 is a schematic diagram showing the position of this average value.

More formally: $\langle x_{t+\tau} \rangle_{x_{t+\tau} \mid x_t} = \int_0^\infty x_{t+\tau} p[x_{t+\tau} \mid x_t] dx_{t+\tau} = x_t + \mu_t. \quad (6.18)$

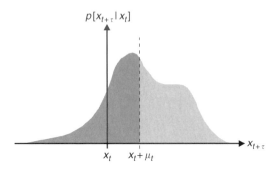

**Fig. 6.8**    Schematic diagram showing the position of the mean of the PDF $p[x_{t+\tau} \mid x_t]$. The two shaded portions have equal area.

However, under unbiased movement of the underlying asset price, the conditional drift term $\mu_t$ will be equal to zero. We are now going to make our *first major assumption*, that $\mu_t = 0$. This gives us: $\langle x_{t+\tau} \rangle_{x_{t+\tau} \mid x_t} = x_t$, and consequently, the summation term of Equation (6.14) is equal to zero. Later we will discuss relaxing this assumption to account for *biased* asset price movements. We can now go ahead and assert the principle of no-arbitrage, which basically states that the option should be written at a 'fair' price—hence neither the writer nor the holder will on average make any money from the contract:

$$\langle \Delta W_T \rangle_{x_0,\dots,x_T} = 0. \tag{6.19}$$

Combining Equations (6.14) and (6.19), we obtain the price of the contract $V_0$:

$$V_0[x_0, X, T] = \langle V_T[x_T, X] \rangle_{x_T} = \int_0^\infty V_T[x_T, X] p[x_T \mid x_0] \mathrm{d}x_T. \tag{6.20}$$

If, for example, we set the payoff function to be that of a European vanilla call, that is, $V_T[x_T, X] = \max[x_T - X, 0]$, then the option price from Equation (6.20) becomes:

$$V_0 = \int_X^\infty (x_T - X) p[x_T \mid x_0] \mathrm{d}x_T. \tag{6.21}$$

### 6.4.3    Implementing the real-world pricing formula

We have constructed a pricing formula for options *without* the need for an underlying asset price model. The only assumption has been that the increments of the underlying asset's price have zero mean. However unlike the Black–Scholes option price formula for a given payoff function, the pricing formula of Equation (6.20) is not in a 'closed-form': we cannot simply drop the formula into a spreadsheet and expect it to spit out a number. This has been a common criticism of the Bouchaud–Sornette approach: practitioners managing portfolios of thousands of contracts need a very fast pricing system. However, it is easy to be scared-off unnecessarily by the integral sign of Equation (6.20). It really can be a very quick process to numerically obtain the PDF $p[x_T \mid x_0]$ and integrate over it. We will demonstrate this with an example using real data. The dataset we will use here is the same as that analysed in Chapter 3: the daily closing values for the NYSE composite index which, at the time of writing, is freely available from http://www.unifr.ch/econophysics. Our analysis of this data will parallel some of the discussion of data analysis in Chapter 3. However, in contrast to Chapter 3 where we used the entire dataset to characterize the statistical properties, here we want to mimic the typical scenario faced in practice whereby the available dataset is not particularly large. Furthermore, we want to provide a step-by-step cookbook of how to implement the statistical analysis of this data in preparation for its use in the formalism, by contrast to the discussion in Chapter 3 which just focused on the end results of this statistical analysis. We will therefore be using a relatively small subset of data. Specifically, we will use daily data for the period 1990–98, instead of the entire record from 1966 onwards.

The first step is to use the series of prices to generate a series of returns over a time increment $\Delta t = T$, the expiry time of the option. This is achieved using the definition of returns (Equation (1.3)):

$$R_t \equiv R_{t,t-T} = \frac{x_t - x_{t-T}}{x_{t-T}}. \tag{6.22}$$

Let us consider a one-month (i.e. $T = 21$ trading days) European call option. Recalling our assumption of an underlying movement with no drift, we need to de-trend these returns by subtracting the mean, that is, $R'_t = R_t - \langle R_t \rangle_t$. Next we need to build a histogram of the de-trended return probability, in order to simulate the PDF $p[x_T \mid x_0]$. Most spreadsheets and analysis packages come with tools to do this automatically; however, the process is simple:

(1) Identify the minimum $R_{min}$ and maximum $R_{max}$ de-trended returns in the series;
(2) Define a bin-size $\Delta R = (R_{max} - R_{min})/\sqrt{n}$ as a guide, where $n$ is the length of the series;
(3) Define a function $n[R']$, which is the number of de-trended returns in the series $\{R'\}$ which have a value in the range $R' \to R' + \Delta R$;
(4) Calculate $n[R']$ at the discrete values $R' = R_{min} + j\Delta R$, for each integer $j$ in the range $j \leq 0 \leq \sqrt{n}$ and assume $n[R']$ is constant within the range $R' \to R' + \Delta R$;
(5) Calculate the frequency $n[R']/n$ for each bin.

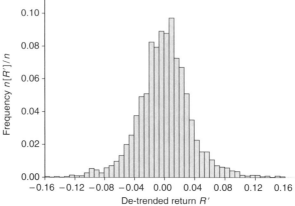

Fig. 6.9　Histogram of one-month de-trended returns on the NYSE composite index for 1990–98.

The histogram of returns looks non-Gaussian, as also found in Chapter 3 for the larger dataset. In fact, the kurtosis $\kappa > 5$ is well in excess of that for a Gaussian. This histogram of returns can be mapped to the PDF we require in the following way. We use the fact that $x_T = x_0 + x_0 R'$ to give

$$p[x_T \mid x_0]\mathrm{d}x_T = p\left[R' = \frac{x_T - x_0}{x_0}\right]\mathrm{d}x_T.$$

The probability $p[R' = (x_T - x_0)/x_0]$ can be obtained from our histogram (see Fig. 6.9). As $n[R']/n$ gives the frequency of occurrence of returns within a return-interval $\Delta R$, then the density of this occurrence is given by dividing by the interval length. In price space $(x_T)$, this interval length is $x_0 \Delta R$. Thus,

$$p[x_T \mid x_0]\mathrm{d}x_T = p\left[R' = \frac{x_T - x_0}{x_0}\right]\mathrm{d}x_T = \frac{n[(x_T - x_0)/x_0]}{n x_0 \Delta R}\mathrm{d}x_T. \tag{6.23}$$

This gives us a PDF of the form needed to calculate the option price: so let us now use it in Equation (6.21). First, let $x[j] = x_0(1 + R_{min} + j\Delta R)$. Then, using Equations (6.21) and (6.23):

$$V_0[x_0, X, T] = \int_X^\infty (x_T - X)p[x_T \mid x_0]\mathrm{d}x_T$$

$$= \sum_{j=0}^{\sqrt{n}-1}\left(H[x[j] - X]\frac{n[R_{min} + j\Delta R]}{n x_0 \Delta R}\int_{x[j]}^{x[j+1]}(x_T - X)\mathrm{d}x_T\right)$$

$$= \sum_{j=0}^{\sqrt{n}-1}\left(H[x[j] - X]\frac{n[R_{min} + j\Delta R]}{n}\left((x[j] - X) + \frac{x_0 \Delta R}{2}\right)\right),$$

$$\tag{6.24}$$

**Fig. 6.10**   The calculated real-world option price $V_0$ as a function of the strike price $X$ for a European call option of initial spot value $x_0 = 500$ and expiry $T = 21$ days on the NYSE composite index.

where $H[x]$ is the Heaviside function. We have used the fact that, due to our method of forming the histogram, the probability is constant in any bin. Equation (6.24) may look complicated, but it is really quite simple and fast to evaluate numerically since the number of terms in the sum (i.e. $\sqrt{n}$) is typically small. The results from pricing an option with initial asset value $x_0 = 500$, and our one month maturity $T = 21$, are shown in Fig. 6.10 for a range of values of the strike price $X$.

This general variation of call option value with strike price is as expected. What we really want to do at this point is to compare this generated 'real-world option price' with the Black–Scholes result from Section 2.4.3. Instead of just putting the two prices side-by-side, we will use the common trick in finance of running the Black–Scholes formula *backwards* from our supposed 'real-world option price'. We then solve for the Black–Scholes volatility $\sigma$ that *would* have resulted in this same price. This quantity is known as the 'implied volatility'.

Figure 6.11 shows the resulting 'implied-volatility smile' (though its shape is often more of a 'smirk' or even a 'frown'). This is the same type of result that one obtains from calculating the implied volatility from actual traded option prices, thereby giving us confidence in the new formalism.[9]

---

[9] As with all numerical implementations, the evaluation of Equation (6.20) described in this section has some intrinsic numerical error. This error arises from the discrete binning of the data when forming the PDF. Equation (6.24) approximates the lower limit of the integral in Equation (6.20) to the nearest bin. For simplicity, we suggested a number of bins of order $\sqrt{n}$. In general, the greater the number of bins, the more sensitive the calculation is to the finite nature of the dataset.

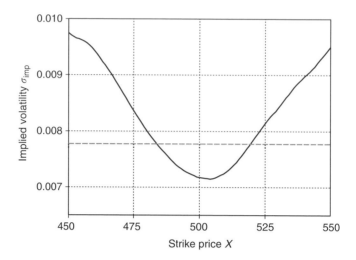

**Fig. 6.11**    Implied volatility as a function of option strike price for a European call option of initial spot value $x_0 = 500$ and expiry $T = 21$ days on the NYSE composite index. The prices used to generate the implied volatility curve were calculated using Equation (6.24). The horizontal dashed line shows the value of the historical volatility.

### 6.4.4    Quantifying the risk analytically

We now turn our attention to minimizing the *spread* of the wealth distribution, and in turn the option writer's 'risk'. We use the term 'risk' rather casually here to imply the uncertainty in the option writer's profit-and-loss situation. We want to keep our approach reasonably general, hence we will consider an adequate measure of uncertainty in an outcome to be an increasing function of the outcome's variance. With this in mind, the minimization of the outcome's risk becomes a minimization of the variance of that outcome. Since we are considering our outcome to be the profit or loss the option writer experiences, that is, the 'variation of wealth' $\Delta W_T$, we therefore need to minimize the variance $\langle (\Delta W_T)^2 \rangle_{x_0,...,x_T} - (\langle \Delta W_T \rangle_{x_0,...,x_T})^2$. We have already asserted however that $\langle \Delta W_T \rangle_{x_0,...,x_T} = 0$ by the principal of no-arbitrage (or equivalently setting a 'fair' option price), hence the variance of the option writer's variation in wealth at expiry is given by:

$$
\begin{aligned}
\mathrm{var}[\Delta W_T] &= \langle (\Delta W_T)^2 \rangle_{x_0,...,x_T} \\
&= \left\langle \left( V_0[x_0, X, T] - V_T[x_T, X] + \sum_{t/\tau=0}^{T/\tau-1} \phi_t[x_t](x_{t+\tau} - x_t) \right)^2 \right\rangle_{x_0,...,x_T} .
\end{aligned}
$$
(6.25)

Expanding Equation (6.25) gives six distinct terms. Remembering that the form of Equation (6.4) is

$$\Delta W_T = \text{value} - \text{payout} + \text{hedging profit}$$

leads us to treat these six terms one by one:

*value × value*

$$\langle V_0[x_0, X, T]^2\rangle_{x_0,\ldots,x_T} = V_0[x_0, X, T]^2 = (\langle V_T[x_T, X]\rangle_{x_T})^2. \tag{6.26}$$

The option price is given by Equation (6.20) and is constant over all realizations of the underlying price process. This is because $x_0$, which is constant for all realizations, is the only asset price on which it depends.

*payout × payout*

$$\langle (V_T[x_T, X])^2\rangle_{x_0,\ldots,x_T} = \langle (V_T[x_T, X])^2\rangle_{x_T}. \tag{6.27}$$

The payoff function is only a function of the underlying asset's price at expiry $x_T$, hence the averaging is over this price alone.

*hedging profit × hedging profit*

$$\left\langle \left( \sum_{t/\tau=0}^{T/\tau-1} \phi_t[x_t](x_{t+\tau} - x_t) \right)^2 \right\rangle_{x_0,\ldots,x_T}$$

$$= \sum_{t/\tau,t'/\tau=0}^{T/\tau-1} \langle \phi_t[x_t](x_{t+\tau} - x_t)\phi_{t'}[x_{t'}](x_{t'+\tau} - x_{t'})\rangle_{x_0,\ldots,x_T}$$

$$= \sum_{t/\tau=0}^{T/\tau-1} \left\langle (\phi_t[x_t])^2(x_{t+\tau} - x_t)^2 \right\rangle_{x_{t+\tau} \mid x_t, x_t}$$

$$+ \sum_{t/\tau \neq t'/\tau} \langle \phi_t[x_t](x_{t+\tau} - x_t)\phi_{t'}[x_{t'}](x_{t'+\tau} - x_{t'})\rangle_{x_0,\ldots,x_T}. \tag{6.28}$$

We first represent the squared sum as a double sum over the time labels $t$ and $t'$, and then split this into two separate parts: one where $t = t'$ and one where $t \neq t'$. We could then use Equation (6.16) on the second of these sums, but this gets messy for the general scenario. Instead we choose to make an assumption about the underlying asset's movement. This will be our *second major assumption*, that the price increments $\Delta x_{t,t-\tau} = x_t - x_{t-\tau}$ and $\Delta x_{t' \neq t, t'-\tau} = x_{t'} - x_{t'-\tau}$ are uncorrelated. With this assumption, the second sum in Equation (6.28) vanishes. We again use our first assumption, that is, $\mu_t = 0$, and perform the averaging over $x_{t+\tau}$ in the first sum:

$$\left\langle \left( \sum_{t/\tau=0}^{T/\tau-1} \phi_t[x_t](x_{t+\tau} - x_t) \right)^2 \right\rangle_{x_0,\ldots,x_T} = \sum_{t/\tau=0}^{T/\tau-1} \left\langle (\phi_t[x_t])^2 (x_{t+\tau} - x_t)^2 \right\rangle_{x_{t+\tau} \mid x_t, x_t}$$

$$= \sum_{t/\tau=0}^{T/\tau-1} \left\langle (\phi_t[x_t])^2 \int_0^\infty (x_{t+\tau} - \langle x_{t+\tau} \rangle_{x_{t+\tau} \mid x_t})^2 p[x_{t+\tau} \mid x_t] dx_{t+\tau} \right\rangle_{x_t}$$

$$= \sum_{t/\tau=0}^{T/\tau-1} \left\langle (\phi_t[x_t])^2 \sigma_{t+\tau,t}^2 \right\rangle_{x_t}. \tag{6.29}$$

In the second line of Equation (6.29), where we explicitly carry out the averaging over $x_{t+\tau} \mid x_t$, we use $x_t = \langle x_{t+\tau} \rangle_{x_{t+\tau} \mid x_t}$. This makes it easy to identify the integral as the variance of the distribution of the underlying asset price between times $t$ and $t + \tau$, which we will call $\sigma_{t+\tau,t}^2$.

$-2 \times$ *value* $\times$ *payout*

$$\langle -2V_0[x_0, X, T] V_T[x_T, X] \rangle_{x_0,\ldots,x_T} = -2 \langle \langle V_T[x_T, X] \rangle_{x_T} V_T[x_T, X] \rangle_{x_0,\ldots,x_T}$$

$$= -2(\langle V_T[x_T, X] \rangle_{x_T})^2. \tag{6.30}$$

The option price is constant, as given by Equation (6.20). The payoff is just a function of $x_T$.

$2 \times$ *value* $\times$ *hedging profit*

$$\left\langle 2V_0[x_0, X, T] \sum_{t/\tau=0}^{T/\tau-1} \phi_t[x_t](x_{t+\tau} - x_t) \right\rangle_{x_0,\ldots,x_T}$$

$$= 2V_0[x_0, X, T] \sum_{t/\tau=0}^{T/\tau-1} \langle \phi_t[x_t](x_{t+\tau} - x_t) \rangle_{x_{t+\tau} \mid x_t, x_t} = 0. \tag{6.31}$$

The option price is constant, hence is unaffected by averaging over realizations. We then used Equation (6.17) and our assumption of zero conditional drift ($\mu_t = 0$) to reduce the summand and hence the entire term to zero.

$-2 \times$ *payout* $\times$ *hedging profit*

$$\left\langle -2V_T[x_T, X] \sum_{t/\tau=0}^{T/\tau-1} \phi_t[x_t](x_{t+\tau} - x_t) \right\rangle_{x_0,\dots,x_T}$$

$$= -2 \sum_{t/\tau=0}^{T/\tau-1} \langle V_T[x_T, X]\phi_t[x_t](x_{t+\tau} - x_t)\rangle_{x_0,\dots,x_T}. \tag{6.32}$$

The summand on the right-hand side of Equation (6.32) contains the asset price at times $t$, $t + \tau$, and $T$. This means that we need to consider realizations that start at $x_t$, pass through $x_{t+\tau}$ and end at $x_T$. We evaluate this complicated conditional average in the following way:

$$\left\langle -2V_T[x_T, X] \sum_{t/\tau=0}^{T/\tau-1} \phi_t[x_t](x_{t+\tau} - x_t) \right\rangle_{x_0,\dots,x_T}$$

$$= -2 \sum_{t/\tau=0}^{T/\tau-1} \left\langle V_T[x_T, X]\phi_t[x_t] \int_0^\infty (x_{t+\tau} - x_t)p[x_{t+\tau} \mid x_t, x_T]dx_{t+\tau} \right\rangle_{x_T \mid x_t, x_t}$$

$$= -2 \sum_{t/\tau=0}^{T/\tau-1} \langle V_T[x_T, X]\phi_t[x_t]\langle\Delta x_{t+\tau,t}\rangle_{x_t \to x_T}\rangle_{x_T \mid x_t, x_t}, \tag{6.33}$$

where $\langle\Delta x_{t+\tau,t}\rangle_{x_t \to x_T}$ represents an average increment in a realization of the underlying asset's price evolution, which starts at price $x_t$ and ends at price $x_T$. The price increment $\Delta x_{t+\tau,t} = x_{t+\tau} - x_t$.

We now have all the terms in the equation for the variance of the variation in the option writer's wealth. We can finally put all these contributing terms (Equations (6.26), (6.27), (6.29)–(6.31), and (6.33)) together to give:

$$\text{var}[\Delta W_T]$$

$$= \left\langle (V_T[x_T, X])^2 \right\rangle_{x_T} - \left(\langle V_T[x_T, X]\rangle_{x_T}\right)^2$$

$$+ \sum_{t/\tau=0}^{T/\tau-1} \left( \left\langle (\phi_t[x_t])^2\sigma_{t+\tau,t}^2 \right\rangle_{x_t} - 2\langle V_T[x_T, X]\phi_t[x_t]\langle\Delta x_{t+\tau,t}\rangle_{x_t \to x_T}\rangle_{x_T \mid x_t, x_t} \right).$$

$$\tag{6.34}$$

Writing the averages in Equation (6.34) out explicitly gives us:

$$\text{var}[\Delta W_T] = \mathcal{R} = \mathcal{R}_c + \sum_{t/\tau=0}^{T/\tau-1} \int_0^\infty p[x_t \mid x_0] \Big( \sigma_{t+\tau,t}^2 (\phi_t[x_t])^2$$

$$- 2\phi_t[x_t] \int_0^\infty V_T[x_T, X] \langle \Delta x_{t+\tau,t} \rangle_{x_t \to x_T} p[x_T \mid x_t] \mathrm{d}x_T \Big) \mathrm{d}x_t,$$

$$(6.35)$$

where $\mathcal{R}_c$ is given by:

$$\mathcal{R}_c = \int_0^\infty (V_T[x_T, X])^2 p[x_T \mid x_0] \mathrm{d}x_T - \left( \int_0^\infty V_T[x_T, X] p[x_T \mid x_0] \mathrm{d}x_T \right)^2.$$

Equation (6.35) gives us an analytical expression for calculating the variance of the variation of wealth distribution. This variance measure can then be used in our chosen model for calculating risk.

### 6.4.5 Risk-minimizing hedging strategy

Our measure of the variance in the variation of the option writer's wealth, depends on the hedging strategy $\phi_t[x_t]$ which is adopted. It is now our objective to find a form for the hedging strategy which minimizes this variance, and hence our chosen risk measure. This is accomplished by means of a functional minimization of Equation (6.35). In practical terms, this corresponds to a simple differentiation with respect to the function $\phi$:

$$\frac{\partial \mathcal{R}}{\partial \phi_t[x_t]} = 0. \qquad (6.36)$$

Combining Equations (6.35) and (6.36) gives us:

$$\sum_{t/\tau=0}^{T/\tau-1} \int_0^\infty p[x_t \mid x_0] \Big( 2\sigma_{t+\tau,t}^2 \phi_t[x_t]$$

$$- 2 \int_0^\infty V_T[x_T, X] \langle \Delta x_{t+\tau,t} \rangle_{x_t \to x_T} p[x_T \mid x_t] \mathrm{d}x_T \Big) \mathrm{d}x_t = 0.$$

$$(6.37)$$

The simplest way to satisfy Equation (6.37) is to set the integrand equal to zero. This ensures that for any general choice of price process PDF $p[x_t \mid x_0]$, the equation will be satisfied and a minimum risk measure then assured. Note here that Equation (6.35) is an upward-curving parabola in $\phi_t[x_t]$ and hence a minimum (rather than a maximum) in the risk is assured by Equation (6.36). Hence:

$$\phi_t^*[x_t] = \frac{1}{\sigma_{t+\tau,t}^2} \int_0^\infty V_T[x_T, X] \langle \Delta x_{t+\tau,t} \rangle_{x_t \to x_T} p[x_T \mid x_t] dx_T. \tag{6.38}$$

Equation (6.38) gives us the 'optimal' hedging strategy $\phi_t^*[x_t]$. The strategy is optimal in the sense that it is the single strategy which minimizes the variance of the option writer's wealth, and hence our chosen measure of risk. We can see how much risk remains by using this form of the optimal strategy in Equation (6.35) for the variance. This gives us a 'residual risk' $\mathcal{R}^*$ given by:

$$\mathcal{R}^* = \mathcal{R}_c - \sum_{t/\tau=0}^{T/\tau-1} \int_0^\infty \sigma_{t+\tau,t}^2 (\phi_t^*[x_t])^2 p[x_t \mid x_0] dx_t. \tag{6.39}$$

The optimal strategy of Equation (6.38) can be simplified further if we make the *additional assumption* that the increments $\Delta x_{t,t-\tau} = x_t - x_{t-\tau}$ are independent and identically distributed (i.i.d.).[10] This means that the evolution of the underlying asset does not change behaviour during the life of the option. Under this assumption, we have:

$$\sigma_{t+\tau,t}^2 = \sigma^2 \tau, \quad \langle \Delta x_{t+\tau,t} \rangle_{x_t \to x_T} = \frac{x_T - x_t}{T - t} \tau, \tag{6.40}$$

where $\sigma$ is the stationary standard deviation of increments $\Delta x_{t,t-1} = x_t - x_{t-1}$. In Equation (6.38), this gives:

$$\phi_t^*[x_t] = \frac{1}{\sigma^2 (T - t)} \int_0^\infty (x_T - x_t) V_T[x_T, X] p[x_T \mid x_t] dx_T. \tag{6.41}$$

For the case of a European call option, Equation (6.41) gives the risk-minimizing optimal hedging strategy to be:

$$\phi_t^*[x_t] = \frac{1}{\sigma^2 (T - t)} \int_X^\infty (x_T - x_t)(x_T - X) p[x_T \mid x_t] dx_T. \tag{6.42}$$

### 6.4.6   Implementing the optimal strategy

The process of taking a set of real financial data and using it to generate a risk-minimizing optimal hedging strategy according to Equation (6.41), seems at first to

---

[10] It is possible that a weaker condition could suffice. Depending on the PDFs of price-increments, it may be enough that the increments are uncorrelated and have identical means and variances. For simplicity, we will impose the more general assumption of i.i.d. increments.

be similar to the process of implementing the option pricing equation. We have to construct the PDF $p[x_T \mid x_t]$ and calculate the variance of price increments $\sigma^2$. Although this seems straightforward following Section 6.4.3, there are some pitfalls when dealing with real financial data. These pitfalls arise mainly due to our assumptions about the data[11]: first that it has zero-mean and is uncorrelated, and then that it is i.i.d.

**6.4.6.1   Using real data.** Let us return to look at the data itself: the NYSE composite index daily values 1990–98, which we used in Section 6.4.3 to price an option. We will take our assumptions one by one, and test their validity for this dataset. Our first assumption was that $\mu_t$, the conditional mean of the increments $\Delta x_{t,t-\tau} = x_t - x_{t-\tau}$, was equal to zero (recall Equation (6.18)). Let us examine this by first forming the series of returns $R_t \equiv R_{t,t-1} = ((x_t - x_{t-1})/x_{t-1})$. The value of $\mu_t$ can then be calculated and compared to $\sigma$:

$$\mu_t \approx x_0 \tau \langle R_t \rangle_t = 5.1 \times 10^{-4} x_0 \tau, \quad \sigma \approx x_0 \sqrt{\tau \langle (R - \langle R_t \rangle_t)^2 \rangle_t} = 7.8 \times 10^{-3} x_0 \sqrt{\tau}.$$
$$(6.43)$$

Hence, for relatively small values of the interval $\tau$, the mean increment in the underlying's price is indeed much smaller than its fluctuations. Next, let us look at our assumption of uncorrelated increments in price: we used this assumption in quantifying the risk analytically in Section 6.4.4. We will calculate the linear correlation coefficient $\rho[x, y]$ defined for time-series $\{x_t\}$ and $\{y_t\}$ in a similar way to Equation (3.3):

$$\rho[\{x_t\}, \{y_t\}] = \frac{\langle (x_t - \langle x_t \rangle_t)(y_t - \langle y_t \rangle_t) \rangle_t}{\sqrt{\langle (x_t - \langle x_t \rangle_t)^2 \rangle_t \langle (y_t - \langle y_t \rangle_t)^2 \rangle_t}}. \quad (6.44)$$

We wish to investigate whether the increment in price at time $t$, that is, $\Delta x_{t,t-\tau}$, is correlated with the increment in price at an earlier time $t' < t$. We therefore examine the autocorrelation, that is, $\rho[\{R_t\}, \{R_{t'}\}]$, where $\{R_{t'}\}$ represents the series of returns $\{R_t\}$ shifted in time such that $t' = t - \Delta t$. Figure 6.12 shows the autocorrelation of the series of returns $\{R_t\}$ and absolute returns $\{|R_t|\}$.

Figure 6.12 shows that there is essentially no evidence of linear correlation in the returns series in our dataset. However, there is a significant degree of correlation in the absolute returns, as reported earlier in Chapter 3 (see Fig. 3.4). This correlation in the absolute returns only decays very slowly and is still non-negligible even after a whole year of trading. Similar results are found for longer increments $\tau > 1$. This then brings us to our assumption that the increments in the underlying's price $\Delta x_{t,t-\tau}$ are

---

[11] The attraction of the more general formalism developed in this chapter, is that these assumptions do not *need* to be made. The formalism becomes more cumbersome if they are not made, but the approach remains valid.

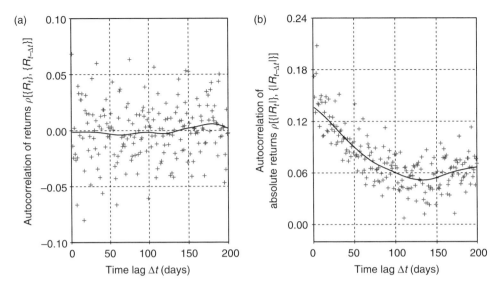

**Fig. 6.12** Autocorrelation of (a) returns and (b) absolute returns against lag time. Crosses represent empirical results and the line gives a moving-average trendline.

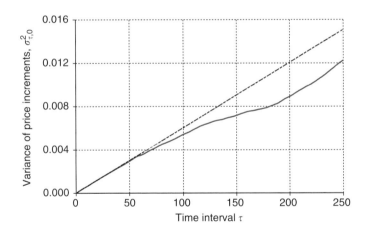

**Fig. 6.13** The non-linear growth of the variance of returns $\sigma^2_{\tau,0}$ as a function of time interval $\tau$ for the NYSE data (solid line). The dashed line represents growth for a random walk model, that is, $\sigma^2_{\tau,0} = \sigma^2\tau$.

i.i.d. We used this assumption at the end of Section 6.4.5 to simplify our expressions for the risk-minimizing optimal strategy. The presence of correlations in the absolute returns in Fig. 6.12, implies that the price increments are not i.i.d. In Section 2.2.3, we showed that for uncorrelated increments with identical variances (and hence for i.i.d. increments as well) we expect the variance to scale as $\sigma^2_{\tau,0} = \sigma^2\tau$. The numerical results for the NYSE dataset yield the graph shown in Fig. 6.13.

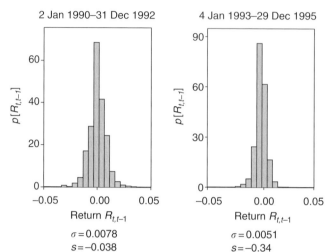
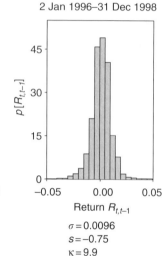

**Fig. 6.14** Histograms showing probability distribution function (PDF) of daily returns from three periods in the NYSE dataset. Under each plot are given the standard deviation $\sigma$, skewness (asymmetry) $s$, and the kurtosis (peakedness) $\kappa$.

As can be seen in Fig. 6.13, there is a marked departure in the real data from the i.i.d. prediction of linear growth of variance. However, this departure seems relatively small for increments $\tau \leq 50$ trading days. Let us also examine the stationarity of the PDF, since this is also part of the assumption of an i.i.d. price process. To do this we split our dataset into three roughly equal parts, each spanning three years. We then construct the PDF of returns $p[R_{t,t-1}]$ for each period by constructing a histogram in the same way as detailed in Section 6.4.3.

Although the three distributions in Fig. 6.14 have a similarly peaked, non-Gaussian shape, the shape parameters $\sigma$, $s$, $\kappa$ demonstrate that the distributions are actually quite dissimilar.

Having discussed the assumptions and their possible limitations, our job is now to develop insight into how deviations from these assumptions will affect our implementation. Recalling Equation (6.42) for the risk-minimizing hedging strategy for a European call option, we see that there are two empirical forms that we need to obtain from our dataset: $\sigma$ which is the standard deviation of increments $\Delta x_{t,t-1} = x_t - x_{t-1}$, and $p[x_T | x_t]$ which is the PDF. Let us start with $\sigma$. The standard deviation of price increments can be approximated as $\sigma = x_t \sigma[R_{t,t-1}]$, where $\sigma[R_{t,t-1}]$ is the standard deviation of the one-timestep returns. However, we need to be careful when dealing with real financial data. Although we made the assumption of i.i.d. increments in order to analytically construct the optimal hedging strategy, we have shown above that the real data exhibit some departure from this assumption. Let us explain why this might concern us here: consider a heavily 'in-the-money' option (i.e. $x_t \gg X$). We would expect that the writer's hedge would be very close to $\phi_t = 1$ since it is almost certain that the asset would be due to be delivered to the option holder at expiry. Let us use the substitution $x'_T = x_T - X$ in Equation (6.42):

$$\phi_t^*[x_t] = \frac{1}{\sigma^2(T-t)} \int_0^\infty (x'_T + X - x_t) x'_T \, p[x'_T + X \,|\, x_t] \mathrm{d}x'_T. \tag{6.45}$$

The limit $x_t \gg X$ gives

$$\phi_t^*[x_t] \rightarrow \frac{1}{\sigma^2(T-t)} \int_0^\infty (x'_T - x_t) x'_T \, p[x'_T \,|\, x_t] \mathrm{d}x'_T$$

$$\rightarrow \frac{1}{\sigma^2(T-t)} \left( \left\langle x_T^2 \right\rangle_{x_T|x_t} - \left( \langle x_T \rangle_{x_T|x_t} \right)^2 \right) \tag{6.46}$$

$$\rightarrow \frac{\sigma_{T,t}^2}{\sigma^2(T-t)},$$

where $\sigma_{T,t}^2$ is the variance of price increments $\Delta x_{T,t} = x_T - x_t$. Equation (6.46) would of course give $\phi_t[x_t] \rightarrow 1$ in this limit under the assumption of i.i.d. increments, because we then have $\sigma_{T,t}^2 = \sigma^2(T-t)$. However, if the real data deviates from the i.i.d. assumption[12] as demonstrated above, then Equation (6.46) will not give the desired limit of $\phi_t[x_t] \rightarrow 1$ for $x_t \gg X$. This incorrect evaluation of the limit of the hedging strategy can seriously affect further numerical calculations. One could correct the limit by choosing a value for the one-timestep volatility $\sigma$ given by:

$$\sigma = \frac{\sigma_{T,t}}{\sqrt{T-t}}, \tag{6.47}$$

where $\sigma_{T,t}$ is the volatility of price increments $\Delta x_{T,t} = x_T - x_t$. However, this misses the point that we used our assumption of independent increments to arrive at $\phi_t^*[x_t]$. If our data deviates from our assumptions, we can no longer assume that the hedging strategy of Equation (6.42) is at all 'optimal'.

Let us now turn our attention to the construction of the PDF $p[x_T \,|\, x_t]$. This is a distribution of price-changes over an interval of $T - t$ timesteps (in our case days). Recall our assumption from Section 6.4.5 that the distribution of price increments is identical for all $t$; if this were true, we would then only have to worry about the time

---

[12] See note 10.

interval of our returns and not the absolute times. We could therefore first generate a
series of returns:

$$R_{t',t'-(T-t)} \equiv R_{t'} = \frac{x_{t'} - x_{t'-(T-t)}}{x_{t'-(T-t)}} \tag{6.48}$$

and then, following the same procedure as Section 6.4.3, de-trend the returns ($R'_{t'} = R_{t'} - \langle R_{t'} \rangle_{t'}$) and bin the data to generate a histogram giving $n[R']$. We then could
construct our PDF by analogy with Equation (6.23) as:

$$p[x_T | x_t] dx_T = \frac{n[R']}{n x_t \Delta R} dx_T. \tag{6.49}$$

However, we saw earlier in this section that the distribution of returns was not in fact
identical for all times within our dataset. We therefore ought to use a sufficiently small
window of past times during which we believe the distribution is indeed stationary.
However, this has the associated problem that without a large amount of data, the error
in constructing the PDF is large. It seems therefore that we either should generalize our
assumptions to cater for the nature of the dataset we are handling, or use a 'surrogate'
dataset containing some of the features we observed in the real data, but lacking
the features which compromised our assumptions. We will follow the second of these
approaches below in order to illustrate the method, and return at the end of this chapter
to consider the effect of generalizing the underlying assumptions.

**6.4.6.2   Using surrogate data.** The basic aim is to construct a new dataset having
the same PDF of one-timestep returns $p[R]$ as the original dataset, but with i.i.d.
increments. We can then use this dataset in place of the original in an implementation
of Equation (6.42) since it will not break any of the assumptions we have made. We
generate the surrogate dataset as follows. First, we need to construct the PDF of one-
timestep returns from the original data. We follow the procedure of Section 6.4.3, by
first forming the return time-series $\{R_t\}$ such that:

$$R_t \equiv R_{t,t-1} = \frac{x_t - x_{t-1}}{x_{t-1}}. \tag{6.50}$$

Then we de-trend the data, $R'_t = R_t - \langle R_t \rangle_t$ and bin it between $R_{\min}$ and $R_{\max}$
such that:

$$p[R'] dR' = \frac{n[R']}{n \Delta R} dR'. \tag{6.51}$$

Having constructed $p[R']$, we need to sample it randomly in order to generate a
time-series of i.i.d. returns $\{R_t^{\text{surrogate}}\}$. We do this in the following way:

(1) define $p_{\max} = \max[p[R']]$, the maximum likelihood value of the de-trended
    returns PDF;

(2) choose a random number $r$ uniformly distributed between $R_{min}$ and $R_{max}$;

(3) choose a random number $p$ uniformly distributed between $0$ and $p_{max}$;

(4) if $p[R' = r] \geq p$, then append $r$ to the series $\{R_t^{surrogate}\}$;

(5) loop back to step (2) until $\{R_t^{surrogate}\}$ reaches the required length.

Once we have our surrogate i.i.d. time-series $\{R_t^{surrogate}\}$, we can compare it to the original de-trended returns time-series generated from the financial dataset. As required, we find that $p[R^{surrogate}] = p[R']$ and that the variance of the surrogate time-series $\sigma^{surrogate}$ scales as $\sigma_{\Delta t,0}^{surrogate} = \sigma\sqrt{\Delta t}$. Also, since we have generated each $R_t^{surrogate}$ independently, there will be no autocorrelation between any functions of the increments. However, since we have eliminated the subtle correlations in the financial data, we will lose the unique scaling behaviour shown in the original data-set. For example, if we look at how the kurtosis (peakedness) of the returns over $\Delta t$ timesteps scales with $\Delta t$, we find that the original financial data does *not* manage to decay to the Gaussian value of $\kappa = 3$ as suggested by the CLT, in contrast to the i.i.d. surrogate data (Fig. 6.15).

**6.4.6.3 Implementation.** We will now implement the optimal strategy. We will do this using the surrogate data since we have manufactured it to obey the assumptions we made earlier in the analytical formalism. We will discuss the optimization process for the original, non-i.i.d. data later on. The process of implementing the hedging strategy is similar to that of implementing the fair option price (Section 6.4.3). We begin by taking the surrogate time-series $\{R_t^{surrogate}\}$ and binning it to generate a histogram

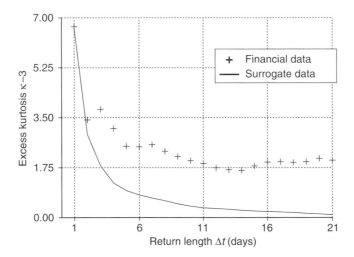

**Fig. 6.15** Excess kurtosis of returns over $\Delta t$ days. Crosses show anomalous decay for NYSE data. Solid line shows (power law) decay for surrogate time-series.

$n[R^{\text{surrogate}}]$. We then construct our PDF as:

$$p[x_T \mid x_t]\mathrm{d}x_T = \frac{n[R^{\text{surrogate}} = ((x_T - x_t)/x_t)]}{nx_t\,\Delta R}\mathrm{d}x_T. \tag{6.52}$$

Defining $x[j] = x_t(1 + R_{\min} + j\Delta R)$ and using Equation (6.52) in Equation (6.42), we arrive[13] at an expression for the optimal hedging strategy:

$$\phi_t[x_t] = \frac{1}{\sigma^2(T-t)}\int_X^{\infty}(x_T - X)(x_T - x_t)p[x_T \mid x_t]\mathrm{d}x_T$$

$$= \frac{1}{\sigma^2(T-t)}\sum_{j=0}^{\sqrt{n}-1}\left(H[x[j] - X]\frac{n[R_{\min} + j\Delta R]}{nx_t\,\Delta R}\right.$$

$$\left.\times\int_{x[j]}^{x[j+1]}(x_T - X)(x_T - x_t)\mathrm{d}x_T\right)$$

$$= \frac{1}{\sigma^2(T-t)}\sum_{j=0}^{\sqrt{n}-1}\left(H[x[j] - X]\frac{n[R_{\min} + j\Delta R]}{n}\right.$$

$$\left.\times\left(\frac{x_t^2\Delta R^2}{3} - \frac{x_t\Delta R}{2}(x_t + X - 2x[j]) + (x[j] - X)(x[j] - x_t)\right)\right). \tag{6.53}$$

Figure 6.16 compares the optimal hedging strategy—implemented using Equation (6.53) together with the surrogate data—to the Black–Scholes delta, at two different times during the option's lifetime. The forms of the two functions are similar as expected, but the risk-minimizing optimal strategy shows a markedly *lower sensitivity* to the underlying asset movement near the expiry time of the contract. At the start of the contract, the Black–Scholes delta-hedging strategy and the risk-minimizing optimal strategy are very similar. This is due to the fact that, with the i.i.d. surrogate data, the distribution $p[x_T \mid x_0]$ has become essentially Gaussian due to convergence under the CLT.

### 6.4.7    The residual risk

We have shown how to derive and implement a method for pricing and hedging options, based on just the historical underlying asset price data. The formalism we used[14] had the aim of minimizing the spread of the option writer's variation in

---

[13] We again consider a European call option as an example.    [14] See note 1.

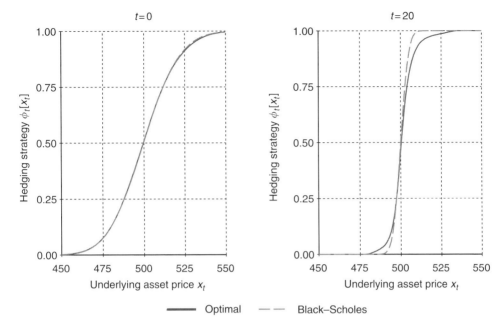

**Fig. 6.16** Comparison of the risk-minimizing optimal strategy (solid curve) and the Black–Scholes delta-hedge (dashed curve). The option is a European call option with strike $X = 500$ and expiry $T = 21$ days, on the NYSE composite index dataset.

wealth. We demonstrated earlier in Section 6.4.1 that in the general case, even if the option writer were able to re-hedge continuously, his/her spread in variation of wealth would be non-zero. Essentially the option writer's portfolio has a non-zero risk. In Section 6.4.5, we showed that this risk could be minimized with a suitable choice of hedging strategy leaving a minimum or 'residual' risk. We now examine the behaviour of this residual risk as a function of different option parameters. This calculation of the residual risk for a real financial dataset will involve a numerical implementation of Equation (6.39). Following the same method as Section 6.4.6 for the implementation of the optimal strategy, we arrive at:[15]

$$
\mathcal{R}^* = \mathcal{R}_c - \sum_{t/\tau=0}^{T/\tau-1} \int_0^\infty \sigma_{t+\tau,t}^2 (\phi_t^*[x_t])^2 p[x_t \,|\, x_0] \mathrm{d}x_t
$$

$$
= \mathcal{R}_c - \sigma^2 \tau \sum_{t/\tau=0}^{T/\tau-1} \sum_{j=0}^{\sqrt{n}-1} \left( \frac{n[R_{\min} + j\Delta R]}{nx_0 \Delta R} \int_{x[j]}^{x[j+1]} (\phi_t^*[x_t])^2 \mathrm{d}x_t \right)
$$

(6.54)

<hr />

[15] We use the surrogate dataset, since the expression for risk was generated with the same assumptions regarding the behaviour of the underlying asset.

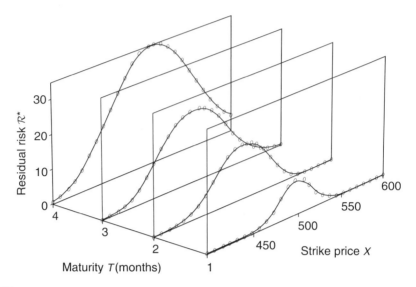

**Fig. 6.17**   Variation of the residual risk vs the two option parameters, maturity $T$ and strike price $X$. The option was re-hedged every day ($\tau = 1$). The initial spot value was $x_0 = 500$, and the data used to produce the risk-minimizing hedge was the surrogate time-series $\{R_t^{\text{surrogate}}\}$ generated from the NYSE data.

with $x[j] = x_0(1 + R_{\min} + j\Delta R)$, and with the returns to be binned given by $R_t^{\text{surrogate}}$. Unlike our earlier numerical implementations, the integral in Equation (6.54) must be evaluated numerically, since the form of the optimal strategy $\phi_t^*[x_t]$ for a given real financial dataset is not a simple analytic function (see Equation (6.53)). This makes the numerical calculation of the residual risk computationally intensive and subject to numerical error. Figure 6.17 shows the dependence of the residual risk on the two parameters of the option, the maturity $T$ and the strike price $X$.

### 6.4.8   Risk premium

In an efficient market, the prices of the same contract offered by many different suppliers should be the same. However, in practice this is not always the case. If the contract is risky for the supplier (i.e. the spread of his/her probable returns is non-zero), the supplier will tend to add a so-called 'risk premium' to the contract price. This seems reasonable, since it is generally accepted that people are 'risk averse': they view uncertainty as a bad thing, and thus require monetary compensation for accepting more uncertainty. However, the extent and manner in which different suppliers of a contract will judge this risk, can be very different: after all, there are many ways of assessing risk and hence calculating an adequate compensatory 'risk premium'. A popular technique involves using the variance of the portfolio in order to calculate a risk premium. For example, under certain assumptions the risk compensation described by Equation (6.55) can be arrived at either from a utility maximization argument, or from a Value-at-Risk (VaR) approach:

$$\langle \Delta W_T \rangle = \lambda \sqrt{\text{var}[\Delta W_T]}. \tag{6.55}$$

Here $\lambda$ represents the degree of risk aversion that the option writer desires. Equation (6.19) in Section 6.4.2, gave the 'fair' option price by setting $\langle \Delta W_T \rangle_{x_0,\ldots,x_T} = 0$. We now ask what would change if instead of simply using the no-arbitrage 'fair' condition for pricing, we used a risk-averse pricing scheme such as Equation (6.55). Recall the equation for the variation of the option writer's wealth $\Delta W_T$, in compact form:

$$\Delta W_T = V_0 - V_T + H, \tag{6.56}$$

where $H$ is the term corresponding to the gain or loss from hedging assets. We can express the variance of Equation (6.55) as:

$$\left\langle \Delta W_T^2 \right\rangle - \langle \Delta W_T \rangle^2 = \left( V_0^2 + \langle V_T^2 \rangle + \langle H^2 \rangle - 2V_0 \langle V_T \rangle - 2\langle V_T H \rangle + 2V_0 \langle H \rangle \right)$$
$$- \left( V_0^2 + \langle V_T \rangle^2 + \langle H \rangle^2 - 2V_0 \langle V_T \rangle - 2\langle V_T \rangle \langle H \rangle + 2V_0 \langle H \rangle \right), \tag{6.57}$$

where $\langle \cdots \rangle$ is our shorthand for averaging over all underlying asset price realizations $\langle \cdots \rangle_{x_0,\ldots,x_T}$. Cancelling and using the fact that for unbiased increments of the underlying asset we have $\langle H \rangle = 0$ (recall Equation (6.17)), we get:

$$\left\langle \Delta W_T^2 \right\rangle - \langle \Delta W_T \rangle^2 = \left( \langle V_T^2 \rangle - \langle V_T \rangle^2 \right) + \left( \langle H^2 \rangle - 2\langle V_T H \rangle \right)$$
$$= \mathcal{R}_c + \left( \langle H^2 \rangle - 2\langle V_T H \rangle \right) = \mathcal{R}, \tag{6.58}$$

which is exactly the same result as Equation (6.35). Hence,

$$\langle \Delta W_T \rangle = \lambda \sqrt{\text{var}[\Delta W_T]} \Rightarrow V_0 - \langle V_T \rangle = \lambda \sqrt{\mathcal{R}} \Rightarrow V_0 = \langle V_T \rangle + \lambda \sqrt{\mathcal{R}}. \tag{6.59}$$

Our risk-averse pricing scheme given by Equation (6.55) has simply resulted in an *additive term* to the earlier option price (Equation (6.20)). This additive term is proportional to the standard deviation in the option writer's variation of wealth. Interestingly, one could use Equation (6.59) to assess an option writer's degree of risk aversion based on traded market option prices $V_0$. This gives an idea of how 'expensive' the option is: the higher the risk aversion $\lambda$, the more the option will cost in excess of the 'fair' price $\langle V_T \rangle$.

### 6.4.9    Black–Scholes as a special case

The numerical results in Section 6.4.1 suggested that if the underlying asset's price movement *was* i.i.d. lognormal, *and* we hedged continuously with the Black–Scholes delta recipe, then the risk of the contract would vanish completely. Here we show that the formalism of Bouchaud and Sornette also predicts this miraculous result, but as a special case: in particular, for a special choice of underlying asset price PDF $p[x_{t_2}|x_{t_1}]$. This special form of PDF can be shown to be lognormal, normal, or quasinormally distributed. To reproduce the Black–Scholes formula, we will here assume a lognormal form for the underlying's distribution of returns such that:

$$p[x_{t_2}|x_{t_1}] = \frac{1}{x_{t_2}\sigma^{BS}\sqrt{2\pi(t_2-t_1)}}e^{-(\ln[x_{t_2}/x_{t_1}]+(\sigma^{BS})^2(t_2-t_1)/2)^2/2(\sigma^{BS})^2(t_2-t_1)}, \quad (6.60)$$

where $\sigma^{BS}$ is the Black–Scholes volatility.

**6.4.9.1    The option price.** We start by looking at the Black–Scholes option price for a European call option. Equation (6.21) gives this price as:

$$V_0 = \int_X^\infty (x_T - X)p[x_T|x_0]dx_T. \quad (6.61)$$

Now let us make the substitution $x_t = x_0e^{y_t}$ in Equation (6.61):

$$V_0 = x_0\int_{\ln[X/x_0]}^\infty (e^{y_T} - e^{\ln[X/x_0]})p[y_T|0_0]dy_T. \quad (6.62)$$

Now we use the return $R_t \equiv R_{t,t-1} = (x_t - x_{t-1})/x_{t-1}$ to give:

$$x_t - x_{t-1} = R_t x_{t-1} \Rightarrow e^{y_t} - e^{y_{t-1}} = R_t e^{y_{t-1}} \Rightarrow y_t - y_{t-1} = \ln[1+R_t] \approx R_t - (R_t^2/2). \quad (6.63)$$

Since $R_t \ll 1$, we have neglected terms greater than the second power of the return in the Taylor expansion of the logarithm in Equation (6.63). For Black–Scholes, the elementary probability distribution of returns $p[R_t]$ is Gaussian: hence from Equation (6.63) the PDF of $y_t$, $p[y_t|y_{t-1}]$, can be calculated using:

$$p[y_t = z] = \frac{\partial}{\partial z}p\left[R_t - \frac{R_t^2}{2} \le z - y_{t-1}\right]. \quad (6.64)$$

The mean of this PDF is $y_{t-1} - \frac{1}{2}(\sigma^{BS})^2$ and the variance is $(\sigma^{BS})^2$. We can now exploit the Black–Scholes assumption of continuous time to say that there have been an infinitely large number of increments $y_t$ in the time interval $0 \le t \le T$. The CLT then implies that the distribution $p[y_T|0_0]$ has converged to a Gaussian with mean

$-\frac{1}{2}T(\sigma^{BS})^2$ and variance $T(\sigma^{BS})^2$. Therefore, we can now calculate Equation (6.62) to be:

$$V_0 = x_0 \int_{\ln[X/x_0]}^{\infty} \frac{\left(e^{y_T} - e^{\ln[X/x_0]}\right)}{\sqrt{2\pi T}\sigma^{BS}} e^{-(y_T + T(\sigma^{BS})^2/2)^2/2T(\sigma^{BS})^2} dy_T$$

$$= x_0 \Phi\left[\frac{\ln[x_0/X] + T(\sigma^{BS})^2/2}{\sqrt{T}\sigma^{BS}}\right] - X\Phi\left[\frac{\ln[x_0/X] - T(\sigma^{BS})^2/2}{\sqrt{T}\sigma^{BS}}\right], \quad (6.65)$$

where $\Phi[x]$ is the cumulative normal distribution function. Equation (6.65) is identical to the Black–Scholes formula for the price of a European call option (see Equation (2.62) with $r = 0$). Hence, by inserting the assumptions about the underlying asset and continuous time into the present formalism, the Black–Scholes result appears as a special case.

**6.4.9.2   The hedging strategy.** We saw in Section 6.4.6 that when our data had almost converged to a Gaussian distribution in the limit of large time-increments, the risk-minimizing optimal strategy of the present formalism almost coincided with the Black–Scholes delta-hedging strategy. We now show that, given the Black–Scholes assumptions, the risk-minimizing optimal strategy analytically reproduces the delta-hedging strategy exactly. We start by recalling that the lognormal distribution of the underlying asset's price movement, which is assumed in Black–Scholes, is very well approximated by a standard Gaussian distribution if the underlying asset price is sufficiently large: in particular, $x_0 \gg \sigma\sqrt{T}$. We will use this as a simplifying assumption in what follows. We first take the Gaussian form of the PDF $p[x_{t_2}|x_{t_1}]$

$$p[x_{t_2}|x_{t_1}] = \frac{1}{\sqrt{2\pi(t_2 - t_1)}\sigma} e^{-((x_{t_2}-x_{t_1})^2)/2(t_2-t_1)\sigma^2}.$$

Then we differentiate to get:

$$\frac{\partial p[x_{t_2}|x_{t_1}]}{\partial x_{t_1}} = \frac{x_{t_2} - x_{t_1}}{\sigma^2(t_2 - t_1)} p[x_{t_2}|x_{t_1}]. \quad (6.66)$$

The risk-minimizing optimal strategy for a European call option, Equation (6.42), is given by:

$$\phi_t^*[x_t] = \frac{1}{\sigma^2(T - t)} \int_X^{\infty} (x_T - x_t)(x_T - X)p[x_T|x_t]dx_T. \quad (6.67)$$

Comparing Equations (6.66) and (6.67), we get:

$$\phi_t^*[x_t] = \frac{\partial}{\partial x_t} \int_X^{\infty} (x_T - X)p[x_T|x_t]dx_T = \frac{\partial V_t}{\partial x_t}, \quad (6.68)$$

where we have identified

$$V_t = \int_X^\infty (x_T - X) p[x_T | x_t] dx_T. \tag{6.69}$$

as the option price at time $t$, by comparison with Equation (6.21). Hence Equation (6.68) gives us exactly the Black–Scholes result from Equation (2.55), that the optimal hedging strategy should be $\phi_t^*[x_t] = \frac{\partial V_t}{\partial x_t}$.

**6.4.9.3    The residual risk.** All that remains to be done now is to show that by using the Black–Scholes pricing and hedging formulae, the risk of option writing disappears altogether. If we differentiate two Gaussian underlying price PDFs, using Equation (6.66), we get:

$$\frac{\partial p[x_{t_2} | x_t]}{\partial x_t} \frac{\partial p[x_{t_1} | x_t]}{\partial x_t} = \frac{x_{t_2} - x_t}{\sigma^2(t_2 - t)} \frac{x_{t_1} - x_t}{\sigma^2(t_1 - t)} p[x_{t_2} | x_t] p[x_{t_1} | x_t]. \tag{6.70}$$

Multiplying by $\sigma^2 p[x_t | x_0]$, and integrating over the intermediate asset value $x_t$ and time, gives:

$$\sigma^2 \int_0^T \int_0^\infty \frac{\partial p[x_{t_2} | x_t]}{\partial x_t} \frac{\partial p[x_{t_1} | x_t]}{\partial x_t} p[x_t | x_0] dx_t dt$$
$$= p[x_{t_1} | x_0] \delta[x_{t_2}, x_{t_1}] - p[x_{t_2} | x_0] p[x_{t_1} | x_0]. \tag{6.71}$$

Recall the form of the residual risk, Equation (6.39). The continuous hedging scenario, where the discrete sum turns into an integral as the step size $\tau \to 0$, gives:

$$\mathcal{R}^* = \mathcal{R}_c - \sigma^2 \int_0^T \int_0^\infty (\phi_t^*[x_t])^2 p[x_t | x_0] dx_t dt. \tag{6.72}$$

If we multiply the identity of Equation (6.71) by the payoff function, and use the fact that $\phi_t^*[x_t] = \partial V_t / \partial x_t$, then the right-hand side yields $\mathcal{R}_c$ while the left-hand side yields $\sigma^2 \int_0^T \int_0^\infty (\phi_t^*[x_t])^2 p[x_t | x_0] dx_t dt$. This implies that the residual risk becomes *zero*, in accordance with the miraculous Black–Scholes result. However, this result of zero risk is *not* general: if we had not assumed an underlying process that was a member of the Gaussian family of processes, *or* we had not assumed that we could hedge continuously, then we would *not* have found this special-case result. Indeed, one can show using the Euler–McLaurin formula for the difference between an integral and a discrete sum, that for small re-hedging times $\tau$, the residual risk is given by:

$$\mathcal{R}^* = \frac{\sigma^2 \tau}{2} P_{>X}(1 - P_{>X}), \tag{6.73}$$

where the cumulative probability distribution $P_{>X} = \int_X^\infty p[x_T | x_0] dx_T$ gives the probability that the option is exercised at the time of expiry. This *remaining risk is not in general small*: for example, for an at-the-money contract ($X = x_0$), we have (using the substitution of $y_T = x_T - X$ in Equation (6.21))

$$V_0 = \int_X^\infty (x_T - X) p[x_T | X] dx_T = \int_0^\infty y_T p[y_T | 0_0] dy_T = \frac{\sigma \sqrt{T}}{\sqrt{2\pi}}, \qquad (6.74)$$

whereas the residual standard deviation in wealth variation can be obtained from Equation (6.73) by using $P_{>X} = \frac{1}{2}$ for an at-the-money option:

$$\sigma[\Delta W_T] = \sqrt{\mathcal{R}^*} = \sigma \sqrt{\frac{\tau}{2} P_{>X}(1 - P_{>X})} = \sigma \sqrt{\frac{\tau}{8}} = \sqrt{\frac{\pi}{4T/\tau}} V_0. \qquad (6.75)$$

Hence, if we have a one-month contract that we hedge every day (i.e. $T/\tau \simeq 21$), then the spread in the option writer's variation of wealth is approximately 20 per cent of the option value. Of course with non-Gaussian underlying asset price processes, the residual risk is much higher and can *never* be hedged away: the differential form of the Black–Scholes formulation cannot take into account the large jumps a real underlying asset may perform, hence the option portfolio cannot be replicated perfectly.

### 6.4.10 Expanding around the Black–Scholes result

We now turn to look at the effect of *non*-Gaussian underlying asset price distributions, by expanding the PDF about the Gaussian. In this way, we will develop systematic corrections to the Black–Scholes results.

#### 6.4.10.1 Expansion of the option price.
We again consider a European call option. The 'fair' option price is given by Equation (6.21):

$$V_0 = \int_X^\infty (x_T - X) p[x_T | x_0] dx_T. \qquad (6.76)$$

Rewriting Equation (6.76) as

$$V_0 = \lim_{Y \to \infty} \int_X^Y (x_T - X) p[x_T | x_0] dx_T \qquad (6.77)$$

and integrating by parts, we have

$$
V_0 = \lim_{Y \to \infty} \left( \left[ (x_T - X) \int_{-\infty}^{x_T} p[x'_T \mid x_0] dx'_T \right]_X^Y - \int_X^Y \int_{-\infty}^{x_T} p[x'_T \mid x_0] dx'_T dx_T \right)
$$

$$
= \lim_{Y \to \infty} \left( (Y - X)(1 - P_>[Y]) - \int_X^Y (1 - P_>[x_T]) dx_T \right)
$$

$$
= \lim_{Y \to \infty} \left( (X - Y) P_>[Y]) + \int_X^\infty P_>[x_T] dx_T \right)
$$

$$
= \int_X^\infty P_>[x_T] dx_T. \tag{6.78}
$$

where $P_>[z] = \int_z^\infty p[x'_T \mid x_0] dx'_T$. In the last line of Equation (6.78), we used the fact that $P_>[Y] \to 0$ faster than $(Y - X) \to \infty$, which must hold to guarantee the correct normalization of the probability distribution. Hence, we have made the transformation of the 'fair' option price in Equation (6.78) such that we can now expand $P_>[x_T]$ around the Gaussian. If we make the substitution $y = (x_T - X)/\sigma \sqrt{T}$, we can expand around the cumulative Gaussian $P_{G>}[y]$ which has mean $z = (x_0 - X)/\sigma \sqrt{T}$ and unit variance. We expand in (rooted) powers of the number of timesteps between writing and expiry $(T/\tau)^{k/2}$ as:

$$
P_>[y] = P_{G>}[y] + \frac{e^{-(y-z)^2/2}}{\sqrt{2\pi}} \left( \frac{Q_1[y]}{(T/\tau)^{1/2}} + \frac{Q_2[y]}{(T/\tau)^1} + \cdots \right), \tag{6.79}
$$

where the functions $Q_k[y]$ are polynomials of the normalized cumulants[16] $\lambda_k$. The first two of these polynomials can be written as:

$$
Q_1[y] e^{-(y-z)^2/2} = \frac{\lambda_3}{6} \frac{d^2}{dy^2} e^{-(y-z)^2/2}, \quad Q_2[y] e^{(y-z)^2/2} = -\frac{\lambda_4}{24} \frac{d^3}{dy^3} e^{-(y-z)^2/2} - \frac{\lambda_3^2}{72} \frac{d^5}{dy^5} e^{-(y-z)^2/2}.
$$

$$
\tag{6.80}
$$

Now we can combine Equations (6.80), (6.79), and (6.78) to give:

$$
V_0 = V_G + \frac{\sigma \sqrt{T}}{\sqrt{2\pi}} \sqrt{\frac{\tau}{T}} \frac{\lambda_3}{6} \int_0^\infty \frac{d^2}{dy^2} e^{-(y-z)^2/2} dy - \frac{\sigma \sqrt{T}}{\sqrt{2\pi}} \left( \frac{\tau}{T} \right) \frac{\lambda_4}{24} \int_0^\infty \frac{d^3}{dy^3} e^{-(y-z)^2/2} dy
$$

$$
- \frac{\sigma \sqrt{T}}{\sqrt{2\pi}} \left( \frac{\tau}{T} \right) \frac{\lambda_3^2}{72} \int_0^\infty \frac{d^5}{dy^5} e^{-(y-z)^2/2} dy + \cdots \tag{6.81}
$$

---

[16] Cumulants $c_n$ are standard parameters characterizing the moments of a PDF. The normalized cumulants are given by $\lambda_n = c_n/\sigma^n$. For example, the third and fourth normalized cumulants $\lambda_3$ and $\lambda_4$ describe the skewness and kurtosis of the distribution: $\lambda_3 = \langle (x - \langle x \rangle)^3 \rangle/\sigma^3$ and $\lambda_4 + 3 = \langle (x - \langle x \rangle)^4 \rangle/\sigma^4 \equiv \kappa$, respectively. For more details, see Gershenfeld (1999) and Bouchaud and Potters (2000).

The integrals in Equation (6.81) are standard.[17] Hence we can easily obtain a cumulant expansion of the 'fair' option price around the Black–Scholes (Gaussian) price $V_G$, as follows:

$$V_0 = V_G + \sigma\sqrt{T}\frac{e^{-z^2/2}}{\sqrt{2\pi}}$$

$$\times \left(-\frac{\lambda_3}{6\sqrt{T/\tau}}z + \frac{\lambda_4}{24(T/\tau)}(z^2 - 1) + \frac{\lambda_3^2}{72(T/\tau)}(z^4 - 6z^2 + 3) + \cdots\right).$$

$$(6.82)$$

We can use Equation (6.82) directly from our knowledge of the moments (and hence normalized cumulants $\lambda_k$) of the PDF of underlying asset price movements, in order to obtain the price correction to the Black–Scholes option price. Alternatively, we can extract from Equation (6.82) an 'implied volatility' as we did in Section 6.4.3, as a function of the moments of the underlying asset's distribution. First, we expand the option price to first order, using Equation (6.78):

$$V_0 = V_G + \frac{\partial V_G}{\partial\sigma}\delta\sigma + \cdots$$

$$= V_G + \delta\sigma\frac{\partial}{\partial\sigma}\int_X^\infty P_{G>}[x_T]dx_T + \cdots$$

$$= V_G + \delta\sigma\int_X^\infty \frac{x_T - x_0}{\sqrt{2\pi\sigma^2}\sqrt{T}}e^{-(x_T-x_0)^2/2\sigma^2 T}dx_T + \cdots$$

$$= V_G + \frac{\sqrt{T}}{\sqrt{2\pi}}e^{-z^2/2}\delta\sigma + \cdots \qquad (6.83)$$

Comparing Equations (6.83) and (6.82), and considering the typical case in which the skewness of the underlying asset price distribution is not the dominant feature as compared to the kurtosis (i.e. $\lambda_3^2 \ll \lambda_4$), we find the implied volatility $\sigma_{imp} = \sigma + \delta\sigma$ to be given by:

$$\sigma_{imp} = \sigma\left(1 + \frac{\kappa_T - 3}{24}\left(\frac{(X - x_0)^2}{\sigma^2 T} - 1\right)\right), \qquad (6.84)$$

where $\kappa_T$ is the kurtosis of the PDF $p[x_T \,|\, x_0]$. Equation (6.84) is parabolic in the strike price $X$. The effect of the skewness term is to skew the parabola to one side or the other. This explains the origin of the implied volatility smile, as seen for example in Fig. 6.11.

---

[17] 'Standard' in the sense that they can be found in formulae books readily so need not be explicitly calculated here.

For typical asset price PDFs, where the excess kurtosis is positive, Equation (6.84) predicts the 'smile' seen in traded option-price implied volatilities. A large skewness and/or anomalous negative excess kurtosis, can turn this 'smile' into a 'smirk' or 'frown'.

**6.4.10.2    Expansion of the optimal hedging strategy.** We will again expand the general result about the Black–Scholes Gaussian case, focusing on the risk-minimizing hedging strategy for a European call option given by Equation (6.42):

$$\phi_t^*[x_t] = \frac{1}{\sigma^2(T-t)} \int_X^\infty (x_T - x_t)(x_T - X) p[x_T | x_t] dx_T. \tag{6.85}$$

We can transform the probability distribution $p[x_T | x_t]$ into a sum over the distribution's cumulants[18] $c_{n,T-t}$. First, we use the definition of the Fourier Transform of the probability distribution $p[x_T | x_t]$, $\hat{p}_{T-t}[z]$:

$$p[x_T | x_t] = \frac{1}{2\pi} \int_{-\infty}^\infty \hat{p}_{T-t}[z] e^{-iz(x_T - x_t)} dz$$

to give

$$(x_T - x_t) p[x_T | x_t] = \frac{1}{2\pi} \int_{-\infty}^\infty \hat{p}_{T-t}[z] \frac{\partial}{\partial(-iz)} e^{-iz(x_T - x_t)} dz. \tag{6.86}$$

We can express the Fourier Transform of the PDF as a sum of cumulants:

$$\hat{p}_{T-t}[z] = e^{\sum_{n=2}^\infty (c_{n,T-t}(iz)^n)/n!}. \tag{6.87}$$

Inserting Equation (6.87) into (6.86), and integrating by parts, we get:

$$
\begin{aligned}
(x_T - x_t) p[x_T | x_t] &= \frac{1}{2\pi} \int_{-\infty}^\infty e^{\sum_{n=2}^\infty (c_{n,T-t}(iz)^n)/n!} \frac{\partial}{\partial(-iz)} e^{-iz(x_T - x_t)} dz \\
&= \frac{1}{2\pi} \left[ i e^{-iz(x_T - x_t) + \sum_{n=2}^\infty (c_{n,T-t}(iz)^n)/n!} \right]_{-\infty}^\infty \\
&\quad - \frac{1}{2\pi} \int_{-\infty}^\infty \sum_{n=2}^\infty \frac{c_{n,T-t} n i^{n+1} z^{n-1}}{n!} e^{\sum_{n=2}^\infty (c_{n,T-t}(iz)^n)/n!} e^{-iz(x_T - x_t)} dz \\
&= \sum_{n=2}^\infty \frac{c_{n,T-t}}{(n-1)!} \frac{1}{2\pi} \int_{-\infty}^\infty (iz)^{n-1} e^{\sum_{n=2}^\infty (c_{n,T-t}(iz)^n)/n!} e^{-iz(x_T - x_t)} dz.
\end{aligned}
$$

$$\tag{6.88}$$

---

[18] See note 16.

The integral in the last line of Equation (6.88) is the $(n - 1)$th derivative of $p[x_T | x_t]$ with respect to $x_t$. This is evident if we look again at the Fourier expansion of the PDF:

$$p[x_T | x_t] = \frac{1}{2\pi} \int_{-\infty}^{\infty} e^{\sum_{n=2}^{\infty}(c_{n,T-t}(iz)^n)/n!} e^{-iz(x_T - x_t)} dz. \tag{6.89}$$

From Equation (6.89), we see that differentiating the PDF $n$ times with respect to $x_t$ will simply pull down successive powers of $(iz)$, just as we require for Equation (6.88). Thus, we have:

$$(x_T - x_t)p[x_T | x_t] = \sum_{n=2}^{\infty} \frac{c_{n,T-t}}{(n-1)!} \frac{\partial^{n-1}}{\partial x_t^{n-1}} p[x_T | x_t]. \tag{6.90}$$

Combining Equations (6.85) and (6.90) gives the cumulant expansion of the optimal hedging strategy:

$$\begin{aligned}
\phi_t^*[x_t] &= \frac{1}{\sigma^2(T-t)} \int_X^{\infty} (x_T - X) \sum_{n=2}^{\infty} \frac{c_{n,T-t}}{(n-1)!} \frac{\partial^{n-1}}{\partial x_t^{n-1}} p[x_T | x_t] dx_T \\
&= \frac{1}{\sigma^2 \tau} \sum_{n=2}^{\infty} \frac{c_{n,\tau}}{(n-1)!} \frac{\partial^{n-1}}{\partial x_t^{n-1}} \int_X^{\infty} (x_T - X)p[x_T | x_t] dx_T \\
&= \frac{1}{\sigma^2 \tau} \sum_{n=2}^{\infty} \frac{c_{n,\tau}}{(n-1)!} \frac{\partial^{n-1} V_t}{\partial x_t^{n-1}}.
\end{aligned} \tag{6.91}$$

In the second line, we used the assumption that the movements of the underlying asset's price are i.i.d., since in this case the cumulants are additive, that is, $c_{n,T-t} = \frac{(T-t)}{\tau} c_{n,\tau}$. The last line of Equation (6.91) includes $V_t$, the option price at time $t$, via Equation (6.21). We now examine our cumulant expansion of the risk-minimizing hedging strategy for the Gaussian distribution, in which case all the cumulants $c_{n,\tau}$ for $n \geq 3$ are identically equal to zero. In this special (Black–Scholes) scenario, Equation (6.91) then gives back the Black–Scholes delta hedging strategy:

$$\phi_{t,G}^*[x_t] = \frac{\partial V_t}{\partial x_t}. \tag{6.92}$$

However, in general this will *not* be true: the presence of kurtosis and skewness, etc., in the real distribution of underlying price movements, will lead to the necessity for higher order corrections to the hedging strategy in order to minimize the risk of writing the option.

## 6.5    Generalizing the formalism

When obtaining the formal results for the option price (Equation (6.20)) and the optimal hedging strategy (Equation (6.38)), we made the following series of approximations

(1)  the risk-free rate of interest $r$ was equal to zero;
(2)  the underlying asset's price-change was unbiased;
(3)  the underlying asset's price-change was uncorrelated;
(4)  the cost of transacting the underlying was zero.

We will now investigate how we might *relax each of these approximations* in turn, in order to obtain more general expressions for the price and risk-minimizing hedge.

### 6.5.1    Finite risk-free interest rate

Recalling Equation (6.8), the variation in the option writer's wealth is given by:

$$\Delta W_T = V_0(1+r)^T - V_T + \sum_{t/\tau=0}^{T/\tau-1} \phi_t \left(x_{t+\tau} - (1+r)^\tau x_t\right)(1+r)^{T-(t+\tau)}. \qquad (6.93)$$

Averaging Equation (6.93) over all realizations of the underlying asset price process, and using the fair game (i.e. no-arbitrage) condition $\langle \Delta W_T \rangle_{x_0,\ldots,x_T} = 0$, we arrive at the 'fair' option price:

$$V_0 = \langle V_T \rangle_{x_T} (1+r)^{-T} - \sum_{t/\tau=0}^{T/\tau-1} \left\langle \phi_t \left\langle \widetilde{\Delta x}_{t+\tau,t} \right\rangle_{x_{t+\tau}|x_t} \right\rangle_{x_t} (1+r)^{-(t+\tau)}, \qquad (6.94)$$

where we have used the notation $\widetilde{\Delta x}_{t,t-\tau} = x_t - (1+r)^\tau x_{t-\tau}$. We note that we could easily have made the risk-free interest rate time dependent; however, this is typically not relevant unless the contract is extremely long term. Now we go back to our approximation of an unbiased underlying asset price movement. In the regime of finite interest rates, this essentially means that the underlying asset appreciates in value at the same rate as a risk-free bond, that is, that $\langle x_{t+\tau} \rangle_{x_{t+\tau}|x_t} = (1+r)^\tau x_t$ and thus $\left\langle \widetilde{\Delta x}_{t+\tau,t} \right\rangle_{x_{t+\tau}|x_t} = 0$. With this approximation, Equation (6.94) gives the 'fair' option price as:

$$V_0 = \langle V_T \rangle_{x_T} (1+r)^{-T} = (1+r)^{-T} \int_0^\infty V_T[x_T, X] p[x_T|x_0] dx_T. \qquad (6.95)$$

The mean of the PDF $p[x_T|x_0]$ is no longer given by the initial spot price of the underlying asset $x_0$, but is instead given by the *forward* price $(1 + r)^T x_0$. Following exactly the same algebra as Section 6.4.4, we obtain the following expression for the variance of the option writer's variation in wealth including the finite interest rate:

$$\text{var}[\Delta W_T] = \mathcal{R}$$

$$= \mathcal{R}_c + \sum_{t/\tau=0}^{T/\tau-1} \int_0^\infty p[x_t|x_0] \left\{ \sigma_{t+\tau,t}^2 (\phi_t[x_t])^2 (1 + r)^{2(T-(t+1))} \right.$$

$$- 2\phi_t[x_t](1 + r)^{T-(t+1)}$$

$$\left. \times \int_0^\infty V_T[x_T, X] \langle \widetilde{\Delta x}_{t+\tau,t} \rangle_{x_t \to x_T} p[x_T|x_t] dx_T \right\} dx_t,$$

$$(6.96)$$

where

$$\mathcal{R}_c = \int_0^\infty (V_T[x_T, X])^2 p[x_T|x_0] dx_T$$

$$- \left( \int_0^\infty V_T[x_T, X] p[x_T|x_0] dx_T \right)^2.$$

The optimization $\partial \mathcal{R}/\partial \phi_t[x_t] = 0$ of Section 6.4.5, gives the risk-minimizing optimal hedging strategy:

$$\phi_t^*[x_t] = \frac{(1 + r)^{-(T-(t+1))}}{\sigma_{t+\tau,t}^2} \int_0^\infty V_T[x_T, X] \langle \widetilde{\Delta x}_{t+\tau,t} \rangle_{x_t \to x_T} p[x_T|x_t] dx_T. \quad (6.97)$$

Hence the imposition of a finite interest rate introduces a shift of reference frame, but does not affect the formalism in any fundamental way.

### 6.5.2   Biased underlying asset price movements

We now consider the case where the underlying asset has a biased price movement:

$$\langle x_{t+\tau} - x_t \rangle_{x_{t+\tau}|x_t} = \int_0^\infty (x_{t+\tau} - x_t) p[x_{t+\tau}|x_t] dx_{t+\tau} = \mu_t \neq 0. \quad (6.98)$$

In the Black–Scholes theory, any bias in the underlying asset's price movement cancels out of the equations, hence neither the option price nor hedging strategy have any explicit dependence on $\mu_t$. The same is *not* true in the more general framework of this chapter. To see this, first consider the 'fair' option price $V_0$. From Equation (6.14) and the no-arbitrage condition $\langle \Delta W_T \rangle_{x_0,...,x_T} = 0$, we have:

$$V_0 = \langle V_T \rangle_{x_T} - \sum_{t/\tau=0}^{T/\tau-1} \langle \phi_t \Delta x_{t+\tau,t} \rangle_{x_{t+\tau}|x_t,x_t}, \qquad (6.99)$$

where $\Delta x_{t+\tau,t} = (x_{t+\tau} - x_t)$. If the bias of the underlying asset price movement $\langle \Delta x_{t+\tau,t} \rangle_{x_{t+\tau}|x_t} = \mu_t$ is small compared with the volatility of that movement—specifically if $\mu_t T \ll \sigma_{t+\tau,t}\sqrt{T}$, which for example was true for our NYSE dataset in Equation (6.43)—then we can use a perturbative approach by expanding Equation (6.99) in powers of $\mu_t$. Typical values for the bias of a stock are of order 5 per cent per year, whereas typical daily volatilities are around 1 per cent. Thus for $T \sim 50$ trading days, we have $\mu_t T \sim 5 \cdot 50/260 \simeq 1$ per cent, whereas $\sigma_{t+\tau,t}\sqrt{T} \sim 1\sqrt{50} \simeq 7$ per cent. Therefore, neglecting the term of order $\mu_t^2$ in the expansion only gives a relative error of around $(1/7)^2 \simeq 2$ per cent. Hence we can proceed with the calculation of the option price for the case of a (small) biased underlying asset price movement, by substituting $\phi_t = \phi_t^* {}_{\mu_t=0} + \delta\phi_t$ into Equation (6.99) and ignoring terms higher than linear order in the small quantities $\delta\phi_t$ and $\mu_t$. For the unbiased form of the optimal hedging strategy $\phi_t^* {}_{\mu_t=0}$, we use a simplified form of Equation (6.38):

$$\phi_t^* {}_{\mu_t=0} = \frac{1}{\sigma_{t+\tau,t}^2} \langle V_T \Delta x_{t+\tau,t} \rangle_{x_T|x_{t+\tau},x_{t+\tau}|x_t}. \qquad (6.100)$$

To first order in the small quantities $\delta\phi_t$ and $\mu_t$, the 'fair' option price is given by:

$$V_0 = V_{0,\mu_t=0} - \sum_{t/\tau=0}^{T/\tau-1} \langle \phi_t \Delta x_{t+\tau,t} \rangle_{x_{t+\tau}|x_t,x_t} = V_{0,\mu_t=0} - \sum_{t/\tau=0}^{T/\tau-1} \langle \phi_t^* {}_{\mu_t=0}\mu_t + \delta\phi_t\mu_t \rangle_{x_t}$$

$$\simeq V_{0,\mu_t=0} - \sum_{t/\tau=0}^{T/\tau-1} \left\langle \frac{\mu_t}{\sigma_{t+\tau,t}^2} V_T \Delta x_{t+\tau,t} \right\rangle_{x_T|x_{t+\tau},x_{t+\tau}|x_t,x_t}, \qquad (6.101)$$

where $V_{0,\mu_t=0} = \langle V_T \rangle_{x_T}$ is the price of an option on an unbiased underlying asset. We now turn our attention to finding the hedging strategy that will minimize the corresponding risk. We revert to the compact notation of Section 6.4.8, where we denote the variation of the option writer's wealth as a sum of the option price $V_0$, the payout $-V_T$ and the profit from hedging $H = \sum_{t/\tau=0}^{T/\tau-1} \phi_t \Delta x_{t+\tau,t}$. Because of the no-arbitrage condition $\langle \Delta W_T \rangle_{x_0,...,x_T} = 0$, the variance of the writer's variation in wealth is given by:

$$\left\langle \Delta W_T^2 \right\rangle_{x_0,\dots,x_T} = V_0^2 + \left\langle V_T^2 \right\rangle_{x_0,\dots,x_T} + \langle H^2 \rangle_{x_0,\dots,x_T} - 2V_0 \langle V_T \rangle_{x_0,\dots,x_T}$$
$$- 2\langle V_T H \rangle_{x_0,\dots,x_T} + 2V_0 \langle H \rangle_{x_0,\dots,x_T}. \tag{6.102}$$

We then carry out the functional minimization of Equation (6.102) as before:

$$\frac{\partial \left\langle \Delta W_T^2 \right\rangle_{x_0,\dots,x_T}}{\partial \phi_t} = 0. \tag{6.103}$$

Before combining Equations (6.103) and (6.102), we note that:

$$\frac{\partial}{\partial \phi_t} H = \sum_{t'/\tau=0}^{T/\tau-1} \frac{\partial}{\partial \phi_t} \phi_{t'} \Delta x_{t'+\tau,t'} = \Delta x_{t+\tau,t},$$

$$\frac{\partial}{\partial \phi_t} H^2 = 2H \frac{\partial}{\partial \phi_t} H = 2 \sum_{t'/\tau=0}^{T/\tau-1} \phi_{t'} \Delta x_{t'+\tau,t'} \Delta x_{t+\tau,t}. \tag{6.104}$$

Thus the minimization gives:

$$\sum_{t'/\tau=0}^{T/\tau-1} \left\langle \phi_{t'}^* \Delta x_{t'+\tau,t'} \Delta x_{t+\tau,t} \right\rangle_{x_t,\dots,x_T} - \langle V_T \Delta x_{t+\tau,t} \rangle_{x_t,\dots,x_T} + V_0 \langle \Delta x_{t+\tau,t} \rangle_{x_t,\dots,x_T} = 0. \tag{6.105}$$

Note the change of averaging in Equation (6.105) that has resulted from a functional minimization at time $t$. The notation $\langle x \rangle_{x_t,\dots,x_T}$ now represents the average over the objective probability at time $t$, with all the information prior to that time available. Splitting up the sum in Equation (6.105) into three parts, $t' = t$, $t' \le t - \tau$, and $t' \ge t + \tau$, gives:

$$\phi_t^* \left\langle \Delta x_{t+\tau,t}^2 \right\rangle_{x_{t+\tau}|x_t} + \sum_{t'/\tau=0}^{t/\tau-1} \phi_{t'}^* \Delta x_{t'+\tau,t'} \langle \Delta x_{t+\tau,t} \rangle_{x_{t+\tau}|x_t}$$

$$+ \sum_{t'/\tau=t/\tau+1}^{T/\tau-1} \left\langle \phi_{t'}^* \Delta x_{t'+\tau,t'} \Delta x_{t+\tau,t} \right\rangle_{x_t,\dots,x_T} - \langle V_T \Delta x_{t+\tau,t} \rangle_{x_T|x_{t+\tau},x_{t+\tau}|x_t}$$

$$+ V_0 \langle \Delta x_{t+\tau,t} \rangle_{x_{t+\tau}|x_t} = 0. \tag{6.106}$$

To first order in (small) $\mu_t$:

$$\left\langle \Delta x_{t+\tau,t}^2 \right\rangle_{x_{t+\tau}|x_t} = \sigma_{t+\tau,t}^2, \quad \langle \Delta x_{t+\tau,t} \rangle_{x_{t+\tau}|x_t} = \mu_t. \tag{6.107}$$

Therefore, to first order in the small quantities $\delta\phi_t$ and $\mu_t$, and using Equation (6.100) in (6.106), we arrive at an approximate formula for the optimal trading strategy $\phi_t^*$:

$$
\phi_t^* = \frac{1}{\sigma_{t+\tau,t}^2} \left( \langle V_T \Delta x_{t+\tau,t} \rangle_{x_T | x_{t+\tau}, x_{t+\tau} | x_t} - \mu_t V_0 - \sum_{t'/\tau=0}^{t/\tau-1} \mu_t \phi_{t'}^* \Delta x_{t'+\tau,t'} \right.
$$

$$
\left. - \sum_{t'/\tau=t/\tau+1}^{T/\tau-1} \left\langle \mu_{t'} \left( \phi_{t'|\mu_{t'}=0}^* + \delta\phi_{t'} \right) \Delta x_{t+\tau,t} \right\rangle_{x_t,\dots,x_T} \right)
$$

$$
= \frac{1}{\sigma_{t+\tau,t}^2} \left( \langle V_T \Delta x_{t+\tau,t} \rangle_{x_T | x_{t+\tau}, x_{t+\tau} | x_t} - \mu_t V_0 - \sum_{t'/\tau=0}^{t/\tau-1} \mu_t \phi_{t'}^* \Delta x_{t'+\tau,t'} \right.
$$

$$
\left. - \sum_{t'/\tau=t/\tau+1}^{T/\tau-1} \left\langle \frac{\mu_{t'}}{\sigma_{t'+\tau,t'}^2} V_T \Delta x_{t'+\tau,t'} \Delta x_{t+\tau,t} \right\rangle_{x_t,\dots,x_T} \right).
$$

$$(6.108)$$

It can be seen from Equation (6.108) that the optimal strategy $\phi_t^*$ at time $t$ has to be obtained by iteration, given the asset price increments from 0 to $t$. For example, the first hedge $\phi_0^*$ is given by:

$$
\phi_0^* = \frac{1}{\sigma_{\tau,0}^2} \left( \langle V_T \Delta x_{\tau,0} \rangle_{x_T | x_\tau, x_\tau | x_0} - \mu_0 V_0 - \sum_{t'/\tau=1}^{T/\tau-1} \left\langle \frac{\mu_{t'}}{\sigma_{t'+\tau,t'}^2} V_T \Delta x_{t'+\tau,t'} \Delta x_{\tau,0} \right\rangle_{x_0,\dots,x_T} \right)
$$

$$(6.109)$$

We have re-derived the 'fair' option price and the risk-minimizing optimal hedging strategy, for managing an option portfolio with a biased underlying asset price movement. Using a cumulant expansion of the PDF as in Section 6.4.10.2, it can be shown for the case where all the moments of the distribution $p[x_{t+\tau}|x_t]$ above order two are identically zero, that the corrections to both the option price and hedge become equal to zero. This recovers the Black–Scholes result that the option is insensitive to the bias of the underlying asset price movement. In general, however, the distribution of asset price movements is *not* Gaussian. Hence this result no longer holds and one should correct the price and hedge according to Equations (6.101) and (6.108), respectively.

### 6.5.3    Correlated underlying asset price movements

The question of how to manage a derivatives portfolio in the presence of an underlying asset which has a degree of autocorrelation, initially seems slightly bizarre. If we have identified that price-changes are correlated, then *in principle* we could make money off this simple fact. The best derivatives portfolio management strategy would then be to simply make as much money from the underlying as possible during the contract's lifetime. More formally, for a correlated underlying asset price process, we have a correlation matrix $\underline{C}$ in which the coefficients $C_{t,t'}$ represent the covariance between the underlying asset price movement at times $t$ and $t'$, that is, $\langle \Delta x_{t,t-\tau} \Delta x_{t',t'-\tau} \rangle = C_{t,t'}$. The mean of the price movement $\Delta x_{t,t-\tau}$ is then explicitly dependent on all the previously realized price movements. We express this mean at time $t$ as follows:

$$\mu_t = \int_{-\infty}^{\infty} \Delta x_{t,t-\tau} \, p[\Delta x_{t,t-\tau} | \Delta x_{t-\tau,t-2\tau}, \ldots, \Delta x_{\tau,0}] \mathrm{d}\Delta x_{t,t-\tau} = m_t^{(0)} + m_t^{(1)},$$
(6.110)

where $m_t^{(0)}$ is an unconditional bias for the price movement and $m_t^{(1)}$ is a conditional mean. Following Bouchaud and Potters (2000), this conditional mean contains the correlation of the current price increment with all previously realized price increments, and has magnitude

$$|m_t^{(1)}| = \left| \frac{1}{(\underline{C}^{-1})_{t,t}} \sum_{t'/\tau=1}^{t/\tau-1} (\underline{C}^{-1})_{t',t} \Delta x_{t',t'-\tau} \right|.$$
(6.111)

In the presence of these asset price correlations, a natural hedging strategy to adopt would be:

$$\phi_t[x_t, x_{t-\tau}, \ldots, x_0] = \mathrm{sgn}[\mu_t].$$
(6.112)

This hedging strategy will thus make an average profit of $T/\tau \times \langle |\mu_t| \rangle$ over the lifetime of the contract, which is comparable in size to the expected payout of the option. The fair game condition $\langle \Delta W_T \rangle = 0$, which gives us $V_0 = \langle V_T \rangle - \langle H \rangle$, might then imply a very small value (or even a negative value) for the option premium $V_0$, that is, the option is essentially worthless. However, autocorrelation in the underlying asset price movement is observable typically only up to timescales of minutes. Using the trading strategy of Equation (6.112) would therefore imply a large number of trades every day. In reality the existence of 'market friction' and transaction costs (see Section 6.5.4) would render this trading strategy unprofitable. The existence of this friction implies that small autocorrelations at small timescales will not be traded upon, and so will remain in the financial time-series.

This leaves us the question of how this residual correlation affects our derivatives portfolio. If we were dealing with a continuous-time model, we would be worried at this stage because we have to consider asset price movements on all scales, and hence we would have to implicitly deal with these short-time correlations. However, as we saw in Section 6.4.6, there is typically no evidence for linear autocorrelation on a daily level. Thus, if our desired trading time $\tau$ is of order one day, then we need not worry at all about the direct effects of correlation. If however we were trading very frequently, we would find that we would have to account for this correlation in order for our derivatives portfolio to be optimal. In this scenario, we could use as an approximation the results of Section 6.5.2 for biased underlying asset price movement, but replace the bias term $\mu_t$ by the sum of the conditional and unconditional biases $\mu_t = m_t^{(0)} + m_t^{(1)}$.

### 6.5.4    Non-zero cost of transacting

In this chapter, we have been discussing a scenario where we manage a portfolio, which is *short* a derivative contract and *long* a certain quantity of its underlying asset. In order to minimize the risk on this portfolio, we have talked about schemes of hedging, that is, buying and selling the underlying asset at regular times $t = i\tau$. So far we have assumed that we are completely unconstrained in our ability to perform such hedging. This led to the natural conclusion that the more we hedge (i.e. the smaller $\tau$ is), the more risk we can eliminate from the portfolio. In practice, of course, there is always a penalty cost from transacting. This penalty cost can arise directly from brokerage costs and 'paying the spread' (i.e. the difference in prices at which the asset can be bought and sold), and indirectly from 'deal slippage'. Deal slippage corresponds to the effect of one's own market impact on the asset price. If you want to buy an asset, you are by definition increasing the demand for it—hence you would expect (by a supply and demand argument) to increase the asset's price which you then pay (see Chapter 1). For these reasons, there exists a per-trade cost for changing the amount of underlying asset held. A general expression for this cost could be written as:

$$K_t = k_1 + (k_2 + k_3 x_t) | \phi_t[x_t] - \phi_{t-\tau}[x_{t-\tau}] |. \tag{6.113}$$

In Equation (6.113), the $k_1$ term represents a fixed cost for executing a transaction, the $k_2$ term represents a cost proportional to the transacted volume, and the $k_3$ term represents a cost proportional to the value of the transaction. In general, the balance and magnitude of terms will depend on the specific market access of the portfolio manager. Note that the Black–Scholes theory does *not* account for such transaction costs.

We return to our derivatives portfolio, which is now managed in the presence of transaction costs $K = \sum_{t/\tau=0}^{T/\tau} K_t$. We assume $\phi_{t<0} = 0$, that is, the portfolio manager does not hold any of the underlying asset prior to writing the derivatives contract. We then have (in the reduced notation of Section 6.4.8):

$$\Delta W_T = V_0 - V_T + H - K. \tag{6.114}$$

Our first step is to assert the no-arbitrage condition $\langle \Delta W_T \rangle_{x_0,\dots,x_T} = 0$ and thus extract a 'fair' option price. Under the assumption of an unbiased underlying asset price movement (which gives $\langle H \rangle_{x_0,\dots,x_T} = 0$) we have:

$$V_0 = \langle V_T \rangle_{x_T} + \langle K \rangle_{x_0,\dots,x_T}. \tag{6.115}$$

Equation (6.115) implies that the average transaction cost of the writer's hedging is passed on to the customer, that is, the holder of the option. It may at first then seem that the portfolio manager (option writer) will not be concerned with the transaction cost and will re-hedge as much as possible to minimize his risk. However, the derivatives market is extremely competitive, hence a manager who can sell a larger number of cheap options can then collect more commissions. Therefore, the objective is not only to minimize the portfolio risk, but also to minimize the option price. Recall from Section 6.4.8, where we discussed adding a risk premium to the option price, that $V_0 = \langle V_T \rangle + \lambda \sqrt{\mathcal{R}}$, and hence a minimization of the option price amounted to the same thing as a minimization of the risk. In the present case of non-zero transaction costs, however, we have $V_0 = \langle V_T \rangle + \langle K \rangle + \lambda \sqrt{\mathcal{R}}$. Hence, a minimization of the option price will mean balancing the reduction of risk (and thus risk premium) with the increase in transaction costs. Let us look more closely at the term $\langle K \rangle$, again using the case of a European call option as an example. The average total transaction cost $\langle K \rangle$ will clearly increase as the number of trades increases (i.e. trading time $\tau$ decreases). However, to balance transaction costs against risk, we need to know how $\langle K \rangle$ increases as a function of $\tau$. To assess this, let us make two approximations: first, that $\Delta x_{t,t-\tau}$ and $\tau$ are small compared with $x_t$ and $T$, respectively. This approximation allows us to express the change in hedging position via the first term of its Taylor expansion:

$$|\phi_t[x_t] - \phi_{t-\tau}[x_{t-\tau}]| \approx \left| \frac{\partial \phi_{t-\tau}}{\partial x_{t-\tau}} \Delta x_{t,t-\tau} + \frac{\partial \phi_{t-\tau}}{\partial (t-\tau)} \tau \right|. \tag{6.116}$$

The second approximation is to say that the variation of the hedging strategy with time is far smaller than the variation with asset price, hence Equation (6.116) becomes:

$$|\phi_t[x_t] - \phi_{t-\tau}[x_{t-\tau}]| \approx \left| \frac{\partial \phi_{t-\tau}}{\partial x_{t-\tau}} \Delta x_{t,t-\tau} \right| = \frac{\partial \phi_{t-\tau}}{\partial x_{t-\tau}} |\Delta x_{t,t-\tau}|. \tag{6.117}$$

We have used the fact that the hedging strategy $\phi_t[x_t]$ increases monotonically with $x_t$ for a European call option, thus ensuring that its slope is always positive. The average total transaction cost becomes:

$$\langle K \rangle_{x_0, \ldots, x_T} = \left( \frac{T}{\tau} + 1 \right) k_1 + \sum_{t/\tau=0}^{T/\tau} \left\langle (k_2 + k_3 x_t) \frac{\partial \phi_{t-\tau}}{\partial x_{t-\tau}} |\Delta x_{t,t-\tau}| \right\rangle_{x_t|x_{t-\tau}, x_{t-\tau}}$$

$$\approx \left( \frac{T}{\tau} + 1 \right) k_1 + (k_2 + k_3 x_0) \sum_{t/\tau=0}^{T/\tau} \left\langle \frac{\partial \phi_{t-\tau}}{\partial x_{t-\tau}} \right\rangle_{x_{t-\tau}} \langle |\Delta x_{t,t-\tau}| \rangle_{x_t|x_{t-\tau}}.$$

$$\tag{6.118}$$

In the second line of Equation (6.118), we have used the assumption that the underlying asset's price process is uncorrelated, together with the approximation that

$$\left\langle (k_2 + k_3 x_t) \frac{\partial \phi_{t-\tau}}{\partial x_{t-\tau}} \right\rangle_{x_t | x_{t-\tau}, x_{t-\tau}} \approx \langle (k_2 + k_3 x_t) \rangle_{x_t} \left\langle \frac{\partial \phi_{t-\tau}}{\partial x_{t-\tau}} \right\rangle_{x_{t-\tau}}.$$

Equation (6.118) gives us an analytic approximation to the average transaction cost for a general underlying asset price distribution. If, however, we make the additional assumption that the underlying asset price follows a Gaussian random walk, we could use the Black–Scholes result that $\phi_t[x_t] = \partial V_t / \partial x_t$. (Since this was the optimal strategy for reducing risk in the *absence* of transaction costs, it can only be used as a first-order approximation for the optimal risk-minimizing strategy in the presence of *finite* transaction costs). Using the Black–Scholes result, gives:

$$\frac{\partial \phi_t}{\partial x_t} = \frac{\partial^2 V_t}{\partial x_t^2}$$

$$= \int_X^\infty (x_T - X) \frac{\partial^2}{\partial x_t^2} p[x_T | x_t] dx_T$$

$$= \int_X^\infty (x_T - X) \frac{\partial^2}{\partial x_T^2} p[x_T | x_t] dx_T$$

$$= \left[ (x_T - X) \frac{\partial}{\partial x_T} p[x_T | x_t] \right]_X^\infty - \int_X^\infty \frac{\partial}{\partial x_T} p[x_T | x_t] dx_T$$

$$= p[x_T = X | x_t]. \tag{6.119}$$

The third line of Equation (6.119) uses the fact that $p[x_T | x_t]$ is only a function of $(x_T - x_t)$, and the following line is a simple integration by parts. Now we can use the result of Equation (6.119) in (6.118) to obtain the final result for the average total transaction cost. For the Gaussian underlying asset price distribution that we are considering, $\langle |\Delta x_{t,t-\tau}| \rangle_{x_t | x_{t-\tau}} = \sigma \sqrt{2\tau/\pi}$. Hence:

$$\langle K \rangle_{x_0,\dots,x_T} \approx \left( \frac{T}{\tau} + 1 \right) k_1 + (k_2 + k_3 x_0)$$

$$\times \left( \phi_0[x_0] + \sigma \sqrt{\frac{2\tau}{\pi}} \sum_{t/\tau=1}^{T/\tau} \int_0^\infty p[x_T = X | x_{t-\tau}] p[x_{t-\tau} | x_0] dx_{t-\tau} \right)$$

$$\approx \left( \frac{T}{\tau} + 1 \right) k_1 + (k_2 + k_3 x_0) \left( \phi_0[x_0] + \sigma \sqrt{\frac{2\tau}{\pi}} \frac{T}{\tau} p[x_T = X | x_0] \right).$$

$$\tag{6.120}$$

Equation (6.120) has a $\tau^{-1/2}$ dependence on the trading time for zero fixed costs, that is $k_1 = 0$. Recalling the result of Section 6.4.9.3 in which the residual risk had a $\tau^{1/2}$ dependence

$$\sqrt{\mathcal{R}^*} = \sigma \sqrt{\frac{\tau}{2} P_{>X}(1 - P_{>X})}, \tag{6.121}$$

we can see that there will in general be an 'optimal' value of the trading time $\tau^*$, which minimizes the option price of Equation (6.115). This trading time will be given by:

$$\frac{\partial}{\partial \tau}\bigg|_{\tau = \tau^*} \left( \langle K \rangle + \lambda \sqrt{\mathcal{R}^*} \right) = 0, \tag{6.122}$$

and hence $\tau^*$ satisfies

$$\lambda \sigma \sqrt{\pi P_{>x}(1 - P_{>x})}(\tau^*)^{3/2} - 2\sigma(k_2 + k_3 x_0)p_X T(\tau^*)^{1/2} - 2\sqrt{2\pi} k_1 T = 0 \tag{6.123}$$

where $p_X = p[x_T = X|x_0]$. Using order-of-magnitude estimates for the parameters in Equation (6.123), we obtain $\tau^* \sim 10^{-1} T$ which is not unreasonable. Returning to Equation (6.120), we can see that the $k_1$ and $\phi_0[x_0]$ terms will dominate for heavily in- or out-the-money-options. For heavily in-the-money options, the writer will expect to have to supply the underlying asset at expiry, and his transaction costs arising from the $\phi_0[x_0]$ term will be of order $k_3 x_0$. Conversely, if the option is heavily out-the-money, the contribution of the $\phi_0[x_0]$ term will be close to zero. Between these regimes, where the outcome of the contract is uncertain, the writer will have to perform more hedging corrections and will incur more cost. Figure 6.18 compares the analytic approximation for the form of the average total transaction cost (Equation (6.120)) with the results of a Monte-Carlo simulation over a range of trading times and strike prices.

Figure 6.18 shows that the analytic approximation of Equation (6.120) has captured the dependence of the average total transaction cost, as a function of both the trading time and strike price. The approximation made in Equation (6.118) accounts for the slight displacement of the analytic dependence on strike price. Similarly, the assumption that $\tau \ll T$ becomes worse as the trading time increases.

Our discussion of transaction costs so far has focused on their impact on the average variation in wealth. We used our analytic approximation for the consequent average total transaction cost, in order to derive an 'optimal trading time' $\tau^*$. This involved balancing the average total transaction cost with the risk premium for the option. In this calculation, we assumed that the risk profile was unchanged by the inclusion of transaction costs in the original variation of wealth: however, this is not in general true.

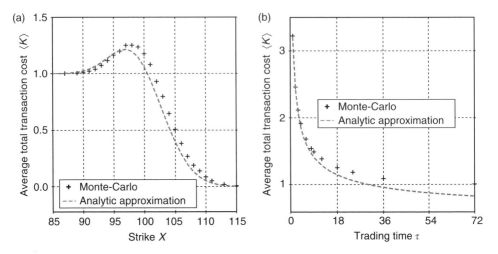

**Fig. 6.18**   The dependence of the average total transaction cost $\langle K \rangle$ on the (a) strike price $X$ at constant trading time $\tau = 24$ days and (b) trading time $\tau$ at constant strike price $X = 100$ cents. The crosses show results from a Monte-Carlo simulation, whereas the dashed line shows the analytic approximation of Equation (6.120). The option being considered is a European call with $x_0 = 100$ cents, $T = 72$ days, $\sigma = 0.5$ cents $\cdot$ day$^{-1/2}$ and a proportional transaction cost of $k_3 = 1\%$.

Adding a transaction cost term to the wealth balance will in fact add an *additional* source of risk. Let us now examine how this extra risk varies with the parameters of the portfolio. First let us look at the dependence of the residual risk $\sqrt{\mathcal{R}^*}$ on the trading time $\tau$. In Equation (6.121) for the residual risk of the portfolio in the absence of transaction costs, we saw that this risk fell monotonically as $\tau^{1/2}$ with decreasing trading time. Figure 6.19 shows that when a modestly large transaction cost is added, this relationship is masked by the transaction cost term, resulting in a risk that actually *grows* as the trading time is decreased.

How can we understand this markedly different behaviour of the portfolio's residual risk when transaction costs are added? Let us examine analytically the variation of the residual risk with the inclusion of transaction costs. First we take Equation (6.114), square it and average. Next, using the no-arbitrage result $\langle \Delta W_T \rangle_{x_0,\ldots,x_T} = 0$, we obtain the variance of the portfolio var$[\Delta W_T]$, which is our risk measure $\mathcal{R}$:

$$
\begin{aligned}
\mathcal{R} = \left\langle \Delta W_T^2 \right\rangle_{x_0,\ldots,x_T} &= \langle (V_0 - V_T + H - K)^2 \rangle_{x_0,\ldots,x_T} \\
&= \Big( V_0^2 + \left\langle V_T^2 \right\rangle - 2V_0\langle V_T \rangle + 2V_0\langle H \rangle - 2\langle V_T H \rangle + \langle H^2 \rangle \\
&\quad + \langle K^2 \rangle - 2V_0\langle K \rangle + 2\langle V_T K \rangle - 2\langle H K \rangle \Big).
\end{aligned}
\tag{6.124}
$$

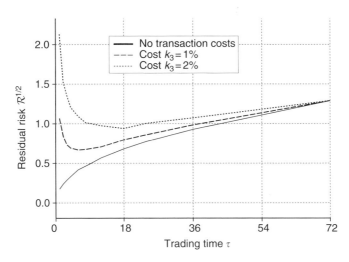

**Fig. 6.19**   The dependence of the residual risk on trading time $\tau$ calculated using a Monte-Carlo simulation. The option being considered is a European call with $x_0 = 100$ cents, $X = 100$ cents, $T = 72$ days, $\sigma = 0.5$ cents $\cdot$ day$^{-1/2}$. The solid line shows the risk in the absence of transaction costs, the dashed line includes a proportional transaction cost of $k_3 = 1\%$, while the dotted line has $k_3 = 2\%$.

Then, we substitute into Equation (6.124) our previous results $V_0 = \langle V_T \rangle + \langle K \rangle$, $\langle H \rangle = 0$, and $\mathcal{R}_c = \langle V_T^2 \rangle - \langle V_T \rangle^2$. After some cancelling, this gives:

$$\mathcal{R} = \underbrace{\mathcal{R}_c - 2\langle V_T H \rangle + \langle H^2 \rangle}_{\text{Term 1}} + \underbrace{\langle K^2 \rangle - \langle K \rangle^2}_{\text{Term 2}} + \underbrace{2\langle V_T K \rangle - 2\langle H K \rangle}_{\text{Term 3}}. \qquad (6.125)$$

Term 1 in Equation (6.125) represents the portfolio variance in the absence of transaction costs, term 2 represents the variance of the transaction costs alone, and term 3 represents the covariance between the portfolio without transaction costs, and the transaction costs themselves. In the covariance term, the $\langle H K \rangle$ term will become zero for uncorrelated, unbiased increments of the underlying asset price since the size of the increment is independent of its sign. The $\langle V_T K \rangle$ term is in general non-zero, but small in comparison to the other terms. Roughly speaking, therefore, the portfolio risk can be approximated by the sum of the risk without transaction costs $\mathcal{R}_{K=0}$ (term 1) and the transaction cost risk alone $\mathcal{R}_K$ (term 2). We examined the form of the risk without transaction costs $\mathcal{R}_{K=0}$ in Section 6.4.4, so let us now turn to examine the form of $\mathcal{R}_K$.

Consider the standard deviation of the transaction cost at each re-hedging time $t = i\tau$, as shown in Fig. 6.20. As the option nears expiry and the hedging strategy becomes more sensitive to movements of the underlying asset around the strike price, then the probability of large re-hedges increases, thereby also increasing the variance of the transaction costs. However, we are concerned now with the dependence of the transaction cost variance on trading time $\tau$. It can be inferred from Fig. 6.20 that the

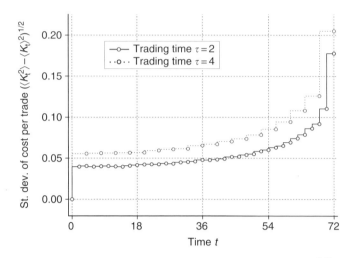

**Fig. 6.20**    The standard deviation of the transaction cost per trade $(\langle K_t^2 \rangle - \langle K_t \rangle^2)^{1/2}$ at each re-hedging time $t = i\tau$, as calculated from a Monte-Carlo simulation. The option being considered is a European call with $x_0 = 100$ cents, $X = 100$ cents, $T = 72$ days, $\sigma = 0.5$ cents $\cdot$ day$^{-1/2}$. The solid line corresponds to $\tau = 2$ while the dotted line corresponds to $\tau = 4$ days.

magnitude of the transaction cost variance for a trading time of $\tau = 2$ days, is more than half the magnitude for $\tau = 4$ days. As the trading time is reduced, the total transaction cost variance would hence be expected to rise, as observed in Fig. 6.19. However, this is not the full story, and cannot by itself explain the very strong dependence of the risk for small trading times which is observed in Fig. 6.19. To explain this, we need to look at the correlations between the separate transaction costs. Thinking about the asset price movement, one can see that if the current asset value is far away from the strike price of the option, the dependence of the hedge $\phi_t[x_t]$ on the asset price $x_t$ will be small. This implies that consecutive re-hedges are likely to be of small magnitude incurring small transaction costs. Conversely, if the asset value is near the strike price, the dependence of $\phi_t[x_t]$ on the asset price $x_t$ is large, hence consecutive re-hedges will be of large magnitude. Hence, large transaction costs tend to follow other large costs, while small costs follow other small costs. This amounts to there being a positive correlation between consecutive transaction costs. Moreover, this correlation becomes greater as the trading time is reduced because the locality of the asset price, and hence the magnitude of $\partial\phi_t/\partial x_t$, are more closely related. All this adds up to a rapidly increasing transaction cost variance as the trading time $\tau$ is lowered.

The form of the transaction cost risk as a function of the strike price $X$ as shown in Fig. 6.21, is also interesting. Unlike the variation of $\mathcal{R}_{K=0}$, which had a maximum risk at $X = x_0$, the transaction cost risk actually exhibits a local minimum there.

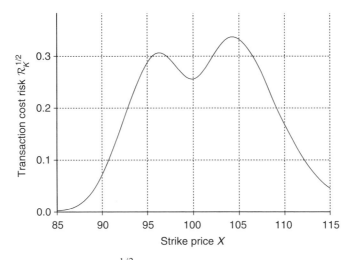

**Fig. 6.21** The transaction cost risk $\mathcal{R}_K^{1/2}$ as a function of the strike price $X$, calculated from a Monte-Carlo simulation. The option being considered is a European call with $x_0 = 100$ cents, $T = 72$ days, $\sigma = 0.5$ cents $\cdot$ day$^{-1/2}$, and $\tau = 24$ days.

To understand this form, let us take the simple case of a European call option where $\tau = T$, that is, the option is only hedged at $t = 0$ (and of course necessarily at $t = T$). The two outcomes of the option, payout for $x_T > X$ and non-payout for $x_T < X$, reflect two different transaction costs:

$$K_{>X} = 2k_1 + (k_2 + k_3 x_0)\phi_0[x_0] + (k_2 + k_3(x_T)_{>X})(1 - \phi_0[x_0]),$$
$$K_{<X} = 2k_1 + (k_2 + k_3 x_0)\phi_0[x_0] + (k_2 + k_3(x_T)_{<X})\phi_0[x_0]. \tag{6.126}$$

Since $\sigma\sqrt{T}/x_0 \ll 1$, we can approximate Equation (6.126) as two delta-functions at $K_{>X} = 2k_1 + (k_2 + k_3 x_0)$ and $K_{<X} = 2k_1 + 2(k_2 + k_3 x_0)\phi_0[x_0]$. The probability weightings for each delta-function would then be $p[K_{>X}] = P_{>X}$ and $p[K_{<X}] = 1 - P_{>X}$, respectively. The two delta-functions representing the probability of a given transaction cost, have a strike-dependent separation arising from the $\phi_0[x_0]$ dependence in $K_{<X}$. When the strike and initial spot are equal (i.e. $X = x_0$), $K_{>X} = K_{<X}$ and the two delta-functions lie at the same place, yielding zero variance. As the strike price is moved away from the initial spot, the two delta-functions move apart, initially with roughly equal weighting. This leads to an increase in the variance. However, as the separation in the strike price and initial spot grows, the weightings become biased and the distribution starts looking more and more like a single delta-function again. The result is a fall in the transaction cost variance for $|X - x_0| \gg 0$. We can see this dependence explicitly from Equation (6.126): let us make the observation that for the Black–Scholes Gaussian case, we have $\phi_0 = P_{>X}$. This then allows us to write out the mean and variance of the transaction cost in a straightforward manner:

$$\langle K \rangle = K_{>X} P_{>X} + K_{<X} P_{<X}$$
$$= (2k_1 + k_2 + k_3 x_0) P_{>X} + (2k_1 + 2(k_2 + k_3 x_0) P_{>X})(1 - P_{>X})$$
$$= 2k_1 + (k_2 + k_3 x_0) P_{>X} (3 - 2 P_{>X}) \tag{6.127}$$

and

$$\langle K^2 \rangle - \langle K \rangle^2 = K_{>X}^2 P_{>X} + K_{<X}^2 P_{<X} - \langle K \rangle^2$$
$$= (2k_1 + k_2 + k_3 x_0)^2 P_{>X}$$
$$+ (2k_1 + 2(k_2 + k_3 x_0) P_{>X})^2 (1 - P_{>X}) - \langle K \rangle^2$$
$$= (k_2 + k_3 x_0)^2 P_{>X} (1 - P_{>X})(1 - 2 P_{>X})^2. \tag{6.128}$$

As shown in Fig. 6.22, the simple forms of Equations (6.127) and (6.128) manage to capture the interesting dependences of both the mean and variance of the transaction cost contributions to the portfolio variation of wealth. This can be seen, for example, by comparison with Figs 6.18 and 6.21, respectively.

Now let us examine $\mathcal{R}_K$, the variance of the transaction costs, in a somewhat more general fashion. We hope here to capture analytically the stylized dependence of the transaction cost variance on both the strike price and on the trading time. The first step is to note that the terms in the transaction cost which are constant for all

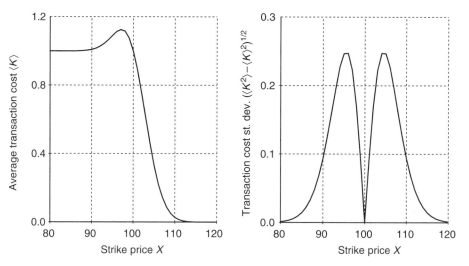

**Fig. 6.22**   The variation of the mean and standard deviation of the transaction cost term from Equations (6.127) and (6.128), respectively. The option being considered is a European call with $x_0 = 100$ cents, $T = \tau = 72$ days, $\sigma = 0.5$ cents $\cdot$ day$^{-1/2}$.

realizations—namely the $k_1$ and $\phi_0[x_0]$ terms—will not contribute to the variance. Using Equation (6.117), we then have the approximate expression:

$$
\mathcal{R}_K = \text{var}[K] = \langle K^2 \rangle_{x_0,\dots,x_T} - \langle K \rangle^2_{x_0,\dots,x_T}
$$

$$
= \sum_{t/\tau=1}^{T/\tau} \left\langle (k_2 + k_3 x_t)^2 \left( \frac{\partial \phi_{t-\tau}}{\partial x_{t-\tau}} \right)^2 \right\rangle \left\langle |\Delta x_{t,t-\tau}|^2 \right\rangle
$$

$$
+ \sum_{\substack{t/\tau,t'/\tau=1 \\ t \neq t'}}^{T/\tau} \left\langle (k_2 + k_3 x_t)(k_2 + k_3 x_{t'}) \frac{\partial \phi_{t-\tau}}{\partial x_{t-\tau}} \frac{\partial \phi_{t'-\tau}}{\partial x_{t'-\tau}} \right\rangle \langle |\Delta x_{t,t-\tau}| \rangle \langle |\Delta x_{t',t'-\tau}| \rangle
$$

$$
- \left( \sum_{t/\tau=1}^{T/\tau} \left\langle (k_2 + k_3 x_t) \frac{\partial \phi_{t-\tau}}{\partial x_{t-\tau}} \right\rangle \langle |\Delta x_{t,t-\tau}| \rangle \right)^2 . \tag{6.129}
$$

We make the same approximations as we did while working out the average total transaction cost—noting that these approximations become increasingly less accurate for the second moment than for the first. We arrive at:

$$
\mathcal{R}_K = (k_2 + k_3 x_0)^2 \left[ \sigma^2 \tau \sum_{t/\tau=0}^{T/\tau-1} \left\langle p[x_T = X | x_t]^2 \right\rangle \right.
$$

$$
+ \frac{2}{\pi} \sigma^2 \tau \sum_{\substack{t/\tau,t'/\tau=0 \\ t \neq t'}}^{T/\tau-1} \langle p[x_T = X | x_t] p[x_T = X | x_{t'}] \rangle
$$

$$
\left. - (2/\pi) \sigma^2 \tau (T/\tau)^2 p[x_T = X | x_0]^2 \right] . \tag{6.130}
$$

Calculating the expectation values of Equation (6.130) then gives the following approximate form:

$$
\mathcal{R}_K = (k_2 + k_3 x_0)^2 \left[ \sigma^2 \tau \sum_{t/\tau=0}^{T/\tau-1} \sqrt{\frac{T+t}{T-t}} \, p[x_{T+t} = X | x_0]^2 \right.
$$

$$
+ \frac{4}{\pi} \sigma^2 \tau \sum_{\substack{t/\tau,t'/\tau=0 \\ t < t'}}^{T/\tau-1} \sqrt{\frac{T+t}{T-t}} \, p[x_{T+t} = X | x_0]^2
$$

$$
\left. - (2/\pi) \sigma^2 \tau (T/\tau)^2 p[x_T = X | x_0]^2 \right] . \tag{6.131}
$$

Counting the terms in the second sum of Equation (6.131) yields:

$$
\mathcal{R}_K = (k_2 + k_3 x_0)^2 \sigma^2 \tau \left(
\begin{array}{l}
\displaystyle\sum_{t/\tau=0}^{T/\tau-1} \left(1 + \frac{4}{\pi}\left(\frac{T-t}{\tau}\right)\right) \sqrt{\frac{T+t}{T-t}} \, p[x_{T+t} = X|x_0]^2 \\[20pt]
-(2/\pi)(T/\tau)^2 p[x_T = X|x_0]^2
\end{array}
\right)
$$

$$(6.132)$$

Equation (6.132) can be seen to have the correct dependencies on trading time and strike price. As the trading time gets progressively smaller, not only are there more terms in the summation of Equation (6.132) but each term is also bigger: this ensures the strong dependence at small trading times which is observed. As a function of strike price, the first line of Equation (6.132) represents a broadened bell-like shape centred on the initial spot value $x_0$. The second line of Equation (6.132) takes a narrower bell-shape away from this broad bell-shape, hence giving the interesting form of the transaction cost risk as a function of strike price shown in Fig. 6.21. This then brings us to the end of our journey in explaining the form and effect of transaction costs on both the first and second moment of the portfolio variation in wealth.

So far we have looked at the portfolio variance $\langle \Delta W_T^2 \rangle = \mathcal{R}_{K=0} + \mathcal{R}_K$ in a Black–Scholes delta-hedging framework. Our main objective is to find another hedging strategy that minimizes the risk in the presence of transaction costs. Although Equation (6.132) gave us an approximation for the variance of the transaction cost part of the portfolio in a Black–Scholes framework, Equation (6.129) is more general and can thus be used for a general optimization process. Of course, any new hedging strategy we arrive at will share the *form* of the Black–Scholes delta-hedge, that is, move monotonically from zero for $x_t \ll X$ to one for $x_t \gg X$ (for a European call, for example). However, it is the *strength* of this variation that is likely to change due to inclusion of transaction costs. For this reason, a useful way of performing the optimization is to take the form of the Black–Scholes delta-hedge for our optimal strategy *but* to replace the volatility by a time-dependent factor $\gamma_t$, which can then be optimized over. In this way, we can tune the strength of the dependence on underlying asset price $x_t$ without losing the algebraic simplicity of the Gaussian framework. Following this optimization process, we can generate an analogue of Equation (6.132) for $\mathcal{R}_K$ as a function of the (time-dependent) factor $\gamma_t$. We then have to perform a minimization of $\mathcal{R}_{K=0} + \mathcal{R}_K$ over all the $\gamma_{t=i\tau}$ values for integers $0 \le i \le T/\tau - 1$. Due to the covariance term of the transaction cost risk, the minimization in this framework has to be performed globally, that is, the minimization with respect to $\gamma_t$ depends on $\gamma_{t'\neq t}$. We therefore have to proceed by forming a grid over $\gamma_{i\tau}$ in a $T/\tau$ dimensional space (one dimension for each $i$), numerically calculating the value of the risk at each grid

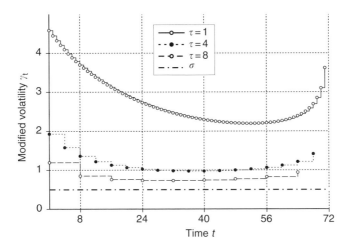

**Fig. 6.23**   The time dependence of the modified volatility $\gamma_t$ which results from a (sub-optimal) local minimization of the portfolio risk $\mathcal{R}_{K=0} + \mathcal{R}_K$, in the presence of a transaction cost term $k_3 = 1\%$. Graph shows $\gamma_t$ for three different values of the trading time. Dashed-dotted horizontal line shows the Black–Scholes value of the volatility. The option being considered is a European call with $x_0 = 100$ cents, $T = 72$ days, $\sigma = 0.5$ cents $\cdot$ day$^{-1/2}$.

point, then finding the global minima. This is necessarily a large computational problem. We can however make a quick approximation to the optimal hedging strategy by assuming that the transaction cost covariance between time $i\tau$ and other times, only depends on $\gamma_{i\tau}$. We can then minimize the risk at each timestep $i\tau$, that is, perform a series of local minimizations as opposed to a global minimization. This sub-optimal minimization is very quick to compute, and gives an interesting time-dependent form for $\gamma_{i\tau}$ as shown in Fig. 6.23.

As can be seen from Fig. 6.23, the value of the modified volatility (which lessens the risk in the presence of transaction costs) always lies above the Black–Scholes value. This result makes sense: the greater the value of $\gamma_t$, the less sensitive the hedging strategy is to the underlying movement and hence the lower the transaction costs (and their inherent risk). As the trading time becomes smaller, the required $\gamma_t$ becomes much larger in order to compensate for the rising transaction cost risk. The form of Fig. 6.23 across time is also very interesting: it suggests that, in order to reduce risk, the sensitivity of the hedging strategy to the underlying asset price movement should be reduced (i.e. $\gamma_t$ increased) both towards the start and end of the option's lifetime. Let us first try and understand this, by looking at the sensitivity of the risk without transaction costs, $\mathcal{R}_{K=0}$, to the 'volatility' used in the hedging strategy $\gamma_t$.

Figure 6.24 shows that the value of $\gamma_t$ which minimizes the risk (in the absence of transaction costs) at each timestep, corresponds to $\sigma = 0.5$ cents $\cdot$ day$^{-1/2}$. This is as expected in this Gaussian framework where, in the absence of transaction costs,

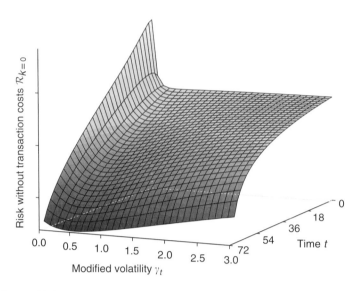

**Fig. 6.24**   The sensitivity of the risk without transaction costs $\mathcal{R}_{K=0}$ to the volatility of the hedging strategy $\gamma_t$ as a function of time. The option being considered is a European call with $x_0 = 100$ cents, $T = 72$ days, $\sigma = 0.5$ cents $\cdot$ day$^{-1/2}$.

the Black–Scholes strategy is the optimal risk-minimizing hedge. Towards the start of the option's lifetime, the risk $\mathcal{R}_{K=0}$ is quite insensitive to increases in the hedging strategy's volatility $\gamma_t$. Towards the option's expiry, by contrast, the risk becomes more sensitive to increases in $\gamma_t$: as we move away from the minimum $\gamma_t = \sigma$, the risk increases more sharply. This explains why our (semi)-optimal volatility modification shown in Fig. 6.23, exhibits a marked rise at the start of the option's lifetime: $\mathcal{R}_{K=0}$ does not greatly increase as we move $\gamma_t$ away from $\sigma$, but $\mathcal{R}_K$ *does* dramatically decrease. Towards the expiry of the option, we know from Fig. 6.20 that the transaction cost risk increases dramatically. This is what then forces the volatility modification $\gamma_t$ up once more, even though it also increases $\mathcal{R}_{K=0}$ more sharply. It is thus the trade-off between $\mathcal{R}_{K=0}$ and $\mathcal{R}_K$ which gives the time-dependent form of Fig. 6.23.

All that remains to be done is test the form displayed in Fig. 6.23 to see if a reduction in the total portfolio risk is actually observed. This is easily carried out through a Monte-Carlo simulation, and the resulting distributions for $\gamma_t = \sigma$ and $\gamma_t = \gamma_t^*$ can be compared directly.

From Fig. 6.25, we conclude that the proposed volatility modification $\gamma_t$, whose purpose was to minimize the total portfolio risk in the presence of transaction costs, is indeed successful. For the option being considered, we not only see a reduction in the total portfolio risk of around 36 per cent but we also see a considerable reduction in the absolute transaction cost. Thus with this system, options can be sold cheaper whilst still presenting less risk to the writer.

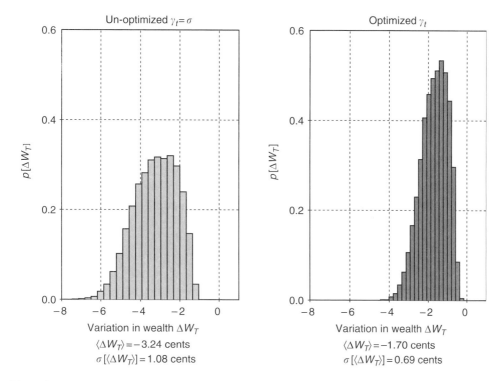

**Fig. 6.25** Resulting minimization in overall portfolio risk and transaction costs, using the modified time-dependent volatility measure $\gamma_t$ from Fig. 6.23. Results show the PDF of the variation of wealth $p[\Delta W_T]$ generated using a Monte-Carlo simulation. The option being considered is a European call with $x_0 = 100$ cents, $T = 72$ days, $\sigma = 0.5$ cents $\cdot$ day$^{-1/2}$, and is priced with the Black-Scholes formula using $\gamma_t$. The trading time was $\tau = 1$ day. The level of the transaction costs was set at $k_3 = 1\%$.

This brings us to the end of our detailed technical tour around the generalized treatment of derivatives. This tour took us back to re-examine the foundations of risk, hedging, and pricing, and through a step-wise process whereby we could examine the consequences of the various Black–Scholes' approximations. In contrast to the 'beautiful but delicate' Black–Scholes theory, the present formulation could be classified as 'uglier but far more robust' since it does not depend on the real market honouring the underlying approximations of Black–Scholes. Given that it is the accuracy of the final answer that is important in financial practice, and given that the Black–Scholes approximations cannot be guaranteed to hold in any particular market, it is this 'ugly but robust' method which we believe will define the future for portfolio risk management and derivative pricing.

A highly speculative, but potentially very exciting, path for future research would be to use the market models of Chapter 4 (and perhaps Chapter 5) to *generate* the

PDFs etc. needed to implement the present risk minimization, hedging, and pricing scheme. The methodology would be: (a) build the microscopic market model, (b) match the model parameters to the present state of the market, (c) project the market model forward in time by letting it evolve, and (d) construct PDFs for the future based on the resulting trajectories of the time-evolving market model. Such an approach, if successful, would do away with the idea of having to obtain such measures by analysing past data. In this case, there would be no reason why the price process would have to be stationary, or even that it have much of a history. For example, the system of interest could be a recent IPO, like our dot-com company *risk-e.com* which featured at the beginning of Chapter 1. In short, one replaces the black-box real market together with its known but limited output from the past, by an approximate output generator for the future.

# 7. Deterministic dynamics, chaos, and crashes

## 7.1 Living with non-linearity

One of the main themes of this book has been the extent to which price series in real markets differ from a random-walk model, and the consequences of such deviations. The deviations themselves were specified in Chapter 3 in terms of the so-called stylized facts of real markets. These stylized facts focus on the *statistical* differences between a random walk and the real market. For this reason, we placed so much emphasis on the appropriate probability distributions of real markets as compared to the Gaussian world of random walks.

Thinking in terms of market speculation, it *might* be possible to use such statistical information to achieve some degree of profit via the direct market, or via the derivatives market: for example, by identifying and trading mispriced options (c.f. Chapter 6). However, traders who look for profit by trying to identify patterns in market price series, are often seeking some kind of *deterministic* signal of future price movements. An example is that of technical analysts or 'chartists' who look to identify definite events such as the crossing point of two moving-averages of past prices, with the averages taken over different time-windows. Chapter 4 looked at the consequences of having a whole population of such chartists, each of whom follows simple determin-istic rules in order to make predictions about future price movements and hence arrive at an investment decision.

Standard finance theory says there is no free lunch. According to the Efficient Market Hypothesis (EMH) discussed in Chapter 2, no profitable information about future movements can be obtained by studying past price series. However, we saw in Chapter 4 that if traders believe that there *is* such a profitable pattern, then their actions alone can in turn produce patterns.[1] It is possible that financial crashes are a particular

---

[1] Of course, the patterns of price movements which *result* from the combined actions of the traders are not necessarily the same as the ones each trader *predicted* would arise.

consequence of this process, as we will demonstrate later in this chapter. In short, common sense tells us that whether *profitable* patterns actually exist in market data or not, there will always be people who try to find them and hence trade accordingly.

The goal of making a deterministic statement about the future evolution of the markets, represents a shift away from considering the stochastic or statistical properties of a market, towards a consideration of the dynamics of the markets. In fact, many people seem to share a desire to instil some kind of predetermined evolution or purpose into the markets: this becomes most apparent through statements in the media that the markets are 'bullish' or 'bearish', or that there is a strong rally underway. The appropriate deterministic dynamics to describe the market, if any such definite dynamics exists, would clearly be *non-linear* given the markets' implicit complexity and strong internal feedback mechanisms. In addition these dynamics should probably include, at least on a longer timescale, the effects of changes in external, macroeconomic factors (e.g. interest rates). This motivates us to end this book by focusing on simple deterministic models of financial markets, with a view to understanding the types of dynamical features that can arise within such a non-linear economic or financial system. For further details on non-linear systems in general, we recommend the excellent book by Strogatz (2001) from which much of the earlier material in this chapter was adapted.

A non-linear dynamical system is characterized by a temporal evolution that is not just given by a linear combination of the separate evolutions of the constituent parts: in short, *more is different*. It has been said that to describe the world as non-linear is like describing the animal kingdom as consisting of non-elephants. Practically all real-world systems are non-linear. Linear behaviour is just a convenient—but actually sometimes misleading—approximation that is used to describe the world, particularly in undergraduate (and even graduate) science and economics courses. A particular class of non-linear dynamical behaviour has attracted the interest of the finance and economics community, in particular practitioners, since the 1980s: this class of behaviour is termed *chaos*. The word 'chaos' carries the idea of randomness, but actually means something more specific in scientific terms. A coin-toss is random, and therefore unpredictable, but strictly speaking it is not chaotic. Unfortunately, the word 'chaos' has no unique definition within the scientific community. However, it is generally taken to mean *a deterministic[2] system which exhibits aperiodic behaviour that depends sensitively on the initial conditions, thereby rendering long-term prediction impossible*. We note that a particular complex system might, or might not, exhibit

---

[2] *Deterministic* implies that, given the state of the system at time $t$ and knowledge of the governing equations, we can in principle deduce the unique state of the system at a later time. *Stochastic* implies that such knowledge is not sufficient to determine a unique state of the system at a later time.

chaos. In fact a small external or internal perturbation might (or might not) take a particular complex system in or out of a chaotic state. Chaos is just *one* of the many varieties of dynamical behaviour that a complex system might exhibit. Each of us, for example, can be thought of as a complex system, and we each exhibit many states during the day—sleeping, eating, running, panicking, relaxing. Some of these states can be thought of as more 'chaotic' than others, yet we move freely between these states according to changes in our environment and changes within ourselves. Hence the labels 'complex system' and 'complexity' do not imply chaos. On the other hand, some relatively simple systems can exist in permanently chaotic states—take for example, a few carefully prepared coupled pendulums which are driven by some external force. In short, one must be careful not to fall in the trap of thinking that 'complex systems equal chaos' and vice versa.

But if long-term prediction in a chaotic system is impossible, why are some people so interested in looking for evidence of chaos in financial markets? The reason is that, somewhat paradoxically, a chaotic system has some intrinsic order. This order is not so regular as to render the system completely predictable, but gives some structure to the dynamics that would otherwise appear totally haphazard. This order comes in the form of the 'fractal structure' of the 'strange attractor' which accompanies a chaotic state.[3] A strange attractor is a low-dimensional object defined by the trajectories of the system (in its 'phase-space' of dynamical variables) in the long-time limit. Such an attractor is 'strange' in that its 'volume' has a fractional dimension (i.e. it is a fractal). This is to be contrasted with a regular (i.e. non-strange) attractor which is either a point (i.e. zero dimensional and hence has no length, area, or volume), a line (i.e. one-dimensional and hence has a length but no area or volume), a plane (two-dimensional and hence has an area but no volume), etc. A strange attractor can quite happily have a dimension such as 1.345, making it lie between a line and a plane. In other words, it appears to have a 'thickness' (which a one-dimensional line should not have), yet does not appear to have enough 'area' to fill a sheet of paper (which a two-dimensional object should). Instead, it is like an infinite set of lines, infinitesimally close together, and hence lies between one and two dimensions. How can this be? Well, an infinite amount of something infinitesimal is an ill-defined quantity and hence can give some surprising results—just think of zero divided by zero, or equivalently zero multiplied by infinity.

So are financial markets chaotic? There are many, many reported studies of empirical financial data in which the authors look for chaotic signatures and, in particular,

---

[3] We are considering dissipative dynamics, as opposed to Hamiltonian chaos. The latter is more suited to isolated few-body physical systems with essentially conserved total energy, such as the Solar System.

the dynamics associated with strange attractors. Unfortunately these empirical studies are generally inconclusive with regards to identifying chaos. They all typically suffer from the problems of a limited-sized (i.e. finite) dataset, plus the non-unique nature of the chaos tests themselves. Hence the jury is still out as to whether low-dimensional chaos exists in financial markets. We do not have the space to pick through the extensive list of empirical tests that could be applied, in order to help determine whether chaotic dynamics can be associated with a given financial data set. We ourselves believe it unlikely that high-frequency financial data represent good examples of low-dimensional chaos. Even if such tests were to appear positive, it is unclear as to which (if any) chaotic model would also be capable of reproducing the stylized facts discussed in Chapter 3. We believe that *if* there is to be any example of non-linear dynamics observable in financial markets, it would more likely arise on longer time-scales driven by some form of systematic, macroeconomic effect. A possible example includes the much discussed business cycles: can these be seen as some kind of limit cycle of the macroeconomical dynamics within a country? Alternatively, how do the quarterly earnings in a given company interact with changes in interest-rates?

While these topics of non-linear dynamics and chaos could fill many books, we will instead explain the basic terminology and features explicitly *by example*, in the next section.

## 7.2   Non-linear dynamical models for finance and economics

Here we explore some simple non-linear dynamical models. As a by-product, our discussion will provide a crash-course on non-linear dynamical systems, in order to illustrate the type of phenomena that could arise in non-linear economic and financial models. Although our main goal here is to illustrate the various non-linear phenomena that can arise as the level of complexity increases, the 'toy' models we present *could* have some financial and economic relevance. In the context of the multi-trader models of Chapter 4, for example, these simple models could be used to link the global resource level $L[t]$ to macroscopic changes in the economy such as business cycles, or to seasonal effects, thereby producing a set of dynamical equations. To orientate ourselves, Fig. 7.1 shows how the deterministic non-linear dynamics to be discussed sits within the general framework of dynamical systems behaviour. Note that if observing only the *output* of a particular system, such as an economy, an outsider might classify that system as being entirely stochastic or 'random' even though it might actually be deterministic and chaotic. Indeed a valid working definition of chaos could well be the following: *chaos is seemingly stochastic behaviour emerging from a deterministic system.*

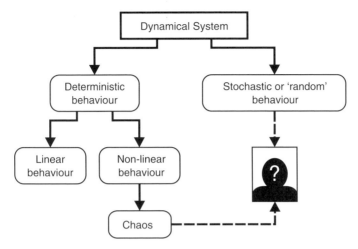

**Fig. 7.1**  Classes of dynamical behaviour for an economic or financial system. As judged by an outsider who is observing the output of the economic or financial system, the system could appear to be stochastic or 'random' even though it is actually deterministic. In practical terms, 'one person's chaos may be another person's noise'.

There are two main types of dynamical equations: differential equations and iterated maps (or difference equations). The former describe the evolution of a system in continuous time—like the Black–Scholes equation of Chapter 2—while the latter describe the evolution in discrete time, like the multi-agent models in Chapter 4. We now turn to the distinction between linear and non-linear, with a focus on ordinary differential equations and hence continuous time. It turns out that one can always rewrite an ordinary differential equation in terms of a set of coupled, first-order differential equations involving $n$ variables $x_1, x_2, \ldots, x_n$:

$$
\begin{aligned}
\dot{x}_1 &= f_1[x_1, x_2, \ldots, x_n] \\
\dot{x}_2 &= f_2[x_1, x_2, \ldots, x_n] \\
&\vdots \\
\dot{x}_n &= f_n[x_1, x_2, \ldots, x_n].
\end{aligned}
\tag{7.1}
$$

The system is said to be linear if the functions $f$ only contain constants or terms proportional to $x$, that is $f$ only contains terms involving $x^p$ where $p = 0, 1$. Otherwise the system is said to be non-linear. The number $n$ of equations gives the dimension of the system. For example, we can rewrite the damped harmonic oscillator equation

$$
\ddot{x} + \alpha \dot{x} + \beta x = 0
\tag{7.2}
$$

in the following way by defining $x_1 = x$ and $x_2 = \dot{x}$:

$$\dot{x}_1 = x_2$$
$$\dot{x}_2 = -\beta x_1 - \alpha x_2.$$
(7.3)

Hence Equation (7.2) for the damped harmonic oscillator is linear and has dimension $n = 2$. As another example, the swinging pendulum is given by

$$\ddot{x} + \beta \sin x = 0,$$
(7.4)

which can be rewritten as

$$\dot{x}_1 = x_2$$
$$\dot{x}_2 = -\beta \sin x_1,$$
(7.5)

and hence is non-linear with dimension $n = 2$. In the case that the ordinary differential equation contains an explicit time-dependence, e.g. the forced harmonic oscillator

$$\ddot{x} + \alpha\dot{x} + \beta x = A \cos t,$$
(7.6)

time itself becomes an extra variable. In other words, $x_3 = t$ and hence Equation (7.6) becomes

$$\dot{x}_1 = x_2$$
$$\dot{x}_2 = -\beta x_1 - \alpha x_2 + A \cos x_3$$
$$\dot{x}_3 = 1.$$
(7.7)

Equation (7.7) and hence Equation (7.6) is non-linear with dimension $n = 3$. In general, non-linear equations are impossible to solve analytically. Instead numerical solutions must be sought.

Table 7.1 demonstrates how the richness of the resulting dynamical behaviour increases as the dimension is increased, for continuous-time equations.

For discrete time equations, the behaviour is much richer for a given $n$. Even equations with dimension $n = 1$ can yield chaos. We will now illustrate this catalogue of behaviours by passing through the various cases.

### 7.2.1   $n = 1$ dimensional systems: continuous time

Consider the following phenomenological model for a financial or economic variable (e.g. interest rate, price) in continuous time:

$$\dot{x} = f[x] \equiv \mu x(1 - \alpha x),$$
(7.8)

**Table 7.1**  Richness of dynamical behaviour increases as the dimension is increased.

| | $n = 1$ | $n = 2$ | $n \geq 3$ |
|---|---|---|---|
| *Dynamical features* | fixed points | can show all the features of $n = 1$ | can show all the features of $n = 2$ |
| | bifurcations and catastrophes | *plus...* | *plus...* |
| | oscillations *not* possible | oscillations | CHAOS |
| | [unless $x$ is defined over a finite range with equivalent end-points] | | associated features include: |
| | | limit cycles | |
| | | Hopf bifurcations | • strange attractor with fractal structure |
| | | | • period doubling route to chaos |
| | ...but chaos *not* possible | ...but chaos *not* possible | • intermittency route to chaos, i.e. chaotic dynamics with pockets of periodicity. |

where $x \equiv x(t)$ is the value at time $t$, while $\mu$ is a multiplying factor reflecting some underlying growth rate. We will assume $x \geq 0$, $\mu > 0$, and the parameter $\alpha > 0$. As an example, $x(t)$ could represent the value of the monthly moving-average of a price or market index at time $t$, that is the average price over the last four weeks, whereas $\mu$ could be the market trend on an annual scale (and hence is effectively constant). The physical behaviour of this system can be understood as follows. For small values of $x$, there is a positive feedback since $\dot{x} \approx \mu x > 0$. However, if $x$ is large, in particular for $x > \alpha^{-1}$, the feedback becomes negative since $\dot{x} < 0$. In the context of prices, this represents a crude model of how a rising market can create momentum to keep itself rising. However eventually the average price reaches a steady value. Setting the left-hand side of Equation (7.8) equal to zero shows that there are two fixed points, $x^* = 0$ and $x^* = \alpha^{-1}$, which correspond to the solutions in the steady state limit $\dot{x} = 0$. But are these solutions stable? We can answer this in two ways. First, we can imagine a small perturbation around the fixed point $x(t) = x^* + \varepsilon(t)$. Differentiating yields $\dot{x} = \dot{\varepsilon}$ and hence using Equation (7.8) for general $f[x]$ we get

$$\begin{aligned}
\dot{\varepsilon} &= f[x] \\
&= f[x^* + \varepsilon] = f[x^*] + \varepsilon f'[x^*] + \cdots \\
&\approx \varepsilon f'[x^*],
\end{aligned} \tag{7.9}$$

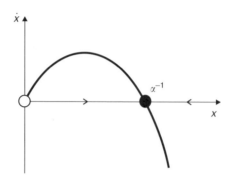

**Fig. 7.2**   Illustration of vector field on a line for the $n = 1$ dimensional system of Equation (7.8).

since $f[x^*] = 0$. (We have used Taylor's expansion.) Equation (7.9) is a *linear* equation for $\varepsilon(t)$. There are various cases:

$$f'[x^*] > 0 \;\Rightarrow\; \varepsilon(t) \text{ grows exponentially} \;\Rightarrow\; x^* \text{ is unstable (i.e. repellor)}$$
$$f'[x^*] < 0 \;\Rightarrow\; \varepsilon(t) \text{ decays exponentially} \;\Rightarrow\; x^* \text{ is stable (i.e. attractor)}$$
$$f'[x^*] = 0 \;\Rightarrow\; \text{need to consider higher order terms in Taylor expansion.}$$

Hence $|f'[x^*]|$ gives the exponential growth/decay rate, and $|f'[x^*]|^{-1}$ is the characteristic timescale for the growth/decay. In the present example $f'[x^* = 0] = \mu(1 - 2\alpha x^*) = \mu > 0$, hence $x^* = 0$ is unstable. For the other fixed point, $f'[x^* = \alpha^{-1}] = \mu(1 - 2\alpha x^*) = -\mu < 0$ hence $x^* = \alpha^{-1}$ is stable. The second method for determining stability is graphical, and involves drawing arrows to the right (or left) on the $x$-axis depending on whether $\dot{x}$ is positive (or negative). In other words, these arrows denote the *flow* of $x$ in time. In this way, we have mapped out a *vector field on a line* (Fig. 7.2).

This graphical method shows clearly that $x^* = 0$ is unstable (open circle) while $x^* = \alpha^{-1}$ is stable (filled circle). It is impossible to overshoot a stable fixed point since $\dot{x} = 0$ at $x^*$. Hence we can see that oscillations in $x$ as a function of time are impossible in such a one-dimensional system. If we now let the growth-rate $\mu$ be either positive *or* negative, and for simplicity set $\alpha^{-1} = \mu$, then Equation (7.8) becomes

$$\dot{x} = \mu x - x^2. \tag{7.10}$$

There is now a 'transcritical bifurcation' which arises as $\mu$ changes from negative to positive (Fig. 7.3). A bifurcation, loosely speaking, is a change in the state of stability of a system. The bifurcation in the above system (Equation (7.10)) corresponds to an interchange of stabilities between the two fixed points at $x = 0$ and $x = \mu$. Plotting out the positions of the fixed points as a function of $\mu$, we obtain the 'bifurcation diagram'

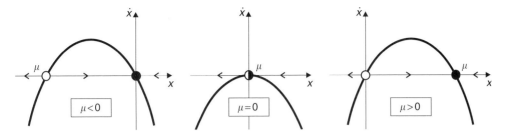

**Fig. 7.3**    Transcritical bifurcation arising for the $n = 1$ dimensional system Equation (7.10).

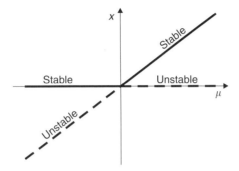

**Fig. 7.4**    Bifurcation diagram arising for the $n = 1$ dimensional system Equation (7.10).

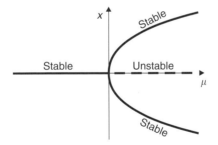

**Fig. 7.5**    Bifurcation diagram arising for the $n = 1$ dimensional system $\dot{x} = \mu x - x^3$.

shown in Fig. 7.4 where the solid lines are the loci of stable fixed points, and the dashed lines are the loci of unstable fixed points. Slightly altering the form of Equation (7.10) yields various types of 'pitchfork bifurcation'. The term 'pitchfork' refers to the shape of the bifurcation diagram. In each of the following examples, depending on the sign of the non-linear term, the arms and stem of the pitchfork are either stable or unstable. For $\dot{x} = \mu x - x^3$, we obtain a 'supercritical' pitchfork bifurcation with the bifurcation diagram shown in Fig. 7.5. For $\dot{x} = \mu x + x^3$, we obtain a 'subcritical' pitchfork

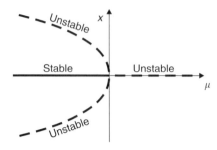

**Fig. 7.6**   Bifurcation diagram arising for the $n = 1$ dimensional system $\dot{x} = \mu x + x^3$.

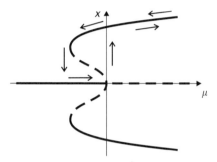

**Fig. 7.7**   Bifurcation diagram for $\dot{x} = \mu x + x^3 - x^5$ exhibits hysteresis or 'memory'. The arrows correspond to changing $\mu$ continuously from large positive through to small negative, then back to large positive again. Notice how the corresponding $x$ value takes on different values for the same value of $\mu$ when $\mu$ is small and negative.

bifurcation, which is particularly important since the system can become completely unstable as the parameter $\mu$ (e.g. growth-rate) increases (Fig. 7.6).

In the case that the equation involves higher order terms, for example $\dot{x} = \mu x + x^3 - x^5$, the bifurcation diagram develops extra branches since, for a given $\mu$, the presence of a higher order (e.g. fifth-order) term means that there are now many more (e.g. up to five) solutions corresponding to $\dot{x} = 0$ (Fig. 7.7). A new phenomenon therefore arises, that of hysteresis or 'memory' in the system. Imagine that $\mu$ represents a market growth-rate which can be controlled by a regulatory body (or 'system manager'), and that this regulatory body wants to restore the value of $x$ to its historical value (e.g. the average annual price level) after some period of erratic behaviour. The hysteresis or memory effect means that the actual value that $x$ takes for a given $\mu$, depends on the *history* of what has happened before. In short, the actual value of $x$ will depend not only on $\mu$, but also on the historical path taken through the bifurcation diagram. (Figure 7.7 shows that for small negative $\mu$, there are three possible stable $x$-values: positive, negative and zero.) Hence resetting $\mu$ may result in a completely different *x* value. This behaviour underlies the phenomenon called a *catastrophe* whereby a system may undergo a *big* and effectively irreparable change in its response *x* for a small change in some control parameter $\mu$. In our financial example, this would mean that even if the market returned to the same growth-rate, the moving average of the price may be completely different from before. The actions of a regulatory body in such a situation would therefore be doing more harm than good.

### 7.2.2 $n = 2$ dimensional systems: continuous time

The issue of stability for an $n = 2$ dimensional system can be treated using a generalized version of the method for $n = 1$ systems. We first outline this approach, before giving a specific example. Consider a general two-dimensional system comprising two coupled equations:

$$\dot{x} = f[x, y],$$
$$\dot{y} = g[x, y].$$
(7.11)

The fixed points $(x^*, y^*)$ can be solved by setting $\dot{x} = 0$ and $\dot{y} = 0$. As before, we can imagine a small perturbation around the fixed point, hence $x(t) = x^* + \varepsilon(t)$ and $y(t) = y^* + \eta(t)$. Differentiating yields the generalization of Equation (7.9):

$$\dot{\varepsilon} = f[x^*, y^*] + \varepsilon \left.\frac{\partial f}{\partial x}\right|_{x=x^*} + \eta \left.\frac{\partial f}{\partial y}\right|_{y=y^*} \cdots \approx \varepsilon \left.\frac{\partial f}{\partial x}\right|_{x=x^*} + \eta \left.\frac{\partial f}{\partial y}\right|_{y=y^*},$$

$$\dot{\eta} = g[x^*, y^*] + \varepsilon \left.\frac{\partial g}{\partial x}\right|_{x=x^*} + \eta \left.\frac{\partial g}{\partial y}\right|_{y=y^*} \cdots \approx \varepsilon \left.\frac{\partial g}{\partial x}\right|_{x=x^*} + \eta \left.\frac{\partial g}{\partial y}\right|_{y=y^*},$$
(7.12)

since $f[x^*, y^*] = 0$ and $g[x^*, y^*] = 0$. Equation (7.12) can be rewritten:

$$\begin{pmatrix} \dot{\varepsilon} \\ \dot{\eta} \end{pmatrix} = \begin{pmatrix} \left.\frac{\partial f}{\partial x}\right|_{x=x^*} & \left.\frac{\partial f}{\partial y}\right|_{y=y^*} \\ \left.\frac{\partial g}{\partial x}\right|_{x=x^*} & \left.\frac{\partial g}{\partial y}\right|_{y=y^*} \end{pmatrix} \begin{pmatrix} \varepsilon \\ \eta \end{pmatrix} \equiv \underline{\underline{A}} \begin{pmatrix} \varepsilon \\ \eta \end{pmatrix},$$
(7.13)

where $\underline{\underline{A}}$ is the *Jacobian matrix*, which is the multivariable analogue of $f'[x^*]$. Substituting in a time-dependence $e^{\lambda t}$ for the small quantities $(\varepsilon(t), \eta(t) \rightarrow e^{\lambda t}\varepsilon(0), e^{\lambda t}\eta(0))$ yields an eigenvalue equation with solutions $\lambda_1, \lambda_2$ corresponding to eigenvectors $\underline{v}_1, \underline{v}_2$. There are four cases to consider:

If Re $(\lambda_1) > 0$ and Re $(\lambda_2) > 0$ $\Rightarrow$ repeller (i.e. unstable node)
If Re $(\lambda_1) < 0$ and Re $(\lambda_2) < 0$ $\Rightarrow$ attractor (i.e. stable node)

If Re $(\lambda_1) > 0$ but Re $(\lambda_2) < 0 \Rightarrow$ saddle node
If $\lambda_1, \lambda_2$ both imaginary $\qquad \Rightarrow$ center (i.e. oscillatory solution)

Suppose that the exchange-rates $X$ and $Y$ between each of two countries and the US dollar, are given by $x(t)$ and $y(t)$, respectively. Suppose also that their coupled evolution is described by the following two equations:

$$\dot{x} = 3x(F - 2x - y),$$
$$\dot{y} = y(2 - x - y). \tag{7.14}$$

The parameter $F$ is assumed to be determined by external macroeconomic variables. We will consider the effect of two different values of $F$:

1. $F = 6$.   The fixed points, obtained by setting the left-hand side of Equation (7.14) to zero, are $(0, 0)$, $(0, 2)$ and $(3, 0)$. The Jacobian matrix is given by

$$\underline{\underline{A}} = \begin{pmatrix} 18 - 12x - 3y & -3x \\ -y & 2 - x - 2y \end{pmatrix}. \tag{7.15}$$

For $(0, 0)$, the Jacobian $\underline{\underline{A}}$ has eigenvalues 2 and 18. Hence it is an unstable node.
For $(0, 2)$, the Jacobian $\underline{\underline{A}}$ has eigenvalues $-2$ and 12. Hence it is a saddle node.
For $(3, 0)$, the Jacobian $\underline{\underline{A}}$ has eigenvalues $-1$ and $-18$. Hence it is a stable node.

The trajectories for the system are as shown in Fig. 7.8. Therefore the currency $Y$ eventually becomes devalued to zero against the US dollar, while the currency $X$ approaches a steady-state value of 3 against the US dollar.

2. $F = 3$.   In this case, the fixed points are $(0, 0)$, $(0, 2)$, $(\frac{3}{2}, 0)$, and $(1,1)$. The Jacobian matrix is given by

$$\underline{\underline{A}} = \begin{pmatrix} 9 - 12x - 3y & -3x \\ -y & 2 - x - 2y \end{pmatrix}.$$

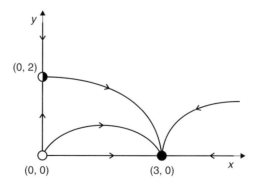

**Fig. 7.8**   Flow of trajectories for the system described by Equation (7.14) with $F = 6$. Any given point $(x, y)$ on a trajectory will flow along that trajectory as time evolves, in the direction of the arrow.

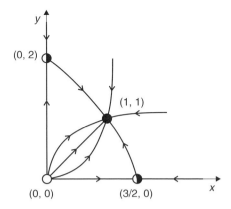

**Fig. 7.9**   Flow of trajectories for the system described by Equation (7.14) with $F = 3$.

For $(0, 0)$, the Jacobian $\underline{A}$ has eigenvalues 2 and 9. Hence it is an unstable node.
For $(0, 2)$, the Jacobian $\underline{A}$ has eigenvalues $-2$ and 3. Hence it is a saddle node.
For $(\frac{3}{2}, 0)$, the Jacobian $\underline{A}$ has eigenvalues $1/2$ and $-9$. Hence it is a saddle node.
For $(1, 1)$, the Jacobian $\underline{A}$ has eigenvalues $(-7 + \sqrt{37})/2$ and $(-7 - \sqrt{37})/2$. Hence it is a stable node.

The trajectories for the system are as shown in Fig. 7.9. Hence the currencies $X$ and $Y$ now *both* approach a steady-state value of 1 against the US dollar.

### 7.2.3   $n = 3$ dimensional systems: continuous time

The situation is far more complicated for $n = 3$ dimensions, since the trajectories now have another dimension in which they can 'twist' around themselves. This gives rise to the possibility of chaos where the attractors become 'strange'. While the full discussion of such details is well beyond the scope of this chapter, we illustrate the possible effects by considering the following model equations:

$$\dot{x} = \alpha(y - x),$$
$$\dot{y} = \beta x - y - xz, \qquad (7.16)$$
$$\dot{z} = xy - \gamma z,$$

where the parameters $\alpha, \beta, \gamma > 0$. These are the famous Lorenz equations. There is a wealth of rich dynamics as a function of the parameters for these equations: here we consider the commonly studied case $\alpha = 10, \gamma = 8/3$. The origin $(0, 0, 0)$ is a fixed point for all parameter values. Considering a

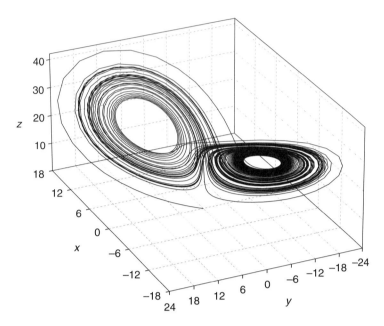

**Fig. 7.10**   Trajectories in the chaotic regime for the Lorenz equations of Equation (7.16), with the parameter values $\alpha = 10.0$, $\beta = 24.2$, and $\gamma = \frac{8}{3}$.

small perturbation around the origin $(0, 0, 0)$ shows that the origin is stable for $\beta < 1$. For $\beta > 1$, the origin becomes unstable, and two stable fixed points emerge at $(x^*, y^*, z^*) = \left(\sqrt{\gamma(\beta - 1)}, \sqrt{\gamma(\beta - 1)}, \beta - 1\right)$ and $(x^*, y^*, z^*) = \left(-\sqrt{\gamma(\beta - 1)}, -\sqrt{\gamma(\beta - 1)}, \beta - 1\right)$. Around $\beta = 24.1$ a strange attractor appears and the system becomes chaotic. Further details can be found in Strogatz's (2001) book. Figure 7.10 gives a typical picture for the trajectories in the chaotic regime, demonstrating the emergence of a degree of *order* associated with the strange attractor.

We now comment on predictability in the chaotic regime. Suppose we let the transients decay so that the trajectory is on the strange attractor. Let $\underline{x}(t) = \{x(t), y(t), z(t)\}$ be a point on the strange attractor at time $t$, and consider a nearby point $\underline{x}(t) + \underline{\varepsilon}(t)$ where $\underline{\varepsilon}(t)$ is a very small separation vector. In numerical simulations, it is found that $|\underline{\varepsilon}(t)| \sim |\underline{\varepsilon}(0)|e^{st}$ and hence neighbouring trajectories separate exponentially fast. Let $A$ be a measure of the acceptable accuracy of a prediction. A prediction therefore becomes unacceptable when $|\underline{\varepsilon}(t)| \geq A$ after a time of the order of $t_{\max} \sim \frac{1}{s} \ln A/|\underline{\varepsilon}(0)|$. Suppose $A = 10^{-4}$ and $|\underline{\varepsilon}(0)| = 10^{-9}$, then $t_{\max} = 5 \ln 10/s$. If we now improve our initial model error to $|\underline{\varepsilon}(0)| = 10^{-14}$, then $t_{\max} = 10 \ln 10/s$, which is only twice as large. This is quite a sobering thought: improving a model's accuracy by a factor $10^5$ yields only a very limited increase in the time-horizon of predictability, if the system is in the chaotic regime.

### 7.2.4 $n \geq 1$ dimensional systems: discrete time

Discrete-time systems can show an incredible richness in behaviour as compared to continuous-time systems of the same dimension $n$. The reason is simple: continuous-time systems involve differential equations and hence deal with variables whose time-dependences require a certain smoothness in order for their differentials to exist. For a discrete-time system, there are no such restrictions. This explains part of the 'problem' with standard finance theory: the time-dependences are just too smooth. As an example we return to our simple one-dimensional model from Section 7.2.1, but now consider a financial or economic variable in discrete time:

$$x_{n+1} = f[x_n] \equiv \mu x_n (1 - x_n), \tag{7.17}$$

where $x_n$ is the value at timestep $n$ (e.g. $x_n$ is proportional to the closing price on day $n$), while $\mu$ is a multiplying factor representing an underlying growth-rate. We will assume $0 \leq \mu \leq 4$ and $0 \leq x \leq 1$. The stability of the fixed points is again determined by expanding around $x^*$, using $x_n = x^* + \varepsilon_n$. Hence

$$x^* + \varepsilon_{n+1} = f[x^* + \varepsilon_n] = f[x^*] + \varepsilon_n f'[x^*] + \cdots \approx x^* + \varepsilon_n f'[x^*], \tag{7.18}$$

since $f[x^*] = x^*$ by definition of a fixed point. Thus $\varepsilon_{n+1} \approx \varepsilon_n f'[x^*]$ which is a linearized version of the non-linear map in Equation (7.17). There are various cases to consider:

$|f'[x^*]| < 1 \quad \Rightarrow \quad \varepsilon_n \to 0$ as $n \to \infty \quad \Rightarrow \quad x^*$ is stable (i.e. attractor)

$|f'[x^*]| > 1 \quad \Rightarrow \quad \varepsilon_n \to \infty$ as $n \to \infty \quad \Rightarrow \quad x^*$ is unstable (i.e. repellor)

$|f'[x^*]| = 1 \quad \Rightarrow \quad$ need to consider higher order terms in the Taylor expansion.

Hence the magnitude of the derivative evaluated at the fixed point, acts like a growth rate. The fixed points of Equation (7.17) are at $x^* = 0$ and $x^* = 1 - \mu^{-1}$. For $\mu < 1$, the only fixed point that exists is $x^* = 0$ and it is stable (i.e. $|f'[x^*]| < 1$); for $\mu > 1$, $x^* = 0$ is unstable. For $1 < \mu < 3$, $x^* = 1 - \mu^{-1}$ exists and is stable; it then becomes unstable for $\mu > 3$. Hence for $\mu < 1$, $x_n \to 0$ as $n \to \infty$; for $1 < \mu < 3$, $x_n$ reaches a non-zero steady state given by $x^* = 1 - \mu^{-1}$. For larger $\mu(\mu \geq 3)$, $x_n$ *oscillates* about this former steady-state solution, yielding an oscillatory

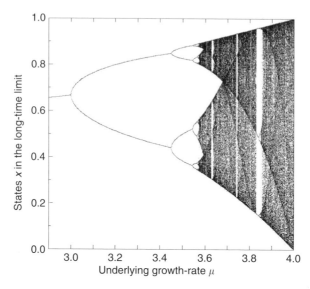

**Fig. 7.11**   Orbit diagram for the $n = 1$ discrete time system given by Equation (7.17). At each $\mu$ value, the values of $x$ are plotted after the initial transients have disappeared.

solution of period 2 (a so-called period-2 cycle). This oscillation is remarkable since the original equation, Equation (7.17), does not have any obvious natural frequencies. Its origin lies in the solutions which arise in the 'second-iterate map' given by $x_{n+2} = f[x_{n+1}] = f[f[x_n]] \equiv f^2[x_n]$, thereby allowing a solution of period equal to two. As $\mu$ subsequently increases towards 3.57, an *infinite* number of period-doublings arise at values of $\mu$ which become *infinitesimally* close. Eventually so many such period-doublings have occurred that the trajectory's period for $\mu = 3.57$ never repeats, that is, the period appears infinite and the system has become chaotic. The evolution of the trajectories in the long-time limit as a function of $\mu$, is shown in Fig. 7.11.

As for Fig. 7.10 in the $n = 3$ continuous-time case, the orbit diagram nicely shows the existence of some order in the chaos. This promise of 'order' and hence some form of predictability, explains the motivation of market-based chaos fans to identify such structures within financial or economic data. As mentioned before, the lack of any requirements concerning smoothness allows chaos to arise for discrete-time maps in one (or more) dimensions, as compared to the three (or more) dimensions required for continuous-time differential equations. Higher dimensional maps can show all the features of one-dimensional maps and more—hence they can also exhibit chaos. It is easy to construct such maps—however it is far less easy to say which ones have any financial or economic relevance.

## 7.3    Financial crashes and drawdowns

### 7.3.1    Extreme behaviour

This chapter has discussed deterministic dynamics, in contrast to the essentially stochastic theme of the rest of the book. Here we bring together both themes to discuss financial crashes, using the microscopic market models of Chapter 4. We have mentioned 'catastrophes' and 'chaos', in addition to discussing transitions between stability and instability in non-linear dynamical systems. To anyone interested in financial applications, these words would probably conjure up images of the market doing something unexpected, such as suddenly heading off in a downward direction. The following question arises. Can we develop a microscopic understanding of how a financial market—whose price series spends much of its time fluctuating around in a stochastic quasi-random way—manages to produce such large, definite price-movements out of thin air?

For the typical investor who is long in the market, it is the large drops in price which are most alarming since they yield direct losses. These large drops are referred to as 'crashes', or more politely as 'drawdowns' or 'corrections'.[4] For the scientist, such large changes are fascinating[5]: after all, to the eye the market usually seems to be behaving randomly, yet it manages to produce these unexpected large changes.[6] Furthermore a given crash may not have an obvious cause. Was it exogenous and hence caused by some external event or piece of news? Or was it endogenous and hence generated from within the system by the action of the traders themselves? Or was it a mix of the two? In the purely exogenous case, the resulting crash will only be as predictable as the external event itself. For example, assuming the 11 September tragedy in the United States was unpredictable one month ahead of time, so was the associated downward movement in the market. However, it was the collective action of the market participants which then determined the duration of the drawdown and the timing of the subsequent recovery. In other words, the duration, magnitude, and mode of recovery of the crash is determined internally by the market participants themselves. Another argument in favour of describing crash dynamics as a primarily endogenous process, is the fact that 'typical' daily news is neither 'good' nor 'bad' for the entire market.

---

[4] This gentler terminology seems to be used during such a slide so as not to further panic the market. We will use the term 'crash' to include any such large changes, happening over a single time-increment or extending over various such time-increments. Since our market-models generally produce symmetric distributions of returns, the analysis in this section is also applicable to the more pleasant phenomena of 'drawups' or 'booms'.

[5] Unless the scientist is also long in the market, in which case the fascination presumably disappears.

[6] Such large changes are often called 'extreme events'. We are not too keen on this terminology since it suggests that there is some definite, albeit unexpected, event associated with the large change. Most historical crashes have no clear exogenous cause.

The possibility therefore arises that financial crashes are telling us something important about the internal forces present within the market. Such forces are usually quite evenly balanced, yielding apparently random fluctuations to the eye and motivating a stochastic view of market dynamics. However, crashes seem to be good examples of moments where these forces become unbalanced, hence producing a large 'quasi-deterministic' movement.[7] It is the spontaneous emergence of such large changes[8] which interests us in this section. Since they are large but infrequent, crashes would be expected to show up in the tails of the probability distribution function (PDF) of price-changes. The tails for real price series are certainly fatter than that for a Gaussian, as we have seen in Chapters 3 and 6, implying that the phenomenon of market crashes cannot be understood within the standard finance paradigm.[9] This is bad news for standard finance theory given the practical implications regarding risk—however, there is worse news. The price-change PDF measured over fixed time-increments does not give us much indication of the real risk from crashes since it tells us nothing about the additional effect of temporal correlations. As mentioned in Chapters 2 and 3, the PDF of price-changes is obtained for a particular time-increment $\Delta t$. However the toy-model in Section 3.6.2 illustrated the fact that higher-order temporal correlations can give rise to price-drop patterns over successive timesteps which cannot be deduced from the single-step PDF of price-changes. Crashes can therefore have a variable duration $\tau_{\text{max}}$, or equivalently, last for a variable number of timesteps $\tau_{\text{max}}/\Delta t$, and hence not show up on the PDF of single-step price-changes. Adding another complication, how do we actually define a crash? One possible candidate is the price-change sequence down $\to$ down $\to$ $\cdots$ $\to$ down $\to$ down which has a duration equal to the number of consecutive downward movements. However, sequences such as large down $\to$ small down $\to$ small up $\to$ large down $\to$ small down will also appear to the eye as a crash. In short, financial crashes have no unique description in terms of size, form or duration, making it extremely difficult to characterize them in terms of statistics. This motivates us to develop a more dynamical approach in order to understand crashes.

---

[7] Followers of the self-organized criticality view of how Nature works would claim that large price-changes (i.e. crashes) are just magnified versions of smaller price-changes, which are in turn magnified versions of even smaller price-changes, and so on. In this sense, there would be nothing 'special' to understand about crashes. However, in addition to the fact that large changes tend to dictate the system's long-term behaviour and hence are of special importance in practical terms, there are reasons for believing that the largest changes may also be 'special' in a microscopic sense. As we have seen in Chapter 3, power-law scaling is only approximately true, and does not apply over an infinite range of scales. Apart from being atomistic at the smallest scale, a population of traders cannot cause any effect larger than the population size itself: in short, the largest changes will tend to 'scrape the barrel' in some way.

[8] There are many other examples of such large changes in complex systems: 'punctuated equilibria' in evolution, unexpected changes in physiological and immunological levels within the body, sudden congestion in internet and vehicular traffic, etc. This ability to self-generate large changes is a defining characteristic of complex systems since it allows for evolution with innovation.

[9] Attempts to go beyond this using 'extreme value theory' are made in practice. However extreme value theory typically says nothing about higher order temporal correlations.

### 7.3.2 Signs of a crash

In Section 4.6 we showed that the El Farol Market Model can generate features that are consistent with the stylized facts of real financial markets. In particular it exhibits crashes[10] as shown in Fig. 7.12.

As indicated in Section 4.7, the El Farol Market Model can be viewed as a stochastically perturbed deterministic system.[11] In particular, the dynamics result from two coexisting effects:

1. Deterministic dynamics driven by 'decided' traders. These 'decided' traders are the ones who, at a given timestep $t$, have a unique best strategy—or equivalently, have two tied strategies with the same prediction—and hence need no coin-toss in order to act. These agents would therefore always take the same action when faced with a particular state of the system. We stress that this group is itself dynamic, that is, a decided trader at one timestep can become undecided in the next timestep and vice versa.
2. Stochastic dynamics driven by either 'undecided' traders, or ties in global supply–demand. The 'undecided' traders are the ones who, at a given timestep $t$, have tied strategies with different predictions, and hence invoke a coin-toss in order to act. These agents would only have a 50 per cent chance of taking the same action if faced again with a particular state of the system. This group is therefore reminiscent of so-called 'noise-traders' with the difference that this group is again dynamic: an undecided trader at one timestep may become a decided trader at the next timestep.

The net effect is to produce stochastically perturbed deterministic dynamics, that is, an underlying deterministic signal with a particular kind of added 'noise'. This suggests that if one averages over this noise, the deterministic dynamics will appear more clearly. We have shown that this is exactly what happens,[12] with the consequence that the equations for the El Farol Market Model become deterministic mapping equations. We will focus here on the crowded regime ($Ns \gg 2^{m+1}$), where the number of strategies in play is comparable to the total number available, since this yields seemingly random dynamics with occasional large movements. This agrees with our intuition that crashes result from some form of crowd dynamics. We will also focus on the Reduced Strategy Space (RSS).

---

[10] All the large changes discussed here represent $> 3\sigma$ events. For additional details about the present crash analysis, see Jefferies, P., Lamper, D., and Johnson, N. F. (2003) *Physica A* **318**, 592; Lamper, D., Howison, S., and Johnson, N. F. (2002) *Phys. Rev. Lett.* **88**, 017902.

[11] A detailed analysis for the simpler case of the Minority Game, is provided in Jefferies, P., Hart, M., and Johnson, N. F. (2002) *Phys. Rev. E.* **65**, 016105. [12] See note 11.

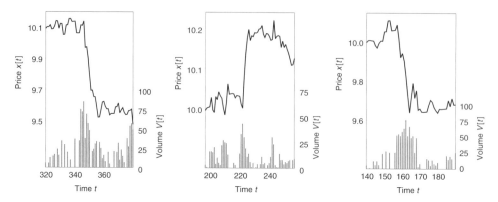

**Fig. 7.12**   Three examples of the type of large change produced by the El Farol Market Model. Parameters for all three simulations: $N = 501, m = 3, s = 2, T = 100, L[t] = 0$ and confidence level $r = 4$.

For simplicity, we will make an approximation to the El Farol Market Model by setting the resource level $L[t] = 0$. Also, instead of 'forgetting' the previous strategy successes or failures smoothly in accordance with Equation (4.12), the agents will recall the past $T$ strategy rewards only, and with equal weight. The strategy score vector $\underline{S}[t]$ is then given by

$$\underline{S}[t] = - \sum_{i=t-T}^{t-1} \underline{a}^{\mu[i]} \mathrm{sgn} \left[ D[(i+1)^-] \right], \tag{7.19}$$

where we have also set the initial strategy score vector $\underline{S}[0] = 0$. This approximation, whilst simplifying the analysis somewhat, will also have consequences for the dynamical behaviour of the system, in particular, the recurrence of crashes. As indicated in Chapter 4, the dynamics of the model can be described by trajectories on a de Bruijn graph, with each transition incurring a particular increment to the score vector $\underline{S}$. There are $P = 2^m$ orthogonal increment vectors $\underline{a}^\mu$, one for each node $\mu$. The $R$th element $a_R^\mu$ corresponds to the action for strategy $R$ given global information state $\mu$. The strategy score vector in Equation (7.19) can thus be written exactly as a linear combination of these orthogonal components:

$$\underline{S}[t] = c_0 \underline{a}^0 + c_1 \underline{a}^1 + \cdots c_{2^m-1} \underline{a}^{2^m-1} = \sum_{j=0}^{2^m-1} c_j \underline{a}^j,$$

where $c_j$ represents the 'nodal weight' for global information node $\mu = j$. In the crowded regime, the strategy scores are highly mean-reverting and hence the nodal weights have a mean value near zero: these nodal weights enumerate the number of negative return transitions from node $\mu$ minus the number of positive return transitions,

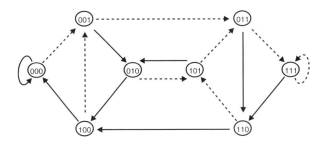

Stable behaviour: path with all transitions equally visited

e.g.   0→0→1→3→6→5→3→7→7→6→4→1→2→5→2→4→...

Crash: path with many negative return transitions

e.g.   0→0→0→0→··· or 2→4→0→0→1→2→4→0→...

**Fig. 7.13**  Paths around the $m = 3$ de Bruijn graph. Dashed-line transitions represent positive demand (i.e. most recent outcome '1' and hence positive return). Solid-line transitions represent negative demand (i.e. most recent outcome '0' and hence negative return). The global information state $\mu$ is shown in binary form at each node. For example, $2 \rightarrow 4$ denotes a transition between $\mu = 2$ and $\mu = 4$, and corresponds to the transition $010 \rightarrow 100$ on the de Bruijn graph.

in the time-window $t - T \rightarrow t - 1$. High absolute nodal weight implies persistence in transitions from that node, that is, persistence in $D|\mu$, which denotes the demand $D$ given the global information $\mu$. Large changes will occur when connected nodes become persistent.

The simplest type of large movement exhibiting perfect nodal persistence would be $\mu = 0, 0, 0, \ldots$ in which all successive changes are in the *same* direction. We call this a 'fixed-node crash'. However, there are many other possibilities reflecting the wide range of forms and durations of the large change. For example, on the $m = 3$ de Bruijn graph in Fig. 7.13, the cycle $\mu = 0, 0, 1, 2, 4, 0, \ldots$ has four out of the five transitions producing demands of the same sign (it is persistent on nodes $\mu = 1, 2, 4$ and antipersistent on node $\mu = 0$). We call this a 'cyclic-node crash'.

Figure 7.14 shows an example of a large change which starts as a fixed-node crash, then subsequently becomes a cyclic-node crash.

Cyclic-node crashes can be treated simply as interlocking fixed-node crashes, hence for clarity we focus here on a single fixed-node crash. The presence of abnormally high nodal weights (particularly on a closed subset of connected nodes $\mu$) will cause a large movement in the system *if* the trajectory of the system hits any of these susceptible nodes in the global information space. This is the signature of a crash-susceptible period within the model.[13]

---

[13] See the publications of Sornette, D. (e.g. Sornette, D., Johansen, A., and Bouchaud, J.-P. (1996) *J. Physique I*, **6,** 167 and Sornette (2000)) for a discussion of possible empirical pre-cursors to crashes.

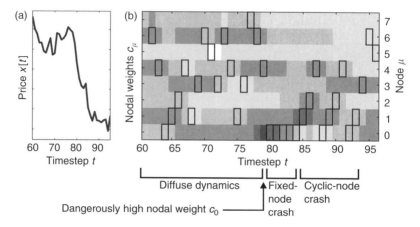

**Fig. 7.14** (a) Example of a crash in the price series generated by the simplified El Farol Market Model with $m = 2$, within the Reduced Strategy Space (RSS). (b) The corresponding weights (with magnitudes indicated by the darkness of the tints) for each node $\mu$, as a function of time through the period of the crash. The global information at each timestep is indicated by the black square. The crash is preceded by abnormally high nodal weight magnitudes (darker tints). The overall crash incorporates fixed-node and cyclic-node crashes.

We now turn to look at how the model market reacts given that it has entered such a crash-susceptible period. In particular we are interested in the form of the demand for assets and the volume of trading during a crash and whether anything can be deduced about the magnitude or duration of the large movement *prior* to its arrival. For the parameter ranges of interest which produce the stylized facts, the choice about whether a strategy is played by an agent is more determined by whether the score of that strategy is above the threshold $r$ required to trade, than whether it is his highest scoring strategy.[14] This is because agents are only likely to have at most one strategy whose score lies above the threshold for confidence levels $r \geq 0$. Making the additional numerically justified approximation of small quenched disorder (i.e. the standard deviation of the entries in the quenched disorder matrix $\underline{\underline{\Psi}}$ is smaller than their mean for the parameter range of interest), the demand and volume become

$$D\left[(t+1)^{-}\right] = \frac{N}{4P} \sum_{R=1}^{2P} a_R^{\mu[t]} \mathrm{sgn}\left[S_R[t] - r\right], \qquad (7.20)$$

$$V\left[(t+1)^{-}\right] = \frac{N}{2} + \frac{N}{4P} \sum_{R=1}^{2P} \mathrm{sgn}\left[S_R[t] - r\right], \qquad (7.21)$$

[14] The threshold to trade $r$ is of order one standard deviation above the mean in strategy scores.

where $r$ represents the usual confidence threshold, but could also be chosen to reflect changes in external economic factors. A fixed-node crash is given by persistence on node $\mu = 0$. Suppose this persistence starts at time $t_0$: how long will the resulting crash last? To answer this, we decompose Equation (7.20) into strategies which suggest to buy, given that the global information is $\mu = 0$ ($a_R^0 = 1$), and those that suggest to sell ($a_R^0 = -1$). First, consider the particular case where the node $\mu = 0$ was not visited during the previous $T$ timesteps, hence the loss of the score increment from timestep $t - T$ will not affect $\underline{S}[t]$ on average since all the vectors $\underline{a}^{\mu \neq 0}$ are orthogonal to $\underline{a}^0$. At any later time $t_0 + \tau$ during the crash (i.e. $\mu = 0$) Equations (7.20) and (7.21) are hence given by

$$
D\left[(t_0 + \tau + 1)^-\right]
$$
$$
= -\frac{N}{4P}\left( \sum_{R \ni a_R^0 = -1} \mathrm{sgn}\,[S_R[t_0] - r - \tau] - \sum_{R \ni a_R^0 = 1} \mathrm{sgn}\,[S_R[t_0] - r + \tau] \right),
$$
(7.22)

$$
V\left[(t_0 + \tau + 1)^-\right]
$$
$$
= \frac{N}{2} + \frac{N}{4P}\left( \sum_{R \ni a_R^0 = -1} \mathrm{sgn}\,[S_R[t_0] - r - \tau] + \sum_{R \ni a_R^0 = 1} \mathrm{sgn}\,[S_R[t_0] - r + \tau] \right).
$$
(7.23)

The magnitude of the excess demand $|D[(t_0 + \tau + 1)^-]|$ decreases as the persistence time $\tau$ increases, and hence the large change ends at time $t_0 + \tau_c$ when the right-hand side of Equation (7.22) changes sign. An estimate of the persistence time or 'crash-length' $\tau_c$ is thus provided by the mean score, prior to the crash, for the strategies which suggest selling, that is, $\tau_c \simeq \langle S_R[t_0]\rangle_{R \ni a_R^0 = -1}$. This quantity can be calculated as follows:

$$
\langle S_R[t_0]\rangle_{R \ni a_R^0 = -1} = \frac{1}{P}\underline{S}[t_0] \cdot \frac{1}{2}\left(1 - \underline{a}^0\right) = \frac{1}{2P}\left(\sum_{j=0}^{P-1} c_j[t_0]\underline{a}^j\right) \cdot (1 - \underline{a}^0)
$$

$$
= -\frac{1}{2P}c_0[t_0]\underline{a}^0 \cdot \underline{a}^0 = -c_0[t_0],
$$
(7.24)

where we have used the nodal weight decomposition of the strategy score vector $\underline{S}[t_0]$, then the fact that $\underline{a}^\mu \cdot \underline{1} = 0$, and finally the orthogonality property of the vectors $\underline{a}^\mu$. In the more general case where the node $\mu = 0$ was visited during the previous $T$

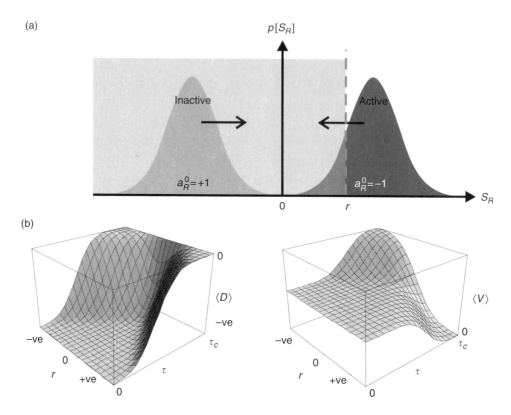

**Fig. 7.15**  (a) Schematic representation of strategy score distribution prior to a large change (crash). Arrows indicate subsequent motion during crash period. (b) Plots of expected demand and volume during crash period, as given by Equations (7.26) and (7.27), showing a wide range of possible behaviours as system parameters are varied.

timesteps, $\tau_c$ is given approximately by the largest $\tau$ value which satisfies

$$\tau = - \left( c_0[t_0] + \sum_{\{t'\}} \text{sgn}\left[D[(t'+1)^-]\right] \right), \tag{7.25}$$

where $\{t'\} \ni (\mu[t'] = 0 \cap t_0 - T \le t' \le t_0 + \tau - T)$. We will assume that the scores have a near-Gaussian distribution, that is, $S_{R \ni a_R^0 = -1}[t_0] \sim N[-c_0[t_0], \sigma]$ as shown in Fig. 7.15. For each strategy $R$ there exists an anticorrelated strategy $\bar{R}$ and hence $S_R[t] = -S_{\bar{R}}[t]$ for all $t$. Consequently, prior to a large change, the score distribution tends to split into two halves. During the crash, the two halves of the strategy score distribution re-converge until an equal number of buy and sell strategies exists above the threshold. The number of buy and sell strategies above the threshold can be calculated easily as a function of time during the crash—this then gives the demand and volume of trading. Averaging Equations (7.22) and (7.23) over the Gaussian score distribution gives the expected demand (and expected volume) during the crash:

$$\langle D\left[(t_0 + \tau + 1)^-\right]\rangle \propto \left(\mathrm{erf}\left[\frac{c_0[t_0] + r + \tau}{\sqrt{2}\sigma}\right] - \mathrm{erf}\left[\frac{-c_0[t_0] + r - \tau}{\sqrt{2}\sigma}\right]\right),$$

(7.26)

$$\langle V\left[(t_0 + \tau + 1)^-\right]\rangle \propto \left(2 - \mathrm{erf}\left[\frac{c_0[t_0] + r + \tau}{\sqrt{2}\sigma}\right] - \mathrm{erf}\left[\frac{-c_0[t_0] + r - \tau}{\sqrt{2}\sigma}\right]\right).$$

(7.27)

These forms are illustrated in Fig. 7.15b. As the spread in the strategy score distribution is increased, the dependence of $\langle D \rangle$ and $\langle V \rangle$ on the parameters $\tau$ and $r$ becomes weaker, hence the surfaces flatten out leading to a smoother drawdown as opposed to a sudden severe crash. As the parameters $c_0$, $\sigma$, $r$ are varied, it can be seen that the behaviour of the demand and volume during the large change can exhibit markedly different qualitative forms, yielding a *taxonomy* of *different species* of large change even within this same single-node family. This result could explain why financial market chartists' rules-of-thumb such as 'volume goes with price trend' are far too simplistic.

### 7.3.3   Birth and recurrence of crashes

We now turn to the important question of what processes cause the buildup of nodal weights that can trigger a crash, and whether history will repeat itself, that is, given that a large change has recently happened, is it likely to happen again? If so, is it likely to be even bigger? It turns out that these questions are linked in the context of the present model. First we address the issue of crash recurrence. Suppose the system has built up a negative nodal weight for $\mu = 0$ at some point in the game (see Fig. 7.16a). The market then reaches the global information state $\mu = 0$ at time $t_0$ producing a crash. The nodal weight $c_0$ is hence restored to zero (Fig. 7.16b). In this model the

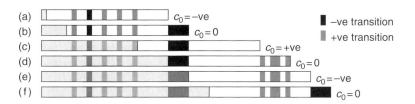

**Fig. 7.16**   Representation of how large changes can recur due to the finite memory of strategy scores possessed by each agent. Light grey area shows history period outside this memory range. This example shows recurring fixed-node crash at node $\mu = 0$.

previous build-up is then forgotten because of the finite-$T$ score window, hence $c_0$ becomes positive (Fig. 7.16c). The system then corrects this imbalance (Fig. 7.16d) through a diffuse set of instances of positive demand. Note that this correction of the positive nodal weight for node $\mu = 0$ will not in general cause an inverse crash (i.e. rally or boom) because the connectivity of the de Bruijn graph does not allow for successive positive return transitions from node $\mu = 0$. Through this diffuse correction, the nodal weight $c_0$ will be restored to $c_0 = 0$. The crash is then forgotten, hence $c_0$ becomes negative (Fig. 7.16e). The system is therefore susceptible to crash again. However a crash (Fig. 7.16f) will only re-appear *if* the trajectory of the system subsequently returns to the susceptible global information state $\mu = 0$.

We have therefore shown that it is likely for history to repeat itself within this model, and hence the tendency exists for a crash to be followed by another crash. This process cannot be solely responsible for *building* a significant crash since there has so far been no suggestion that the next large change will be any bigger than the last. However there is a mechanism within the system which *can* convert a previously modest drawdown into one of much greater magnitude. To understand this mechanism, we return to consider Equation (7.20) for a modestly low value of the threshold to trade, $r \leq 2\sigma[S_R[t]]$. It can be shown[15] that for a large fraction of all timesteps, the outcome $(\text{sgn}[D[(t + 1)^-]])$ is well-described by the following expression:

$$\text{sgn}\left[D[(t + 1)^-]\right] = \text{sgn}\left[\underline{a}^{\mu[t]} \cdot \underline{S}[t]\right] = \text{sgn}[c_{\mu[t]}]. \tag{7.28}$$

However, when the nodal weight $c_{\mu[t]}$ is zero, Equation (7.28) is no longer a reliable predictor of the outcome of the system. In these cases, it tends to be the asymmetry in the population of strategies which has the dominant effect on the outcome. In the presence of such a non-flat strategy allocation matrix as discussed in Section 4.7, the demand function in Equation (7.20) generalizes to give the following approximate form[15]:

$$D[(t + 1)^-] = \frac{1}{2}\sum_{R=1}^{2P} a_R^{\mu[t]} \sum_{R'=1}^{2P} \Psi_{R,R'} + \frac{1}{2}\sum_{R=1}^{2P} a_R^{\mu[t]} \, \text{sgn}\,[S_R[t] - r] \sum_{R'=1}^{2P} \Psi_{R,R'}$$

$$= \frac{1}{2}\underline{a}^{\mu[t]} \cdot \underline{\psi} + \frac{1}{2}\sum_{R=1}^{2P} a_R^{\mu[t]} \, \text{sgn}\,[S_R[t] - r]\,\psi_R, \tag{7.29}$$

where $\psi_R = \sum_{R'=1}^{2P} \Psi_{R,R'}$. For the cases where the nodal weight is zero, that is, $c_{\mu[t]} = 0$, the first term of Equation (7.29) should dominate in determining the outcome. This dominant first term arises purely from the unevenness in the quenched

---

[15]  See note 11.

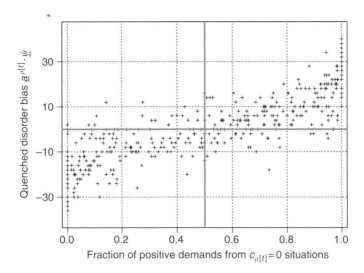

**Fig. 7.17**   The fraction of instances at which a positive demand transition follows a situation of zero nodal weight $c_{\mu[t]} = 0$, compared to the quenched disorder bias for that global information state, that is, $\underline{a}^{\mu[t]} \cdot \underline{\psi}$. Crosses represent the results for each of the $2P = 8$ nodes over 50 runs of 1000 timesteps.

disorder matrix $\underline{\underline{\psi}}$. In Fig. 7.17, we show the fraction of instances for which a positive demand (rather than a negative one) follows from a situation where $c_{\mu[t]} = 0$, compared to the bias for that value of the global information (i.e. the first term of Equation (7.29)). As can be seen, there is a definite positive correlation between these two variables confirming the proposition that it is the quenched disorder bias which essentially determines the sign of the demand in situations of zero nodal weight. This quenched disorder bias arising from the situations of zero nodal weight, can lead to a build-up in the size of a recurring large movement. Suppose that every time the nodal weight becomes zero (e.g. see Fig. 7.16b,d,f) the quenched disorder bias decides the sign of the transition (i.e. demand). If this bias produces the correct sign, then the magnitude of the nodal weight and hence the impending crash will grow with every recurrence. The quenched disorder in our simplified El Farol Market Model, can therefore act as a *catalyst* for building up very large price movements.

We have therefore deepened our understanding of crashes within the simplified El Farol Market Model. But what about real markets? A financial analogy to the triggering of a crash-buildup as a result of quenched disorder bias, would be the following. Suppose there is an excess of agents who have a predisposition to buy assets after they have seen the price fall on a number of consecutive timesteps during diffuse market behaviour. Their activity will leave an 'imprint' in the market. This imprint comes from the fact that the strategy of *selling* assets after seeing they have fallen, then becomes a very successful strategy. Therefore the next time the agents are faced with the decision about which way to trade when the price has fallen for several consecutive timesteps, a large proportion of the agent population will consequently rush to the market with sell orders. A large proportion of agents will then continue selling until they realize that this has become a poor strategy.

So how might financial crashes be avoided? It is clear that a crash can be seen to be brewing in the very simple framework of nodal weights described here. A large nodal weight on a subset of connected nodes is a crash-susceptible situation. In real terms, this means that patterns must be avoided which lead to the following viscious circle: pattern induces trade, induces pattern, induces trade, and so on. However in order to remove such patterns, one needs to have significant market impact. While this may be outside the control of any individual institution, the possibility exists that a market controller could indeed take such steps. The feasibility of such on-line complex-system management awaits further study.

## 7.4  Predicting the future: who wants to be a Millionaire?

It has been said that one should never make predictions, particularly about the future. It has also been said that econometricians can predict five out of the last three market crashes. Econophysicists would possibly manage six! However the potential rewards for making *any* kind of prediction about markets are so huge, that people will keep trying. And as Doyne Farmer of the Santa Fe Institute and Prediction Company has aptly remarked: the nice thing about financial markets is that you do not have to predict very much to do an awful lot.

So how good are the prediction techniques that one hears about? What about 'chaos theory' and its spin-offs such as attractor reconstruction? Genetic algorithms? Neural networks? Or how about the log-periodic oscillation precursors of large market movements, as proposed by Didier Sornette?[16] And what about some of the more statistical techniques related to entropy (i.e. information theory) measures? To start with, each of these labels is quite imprecise. The number of possible bells-and-whistles that one could add within each technique is enormous. Any one bell-and-whistle might hold the magic ingredient to predict markets. Worse still, if we think back to the non-linear theme of this chapter, it might be that a particular combination of bells-and-whistles proves crucial. Hence it is difficult to dismiss any of these techniques at face value. The academic papers which report the application of such techniques to predicting financial markets, tend only to suggest modest success rates, if any. It is therefore unclear

---

[16] See note 13.

whether real profits could be made after accounting for transaction costs. Maybe this lack of success in reported studies is to be expected: after all, who would want to publish the details of a prediction model if it actually worked?

Since this is a section about predicting the future—and since people only tend to remember those predictions that actually come true—we ourselves will hazard a guess as to where the most reliable market predictions might lie. Only time will tell if we are right. As physicists, our tendency is to put our trust in models which are micro-scopically realistic, and where the model parameters hold some physical meaning. Hence, any prediction model for financial markets which does not have at its heart a description of the dynamics of trader activity, would be less likely to succeed in our opinion. An example of such a non-physical model for financial markets would be that of neural networks: the individual perceptrons, while possibly meaningful for brain researchers, have no clear significance in a financial market. It turns out that this belief in the importance of a physically relevant model, is also becoming popular in a completely different prediction community: that of weather forecasting. This latter community is now tending to focus on weather prediction models which have phys-ically realistic features, as opposed to pure time-series prediction techniques where the time-series could equally well be the weather, the stock market, or the number of cars on the road. To summarize, therefore, we believe that a successful financial market prediction technique should, at some level, account for the microscopic details of the market: in particular, the presence of traders, who buy/sell according to their individual agendas and strategies, and who change their minds as time goes on—this is reflected in our emphasis on such agent-based models throughout this book. Abstract time-series techniques, where the nature of the system producing the time-series is irrelevant, will always be unreliable in our opinion.

It would be impossible for us to describe all the practical details behind the imple-mentation of a given prediction technique in a given market—even if we knew all these details ourselves. Hence we decline from any further discussion of prediction techniques in this book. There really is no point since the 'devil is in the details'—any one, or combination, of the bells-and-whistles may prove crucial for the successful prediction of a given market over a given period of time. We prefer to refer the inter-ested reader to the Econophysics website *www.unifr.ch/econophysics* and to the list of *Further reading* at the end of this book. Or better still, download some of the freely available financial data from the web and try out some prediction models for yourself. Maybe you will find the appropriate bell-and-whistle. If you do, you may want to think twice before publicizing it—but do please let *us* know!

# Further reading

The following books are recommended for providing further material and different perspectives. Our discussion of market structure, probabilities, Black–Scholes option-pricing, and non-linear dynamics are heavily influenced by some of these books.

Wilmott, P., Howison, S., and Dewynne, J. (1996) *The mathematics of financial derivatives*, Cambridge University Press.

Bouchaud, J. P. and Potters, M. (2000) *Theory of financial risks*, Cambridge University Press.

Mantegna, R. N. and Stanley, H. E. (2000) *An introduction to Econophysics*, Cambridge University Press.

Wilmott, P. (1998) *Derivatives*, Wiley.

Gershenfeld, N. (1999) *The nature of mathematical modelling*, Cambridge University Press.

Feller, W. (1968) *An introduction to probability theory and its applications*, Wiley.

Voit, J. (2001) *The statistical mechanics of financial markets*, Springer.

Strogatz, S. (2001) *Non-linear dynamics and chaos*, Perseus.

Sornette, D. (2000) *Critical phenomena in natural sciences: chaos, fractal, self-organization and disorder*, Springer.

Campbell, J. Y., Lo, A. W., and MacKinlay, A. C. (1997) *The econometrics of financial markets*, Princeton University Press.

Pilbeam, K. (1998) *Finance & financial markets*, Macmillan Business.

# Index